LEADING, TEACHING, *and* MAKING DISCIPLES

*World–Class Christian Education
in the Church, School, and Home*

DR. MICHAEL R. MITCHELL

CROSSBOOKS
PUBLISHING

CrossBooks™
A Division of LifeWay
1663 Liberty Drive
Bloomington, IN 47403
www.crossbooks.com
Phone: 1-866-879-0502

First published by CrossBooks 7/19/2010

Library of Congress Control Number: 2010907034

ISBN: 978-1-6150-7040-4 (sc)
ISBN: 978-1-6150-7240-8 (hc)

Printed in the United States of America
Bloomington, Indiana

This book is printed on acid-free paper.

Dedications

This work is dedicated to the Mitchell Family:
My wife, Sharyn Ann, who has supported, encouraged, and been there
with me every step of the way, whose "children arise and call her blessed;
her husband also, and he praises her"
(Proverbs 31:28)

My son and daughter, Michael Jr. and Charis, well-disciplined children
who bring peace and are a delight to their father
(Proverbs 29:17)

And my sister, Patti Zielke, in memory of our parents, Ken and Betty,
who revealed by words and deeds how to "walk in the ways of good men"
(Proverbs 2:20)

Contents

Prologue

Stepping out of my office for a break, I was immediately confronted by a student who asked for a few minutes to talk. He came to the seminary, after three years of missionary service, in search of a universal design for discipleship and education ministry. His goal was to identify a curricular approach that he could utilize on the mission field in poor villages, among the illiterate, with all age groups, and yet be equally effective in the children's ministry of his local church. This young scholar was looking for a solid core of information, a simple delivery system, and an educational strategy that did not demand literacy or technology so that he could employ it worldwide.

The requested few minutes grew into an hour as we contemplated my initial recommendation to examine Jesus' ministry and observe the messages and methods he used in such an environment: What did he say? How did he say it? To whom? In what settings? In this context, we also considered the use of texts, technology, and the irreducible minimums of education.

At one point during the conversation, the student stated that he had come to one tentative conclusion: content needed to be reduced to an easily produced and reproduced "bulleted list" such as the Ten Commandments or the early church creeds. I replied that a teacher could supplement these with stories, especially in informal group settings, to flesh out the principles and visual symbols necessary to stimulate recognition and memory. We also considered theater and pageantry as possibilities for further dramatic enhancement and enrichment.

Finally, we briefly reflected upon the practice of age grading that occurs in compulsory public education and how it has affected church ministry. He expressed a specific concern for adults who accept Christ and feel called to the ministry but are in a career. Within this discussion we looked specifically at the issues of adult converts: Do they attend Sunday school with children? Do we provide a new believer's class? For how long, and in what way, must they be trained before starting to serve? Is there a model we can follow and implement? Again, how did Jesus do it? With limited time available, I simply recommended that he consider multi-generational small groups, one-on-one mentoring, and discipleship. These eliminate or cut across generational and educational lines and barriers, allowing personalization and application in a real-life environment.

There was nothing new or exclusively contemporary in these methods and approaches. They have informed and inspired illiterate masses all over the world for centuries, and we could not conceive of any good reason not to employ them today. In fact, they exemplify exactly what we were trying to identify: a conception of "world-class" leadership and education whose product is really good and really global. After all, if our commission is to present the gospel to the entire world, we must have the ability to reach anyone, anywhere effectively.

In one brief conversation, we had addressed many of the critical questions that provide design to the processes of education and discipleship ministry. In doing so, we joined noted educator Robert Pazmiño in his attempt to identify and affirm "transcultural universals which may then guide all educational conceptions and efforts" in his work *Foundational Issues in Christian Education* (Pazmiño 1997). In conclusion, I also recommended that the student read this book in that it asks and attempts to answer the very inquiries we were addressing.

Transferable Principles

The considerations generated by this conversation reminded me of another encounter that occurred early in my ministry career. When a church invited me to conduct teacher and leader training for their staff, a couple who were former members of the youth ministry team provided room and board. One evening after a training session, I sat down with the wife for a piece of pie, a cup of tea, and some conversation. Rambling and disjointed dialogue finally found focus as we discussed the ten years she and her husband had spent as very effective Sunday school and youth group leaders. After a season of much-needed rest, they were contemplating volunteering once again. They were, however, hesitant because they were not certain they would be able to duplicate their former success. Therefore, she was vitally interested in the training that I was presenting; she wanted to know if anything they had previously experienced was transferable to a new setting.

When I shared the basic principles and the design for ministry that I was providing for the present staff, her face lit up as she realized that they had intuitively followed this very instruction. She quickly grasped the implication: when one understands *why* something is effective, the necessary resources can be crafted to implement the *how*. Whether it is determining which lesson to teach, creating a lesson plan to teach it, or finding ways to discipline an unruly student, good theory promotes the good ideas that produce good practice. This couple had done the right things, and I encouraged her that they could indeed do them again, this time intentionally.

Five Questions

Reflecting upon these issues with the young missionary and the youth minister caused me to reminisce upon my first encounter with the questions they asked and the debates they inspired.

As I commenced my first full-time church ministry, two factors generated a sense of personal insecurity and professional uncertainty. The first was that I had grown up and served in a small local church that was congregational and democratic in polity. Now, however, I was one of the assistant pastors at a megachurch with a metropolitan demographic, a board-run governance structure, and an autocratic senior pastor. The second, more critical factor was that I had assumed responsibility for the oversight of a very large children's ministry for which I had very little formal training, since my academic preparation had focused on youth. I was equipped with practical experience, having been a schoolteacher and an outdoor educator in other organizations, but this was my first opportunity to lead and direct a formal educational program. I discovered quickly that I was in over my head.

"Help! I need answers, and I need them now!" was my constant prayer. Believing it was a simple request, I assumed the Lord would hear me and respond promptly in my hour of need. Instead, there was silence for weeks. After nearly a month of beseeching the Lord, I came to the inspired realization that I would not receive the answers I needed until I asked specific questions. Therefore, with pen and pad in hand, I began the process of reflecting upon what I wanted to know and recording thoughts that eventually took the shape of inquiries. I narrowed the parameters to five vital investigations, and with these queries, I petitioned the Lord for direction as to what to do and how to do it:

1. **What is (Christian) education?** *What is the nature of my work, and what are its purposes and goals? In essence, asking, "What am I doing here?" and "What makes it Christian?"*

2. **What is the content of education?** *How do I know what to teach? What curricular guidelines might there be?*

3. **What are the processes of education?** *How do people learn? How do I teach? Are there any plans I can follow? What do I need to know about methods?*

4. What is the context of education? *How do I best group students for learning? What about the organizational structure for my program?*

5. Who are the people involved in education? *What are the roles of the Godhead? What do I need to know about people? What do I need to know about parents, teachers, and students?*

The Lord did direct my studies, and within a month, I had fashioned the basic biblical outline that framed a response to my inquiries and gave direction to further studies. Within three months, I had formulated a strategy and structure for the assignment before me. Within a year, I had established the essential activity required to implement the critical components of each inquiry.

The Structure of the Discipline

In the years that followed my initial investigation, I read a number of texts that, in essence, addressed the same questions and concerns. The specific terms, sequence, and number of inquiries differed, but the concepts were clearly complementary to those I was exploring. For example, Thomas Groome ventured to ask in his penetrating *Christian Religious Education: Sharing our Story and Vision:* 1) What is the nature of Christian education? 2) Why is Christian education essential? 3) Where is Christian education undertaken? 4) How is Christian education conducted? 5) When is it appropriate to share particular Christian truths and experiences? and 6) Who is interacting in Christian education? (Groome 1980).

Later, in reading George Knight's *Philosophy and Education* I discovered that in the chapter entitled "A Christian Approach to Education," the author identified the same five considerations I proposed. His headings were: 1) The Nature of the Student and the Goal of Christian Education, 2) The Role of the Christian Teacher, 3) Curricular Considerations, 4) Methodological Considerations, and 5) The Social Function of Christian Education (Knight 1998).

Recently, James Estep observed in *A Theology for Christian Education* that there were "seven common elements of every approach to education." Not surprisingly, they address the same issues, although, again, in different words: "(1) the purpose and objectives of education, (2) the role of the teacher, (3) the role of the student, (4) the relationship between the teacher and the student, (5) the curriculum content, (6) the learning environment and methods, and (7) the means of evaluation" (Estep, Anthony, and Allison 2008).

Over time, I came to understand that these topics were framing and informing what is referred to as "the structure of the discipline." It was encouraging to realize that I had identified the same issues that other scholars and researchers were addressing and exploring: the definition, content, process, context, and people of Christian education. The primary differences that separate us, of course, are in the answers we provide.

Essential Activities of Education

Academic considerations and practical applications complement and balance each other. Therefore, as I contemplated the scholarly issues, I was also confronted with the need to acquire and establish an administrative team, a support staff, and a teaching faculty. With each appointment, a new voice with a fresh approach joined the team and contributed to the investigation of the five questions. In order to consider the possible applications of the principles emanating from our exploration, we frequently gathered to share our discoveries and emerging perceptions.

Some of our early observations compelled us to consider how the answers we were uncovering affected actual classroom educational activity. As fascinated as the administrative team was with the theory and foundations for the five questions, the faculty simply wanted to know how to teach and what to do in a room with students. The need for an appropriate balance between theory and practice fueled a lengthy debate over the primary focus for our training program. If we did not provide enough skill training, the teachers would walk into their classrooms unprepared for their ministry. If we did not provide enough theoretical foundation, the teachers would walk into their classrooms facing the same fears as the retired youth ministers – they would consistently wonder if they were just fortunate when something worked or if the techniques that worked were transferrable.

The fusion of academics and applications was evident as we simultaneously grew in our theoretical convictions and developed in our ability to provide necessary skills training. As a result, we identified a core set of basic and necessary behaviors and competencies that correlated with the questions and issues we were exploring. We labeled these behaviors the "Essential Activities of Education," as they formed the framework for the skill set required of a teacher. We expected our faculty to be able to:

1. Make a Disciple who Worships Jesus (answering the What question)
2. Construct a Curricular Plan (answering the Content question)

3. Prepare a Plan for Teaching and Learning (answering the Processes question)
4. Establish an Environment for Education (answering the Context question)
5. Have a Heart for and Serve People (answering the People question)

It is my continuing conviction that these five essential activities provide the blueprint and the foundation for a well rounded, biblically based, and effective disciple-making experience. I still utilize them as the structural framework for any training program intended to prepare Christian leaders and educators for a classroom, small group, or corporate discipleship ministry. I have even used an edited version in a public school venue.

Applications: Ministries and Models

Even though I quickly identified the core constitution of the discipline, and was learning to apply many of the essential activities, I realized something profound while leading, teaching, and making disciples. I discovered that the responses to the five framing inquiries informed not only my perspective on educational ministries, but also my ideas on leadership as well. In fact, the answers to the questions inform and shape the outline of an approach to any ministry or service, regardless of its title or label.

Master and Rabbi: Leader and Teacher

Throughout my lifetime, a number of "dynamic duos" have graced the screens of the motion picture and television industries, the music business, and other aspects of popular culture: George and Gracie, Bob and Bing, Bogie and Bacall, Batman and Robin, Lucy and Ricky, Lennon and McCartney, Sonny and Cher, Simon and Garfunkel, and let us not forget Calvin and Hobbes, Kermit and Miss Piggy, and everyone's favorites, Mickey and Minnie. These dyads teamed up to entertain, encourage, and educate generations of culturally literate citizenry and have left their mark on our society.

Christian ministers, whether full or part-time, paid or volunteer, have a pair of equally influential, life-altering forces at their disposal. The partnership of the twin sisters, *leading* and *teaching*, provides the followers of Jesus with the inspirational mindset and influential skill set necessary to make disciples and turn their world upside down. Unlike the complementary yet distinct elements of the pairs mentioned above, leading and teaching share many components. Both of them exert influence, require effective communication, and utilize modeling and imitation as key methodologies. They equally commence with a mission and a message and conclude with a change of behavior and performance.

These similarities explain why Jesus, equally skilled in each, is acknowledged as both Master (leader) and Rabbi (teacher). To come and follow him demands simultaneously submitting to his influence and his instruction. To imitate him and follow his example demands that we engage in these activities as well.

On the Structure of this Work

These two concerns, then, provide the framework for the outline and structure of this work. Part I ("Come, follow me") introduces the concepts of leadership and followership by way of the biblical text and personal experiences. Part II ("Come, learn from me") presents a biblical model for instruction inspired by King Solomon's effort to prepare his prince for the throne, and offers a classic illustration of the integration of leading and teaching. Part III ("Go, make disciples") ties it all together by articulating answers to the five questions that initiated this study and suggesting a design for an effective disciple-making environment. They effectively address the research concerns of the seminarian whose search for a universal model opens this prologue: 1) What am I trying to accomplish? 2) With what messages? 3) Transmitted how? 4) In what kind of environment? 5) Inhabited by whom?

Collectively, the three parts provide insight into the methods our Master and Rabbi utilized to transform everyday fishermen into dynamic disciples. So I extend an invitation: join me in the adventure of exploring the principal principles of leading and teaching revealed in the Word and applicable to our lives and ministries as we "go and make disciples." We will investigate the key terms, concepts, and theories that form the "unchanging framework" of the discipline of any ministry, but especially those of education and leadership.

Frameworks and Filters: Coat Hangers and Screen Doors

As we explore this theoretical structure for disciple making, we will simultaneously be constructing a biblical and practical framework for the Christian minister to utilize in the course of both personal and professional growth and development. In a manner similar to the use of hangers to sort and store clothing, we will create a conceptual closet with hangers for the mind and skill sets we will attain. For example, I recently read a text that discussed ancient wisdom literature. Because I had a mental hanger in place to receive, sort, evaluate, and store the data, I was able to make use of this new information to enrich my understanding of one of the five inquiries. We will experience the same dynamic in Chapters 2 and 6, when we will construct hangers upon which to drape our gleanings on leadership behaviors and the teaching-learning process.

This framework can also be employed as a filter to help us winnow out the perilous and unprofitable influences encountered in the journey of living, learning, and leading. The result will be an "academic screen door" that allows in the breezes of fresh air but keeps out pests and irritating bugs. The tighter the weave of the mesh, derived from study and experience, the more effective the filter will be. My ministry career would have been so much more effective, and probably easier, if I had my hangers and screen door in place earlier and had known then what I know now about leadership, education, and disciple making.

Sources and Experiences: Life and Doctrine

A prologue is a logical place to acknowledge the sources of thoughts and insights that enable the construction of such a multipurpose framework. For this study, they are nothing more or less than reflections upon pertinent precepts or doctrines and life experiences. This text, therefore, is laced with references to the biblical scriptures, my primary source. I have depended upon them for both information and inspiration. If I have accomplished anything, I hope it is to have established a biblical base for the theories and models presented. When my initial research into the five inquiries began, my intention was to back up every human resource with six biblical references. This six-to-one ratio was a dream that I did not accomplish, but it should be obvious that this work is substantially an interpretation of the Master and Rabbi's teaching.

It is interesting, though, to note that often the biblical revelations came on the heels of personal experience or breakthrough "ah ha!" moments. Many times, I reflected upon an experience, wrote a note or a thorough outline, and then discovered that very truth embedded in what had been a concealed or neglected portion of Scripture. When the Apostle Paul instructed Timothy to "watch your life and doctrine closely" (1Timothy 4:16), he could have just as easily been looking down through the ages to people like me whose lives and ministries would be influenced and informed by their life experiences confirmed by the doctrine of God's Word.

The second source to acknowledge, therefore, is the life that I have been privileged to experience and upon which I now expound. My occupations have spanned the gamut. I have served as a senior pastor, executive pastor, associate pastor, age group director, camp director, Bible institute and day school teacher, and administrator, among others. As of this writing, I am a seminary professor. My career prior to this assignment was book-ended by two stints as a school administrator that I served concurrently with church ministry positions. In total, these two opportunities spanned fifteen calendar years, but they provided nearly a lifetime of experience.

I have made it a personal and professional commitment to watch both my life and my doctrine carefully. I have done so in both the public and private school systems, in church and in my home, affirming the universal nature of the principles and practices we will discover and explore. Thus, from a lifelong investigation of the foundations supporting and informing the answers to five definitive questions, *Leading, Teaching, and Making Disciples* has emerged. It is one man's attempt to weave a verbal tapestry composed of strands of scholarly insights, personal experiences, and practical applications that can also provide the mesh for our screen doors and filters.

This symphony of words chronicles my educational pilgrimage and reflects upon my conviction that God has provided the design for both the principles and the processes of making disciple-followers. My expectation is that the lessons imparted here will be transformative. I anticipate that this introduction to leadership, education, and discipleship will spur leaders and teachers to explore further the greater breadth and depth of their ministries and to experience personally the renovation proffered them.

PART I
"Come, follow me"

"Come, follow me, and I will make you fishers of men" (Matthew 4:19).

Preview Pane:
Outline and Chapter Synopsis

Chapter 1 – Definitive Concerns: What Is Leadership?

Leaders induce and influence followers to engage in activities that fulfill a mission. The model of Jesus' ministry that produces that perception and facilitates a biblical and practical approach to leadership and management is the focus of this chapter. Attention is given to followership, paradigm shifts, and the biblical gifts of administration. The term *disciple-follower* is introduced, while a formal definition of leadership is provided to complete the investigation.

Chapter 2 – Leadership Behaviors: What Does a Leader Do?

Leaders determine, declare, and direct the implementation of their message, mission, and vision. This chapter explores each of these behaviors and provides an introduction to administration. The procedures and phases of leadership that facilitate transaction and transformation close the chapter.

Chapter 3 – Administrative Functions: How Does a Leader Do It?

Leaders implement five functions of administration: planning, organizing, staffing, developing, and controlling. Building upon the examples of Moses and Jesus, this chapter explores each process through biblical and practical lenses. Proposed are a unique set of principles and procedures for each function, including original perceptions and prescriptions for recruiting, motivating, and organizing, among others.

Chapter 4 – Leader Competencies: The Tools of the Trade

Leaders must acquire the mind and skill sets essential to the fulfillment of the mission. This chapter reviews four popular catalogues and recommends five requisites for leadership. A practical feature is a recommended set of values and strategies for everyday administrative function.

One

DEFINITIVE CONCERNS: *What Is Leadership?*

*"Come, **follow** me, and I will make you fishers of men" (Matthew 4:19; Mark 1:17).*

He could not have stated it with more clarity or simplicity. With this piercing and poignant declaration, the Master revealed the heart of his perception of a leader's role and function. Consequently, he established a template for not only those who would follow him directly, but also for those who would emulate his ministry. When adhering to the pattern of Jesus, a leader engages others to *comply* with direction (learning to follow) and *commit* to a life-changing adventure (learning to fish).

Even though the Gospels present multiple renditions of the same stories, the realization that they record Jesus as saying, "Follow me" more than twenty times is still impressive. It lends credence to the common conception that a leader is one who has followers, or as the creators of Situational Leadership state, "There is no leadership without someone following" (Hersey, Blanchard, and Johnson 2001). Although the full implications of this popular dictum may be debated, the reality is that to be acknowledged as a leader, one must be able to turn around and see someone coming along behind. Christian leaders first follow Jesus; then they provide a path for others to travel as they learn to follow and learn to fish.

Let's Talk About Followership

Jesus expected his disciples to follow him, experience life change, and participate in something remarkable. Contemporary leaders must anticipate and prepare for the same. In fact, perceptive leaders concede that success in an endeavor is to a great degree dependent upon the condition, character, and competence of the disciple or follower. As St. Augustine noted 1600 years ago, the leader must make certain his hearers are "friendly, attentive, and ready to learn, whether he has found them so or he has made them so" (Augustine 1997).

On Following

I find it striking that after briefly surveying the tables of contents and the indexes of more than three dozen texts on leadership and management,

I discovered only four with any reference to "followers" or "following." Additionally, one of my students in a church administration course, in order to construct an annotated bibliography on followership, conducted an extensive search and found a mere nineteen sources – three books devoted to following, six with chapters on the subject, and ten related journal articles – with only two of the authors being clearly identified as Christian. Finally, a colleague reviewed a collection of homiletics texts and observed that for all the attention given to preaching, there was next to none given to the listening skills of the congregants. It appears that even though preachers, teachers, and leaders all share the conviction that effective communication demands both a sender and a receiver, in practice they pay little attention to the receiver.

In my survey, two of the four leadership texts that referred to followers were secular texts. Eugene Habecker's *The Other Side of Leadership* is the only Christian book on leadership containing any significant discussion of following (Habecker 1987). Considering the titles, the absence is also notable when no discussion of following can be found in Kenneth O. Gangel's article, "Toward a New Testament View of Leadership" (Gangel 1974) or his entire work on *Leadership for Church Education* (Gangel 1970). Gangel, however, does reference the contribution of William Litzinger and Thomas Schaefer in his *Team Leadership in Christian Ministry*. Their work focuses on the leadership training strategy at West Point, and their research indicates that a leader must first learn to be a follower (Gangel 1997).

Douglas K. Smith includes a chapter on "The Following Part of Leading" in *The Future Leader* (Hesselbein, Goldsmith, and Beckhard 1996), but his interest in following is as a means to ensure results, such as producing performance for the organization, rather than changing the life of the follower. Hersey, Blanchard, and Johnson's Situational Leadership model (2001) likewise focuses upon a leader's response to a follower and his performance, not the follower's response to the leader. In other words, little is written about the follower unless it is to promote activity and accomplishment within the confines of the institution. This work also focuses on the behaviors of leaders, but it does so cognizant of the fact that if no one responds, the leader is not leading. In fact, one of the underlying dynamics of leadership to which I adhere proposes that leadership involves influence, instruction, and inspiration, therefore anticipating responsive devotees who not only hear but also react and conduct themselves in harmony with the leader's direction.

Our culture, however, relegates following to a secondary status, as symbolized by an automobile manufacturer's recent advertisement: "It's greater to lead than follow." Coach Phil Jackson's journal of the Los Angeles Lakers' 2003-2004 NBA basketball season also illustrates this in a most profound and telling way (Jackson 2004). While they enjoyed a successful season by most standards, it fell short of the expected championship envisioned by a team with four future Hall-of-Famers on its roster. In Jackson's attempt to dissect the reasons for the failure, he mused, "Maybe I was incapable of communicating the selfless concepts required to produce success." While taking the blame on himself and accepting his failures as a leader to unite and inspire his team, Jackson also asserted throughout his book that it was critical for each individual player to make the choice to submit to the system and work for the good of the team, rather than for personal accomplishments and statistics. Most of today's NBA players appear to believe it is greater to lead than to follow, but rejecting direction and instruction seldom produces consistent victory. In fact, following is the prerequisite to leading. No wonder so many of the truly effective coaches were not stars when they played the game; they learned to follow before they led.

On Followership

With penetrating insight, Manfred F. R. Kets de Vries and Elizabeth Florent-Treacy expand this discussion by observing, "It is essential to remember that there is no *leadership* without *followership*" (Chowdhury 2003). The core of any definition of exceptional and life-changing leadership is the expectation that a leader is one who exerts enough influence in another's life that ultimately *followership* and not just *following* ensues.

Followership is more than a position of submission. It is a commitment to change, a willingness to be transformed into the image, style, and behavior of the leader. *Following* may simply indicate trailing behind another or even adhering to the directions of someone who can point the way to a desired location. *Followership*, on the other hand, implies a condition of relationship and accountability. The invitation of Jesus to follow him offered a transformation of life and lifestyle that involved more than just shadowing him from town to town and miracle-to-miracle, observing and not participating. Many people followed him, but only a few chose to accept his invitation to followership and discipleship.

Disciple-Followers

Dallas Willard stated in an interview that he believes "discipleship as a term has lost its content." Therefore, to "redeem the idea of discipleship," the current generation has resurfaced the ancient phrase *spiritual formation* to infuse ministry processes with meaning and application that *education* and *discipleship* have apparently lost (Willard 2005). It is, however, my conviction that by uncovering timeless truths, framed in both biblical and contemporary language, we can rekindle the embers smoldering in the term *discipleship* and restore its inherent power and proper place in the practice and vocabulary of Christian ministers.

While pastoring a small suburban congregation, my preparation for a series of sermons on Jesus' expectations of his disciples deeply affected me. I discovered that the noun form of the word *follow* (i.e., "follower") is utilized only once in the New Testament, but the term *disciple(s)* is found 294 times. The implication is that to "come follow me," the Lord's respondents had to be disciples, and that implied more than mere presence. In fact, the conditions of discipleship articulated by the Master included self-denial, renunciation and leaving all, steadfastness, fruitfulness, and love. Jesus frequently confirmed the necessity of meeting these conditions by stating, "You cannot be my disciple unless…" (e.g., Luke 14:27, 33). In other words, he demanded perseverance and personal commitment, as did the Apostle Paul in 1Corinthians 11:1, when he instructed the church to "imitate" him. It is noteworthy that the Greek word Paul employed is also translated "follow," implying that the biblical perception of following involves imitation. In essence, Jesus and Paul both redefined the term *follow* to denote a commitment consistent with the terms *discipleship* and *followership*. To reflect this enhanced meaning, I have coined the term *disciple-follower*; I perceive and utilize it as virtually synonymous with an enriched understanding of follower or learner.

Let's Talk About Leadership

Leadership will be defined more completely at the end of this chapter. Nonetheless, a preliminary description of the behaviors of leadership may be submitted. Considering the evidence encountered so far, we can describe leadership as a behavior or activity that induces a person or group to choose to *come* and influences an individual or group to *follow*.

An Emerging Paradigm

Leadership of any kind or at any level demands the utilization and application of skills that induce and influence followers. Researchers have attempted to identify what those skills, traits, or characteristics may be and how they can effectively be applied in a leadership situation. However, the summary judgment of those investigators provides credibility to the perception that there is no universally agreed upon set of leadership characteristics. Consequently, they assert that leadership is exercised most effectively when the situation is taken into consideration. This is very similar to a golfer who chooses his club and plays his shot based on the lie of the ball; everything is relative.

This approach to leadership theory was extended by the *In Search of Excellence* phenomenon (Peters and Waterman 1982), which was built upon the assumption that an entirely new way to look at leadership is required because the milieu in which business is conducted has changed drastically from the economic culture prevalent during the Great Depression and World War II. Many approaches to leadership still share this basic premise, and it has proven to be the catalyst for the discovery and establishment of an entirely new paradigm for leadership theory and application.

In the formulation of this emerging paradigm, two parallel concerns inform and constrain the process. The first concern consists of the observation that leadership is normally defined, described, theorized, and preached from a unique and limited individual perspective. No one human's perspective, however, is adequate or complete. In fact, twenty years ago there were more than 350 definitions of leadership and thousands of empirical investigations, and "no clear and unequivocal understanding exists as to what distinguishes leaders from non-leaders, and perhaps more important, what distinguishes effective leaders from ineffective leaders" (Bennis and Nanus 1985). The fact that the underlying research on leadership has gone from the study of great men, to the identification of common traits, to the anticipation of attitudes and styles, and finally to analytic grids indicates the theoretical base is constantly changing. Hersey and Blanchard, therefore, created a metatheory called Situational Leadership to incorporate all of this research into a unifying structure, leading one to believe the key to leadership is not just the accumulation of attitudes and techniques, but finding an underlying relationship and approach to the followers.

The second concern in identifying and establishing the new paradigm is similarly restrictive. Much of the current theorizing on leadership is focused upon the need to be able to respond to the rapidly changing world in which we live. These changes, fueled by technology and forged in the furnace of prevailing postures, force the leader of today into a novel set of attitudes and behaviors not anticipated by previous generations. In this rush to originality, however, the modern leader must be careful not to reject the wisdom and experience gathered from the past. Contemporary leadership must not abandon ancient wisdom or proven traditional methods. After all, leaders have risen and influenced followers throughout history.

Thus, the situation in which leaders find themselves today demands the practical integration of the new with the old. Contemporary Christian leaders, therefore, find in a synthesis of the tried and true with the new and improved a model that is consistent, global, and not dependent upon technology to generate change.

Three Themes

Tempered by these two concerns, and extrapolated from a preliminary perception of the emerging paradigm, we can identify three dominant themes that have a dramatic impact upon our understanding of leadership and even management. In his classic work *Visionary Leadership*, Burt Nanus (1992) also acknowledges the same three as primary influences among the eight forces shaping twenty-first century organizations. The first theme is that a shrinking world demands a leader to think globally. The second states that this mentality is due primarily to the incredibly massive infusion of technology into every aspect of life. The third recognizes that this phenomenon has produced change on a scale never before experienced or encountered by humankind. In summary, global technological changes are driving our culture as never before.

A Personal Paradigm

What happens, then, if the technology breaks down? What do we do if our resources are limited? I use my computer to write books, communicate online, balance my checking account, manage my schedule, maintain an address book, and study Greek words in a Bible program. It is a very useful tool and resource. However, what if there is no power to drive it? A student in one of my Sunday school classes came each week with a laptop computer. He used it to read the text, to check my facts in his digital study books, and take his personal notes. Every time I looked in his direction, his face was focused on the screen or looking down at the keys. During one of these classes, I heard a beep and looked over to see him closing his "Bible." His battery had gone dead, and so did his study for that morning. No contemporary technology can improve upon the word found in manuscript or in the heart.

In addition to technology, the climate of constant change in our culture is the underlying thesis of nearly every contemporary book or article on leadership. Within the text *The Leader of the Future* (Hesselbein, Goldsmith, and Beckhard 1996), five of the first seven chapters refer to the influence and effect of technology on our culture and its leaders. In one of these chapters, John W. Work states, "The world as we have known it is changing at a dizzying pace, fueled by advances in technology and innovation." When we examine them closely, however, today's leaders possess the very qualities and characteristics found in the biblical leaders of other eras. In fact, Kenneth Blanchard in the same work (Chapter 8, "Turning the Organizational Pyramid Upside Down") utilizes Moses as an illustration of the need for leaders to be the ones who set the mission, vision, values, and major goals.

In establishing a personal approach to leadership and management, I am challenged to strip away those components which are only contemporary and temporary – determined by the swiftly changing currents of our culture, especially those technology fuels – and discover the underlying, foundational, trans-generational and trans-cultural, universal character and application of leadership. To summarize and emphasize this point, consider the following quotation from a paper I wrote during my doctoral studies:

> I am convinced a leadership philosophy must be rooted in principles that transcend the culture and its strengths and limitations. I want to be a leader even if I don't have my computer and technological resources. I want to be able to minister to people's lives if our economy crashes and we all become agrarian again (a labor-dominated work force instead of our present information-driven one)! I want to be a leader if the church in America finds itself persecuted and driven underground and not allowed access to the pool of resources and privileges it now enjoys. I want to be a leader in my home, in my neighborhood, when I coach little league sports, or when I'm confronted with a ministry call in the middle of the night.
>
> My philosophy and approach to leadership must be universal in scope and operation. It then can integrate and apply whatever perceptions, skills, and resources are available at the time, but not be limited by them. My desire, then, is to find a "metamodel" that gives me the framework upon which I can hang any new theory, skill, technique, or resource and

9

yet still have a viable, working leadership model no matter the environment or culture (or how fast or slow things are changing around me).

So where do we begin in our attempt to construct a global, change acknowledging, technologically independent, metamodel for leadership and its behavior? In essence, we need to ask the questions that will enable us to identify, describe, and articulate the structure of the discipline *leadership*. Therefore, commencing with the next section and continuing in the following two chapters, we will address these three critical concerns:

1. What is leadership?
2. What does a leader do?
3. How does a leader do it?

Leadership: What Is It?

Our examination so far has lead us to perceive leadership as a behavior or activity that induces a person or group to choose to *come* and influences an individual or group to *follow*. Utilizing the Bible as our primary guide, we will now explore the concept of leadership in more depth and develop a more comprehensive definition. As disciples of Christ, we must approach the Word of God as the base upon which we can build a universal metamodel for leadership behavior. Since Paul could tell believers that their experiences in Greek-dominated Thessalonica were the same as their Hebrew brothers in Jerusalem (1Thessalonians 2:14), it should not be difficult to understand leadership in a similar cross-cultural way.

My intention is to craft a biblical and universal conception of leadership that establishes and informs a paradigm shift of global proportions. Our investigation, then, will lead us to a description and formal definition that is not bound by cultural constraints, generational quirks, or technological advances or retreats.

As we begin, it is important to note that it is necessary to set aside pre-conceived notions, assumptions, and even cherished perceptions of terms and definitions. *Leadership, management,* and *administration* are terms utilized in business, religious, and educative contexts with often overlapping or even contradicting applications in diverse venues. I am going to present a unique approach to these concepts and terms that contains scholarly, biblical and practical components, thereby adding to that diversity.

Transactions and Transformations

As a result of James MacGregor Burns's classic volume, *Leadership*, it is common today to distinguish between "transactional leadership," where an exchange occurs, and "transformational leadership," where change occurs (Burns 1978). In transactional leadership, an exchange between the leader and the follower facilitates the fulfillment of an objective or the accomplishment of a task, enabling an alteration in location, information, or even product. In transformational leadership, a substantive change occurs in the nature or character of either the followers or the organizations of which they are part.

Jesus' approach to leadership included both. Obviously, there were transactions involved, both personal and professional, in which Jesus and his followers engaged in mutual interaction, a spiritual version of give and take. Equally present, however, was the expectation of change and the insistence his followers become something different than they were before the encounter. Transformation was his ultimate goal.

"Come, follow me and I will make you fishers of men" is, therefore, more than a transactional imperative uttered by Jesus and offered to a select cadre of first century fishermen, tax collectors, and unlearned disciples. This offer was an invitation to transformation proffered not only to the disciples, but also to the citizens of a hurting and needy nation suffering through the enduring consequences of national and individual sin and disobedience. This offer is now tendered to contemporary leaders and followers. Jesus is providing an example to emulate, as well as an opportunity to experience the transformation available to all who will heed his call.

Stated simply, to allow Jesus to lead is to accept his invitation to be a *disciple-follower* while simultaneously growing in the ability to make disciple-followers of others. I have personally acknowledged and responded to his invitation, and I encourage those who will to join me in a quest to discover and implement this style and manner of biblical ministry. It will challenge us not only to be, but also to make, "fishers of men," allowing ancient wisdom to inform and inspire our efforts in contemporary Christian ministry.

We will discuss in Chapter 2 the fact that transaction and transformation often work in concert, in consecutive phases, and in practice may actually include or imitate each other. Although they share numerous commonalities, a cursory investigation of both biblical testaments affirms a distinction between these two dimensions of leadership. In this chapter, therefore, we will examine them individually.

Transactional Leadership

Let us investigate first transactional or functional leadership. Habecker does a wonderful job of discussing this aspect, and he examines both the words involved and the context of their usage in the New Testament (Habecker 1987). His research indicates that anyone can function as a transactional leader, providing information, direction, assistance, and skills that influence others to go somewhere or do something different then they had been previously. Parents, teachers, friends, colleagues, or anyone who exercises random acts of "roving leadership" can practice this influential behavior (De Pree 1989). Anyone who receives and acts upon this information, direction, or influence is following the lead of another person.

A student in one of my leadership courses was discussing the fact that she was having a hard time finding a church since she had relocated from another town. One of the other students offered, "Come to my church this week, and I will introduce you to the pastor and show you around." I pointed out to this second student that she had just exercised leadership, and it caught her by surprise. "Are you not giving direction, showing the way, and asking the other to follow you?" I asked. Then I noted, "You just practiced a form of functional leadership." From this perception of leadership as a function, it is obvious that anyone may lead, and at some point, everyone is a follower. The concept of leadership as a transaction between individuals is evident.

In the New Testament, three primary words for "lead" are utilized for this conception and function of leadership. Table 1 contains a brief definition of the Greek terms employed along with a practical description of some of the behaviors in which leaders engage. Before proceeding with our investigation, a careful review and reflection upon the implications for Christian leaders is beneficial.

Table 1. Biblical Terms for the "Function of Leadership"

Biblical Term	Definition
Ago	"To bear, bring carry" > Lead
"Take my hand and come with me" OR "climb aboard I'll help you" ("led" to a place)	
Hedegeo	To lead (Ago) + "Away"
"Follow me (away from here) and I'll get you there (where we're to be)" - ("led" away)	
Kubernao	"To guide, steering, pilotage"
"Listen; I'll point you in the right direction" OR "Follow; I'll guide you" ("directed")	

Transactional leadership may well be exercised as an individual and personal response to a need, a request for direction, or a private drive to accomplish some task. It can also be exercised, however, in corporate and organizational contexts. At some point, we all find ourselves serving an organization or someone who is in headship over us. This position may have different titles, such as CEO, president, boss, or simply "master" (which is derived from the Latin *magistratus*, although today a "magistrate" is considered a minor civil official), but the function is the same. This master directs the affairs of the enterprise and determines, controls, commands, orders, points, and guides others toward a goal, thus performing as a transactional leader in a corporate context.

Transformational Leadership

Burns suggests transformational leadership "occurs when one or more persons engage with others in such a way that leaders and followers raise one another to higher levels of motivation and morality." Although he is not writing from a biblical or Christian perspective, Burns also observes that, "Transforming leadership ultimately becomes moral in that it raises the level of human conduct and ethical aspiration of both leader and led, and thus it has a transforming effect on both" (Burns 1978).

This aspect of leadership demands an endowment, whether naturally at birth or supernaturally at new birth, which enables an ability to influence others. This grace is available to and may be exercised by anyone the Lord chooses to have minister in a leadership capacity in an organization, whether it is a church, a business, a family, or even a recreational group. In its fulfillment, someone or something will be transformed and truly follow the leader. This is in contrast to transactional leadership that simply and only accomplishes a specific task.

Clearly, this is the kind of leadership Jesus had in mind when he appointed The Twelve to be with him (Mark 3:14), converted them into fishers of men (Matthew 4:19), and anticipated that they would go and make other disciples (Matthew 28:20; cf. John 17:20).

The relationship between transactive and transformative leadership, especially in the context of an institutional or corporate venue, will be addressed in detail in Chapter 2. For this discussion, it is sufficient to state that the influential activities of a Christ-following leader are intended to accomplish more than simply carrying out the mission and fulfilling the purposes of an organization. Ultimately, the goal is to promote a conversion and transformation of both the followers and the institution of which they are a part.

Let's Talk About Administration

In order to appreciate fully the application and function of leadership, it is necessary to identify and explore the dynamic environment or milieu in which it operates. The transactions and transformations of leadership are not achieved within a lifeless vacuum; they exist and find their fulfillment within a living context. Specifically, such an environment is established when a unique contribution or specialized support is required to fulfill the mission of an institution, and the head of the organization appoints accomplished *administrators* to assist in the implementation of the program. The term *administrate*, as with the word *master*, comes from the Latin and means "to be an aid to," from the roots *ad* (to) and *mei* (inferior, servant; hence, minister). In other words, an administrator carries out the directions and will of another, thus serving as a ministering agent (Picket 2000).

The implication for Christian leadership is obvious. Jesus Christ is the Master, the head of the Church, and while he has the power and authority to accomplish his mission directly and personally, he chooses to involve his people in productive service. In fact, every believer is expected to make a significant contribution to the commission through utilizing the gifts of the Spirit in mutual ministry. As the program designed to implement the mission unfolds, those who, among other gifts, teach, serve, give, help, and share knowledge or wisdom, all contribute to its fulfillment. There are, however, some who are gifted or anointed with special calls to the administration of Christ's church and serve its related institutions, enterprises, and programs.

Since God is sovereign over all of creation, and since Paul and Peter both assert that governments are under God (Romans 13:3, I Peter 2:13), it is possible to include secular leaders and their organizations in this discussion as well. Therefore, ministers are not limited to service in the church. For example, administrators in democratic governmental departments and agencies often carry titles such as "Minister of Finance" as they implement what the current party in power perceives as the will of the people. That is why they are called "the current administration" – their responsibility is to administrate the will of the people as the elected representatives discern it.

Leadership and Management

As these administrators serve their masters, their duties fall within one of two broad categories: *leadership* or *management*. Here, then, we find and identify a context for the function of leadership. In the same manner that teaching collaborates with training in the process of education (see Part II), leadership collaborates with management in the process of administration. These functions closely coincide with the two spiritual gifts whose descriptions and functions are noted in Table 2, although not every administrator is spiritually gifted. Despite the fact that both gifts are often perceived as being involved in leading, a more accurate translation of the terms would be "leadership" for *proistemi* and "management" for *kubernesis*.

Table 2. Biblical Terms for the Gifts of Administration

Biblical Term	Definition
Proistemi (Romans 12:8)	"To stand before"
Other possible translations – "Leadership"; "Leads"; "Ruleth" The gift of leadership is the grace which allows a person to hear from God concerning the vision, direction, and purpose of a ministry and to be able to "stand before" the church and communicate that direction in such a way that people respond, follow, and implement the course, as so directed.	
Kubernesis (1Corinthians 12:28)	"To pilot, guide, govern"
Other possible translations – "Government"; "Administration" The gift of governments is the grace which allows a person to see to it that the church stays "on course" through administrative procedures such as planning, organizing, scheduling, and guides its implementation through communication and organizational systems.	

Current scholarly literature debates as to whether or not a sharp distinction exists between these two terms. Biblical literature is not so bifurcated. Instead, the Bible confirms the distinction, as exemplified in the administrative practices contained in both Testaments. In Exodus 31, for example, the Lord appoints and anoints skilled artisans to manage the resources necessary to construct and outfit the Tabernacle, and then assigns Moses to the leadership task of speaking for the Lord when standing before the Israelites. In the New Testament, when a dispute arises over the handling of food in Acts 6, "the Twelve gathered all the disciples together and said, 'It would not be right for us to neglect the ministry of the word of God in order to wait on tables. Brothers, choose seven men from among you who are known to be full of the Spirit and wisdom. We will turn this responsibility over to them and will give our attention to prayer and the ministry of the word'" (Acts 6:2-5). In both instances, we observe what is

15

commonly referred to as a division of labor; the distinction and separation of the functions is patent.

A contemporary articulation of the distinction was evident during the 2008 primary campaign for President of the United States when one of the candidates, John McCain, attempted to distinguish himself from one of his rivals, Mitt Romney. McCain noted and compared the practical differences between the two administrative functions, as the Los Angeles Times (January 25, 2008) reported:

> *Arizona Sen. John McCain swiped at his chief rival, former Massachusetts Gov. Mitt Romney, at a news conference.*
>
> *"I have led, not managed," McCain said.*
>
> *"Governor Romney is touting his qualities and his experience and resume as a manager," McCain said. "I am telling the American people, and they know it, that I am a leader.*
>
> *"You can hire managers all the time, people who do the mechanics, people who implement policies, people who are good with assets," McCain said. "Leadership is the ability to inspire and the ability to make Americans serve causes greater than their self-interest."*

My theory and observation of practice falls in line with McCain's perception of the distinction. It is also in line with Bennis and Nanus, who have been quoted so frequently that it is almost to the point of being axiomatic:

> *The problem with many organizations, and especially the ones that are failing, is that they tend to be over managed and underled... There is a profound difference between management and leadership, and both are important. "To manage" means "to bring about, to accomplish, to have charge of or responsibility for, to conduct." "Leading" is "influencing, guiding in direction, course, action, opinion." The distinction is crucial. Managers are people who do things right and leaders are people who do the right thing. The difference may be summarized as activities of vision and judgment-effectiveness versus activities of mastering routines-efficiency (Bennis and Nanus 1985).*

In summary, leaders spend most of their time and attention focusing upon the mission, vision, goals, and direction of the enterprise and thus deal most directly with the people involved. Managers, on the other hand, spend most of their time in the manipulation of the tools, resources, and objects of the enterprise. Put perhaps much too simplistically, leaders minister to people while managers manipulate the things that are utilized to facilitate that ministry. For this reason, "the responsibility of leaders is not to manage the church," but to equip and shepherd the people (Richards and Hoeldtke 1980). In practice, this principle can be applied to other organizations and programs as well.

Administration in Action

Despite their differences, leadership and management are not competing forces. Rather, they complement each other in addressing the activities necessary to fulfill a master's will and direction. After all, leaders do manage resources, and managers often lead others who share the management responsibilities. Nonetheless, acknowledging the distinction is helpful.

Since many leaders are not equipped with the passion or skills needed for day-to-day management, their recognition of this deficiency and deference to a gifted manager is critical. Even with competent leadership, an organization that is not managed well may fail to fulfill its vision. When the Gulf Coast of the United States was devastated by a series of hurricanes in 2005, no one argued about the leadership's vision for disaster relief. The inevitable criticisms leveled against local, state, and federal administrators were due to a perception of mismanagement of the available resources and the devastation those unfortunate actions produced. Stated concisely, for the administration of an enterprise to flow smoothly, leaders and managers must learn to work together, appreciating and taking advantage of each other's contributions. In most instances, the establishment of a team including both a leader and a manager, or multiples of each, provides the most effective and efficient administration.

Experiencing a Team

Early in my career, I experienced a positive and productive combination of leadership and management that provides a practical example of an administrative team in action. While serving as the principal of a church's school, and after filling both leadership and management roles for a number of years, I desired to hire a business manager. My supervisor cautioned me to be careful because a business manager can "make you or break you." I took the risk and hired a young man who had been a member of our faculty but had also evidenced managerial aptitude as a department coordinator. In the years that followed, it proved to be a wise decision that literally paid dividends.

During our time together, we discovered the differences between a *leader* and a *manager* and forged a partnership that was effective and efficient. One afternoon during a meeting with my department coordinators, we decided that we wanted to spend some money on a certain ministry project. I called the manager into the meeting to discuss the idea and, of course, the first words out of his mouth were, "We don't have an account for that." I suggested that he create one, and with a smile he said, "I'll be right back." A few moments later, he returned with a check in hand, and we proceeded with the project. He managed the resources to make it happen. Additionally, by the end of the year, he had generated enough of a surplus to give each member of our staff a bonus. I had only been able to balance the budget; he made it work profitably. He honored my mission and vision, followed my lead, and manipulated resources rather than people to make the dreams come true. I respected his judgment, relied upon his skill, and submitted my leadership to his managerial expertise. Together, we practiced administration.

Leader or Manager?

Countless numbers of other leaders and managers have also been liberated and empowered to serve as they have identified and embraced their place and involvement within an organization, program, or project. They have found it beneficial to identify the spiritual gift, natural endowment, or personal service preference – leadership or management – with which they resonate and operate. To assist in this process of personally identifying and embracing a role, I have described the distinct but complementary nature of these functions in Table 3. It contains a chart summarizing the characteristics and purposes of both leadership and management. Reflecting upon the nature and function of each, and their relationship to people, positions, and processes, can facilitate the discovery or affirmation of an individual's primary means of service.

Table 3. The Functions of "Administration"

"Leadership"		"Management"
"Lithan" - to go; "Lad" - "a course"	Definition	"To control or direct; using for a purpose"
Ministry	Function	Manipulation
People	Object	Ideas & Things
Family Tree	Structure	Organizational Chart
Active	Involvement w/ People	Passive
People's Possess things/ideas, not people	"Ownership" of program & resources	**Yours** Ideas, things, people, resources
Leaders serve people, not things, programs or plans	Summary	**Managers support leaders** by manipulating things
"Leadership" *Proistemi*	Biblical Gift	"Governments" *Kubernesis*

Leadership and management are literally two sides of the same coin, unique but integrated, complementary and not competitive, and without hierarchy. In fact, where an individual is located on an organizational chart is determined by the group's structure not by whether he is a leader or a manager. A teacher, for instance, may be relegated to a relatively lower place on a school's orgchart, yet still function as a classroom leader with as much, or more, influence than a district administrator who rarely sees a student. In other words, to fully comprehend the nature of administration and the functions of leadership and management, it is necessary to separate them from organizational hierarchy and the identity of personnel, and perceive of them as functions and activities that enable administration.

Each of these functions is essential for the effective and efficient administration of any organization or enterprise, especially the Body of Christ, the Church. The focus of this work, however, is on leadership, not management, so I defer further exploration of management to any number of other texts (secular or religious – there are quite a few specifically geared to church management). David Pollock, for example, has created a resource manual, *Business Management in the Local Church*, containing instructions, tables, charts, displays, and sample forms that a manager would find very helpful in the manipulation of finances, facilities, and the various legal and business responsibilities, including a brief section on pastoral compensation (Pollock 1996). He also integrates his recommendations around biblical principles, allowing the thoughtful and reflective leader to be comfortable in the implementation of his suggestions.

In Conclusion: A Definition of Leadership

Administration consists of leadership and management. A *leader* is one who possesses a clear mission with an attendant vision, stands before others effectively conveying the messages, and efficiently supervises the actions needed to fulfill the mission. A *manager* is one who controls and manipulates the resources necessary to keep the enterprise on course and actively engaged in progress towards its objectives.

In communicating these concepts in workshops, courses, and training programs, I have found that a graphic visualization of the relationships between administration, leadership, and management can be helpful. These relationships can be visualized as an umbrella with two ribs, a wheel with two spokes, or a tree with two branches, as presented in Display 1. Unlike an organizational chart, this depiction does not represent a hierarchy or specific individuals; in many cases, one person must function as both a leader and a manager, as I did before I hired the business manager. As with Table 3, many leaders find it beneficial to consider the implications for, and effects upon, the people, positions, or processes of the function represented by each box in the diagram.

Display 1. The Administration Tree Chart

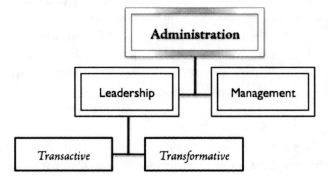

In concise terms, I define leadership as "an aspect of administration in which others are induced and influenced to come, follow, and contribute to the accomplishment of a mission." With this definition in mind, we shall now explore a description of a leader's behavior in Chapter 2. To do so, we will address the second of our three critical inquiries that outline Part I and facilitate the uncovering of the structure of the discipline leadership: "What Does a Leader Do?"

Transactional leadership: Orders, points, and guides others toward a goal.

Transformational leadership: leaders and followers raise one another to higher levels of motivation and morality.

Leader: One who posses a clear mission with an attendant vision; stands before others effectively conveying the message; and efficiently supervises the actions needed to fulfill the mission.

Manager: One who controls and manipulates the resources necessary to keep the enterprise on course. And actively engaged in progress towards its objectives.

Leadership: an aspect of administration in which others are induced and influenced to come, follow, and contribute to the accomplishment of a mission." Dr. Mitchell

Reflection and Response

If you expect this book to make a significant impact on your life, learning, or leadership, you will need to give consideration to two questions: "What do you think about what you have read?" and "What are you going to do about it?" To encourage and facilitate this process, each chapter will conclude with an opportunity to reflect upon and respond to several selected questions, comments, or issues.

Agree - Disagree Exercise

Listed below are a number of statements representing a variety of leadership issues addressed in Chapter 1 or will be addressed in chapters to come. Read each one and determine: A if you agree with it or D if you do not, reflecting upon why. When you have finished reading the rest of Part I, return to this page and see if your responses or reasons have changed.

A D   Leadership is the key to all effective ministry.

A D   Leaders are born, not made.

A D   Leadership is more important than followership.

A D   Understanding and utilizing technology is essential for today's administrator.

A D   There is no leadership without someone following.

A D   Leadership is a behavior or activity that induces a person (or group) to choose to come and influences an individual or group to follow.

A D   Leaders minister to people, managers manipulate things.

A D   A formal, written mission statement is mandatory for success.

A D   Communication is the key to all effective and efficient administration.

A D   It does not matter what organizational structure is utilized, as long as it is effective.

A D   Setting the bar too high is a hindrance in recruiting volunteers.

21

A   D   Controlling another person's behavior is a necessary function of management.

A   D   Secular leaders, especially executives, are not appropriate models for Christians to follow or imitate.

A   D   Who a leader is, is not nearly as important as what the leader does.

A   D   A leader's skill set is more important than his mindset.

A   D   I have a clear personal definition, philosophy, and approach to leadership.

Two

LEADERSHIP BEHAVIORS: *What Does a Leader Do?*

> *The kings of the Gentiles lord it over them... But you are not to be like that... the one who rules [is] like the one who **serves** (Luke 22: 25, 26).*

In a seminary course I presently teach, students choose the topic of servant leadership as the subject of their research paper by a three-to-one ratio over all other topics except the ordination of women. In contemplating the possible reasons for this popularity among seminary students, three explanations rapidly present themselves. First, the idea of servant leadership has taken on the quality of a catch phrase or buzzword in leadership and management circles ever since Robert Greenleaf made it popular in his text *Servant Leadership* (1977), and Hersey, Blanchard, and Johnson applied it to managing followers in their Situational Leadership model (2001). Second, the concept itself is centuries old, finding its genesis not in contemporary management theory, but in ancient biblical leadership. Jesus himself pronounced the summary statement in Luke 22. Third, it provides not only a description of an approach to leadership, but also articulates a prescription for the function of a leader. In essence, "servant leadership" encapsulates in two words an introduction to a biblical response to the second question framing our discussion of leadership: "What Does a Leader Do?"

Servant leadership appears to be self-explanatory: it is the responsibility or the mission of the leader to serve his followers. The application, however, is to a great degree dependent upon how one defines "serve." It has been applied on a continuum from slaves, who are at their master's disposal for any menial task, to elected politicians or conquering warriors, who attempt to persuade the populace that their agenda is truly for the good of the people.

The contemporary Christian educator and leader must walk a line of balance between these two extremes of imposed servitude and beneficial service. On the one hand, to serve my followers, I influence, instruct, advise, and share my life in a way that brings change for the better. In this process, I admonish, correct, discipline, and expect response. To state it simply, I give direction that I anticipate being followed; my service is in being, as Jesus named it, a "ruler." On the other hand, I acknowledge I am but an experienced fellow traveler and am at their disposal to lend a hand in the activities they have determined to be essential and require assistance.

In attempting to describe the character and qualities of a person who chooses to live life as a steward and administrator of Christ's kingdom, I examined the scriptures with a focus upon the directives presented and arrived at the conclusion that a servant exhibits certain characteristics that can be summarized in the following acrostic.

A SERVANT is one who:

S: Shares his life message (2Cor. 2:3-8; 1Thess. 2:8; 1Tim. 4:16)

E: Exemplifies that message (Phil. 3:17; 1Thess. 1:6, 7; 1Cor. 11:1)

R: Represents his master correctly (1John 4:20; 1Peter 2:12)

V: Verbalizes his master's thoughts (1Cor. 5:20; 1Peter 4:10, 11)

A: Acquiesces to authority and shares leadership (2Cor. 1:24; 1Peter 2:13 – 3:7)

N: Needs are met (Acts 4:32-35; 2Cor. 8)

T: Teaches and trains (Acts 20; 20, 27; Titus 2; 1Tim. 3:2; 2Tim. 2:2, 14)

Embedded within these characteristics are the activities that constitute the behaviors of leaders: hearing, speaking, and doing. Before we examine these behaviors, I want to make a critical observation. The "R" component suggests a servant serves the master. The question, though, must be asked: Who is the contemporary leader's master? Whom does the leader truly serve and represent? In business, the answer is the bottom line. In corporate America, the response is often the firm or the company. In the service industry or people business, it is supposed to be human beings. Doctors, teachers, and ministers are all called to serve, assist, and facilitate people in meeting their needs – the "N" component. Far too often, these leaders and their organizations fall prey to the siren calls of production, prosperity, and profitability. The nurture and development of people becomes not an end in itself, but a means to an end.

To whom or what a servant leader is submitted and actually serves is therefore one of the critical considerations that must be addressed for an administrator to truly be effective. How does one reconcile the human master's instruction to "Go make a dollar," with the heavenly master's instruction to "Go make disciples"? It dramatically affects a variety of issues including staffing, budgeting, and policy decisions. There are probably no easy answers, but before proceeding to discover what leaders do, we at least needed to address the question. As the Bob Dylan lyric states, "You gotta serve somebody." Each of us is faced with the definitive inquiry, whom do you serve? How one responds determines how one will behave, and how a leader behaves is critical to the growth and development of the organization and the constituency it serves.

Describing Leadership: What Does a Leader Do?

Whether *transactional* or *transformational*, leadership is exercised in a variety of situations that require the comprehension and implementation of a wide selection of leadership skills. Since the skills and the resources needed to carry them out will vary, it is important to find a metamodel a leader can depend upon regardless of the circumstances or the resources available. Identifying and illustrating the activities of biblical leaders in both the Old and New Testaments provide a functional framework for a metamodel of three leadership behaviors, as shown in Table 4.

Table 4. The Behaviors of Biblical Leaders

A Biblical Illustration: *Moses*

Moses' Action	Exodus 6	Exodus 7	Exodus 8
HEARING	"Then the Lord said to Moses..."		
SPEAKING	"Moses reported to the Israelites -"Tell Aaron"; "Tell Pharaoh"		
DOING	"Moses and Aaron did just as the Lord Commanded"		

A Biblical Illustration: *Joshua*

Joshua's Action	Joshua 3:7-14ff	Joshua 4:1-8ff	Joshua 4:15-18ff
HEARD FROM GOD	"Tell the Priests"	"Choose 12 men"	"Command the Priests"
SPOKE TO PEOPLE	"Come and listen"	"Called the 12"	"Commanded the Priests"
DID THE JOB	"Priests carry ark"	"So Israelites did"	"Priests came up"

A Biblical Illustration: *Nehemiah*

Nehemiah's Action	Nehemiah 1:1 – 2:17	Nehemiah 2:17 – 18	Nehemiah 2: 18b ff
REPORT RECEIVED	"Send me to the city in Judah... so I can rebuild it." 2:5		
CHALLENGE SHARED	"Come, let us rebuild the wall of Jerusalem." 2:17		
TASK BEGUN	"Let us start rebuilding." So they began this good work. 2:18b		

A Biblical Illustration: *the Apostles*

The Action	Acts 6:1-6	Acts 9:10-19	Acts 15:5-31
ISSUES ARISE	Heard a complaint	Lord spoke to Ananias	An issue arose
SOME SPEAK TO IT	Spoke to disciples	Ananias spoke to Saul	Paul/Barnabas speak
ACTIVITY ENSUES	Disciples chose	Saul healed	A decision made

In this sampling of biblical sources, we find a simple, but not always easy, three-step template for the procedures of leadership. What does a leader do? Leaders first receive, from some source, a mission and an attendant vision for an enterprise to be undertaken. Then they communicate the mission and vision statements to the leadership team and the followers. Finally, the leader oversees, supervises, and directs the program of activities necessary to accomplish the mission's goal and objectives. As evidenced in John 16:13, even the Godhead adheres to this pattern. In preparing his disciples for his departure, Jesus informs them that, "When he, the Spirit of truth, comes, he will guide you into all truth. He will not speak on his own; he will speak only what he hears and he will tell you what is yet to come." Identifying the message (truth), passing it on (speak), and providing information and direction (what is to come) are inspired and inspirational activities.

Confirmation by Contemporary Scholars

Drawing from a study of the life and leadership of Moses, LeRoy Eims provides a summary catalogue of a leader's conduct. He also discloses his perception of the essential activities of an effective leader: receiving direction, communicating with people, and delegating responsibility (Eims 1981). In doing so, he joins other scholars and researchers in identifying the three behaviors of leaders.

Burt Nanus, writing for a secular audience, concurs. To be successful, leaders

> *adopt challenging new visions of what is both possible and desirable, communicate their visions, and persuade others to become so committed to these new directions that they are eager to lend their resources and energies to make them happen. In this way, effective leaders build lasting institutions that change the world (Nanus 1992).*

Hersey, Blanchard, and Johnson also affirm three general skills or competencies of leadership:

> *Leading or influencing requires three general skills, or competencies: (1) diagnosing—understanding the situation you are trying to influence; (2) adapting—altering your behavior and the other resources you have available to meet the contingencies of the situation; and (3) communication— interacting with others in a way that people can easily*

understand and accept (Hersey, Blanchard, and Johnson 1996).

Leighton Ford asks rhetorical questions that reveal the strategy of the Master.

Who had greater visions than Jesus? Who knew better how to communicate with his followers through everyday stories? Who was more trustworthy, credibly positioned and believable than Jesus in carrying through his mission? And who has ever been able to empower others more than he, through his own wonderful self-knowledge and the total positive giving of himself? (Ford 1991).

Sara E. Melendez, in "An Outsiders View of Leadership," may have the conclusive word:

The leaders I admire have a clear vision of how things should be. They are able to communicate that vision so others can share in it, and then get others to work together as a unity, each contributing his or her best toward the achievement of that vision (Hesselbein, et al 1996).

Illustrated by the biblical models and confirmed by contemporary authorities, this sequence of behaviors is succinctly summarized in the *NIV Study Bible's* notes on Joshua 1:

The chapter consists of speeches significant in their content and order: The Lord commands Joshua as his appointed leader over his people (vv. 1-9); Joshua, as the Lord's representative, addresses Israel (vv. 10-15); Israel responds to Joshua as the Lord's representative and successor to Moses (vv. 16-18).

Behaviors of Leadership

Extracted from these ancient and contemporary foundations of leadership activity, a practical pattern of three stages or steps emerges. I refer to these as "The Behaviors of Leadership":

1. Determine the Mission,
2. Declare the Mission, and
3. Direct the Mission.

Whether in the boardroom or the backroom, the courthouse or the clubhouse, the upscale restaurant or the downtown fast-food establishment, people are attempting to induce and influence others to follow them. The common denominator to every effective interchange is a commitment to these three simple behaviors.

I encountered an example of this in a conversation I overheard in a restaurant between an apparent entry-level management applicant and the supervisor who was interviewing him. Throughout the conversation, the interviewer repeatedly made the following statements to the candidate: "Know what you're talking about," "Utilize the operations manual," "Communicate effectively," "Lead by example," and "Have an impact." In other words, the supervisor instructed the applicant to know the job (i.e., determine the mission), assist others in discovering theirs (i.e., declare the mission), and get something accomplished (i.e., direct and implement the mission).

A Metamodel for Leadership Behavior

The metamodel for both transactive and transformative leadership behavior is plain and practical. A leader *determines*, *declares*, and *directs* a mission, which often transforms not only followers but the organization as well. This model is not only simple; it is global. Bosses, pastors, coaches, parents, and anyone who aspires to influence others can implement this procedure wherever they are, whatever the resources available, and no matter whom they are leading. The model is neither determined by, nor dependent upon, any particular skill or style of leadership. However, any leadership skill acquired, attitude developed, or paradigm shift proposed can be implemented at the appropriate stage of the process. The model is not dependent upon technology, is global and universal, and can handle the varieties of life and circumstances rapid change produces. Both wise and foolish leaders may exercise it in every generation, cultural setting, and enterprise. It is an integrated whole but may be examined one component at a time, and that is exactly what we will do.

Determine the Mission

The initial behavior of a leader is to identify and *determine the mission*. Therefore, a mission statement is a critical component in a leader's understanding of the task to be undertaken. Without it, one is left to flounder about, trying to figure out what is to be accomplished and how to implement it. I learned this lesson the hard way.

It began as many ordinary days do. I was sitting at my desk in a private Christian K-8 school and having a very positive and encouraging conversation with a mother who was expressing her gratefulness for us having "saved her son." He was a troubled middle school student who had been expelled or driven from three other schools, and we were her last hope. Something apparently connected, and he was making great improvement. Mom was now hopeful.

As I accompanied her to the exterior exit door of my office, another mother was being escorted through the interior entry door. This mother was enraged at me. She was on the verge of removing her child from our school because of the terrible influence one student in particular was having on her son. She confronted me with a barrage of questions: How could I have allowed a coarse, bullying, disrespectful, ungodly student in our Christian school? Did I not realize the negative impact he was having on the good kids? What was I going to do about it?

It was a classic "no-win" situation because both moms were referring to the same student. One was grateful we had saved her son; the other was incensed we would sacrifice others for the sake of this one. In reflecting upon these conversations, I asked myself a few simple questions: To whom was this school designed to minister? Sure, we are a "Christian school," but what does that mean? What is our purpose? What are we trying to accomplish? What is our mission? Who is our target? No one had informed me, and I was not aware of the board ever discussing these questions.

Someone in every organization, however, must address them, and when they do, two critical concerns come to the front. The first is the issue of extracting and determining the mission from its source or origin, and the second is the matter of identifying and cataloging its components. We will address these two concerns in that order.

Sources of the Mission

For the Christian leader, especially in a Christian context, hearing from God is the primary source for the establishment of a mission and its vision, along with the appropriate message, strategy, and plan. The critical question that needs to be asked, then, is "How does God communicate his intentions and desires for a ministry?" This is an intensely debated issue among believers today, and it is deserving of some attention as we consider the need for a leader to determine the mission.

Although the Christian leader would appreciate hearing from him directly, the Lord also speaks through creation, our constitutional makeup, his providential work in human affairs, and directly through the human master (cf. Proverbs 21:1). These manifold vehicles of his revelations are all valid sources for an administrator's message, and they need to be seriously explored and considered.

In addition to the classic processes involved in determining God's will, the leader extracts the mission and message from four primary sources. In a manner similar to a teacher establishing a curricular plan and selecting messages for a lesson, a leader likewise determines a message, as Paul illustrates in 1Corinthians 2:1-5, 6-10, 3:1-4 and 10-15, and as Peter illustrates in 2Peter 1. These sources may be defined and described as follows:

Tradition: the messages/lessons embedded in and extracted from the "heritage of the race" (J. M. Gregory, 1888)

Description: The living words of the community. The historical "stuff" that societies codify in their texts and contain in their treasures to describe and perpetuate their culture (the "content" of socialization)

Observation: the messages/lessons embedded in and extracted from the life experiences of the followers

Description: The life needs of the disciple-follower. The raw "stuff" that every individual brings to the enterprise to be refined and cultured

Participation: the messages/lessons embedded in and extracted from the life experiences and activities of the leader

Description: The life message of the leader. The refined "stuff" that each administrator brings to the experience to share with others (The Law of the Teacher)

Inspiration: the messages/lessons embedded in and extracted from divine disclosure (the instruction and direction of the Holy Spirit)

Description: The leading of the Lord. The anointed "stuff" that the teacher receives from above to transmit here below; often perceived of as intuition or "insight" – an innate sense of what is

To condense and summarize, a leader is assisted in selecting the messages that support and determine the mission from: 1) experience and tradition, transmitted in both oral and written expressions, such as pertinent documents and in the case of Christian ministry, the Bible; 2) the life experiences and needs of the followers as they are witnessed and interpreted by the leader; 3) the life experiences of the leader as they confirm and impact the mission objectives to be fulfilled; and 4) the immediate direction and prescription of the Holy Spirit as the leader seeks guidance from the divine source.

Throughout this text, reference is made to the "will of the master" when referring to the determiner of the mission and vision along with the goals and objectives of the institution, organization, or enterprise undertaken. For the Christian, that master is the Lord whose providential and sovereign rulership of the universe will ultimately culminate with all humanity bowing before him. In practice, however, his will is often manifest through the instruction of human leaders, the combined wisdom of the community throughout history, life experiences and the resultant lessons learned, and even occasionally through the direct intervention and inspiration of the Lord himself. The wise leader listens to and observes intently all of these sources to discern and determine the appropriate mission to engage.

Regardless of the source that inspires and informs the leader, the godly administrator recognizes that it is not his will that is of primary importance, but it is acknowledging, serving, and administrating the will of the master, whether human or divine. As Leighton Ford suggests,

> *Our task is not to dream up visions or to develop strategies, but to see Jesus' visions and understand what the Father's strategy is for our lives.*

He even goes so far as to observe,

> *Vision is not used in the Bible in our sense of an entrepreneurial 'visionary.' In the Scriptures, the word vision is commonly used of an ecstatic experience in which saintly people with an awareness of God receive a special word from him (Ford 1991).*

Substituting the word *dream* for *vision*, Jerry Falwell writes,

> *If you work up a dream in your own energy, it may not come to pass. If it's something you want for selfish reasons, it may or may not happen. I realize many accomplish their life's dreams even though they have nothing to do with God. But when God gives you a dream, it will possess you. The dream will motivate you, and you will sacrifice your life for it (Falwell 2005).*

This attitude and perspective is in contrast to both historic empire building and modern western democratic government, which manifests the will of the people, but not necessarily that of God. The true servant leader identifies both the master and the mission. A young man in a church I served was considering running for the state legislature. During a lunch appointment, I told him one of the critical issues he faced was the all-too-common conflict between the personal values and views of an elected official and those of the populace. He told me it would be no problem; he would always do what was right, no matter what the people thought. He did win his race, but he only lasted one term in office. It became very apparent that his mission's agenda was not the same as the majority of the electorate, and those he swore to serve rejected his leadership.

Components of the Mission

Once determined, a leader's mission and message is comprised of at least four major components:

1. The assignment itself,
2. A vision for its implementation,
3. Goals and objectives for its accomplishment, and
4. A strategy and a plan for doing so.

A *mission* is the task or assignment undertaken. "What is to be accomplished?" is the simple question here. A *vision* is what one sees occurring in the fulfillment of the mission. What will it look like? What will people be doing? What kind of people will be involved? Answers to these questions, and others similar to them, determine vision. It is, in essence, "a realistic, credible, attractive future for your organization. It is your articulation of a destination toward which your organization should aim, a future that in important ways is better, more successful, or more desirable for your organization than is the present" (Nanus 1992).

Some administrators believe that the vision drives the mission. The concept behind this approach is that a leader formulates a mental picture of what is to be accomplished, the vision, and then figures out how to do it, producing the mission. It may be the chicken or the egg debate, but it has been my experience that being vision-driven does not always produce the desired outcome(s), but being mission-driven usually does. It is too easy to be sidetracked by visionary activities that please but are not mission productive.

The approach presented here begins with the acknowledgement of a mission followed by the description of the vision. The distinction in practice can be patent. I once met three women who shared a common mission: to provide a shelter for battered and abused women. Within ten minutes of conversation, though, it was apparent that they had three different visions of what that ministry would look like, whom it would serve, and how it would be carried out. Many church education departments attempt to fulfill the Great Commission, but their visions for doing so are distinct. It is the vision that distinguishes the activities of one organization from another.

Goals and objectives are the specific stepping-stones one takes to reach the ultimate accomplishment of the mission. In order for a leader to set his goals, there are questions that must be asked: Where are we going, and what do we need to do to get there? These inquiries are followed by other questions: Is there a specific procedure we should follow? What if this occurs? What if it does not? Where do we go after we have done this? Equipped with answers derived from this investigation, the leader determines the plan and strategy to reach the goals and accomplish the objective. This is the fulfillment of the mission.

The critical concern for the Christian leader is whether this emphasis upon mission, vision, and goals is appropriate and biblically based. In order to address this concern, we can review the approach Jesus employed while addressing his disciples in what has become commonly referred to as the Great Commission.

The Great Commission

Jesus frames the discussion by acknowledging his perception of authority, identifying the tasks of going and making, articulating the objective of discipleship, describing the processes of baptizing and teaching, and, as recorded in Acts 1:8, prescribing the procedure of witnessing:

> *Then the eleven disciples went to Galilee, to the mountain where Jesus had told them to go. When they saw him, they worshiped him; but some doubted. Then Jesus came to them and said, "All authority in heaven and on earth has been given to me. Therefore go and make disciples of all nations, baptizing them in the name of the Father and of the Son and of the Holy Spirit, and teaching them to obey everything I have commanded you. And surely I am with you always, to the very end of the age" (Matthew 28:16-20).*

No simpler description of a mission can be anticipated. He provided a glimpse into his worldview and value system while articulating a discrete mission, clarifying his goals, envisioning their behaviors, and setting a strategic course for his followers. It is fair to state that determining the mission is the first behavior of the biblical, Christ-following leader.

Declare the Mission

The experience of an undercover police officer that was one of my students illustrates the importance of implementing the second step in the metamodel for leadership behavior: *declare the mission*. This officer kept his classmates enthralled with the exciting stories he shared; from teenage drug busts to celebrity traffic violations, we were introduced weekly to the other side of life. One of the ongoing assignments in this course was for each student to keep a leadership journal, and I looked forward to reading this student's entries. They were, as suspected, filled with cop stories and examples of how he was trying to apply the principles from class in his work. In his fourth entry, he had one of those *eureka* moments. This experienced police officer had been trying for weeks to identify the mission for each case he was working. In this entry, however, he realized how critical it was to communicate the task to the other members of his team. When he sat down with them and shared the mission, their success startled him. The one time he forgot to inform them of the goal, the team was ineffective, botched part of the investigation, and had to redo it. He became committed to not only knowing his assignment, but also to being diligent to declare the mission to all who were involved in the case.

The Lord instructed the prophet Habakkuk to write down the revelation given to him so that he could distribute it among the people (Habakkuk 2:2). In the same way, the contemporary leader, after determining the mission, declares it to others. Seldom is a mission, vision, or dream given to an individual for personal implementation. Concerning church ministry, Jerry Falwell simply opines, "No dream from God is strictly a personal matter" (Falwell 2005).

Therefore, after discerning and determining the mission, it is the leader's responsibility to effectively communicate and relate this intention to the leadership team and the followers so they are motivated to proceed. As Ford notes, "Vision is the very stuff of leadership – the ability to see in a way that compels others to pay attention" (Ford 1991). In fact, this lies at the very heart of any assignment; as noted in Chapter 1, engaging others to join in the quest defines the very nature of leadership.

This simple but critical concept can be illustrated no more effectively than in the story of the city and tower of Babel recounted in Genesis 11. Using sanctified imagination, we can witness one of the most transformative events in the history of humanity. It is instructive to observe the behavior of the Lord as he deals with humankind throughout this event.

Communication: The Key to Any Enterprise (Genesis 11:1-9)

It begins, as most stories do, in the beginning; and in the beginning, it was good. There came a time, however, when the Creator looked down upon his dearly loved children and observed behaviors that he knew he must confront and discipline.

God's Intention

At the commencement of history, in the Garden of Eden, God created human beings in his own image with two specific intentions. The first was that this creation would reflect his image (Genesis 1:17), and the second was that humanity would fill and subdue the earth (Genesis 1:28, 9:17). Inherently implied in both of these intentions was the expectation that people would take to their knees in humility and submission, respectfully worshiping, serving, and obeying their Creator.

Man's Intention

Men and women, however, manifested in a short period that they had ideas and intentions of their own. As they scattered, in the initial fulfillment of the first commission to fill the earth, they settled in a plain and began construction on what has traditionally been referred to as "The Tower of Babel."

The text makes clear, however, that the project was to begin with the city in which the tower would reside. This was not a pillar for worship or a memorial for educating the next generation, as is evident throughout much of the Old Testament. The stated intention was, "Let's build ourselves a city with a tower so that we make a name for ourselves and will not be scattered" (Genesis 11:4). In other words, their goal was to free themselves from their dependence upon the Lord, rebelling against both the commission to scatter and the expectation to bring glory to his name.

God's Intervention

Depending upon one's worldview, what happened next is either manipulation or mercy. The following few verses describe God's strategic response. They reveal, in sequence: God's perception, plan, purpose, and product. Valuable lessons unfold as we observe God's reaction and rejoinder to this rebellion.

His Perception:

> *But the Lord came down to see the city and the tower that the men were building. The Lord said, "If as one people speaking the same language they have begun to do this, then nothing they plan to do will be impossible for them."*

The first and possibly most critical observation is the perception of the Lord himself that if people are in unity and communicate with understanding, they can do anything. In this case, the plans and intentions of the people were evil, selfish, and rebellious. Imagine, though, what righteous, godly, and selfless people could accomplish if they would simply speak the same language and plan together. The necessary expenditure of time and energy discussing, planning, and organizing is clearly worthwhile and essential to our enterprises. Whether teaching or leading, the Lord's ministers must communicate and strategize with each other and with their disciple-followers. Likewise, we find the Lord formulating and implementing a plan of his own.

His Plan:

> *"Come, let's go down and confuse their language..."*

Of all the possible methods, means, and manipulations that were available to the Lord to quench the rebellion, the one he knew to be most effective and efficient was the confusion of language and the disruption of the communication system. It is no wonder, then, that some of the most intriguing and thought-provoking stories to come out of wartime are the ones that center around breaking codes, intercepting signals, and deploying false messages to confuse and disrupt the enemy.

His Purpose:

> *"...so that they will not understand each other."*

The Lord disrupted their communication with a very simple strategy – cause them to not be able to understand each other. His approach affirmed the Law of the Language proposed by John M. Gregory, "The language used in teaching must be common to teacher and learner" (Gregory 2003). Therefore, regardless of how we define and describe the process of communication, the concern to understand each other must be paramount. In practical terms, this understanding is dependent upon a common language; confused language produces a lack of understanding and hinders the communication process.

His Product:

> *So the Lord scattered them from there over all the earth,
> and they stopped building the city. That is why it was called
> Babel—because there the Lord confused the language of the
> whole world. From there the Lord scattered them over the face
> of the whole earth.*

The result was that humankind was required to return to the commission with which God originally entrusted them. They were indeed scattered over the face of the earth, and the lordship of Jehovah was reinstated. Nevertheless, this is not the end of the story. It is my contention that during this entire episode Satan was present, evoking the rebellion and selfishness that prevailed. He also observed God's response and became aware of the importance of communication. As he saw his malevolent plan crumble before his very eyes, he also took note of the means by which it was accomplished. His plan was thwarted when the Babelites could no longer communicate with each other. Satan realized he could use this same method for his benefit by disrupting the communication networks among God's people. Communication breakdowns destroy marriages, families, businesses, sports teams, friendships, and other personal relationships – not to mention hundreds, if not thousands, of churches – every year. If it is a divine intention for men and women to communicate, and thus be able to accomplish every plan, it is likewise a device of the enemy to disrupt and destroy that very communication. If communication is indeed the key to every enterprise, then education and leadership are not exceptions. It is the first essential activity of the processes of Christian education and an indispensible skill and behavior of a leader.

What Is Communication?

Building upon this biblical and conceptual background that demonstrates the necessity of communication, it is incumbent upon us to identify both a definition of communication and a description of its critical components. These elements will establish the foundation essential to an understanding of the leader's behavior in declaring his mission.

I have examined both dictionary and textbook definitions of communication because of its essential nature in both teaching and leading. I found little agreement among the authorities; from the absurd proposition that communication was simply "self expression" to the preposterous notion that communication was "agreement," even the experts could not decide upon a common definition.

With a concrete definition eluding me, I turned my attention to a description of communication. Among the experts consulted, I discovered communication described as sharing something with another person, coming to understand another person, and finally having something in common with another person. At that point, Gregory's laws of teaching again came to mind. In the original edition of his work, he defined teaching as the "communication of knowledge." He then went on to speak of communication "… not in the sense of the transmission of a mental something from one person to another, but rather in the sense of helping another to reproduce the same knowledge and thus make it common to the two" (Gregory 2003). The focus, therefore, is not upon the transmission of a message as in the "self expression" definition, but upon the reproduction of a concept or a consequent behavior or skill.

Like dominoes tumbling one after another, a number of tentative conclusions began to fall into line. Communication involves sharing and helping one person to understand or preferably experience some concept or skill another person has experienced. In essence, the intention is that the participants come to have this knowledge or experience in common. In other words, communication means the commonality which produces unity; hence, communication = common + unity. To apply this on a personal level, something exists within me that I attempt to share and have in common with another. While this may not be a complete or satisfactory definition, I have found it to be helpful in understanding my relationship with other people and the process by which I can experience *koinonia* in communion with others, sharing diverse experiences rooted in commonality.

At this point in our discussion, it is appropriate to acknowledge the fact that we are primarily concerned with and considering interpersonal communication as opposed to mass communication (i.e., broadcast, print, or even rhetoric). Authors from both the near and distant past can communicate their messages and leave an impression upon readers today. Orators may address disciple-followers they have never met on film or video. Teachers and trainers from art to athletics utilize contemporary media to instruct and inform distance learners. We, however, are reflecting upon the proximate and interpersonal work of educators and leaders, and my comments and explanations will focus upon their needs and expectations.

How Does Communication "Work"?

The question, then, that must be addressed is how exactly this interpersonal commonality is produced. In other words, how does communication "work"? Display 2 graphically describes the conclusions I have come to concerning the communication process and how it unfolds. After a brief introduction, I will take a few paragraphs to describe my metamodel and utilize the experience of the attempted communication that is occurring between us to illustrate this process.

Foundations for Communication

Before we can begin, however, it is necessary to lay three foundation stones. These foundations are vital and will be addressed again in our discussions of educational psychology and the teaching-learning process in Part II. The first stone, to hearken back to our discussion of Genesis 11, is an acknowledgement that God created humankind in his own image. For the sake of this discussion, we will limit our focus to the constitutional image of God in human beings, specifically our trinitarian makeup of body, soul, and spirit.

This constitutional and trinitarian image is also replicated within the soul, which is equally composed of three components or functions: the cognitive, affective, and volitional activities of the intellect, emotion, and will. The second foundation stone, then, is the acknowledgment that human beings think, feel, and make decisions. Authorities variously label the source of these functions as the *soul* or the *heart*. Some even refer to it as the *spirit* of man, while others simply label it the *mind*. Regardless of its definition or designation, the recognition of the three functions is the critical component of this foundation.

The third foundation stone consists of the perception that within the soul an experience occurs that forms the heart of the message to be communicated. This experience may be one of acquired knowledge, applied wisdom, emotional episode, practiced skill, or a host of other experiential possibilities. Again, the label is not critical; we may refer to it as an event or any number of other terms and descriptions. The critical concern is that something vibrant and vital occurs within the inner state of an individual that precipitates an experience that he desires and intends to share with others.

With these introductory foundations of definition and description in place, let us explore in some detail the functional model for communication depicted in Display 2. On the surface, the graphic appears to illustrate and illuminate a *linear* communication model. Upon closer inspection, it is clear that the model also incorporates elements of *interactive* and *transactional* models for communication. It may be helpful to perceive the graphic as three-dimensional and the interactions as dynamic. It may also be helpful to photocopy, or even hand copy, the diagram, in order to refer to it while reading and reflecting upon this component of a leader's behavior and skill set.

We will examine the components and functions of the participants and proceed sequentially through the process. In analyzing and applying this model, the impact is enhanced when it is remembered that it was the Lord who observed, "If as one people speaking the same language they have begun to do this, then nothing they plan to do will be impossible for them."

Display 2. A Model for the Communication Process

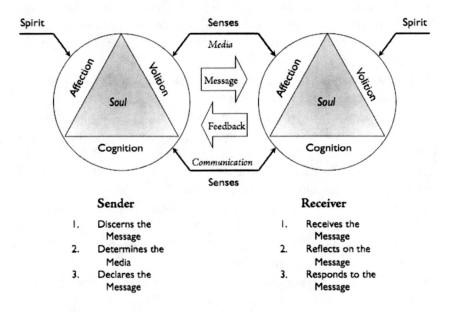

Sender		Receiver	
1.	Discerns the Message	1.	Receives the Message
2.	Determines the Media	2.	Reflects on the Message
3.	Declares the Message	3.	Responds to the Message

Utilizing the components of this model, we will identify and investigate six specific and sequential activities that enable effective and efficient communication. In brief, communication: 1) commences with an experience; 2) that is processed in the soul of the sender; 3) and transmitted as a message by the senses of the sender. This message is then: 4) accepted by the senses of the receiver; 5) processed in the soul of the receiver; and 6) produces a new experience that, in turn, generates a new sequence.

Activity 1: The Sender Discerns the Message

The primary and critical concern for this discussion of communication is that the first action in the model consists of the sender discerning the message. In other words, the communicator must identify both the experience to be shared and the articulated message that will represent it. Whether communicating as a leader or as a teacher, this first step answers the question, "What do I know that I want to have in common with others?" The communicator must determine the message that contains the mission statement, the subject matter, or any dimension or aspect of the communicator's experience.

As I was describing the contents of this book to a friend, I referred to it as my personal educational memoirs. The cognitive, affective, and volitional experiences of my life constitute the core and framework for the messages of my work; they reside simultaneously deep within my soul and yet ever presently close to the surface. It is my goal, intention, and desire to share these in such a way that another person can understand, appreciate, and practice these principles. In that way, we grow to have them in common and thus experience communication. That is the end line, but the process must begin somewhere. In language foreshadowing issues to come, communicators acknowledge that they must have something to say, and must know it well, because as the colloquial adage goes, "You can't give what you don't got!" To employ yet another analogy, this experience fuels the furnace that fires communication.

Activity 2: The Sender Processes the Message

Soulish activities such as critical thinking and analysis, personal and emotional reflection, and choosing to have experience and interaction with the message, enhance and facilitate this "knowing it well." In other words, the sender is not simply acquainted with the content of the message but has "processed" it to the point that some level of competence and confidence has been experienced and can now be transmitted. This step therefore addresses the concern, "Do I understand this message well enough to share it with others?" Probably more than anything else, attaining this mastery enables the effective communication of the message.

The authority and credibility of the sender is often determined at this juncture. Based upon previous experience, the receiver's willingness to accept and pay attention to the message is often decided before the message is actually sent. In the case of this book, I have been reflecting upon and ruminating over these principles and practices for over three decades. I trust that this has been reflected in my writing and influences the reception of it.

Activity 3: The Sender Transmits the Message

Determining and selecting the appropriate methods and materials for transmitting a message that represents a soulish experience is a crucial next step in the process. In making these decisions, it is necessary to recognize that both teaching-learning and communication theories acknowledge that the amount of sensory stimulation directly affects the efficiency of the transmission of the message and the effectiveness of the production of the communication attempt itself. Therefore, the second and third actions in the model find the sender choosing and using a variety of instruments to send the message, thus answering the inquiry, "How can I effectively share my message with others?"

Since the senses are "the gateway to the soul," communicators make use of their five senses to fabricate and employ the vehicles that carry the message. We shall establish and extensively explore this assertion from the educational perspective in Chapter 6.

It is also necessary in this step to acknowledge the fact that obstacles of many kinds, often referred to as noise, interfere with and disrupt the process. The communicator must confront and deal with these interferences to be effective. Consistent, congruent, and redundant means of communication, unencumbered by obstacles and noise, facilitate the transmission from sender to receiver.

In a very real sense, the selection of the media employed in sending the messages of this book limits my ability to communicate. I am restricted to the use of words and graphics printed on paper to transmit knowledge, feelings, and a lifetime of experience. My preferred method of communication would be to share and demonstrate my message in person. I take comfort in the fact that books have been utilized to transmit tradition and experience for thousands of years. I trust it will be effective in this situation as well.

Activity 4: The Receiver Accepts the Message

Once the sender has completed the work of determining, designing, and actually deploying methodology to stimulate the recipient's senses, the receiver must make a conscious decision to accept those messages and their input and imprint upon his senses. Whether the message is sent visually, auditorially, or kinesthetically, the receiver responds to stimuli and allows the neurological impulses to do their job. Signals travel along the neurological highway, ultimately reaching the destination of the brain and the complex processes encountered there.

The process of reading this book can effectively illustrate this activity. As one reads, there is probably little awareness of the extreme physical reactions that the body encounters and facilitates while participating in the activity, but that does not lessen the reality of the experience. While I, as the author (sender), considered the most efficient way to stimulate the senses of the recipient, the reader (receiver) shares the responsibility for effective communication by consciously choosing to open the gateway to the soul, and answering "Do I want to have this message in common with the sender?" in the affirmative.

One reads with the eyes but should not be satisfied until reading has occurred in the mind or the soul. It is this distinction between the eyes and the mind that sets us up for the next step in the process and allows us to proceed with high expectations for communication.

Activity 5: The Receiver Processes the Message

Communication, to be effective, demands the active participation of the soul as well as the senses. "It is the painting in another's mind the mental picture in one's own – the shaping of the pupil's thought and understanding to the comprehension of some truth which the teacher knows and wishes to communicate" (Gregory 2003). In this stage of the communication process, the receiver reflects upon the message and initiates the process of making it his own. Borrowing imagery from the Parable of the Sower, the messages take root in the soul, sprout as they are manifested through the senses, and bear fruit in one's life, producing something new.

Activity 6: The Receiver Completes the Cycle and Generates a New Experience

The recipient(s) of the message should respond, react, and choose to do something about what they have heard, seen, read, and reflected upon. Thus, in a manner reminiscent of the leader who had been the follower, it is at this point that the receiver becomes a sender by reacting to the concern, "How am I going to respond to the message?"

The message in response may be one of affirmation or clarification; a question may need to be answered, an explanation proffered, or further clarification of a complex issue required. The sender may want to argue or refute the proposition presented or offer thanks and appreciation for new information, an acquired skill, or an adjusted attitude. Regardless of the message sent as feedback, the cycle is now complete and communication begins again around these new experiences and messages.

Many attempts at communication break down at this point. This is also the juncture where the communication intended in this book has the potential to be disrupted; the ability to respond to me is problematic. If my address, phone number, e-mail address, or the possibility of personal contact is not available, there is no opportunity for sending or receiving feedback and completing the loop. Even though I may have made myself clear at every turn, and the reader may have understood every argument, the communication remains open and susceptible to distortion and misunderstanding until the cycle is complete. The process of communication may be complete without a response, but feedback mitigates the presence of misunderstanding and confusion.

Looking at it Another Way

Myron Rush includes a helpful discussion of the communication process in his text on leadership theory, *Management: A Biblical Approach* (1983). He provides a six-step model that basically restates the process I have outlined. Rush, however, does not prescribe a specific step for the utilization of the medium to actually deliver or transmit the message. When I use this model in training sessions, I inject Step 3.5: "Transmit the message utilizing the appropriate medium." With this suggested addition, I have reproduced his model here as a summary conclusion, providing a basically redundant, yet complementary, approach that may enrich an understanding of the process of communication:

1. *Develop a clear concept of the idea or feeling to be communicated*
2. *Choose the right words and actions to convey the idea or feeling*
3. *Become aware of the surrounding communication barriers and work at minimizing them*
4. *The receiver must absorb the transmitted information by listening to the words and observing the actions*
5. *The receiver must translate the words and actions*
6. *The receiver must develop correct ideas and feelings*

Direct the Mission

We were gathered around a table at one of our weekly church staff meetings when we realized that unless someone *directs the mission* – which is the third and final step of the metamodel for leadership behavior – and takes responsibility for implementing a plan, even the best ideas come to naught.

Business was proceeding as usual until the pastor inquired about how a certain project was progressing. The associate staff looked at each other with quizzical expressions and had to answer, "Nothing is happening; we didn't know we were supposed to be doing anything!" This angered the pastor, but he quickly realized no one had been assigned to the task. Two months earlier, we had spent over an hour brainstorming ideas and suggestions regarding this matter, but that was as far as it went. No decisions were made, no tasks assigned, and no one thought about it again.

Despite popular practice to the contrary, just declaring the mission is not enough. Telling people what to do or even how to do it does not ensure it will be done or done effectively. The leader, therefore, must also devote himself to the time, energy, practice, skills, and sometimes-monetary issues necessary to influence and direct the fulfillment of the mission and vision. In doing so, the leader engages in two primary activities: influencing the people and influencing the process.

Influence the People. Jesus provides us with an excellent example of directing a mission by influencing followers. In the tenth chapter of his gospel, Matthew brings together a variety of Jesus' instructions that Mark and Luke spread over a number of incidents (see especially Luke 9 and 10). The context the apostle utilizes to summarize these directives is the sending out of The Twelve to minister and to heal. After recording Jesus' declaration of the mission in Verse 1, Matthew uses the rest of the chapter to frame the Master's instructions with three simple ideas: how he wanted them to go and minister (Verses 5-20), what they needed to know in going (Verses 21-31), and why they should go and obey him (Verses 32-42). Put simply, he instructed, informed, and inspired his disciples.

The first aspect of directing, *instruction*, involves the communication and explication of the plans, strategy, programs, and methodology of the enterprise, providing an education that facilitates followership. Through a training and development program, disciple-followers are equipped with the skill set essential to the implementation and fulfillment of the mission and vision. Consequently, as a pastor-teacher, I take the implied injunction of Ephesians 4:11 to heart. My primary job description is to equip and train members of Christ's body for their "works of service."

Information, the second dimension of influencing direction, involves the communication and explication of the mindset that undergirds the manner in which the mission is to be engaged. The leader provides essential knowledge regarding the enterprise, its mission and vision, and a sense of the procedures utilized to accomplish its goals. This information establishes the references employed in the formation of guidelines for the follower's activity and behavior.

Finally, *inspiration* involves persuading and motivating followers. Motivation may be defined as: "To provide with an incentive; move to action; impel" (Picket 2000). It can be described as: that which excites to action; that which determines the choice or moves the will; cause; or inducement causing motion or action. In other words, we are moving someone somewhere, inducing an alteration in either the physical or psychological condition. As Nanus (1995) observes, the leader becomes an agent of change. Understanding how to influence and implement change in a person or an organization is an essential aspect of leadership. Elmer Towns, in fact, believes that "guiding followers is the same as the task of introducing change and to initiate change is to apply the laws of leadership" (Barna 1997). It is justified, then, that virtually every modern definition of leadership acknowledges the influence factor. To put it simply, inspiration provides the reason and motive to follow and support the mission.

It is instructive to note that to "inspire" someone also involves stirring the emotions and generating creativity. Theologians and artists alike draw from the Latin origin, "to breathe into," a mandate to stimulate soulish activities such as critical thinking, reflective assessment, and worship. The inspirational, and Christian, leader motivates disciple-followers not only to come, follow, and fulfill the mission, but also to do so with excitement, enthusiasm, and creativity.

In summary review, Jesus directed his disciple-followers by:

- *Instruction* or education, providing the detailed blueprint for, and the training in, the methods utilized to accomplish the mission.
- *Information* or illumination, providing the necessary knowledge needed to understand the manner by which the mission is to be accomplished.
- *Inspiration* or motivation, providing the driving force and necessary zeal to persevere to the finish and comprehend why it is necessary to fulfill the mission or accomplish the task.

The charge given by Jehovah to Joshua as he takes command of the Israelite forces after the death of Moses provides further evidence of the necessity and practicality of these three functions in the directing component of administration. In Joshua 1:1-9, we find the Lord: 1) instructing Joshua as to the task (to cross the Jordan in three days and take the land as an inheritance), 2) informing him of his obligations (to obey all of the law and do everything written there), and 3) inspiring him (to be strong and courageous – because the Lord will be with him wherever he goes). Both the Heavenly Father and his Son directed their charges by instructing, informing, and inspiring. Their administrators wisely follow their lead and do likewise.

Influence the Process. In addition to the responsibility of influencing followers, an administrator also faces the task of influencing the process and effectively and efficiently accomplishing the goals that fulfill the mission.

In the direction of the mission, leaders fulfill the first component – influencing the people – by primarily employing the three functions initiated by the Master: instruction, information, and inspiration. They fulfill the second component, the activity of influencing the process, by administration. Over the years, a number of administrative models and strategies have emerged to aid a leader in implementing the mission and vision of the organization. Hersey, Blanchard, and Johnson suggest, "Many authors consider the managerial functions of planning, organizing, motivating, and controlling to be central to any discussion of management" (Hersey, Blanchard, and Johnson 1996). Early in the twentieth century, French executive Henry Fayol reached a similar conclusion as he developed the "process approach" to management, identifying five basic functions of a manager:

- Foresight and planning,
- Organization,
- Direction,
- Coordination, and
- Control

More recently, "coordination" and "direction" have been combined, and "staffing" has been added to produce a list similar to Robert Bower's: planning, organizing, delegating, staffing, coordinating, and controlling (Bower 1964). These foundational approaches and works paved the way for a breakthrough paradigm in the systems approach, generated by R. Alec Mackenzie as published in the *Harvard Business Review* (November-December 1969). My mentor, Bill Bynum, provided me with a copy of the management cycle diagram produced in that article, and I have referenced it in leadership training programs for over thirty years. It was a pleasant surprise to see that Michael Anthony and James Estep have used it as the basis for the outline of their text *Management Essentials for Christian Ministries* (2005). Based upon the definitions and descriptions I have presented, I would have titled their work *Administrative Essentials*. Nonetheless, I recommend it as essential reading for the practical details of and skills necessary for activities such as working with boards and conducting meetings.

After a leader has determined and declared the mission and message, the final component of the process is to direct its implementation. The effective leader turns to these five functions for guidance and assistance in fulfilling the mission:

- Planning,
- Organizing,
- Staffing,
- Directing, and
- Controlling.

In establishing a Christian, biblically based approach to leadership and management, we must inquire as to whether this approach is sound and appropriate for a Christian leader. Do these five functions find scriptural support? It should come as no surprise that we find confirmation in the life and ministry of Moses. In Exodus, the Lord reveals his plan and literally steps Moses through each of these functions: *Planning* in Chapters 3 and 4, where the Lord reveals a sequence of events and encounters with the Israelites and with the Pharaoh; *Organizing* and *Staffing* in Chapter 4, where the structure of the plan is revealed and Aaron joins Moses; *Directing* in Chapter 5, where Moses confronts Pharaoh and sets the plan in motion; and *Controlling* in Chapter 6, where the intervention of the Lord assures the fulfillment of the mission.

These illustrative activities provide the modern leader with an indication of a template for leadership behavior that is as appropriate today as it was 3500 years ago. In Chapter 3 of this work, we will examine each of these administrative functions in order to answer the third question of Part I, "How Does a Leader Do It?" Before we conclude this portion of our study, however, let us explore the phases of leadership – two variations on the objectives of a leader.

Phases of Leadership

There are two discrete yet complementary phases in which leaders practice the activities of inducement and influence for distinct purposes and unique outcomes. During these phases, we observe the coordinated interaction between the three behaviors and the two dimensions of leadership, generating and facilitating the transactions between leaders and followers and the potential transformation of each.

In its initial transactional phase, as depicted in Table 5, leadership is a simple exchange: one leads, other(s) follow, and they do a job.

Table 5. Phase I Leadership: Transactional

Metamodel	Leader	Follower
Determine the Mission	Inspiration	*Conceptualize:* identify the message
Declare the Mission	Instruction	*Internalize:* receive and accept the message
Direct the Mission	Influence	*Externalize:* follow and implement the message

As we have seen, however, leadership often extends beyond the completion of a task or the fulfillment of an objective. Although it may manifest itself in changes in the corporate or even societal culture, this effort is clearly intended to change the follower. The successful completion of the task provides the foundation for the transformative phase of leadership. True servant leaders, especially Christian ones, expect their labors to transform both their organizations and the people they serve. To turn fishermen into fishers of men, Jesus had to transform followers into leaders. This is exactly what occurs in Phase II Leadership, as shown in Table 6. Burns also anticipates this when he states that transforming leadership "converts followers into leaders" (Burns 1978).

In Phase II, the emphasis shifts to the expectation of the follower "buying in" and joining with the leader in the administration of a master's direction. While also beginning to formulate a personal perception, the follower will then own the message, share it with his newfound followers, and continue to fulfill the original mission. In other words, disciples will now "Go, make disciples."

Table 6. Phase II Leadership: Transformational

Phase	Metamodel	Leader	Follower
TRANSACTION	*Determine the Mission*	*Inspiration*	*Conceptualize: identify the message*
	Declare the Mission	*Instruction*	*Internalize: receive and accept the message*
	Direct the Mission	*Influence*	*Externalize: follow and implement the message*
TRANSFORMATION	**Determine the Mission**	**Infusion: anoint new leadership (a>r>c)**	*Internalize (Determine):* "own" the mission & vision
	Declare the Mission		*Externalize (Declare):* "share" the mission & vision
	Direct the Mission		*Operationalize (Direct):* "fulfill" the mission & vision

Authority, Responsibility, and Commitment

One of the critical concerns a leader faces in the transition from Phase I to Phase II is how to actually facilitate and implement the transformation of a follower to a leader. The most common method follows this pattern: commitment -> responsibility -> authority. The administrator recognizes a need or desire to recruit a new leader, so he scans the follower pool to find those who have exhibited *commitment* to the mission and objectives of the organization. The intention is to identify people who attend, help, and generally indicate a dedication to the organization or the leader. If one or more of these faithful or available people are identified, they are given an opportunity and a trial period to see if they can handle the job. Once the internship is completed, they are assigned a more permanent *responsibility*. Over time, emerging leaders may evidence those special characteristics that set them apart from others, compelling consideration for a position of *authority*. At each juncture along the way, from commitment to responsibility to authority, the pool narrows and gets shallower while capable people rise to the top of the organization.

Although this method is common, there are a number of weaknesses with this approach. The first area of difficulty is rooted in the assumption that attendance equals commitment. This generates two problems for the recruiter. The first is that many regular participants are there for the wrong reasons, i.e. to fulfill personal needs rather than serving Christ. They may have a level of competence, but are nonetheless inappropriate candidates for Christian leadership. The second problem is that simple attendance or participation does not insure an acceptable level of competence.

An additional difficulty and weakness with this approach concerns the emerging leader's commitment to the mission and vision, along with the assumption of authority. Both remain superficial because the original leader retains the ownership. The promising leader must internalize the message in order to be successful in sharing it with others.

If this widespread approach to facilitating and implementing emerging leadership is faulty, what is the alternative? The answer is actually quite simple: reverse the process. Based, in part, upon the competency and commitment required of a candidate, the administrator determines the level with which he can be comfortable allowing a new leader to operate. The administrator then selects a candidate for a specific task or project as a result of the recruiting process (see Chapter 3, "Staffing"), and gives this individual full *authority* for the assignment, with the privilege of making the necessary decisions to run the program, department, team, or class. The new leader is now experiencing true ownership and with this comes the *responsibility* and accountability attendant to that authority. Now the leader has the right to make decisions within the established limits. When the emerging leader is empowered to make decisions, be responsible, and held accountable (see Chapter 3, "Controlling"), the *commitment* level goes sky high. The result is a competent and dedicated leader who will continue to implement the mission and vision of the organization, but will not be dependent upon the original leader to sustain growth and momentum.

Authority, responsibility, and commitment, when implemented in the suggested sequence, are critical components and expectations of Phase II leaders. Administrators should look for candidates with character and competence, give them authority to do their jobs, and watch them soar as they exercise and put into service their leadership potential.

In Conclusion

Dathan Hale, a local church's children's pastor, recently completed one of my courses on the administration of a children's ministry and utilized the experience to reflect upon his leadership practice. In the form of an e-mailed testimony, he stated:

> As I looked back at past ministry successes, I discovered that I followed this practical leadership model. When I looked at my ministry failures, I found that it was in one of the three that I had failed, usually in declaring my message.

Dathan and the other leaders whose anecdotes appear throughout this chapter have confirmed in practical experience that the three behaviors of the model – determine, declare, and direct – are both effective and efficient. Regardless of the specific procedures or practices utilized, successful administrators make certain that these three activities characterize the strategy employed in influencing followers. They provide a sufficient answer to the question, what do leaders do? They also frame the context in which our definition of leadership is described:

> *A leader is one who possesses a clear mission with an attendant vision, standing before others efficiently conveying the messages, and effectively supervising the actions needed to fulfill that mission. In more concise terms, leadership is "an aspect of administration in which others are induced and influenced to come, follow, and contribute to the accomplishment of a mission."*

Reflection and Response

Reflections on the Behaviors of Leaders

Determine the Mission: Reflection on Vision

Reproduced below is a proposed vision statement for a local church Christian education program. Would you endorse it? Why or why not? What would you add or delete?

After reviewing this one, create your own mission and vision statements.

To fulfill the mission of Christian Education, we envision a ministry that will produce...

1. **A Cross-cultural community** of disciples (of all ages, races, economic, or marital status, etc.) who form a "body of believers" united in Jesus, but diverse in style, personality, and giftedness - an open system.

2. **Educational units** that simulate family groups where our students are loved, accepted, nurtured, and discipled into and in Jesus' life.

3. **A leadership team** of world-class people doing world-class Christian Education - mature and godly men and women who know the Bible, who know how to lead, and who know how to educate.

4. **A faculty** of well-trained, well-equipped, and well-supported Christian educators who could teach (and perhaps organize and lead) in any educational environment.

5. **Students/disciples** who know and love Jesus, know his Word and apply it in their daily lives - well-balanced lives that produce discipleship and worship.

6. **An "educational system"** that, by its effective nurture of faculty and students, provides a model for Christian families to follow in the discipling and nurture of their own natural children at whatever stage of personal or spiritual growth.

7. **A system (church)-wide curriculum** that is Jesus-centered, Bible-based, life-oriented, practical living-focused, and evangelistically applied.

8. **A Christian education ministry** <u>in relationship with</u> and in cooperation with the other ministries of the church in order to accomplish the mission and fulfill the vision of the church.

After you finish reading this book, revisit this statement and update your own vision statement.

Declare the Mission: Reflection on Communication

Read John 4 carefully, and then reflect upon Jesus' manner of communication by answering the following (possible ideas are in parentheses – you create your own):

* If you were to try to explain to another person why Jesus was effective as a communicator, you would use words (or phrases) like…
(*He understood people*)
* If you were to use Jesus as your model for being an effective communicator, you would try to imitate his…
(*Use of analogy and parable*)
* When you lead, you find the following communication activities to be like those of Christ's…
(*I try to use illustrations and examples to make my points*)
* However, you would like these communication behaviors to be more like Christ's…
(*I want to be more sensitive to people's real needs*)
* You would be willing to make the following changes to do so…
(*I will actively listen to others in order to understand them*)

Direct the Mission: Reflection on Influence

Read Matthew 10 and Joshua 1 carefully, and then reflect upon the manner by which both the Father and the Son influenced their followers by answering the following:

* If you were to try to explain to another person how divine influence is accomplished, you would use words (or phrases) like…

* If you were to use Jesus as your model for influencing others, you would try to imitate his…

* When you lead, you find the following influence activities to be like those of the Father...

* However, you would like these influence behaviors to be more like Christ's...

* You would be willing to make the following changes to do so...

Three

ADMINISTRATIVE FUNCTIONS: *How Does a Leader Do It?*

As the son of a professional firefighter, I learned at an early age that fire occurs with the merger of three critical components: heat, fuel, and oxygen. When these elements combine in close enough proximity, fire is created, generating heat and light. When they are separated or one is eliminated, the fire is extinguished, leaving only smoldering embers.

As the son of a volunteer lay minister, I learned early in my apprenticeship that there is also a combination of critical components necessary for the effective and efficient fulfillment of a mission. When these elements combine in close enough proximity, leadership is enabled, and goals are accomplished. When they are separated or one is absent, leadership is crippled, leaving the potential for unfulfilled hopes and dreams. Formed in the workshop of observation and fixed in the kiln of experience, I have identified five "lessons for leaders" that constitute these critical components:

- Plan your work and work your plan – don't be afraid to be a visionary;
- Structure will help or hinder, but it won't make or break – don't be afraid to be organized;
- Personnel will make you or break you – don't be afraid to be selective;
- Your voice must be heard – don't be afraid to be assertive; and
- Commend and correct as is appropriate – don't be afraid to be encouraging.

Interestingly, and not coincidentally, these lessons align perfectly with the five functions of the Administrative Cycle that were introduced in the previous chapter:

- **Planning** – *predetermining a course of action (envisioning the potential)*
- **Organizing** – *arranging and relating work, and people, for effectiveness (arranging the pieces)*
- **Staffing** – *choosing competent people for positions in the organization (selecting the participants)*

- **Directing** – *bringing about purposeful action toward desired objectives (influencing the process)*
- **Controlling** – *ensuring progress toward objectives according to a plan (managing the progress)*

How Does a Leader Do It?

At first glance, the answer to the question, "How does a leader do it?" appears to have a simple answer: the leader follows the steps of the Administrative Cycle. This simplicity, however, must be counterbalanced by at least two caveats that also provide additional texture to our understanding of the process of leadership.

The first of these caveats is an acknowledgment and recognition that leadership is an art. Despite the fact that these administrative functions are essentially sequential and technical, a leader must be creative in the implementation of the mission and its procedures, exercising sensitivity to the situation and to the followers. The second caveat affirms and addresses the fact that Christian leadership is spiritual. In the administrative example provided in Exodus 1-6 noted in the last chapter, we find in 6:1-8 that the Lord assumes responsibility for his intention concerning the Israelites and for all of its implementation. In fact, he utilizes the terms "I" or "my" twenty times in these eight verses. The administrative functions, therefore, are not our responsibility to plan and then implement for the Lord. Our task is to discern his intention and administrate it by his help and direction. He is the Master; we are only his administrators. In other words, he not only determines and declares the mission, but he also plans, chooses people, creates structure, and generally adheres to the administrative cycle. We simply follow his lead.

With these stipulations in mind, and in order to comprehend all that is involved in administrative leadership, we will now examine the five functions of the Administrative Cycle in sequence. These functions enable leaders to fulfill their responsibilities and accomplish their missions. They provide a concise response to the third inquiry that gives shape to and informs our investigation of leadership: "How Does a Leader Do It?"

Planning

The Bible is paradoxical in its presentation of the value of *planning*, the initial component of the cycle's sequence. On the one hand, we are encouraged to take counsel, store up, prepare, and anticipate (e.g., Proverbs

20:18). In the example of administration and leadership provided by Moses, we note that the Lord composed the planning and then revealed it to his servant administrator through a variety of sources, including his family, his experiences, and the combined wisdom of the national community (cf. Exodus 3:10 - 4:17). Moses then communicated this plan to the Israelites, often to the elders first, and then he carried it out.

On the other hand, we are to take no thought for tomorrow and trust the Lord to direct and provide (e.g., Proverbs 3:5). Until recently, I leaned more heavily toward the planning and forecasting end of this continuum, frequently establishing plans a year and more in advance. A few years ago, though, the Lord took me through a two-week experience of going to bed each night with the knowledge I had not accomplished anything I had planned for that day. Every day a phone call, letter, email, or surprise contact altered my agenda to conform to his. Since that time, I have come to appreciate Jesus' advice to live one day at a time (Matthew 6:34).

In this experience, I came face-to-face with the dilemma: how does a leader balance the apparently conflicting approaches to planning? It is clear that planning is a process in which leaders are involved; however, the Lord and the timing of his revelation determine to what extent. My method now is to realize and trust that God does have plans for my life and my ministry. When he chooses to reveal those plans, I can then cooperate with him in their implementation as a fellow worker and as an administrator in his church. Whether he reveals a plan to me in enough time to participate in its development and communication (i.e., I plan) or whether he reveals it in just enough time to hang on and go for the ride as he directs it (i.e., he has planned) is of little concern to me. My job is to hear from God as best I can and proceed accordingly, just as the Israelites waited for the cloud to move in order to determine when to leave and where to go.

Regardless of the manner in which the leader determines the plan, it is important that time is taken to strategically consider what needs to be done and the order of events that must unfold in the fulfilling of the mission. Proceeding in the most profitable manner demands a sense of sequence and the prioritization of items and events. How one mechanically goes about the process of determining priority and sequence is probably not a major concern, although I recommend utilizing Myron Rush's "Priority Ranking Instrument" (Rush 1983).

Ideas, Strategies, and Plans

In a previous section, "Determine the Mission" (Chapter 2), I briefly addressed the concepts of goals, objectives, and plans. Now I would like to expand upon that foundation and explore how they relate to strategic planning.

To begin, we must distinguish *ideas* from *strategies* and *plans*. *Ideas* are random or reasoned thoughts that suggest a possible course of action. They are the notions, impressions, impulses, and concepts we consider, debate, manipulate, and refine until we agree upon a direction. *Strategies* are envisioned schemes that give direction to an overall course of action. They are conceptually devised plans of action to achieve a goal. *Plans* are proposed designs for the accomplishment of an objective. They are the specific intentions, usually formalized, which take shape in activities designed to fulfill the idea and implement the strategy.

Research and anecdotal evidence suggest people utilize only seven percent of their ideas, indicating that there are ninety-three unusable ones for every seven employed. Therefore, it is important to not announce ideas, to not write them into formal documents, and to not commit to them. One should only announce *plans*. A leader can dream, brainstorm, manipulate, and create ideas, but nothing should be formalized until it is clearly one of the useable seven ideas. I was in a church meeting when the entire staff was surprised to hear our senior pastor announce an upcoming event no one had heard about. It seems he had an inspiration for a conference while preaching and announced the idea in the pulpit as it was being broadcast on the radio. For six months, we fielded questions about this event that was never planned. A year later, we finally had the conference, but our reputation suffered because we announced an idea before it became a carefully designed plan.

Once an idea takes the shape of an intention, strategic planning begins in earnest. The term *strategy* is a combination of two Greek words (*stratos + ago*) that denotes leading an army, and implies maneuvers (stratagems) that surprise the enemy. It suggests a carefully devised plan of action to achieve a goal, or the art of developing or carrying out such a plan. Hence, the intentions of the leader (as with a general) must be clear before devising a scheme to accomplish them. It would be beneficial, therefore, to explore a primer on goals, objectives, and aims. In order to avoid unnecessary repetition, please note that the preceding definitions as well as those found in the following section are from *The American Heritage Dictionary of the English Language*, 4th edition.

Goals, Objectives, and Aims

A *goal* is "the purpose toward which an endeavor is directed." It is the intended end of the labor. Consider for a moment: what is the goal of the organization? Obviously fulfilling the mission statement is critical, but what does that mean specifically? What is the team trying to accomplish? What will be happening when it is completed?

Objectives are often perceived synonymously with goals and aims, but they are more discrete, hence the definition, "Something worked toward or striven for." That sounds like a goal, but it may not necessarily refer to the end originally sought, and it could even be in conflict or inconsistent with the goal. For example, an organization may have fiscal profitability as a goal, yet one of their objectives is to modernize or beautify their plant. This objective, which may not even be stated, may reduce the financial resources and perhaps work against the goal. One needs, therefore, to be careful to create objectives consistent with the goals of the organization or any given department or segment in particular. Accessing data, recognizing facility limitations, and desiring to spend wisely the primary resources of time, energy, and money force a leader to focus on appropriate and attainable objectives.

Finally, *aims* are statements of "purpose or intention toward which one's efforts are directed." The verb means "to direct toward an intended target; intend for a particular goal." In other words, effort is directed or pointed toward some specific activity or purpose that the administrator has determined will assist in goal fulfillment.

A Goal and a Plan: in Illustration

The following two anecdotes exemplify a flowing sequence of concepts and behaviors, generated by goals and objectives, which produce specific ideas, strategies, and plans to fulfill the mission and vision statements.

The first example consists of a professional development program that I created and developed for the faculty of a charter school in order to facilitate a content-rich, academically rigorous educational program. In line with our mission statement, I envisioned a "world-class faculty." In fact, world-class ministry is a component of every vision statement I compose (see Reflection and Response at the end of Chapter 2). To me, world-class involves two aspects: being great (cf., e.g., "world-class" athletes) and being global (i.e., able to teach anything, anywhere in the world). That was my goal – Olympian educators who were really good and really global. My first objective, then, was to help my staff understand and implement a universal five-stage learning and teaching model in their pedagogy. The second objective was to help them grasp and structure their educational programs around the five essential activities of a superior education system. To accomplish these, I pointed them to certain concepts and skills that would allow them to teach and conduct educational activities capable of attaining our goals and objectives. The strategic plan was to take advantage of sequential in-service and faculty meetings, utilizing certain techniques and methods to point them in the right direction and equip them with world-class skills.

Although it had not been formulated in a plan, I also had an idea I hoped to implement: I wanted to create a five-chapter extension of the program, outlining and codifying these models and activities for future use and development. Although I did create the outlines, I was unable to complete writing the chapters. However, they are now incorporated in Part III of this work, which is a classic example of how one of the ninety-three unusable ideas becomes one of the seven useable ones.

These concepts can also be illustrated and summarized in an example from children's ministry. One of the goals or objectives extracted from a mission statement will no doubt include and address some form of child evangelism. So, someone comes forward in a meeting and states, "I've been thinking about child evangelism and had a thought: why don't we have a block party..." This is a classic case of a random or reasoned thought that offers a possible course of action; in other words, it is an idea. After some discussion, another person suggests, "We can reach more children by having a block party that is followed up with a Good News Club and possibly a weeklong Vacation Bible School." Here we see a strategy in the early stages of formulation. The group has envisioned a policy or overall plan of action. Finally, another member of the team proposes a design for the accomplishment of the evangelistic objective, i.e., a plan: "Let's have three block parties, one in each month January through March, and after each we will start a Good News Club one week later. Then in April, during spring break, we will hold a nontraditional Vacation Bible School." The entire program commenced with an idea and concluded with a strategic plan of action.

Planning, therefore, is the critical first step in a leader's fulfillment of the organization's mission. It is a top priority to strategically discern plans from ideas and insure that they are supporting the goals of the enterprise.

The Master's Plan

Then the eleven disciples went to Galilee, to the mountain where Jesus had told them to go. When they saw him, they worshiped him; but some doubted. Then Jesus came to them and said, "All authority in heaven and on earth has been given to me. Therefore go and make disciples of all nations, baptizing them in the name of the Father and of the Son and of the Holy Spirit, and teaching them to obey everything I have commanded you. And surely I am with you always, to the very end of the age (Matthew 28:16-20).

After his resurrection, Jesus met his disciples in Galilee and shared with them one of his final messages – his vision and intention for their ministry. In the master plan, commonly known as the Great Commission, Jesus provided his disciple-followers with a glimpse into his worldview and value system while affirming their mission, clarifying his intention, envisioning their behaviors, and setting a strategic course for them to follow. In doing so, he framed the discussion ("authority"), identified the task ("go and make"), articulated the objective ("disciples"), described the process ("baptizing and teaching"), and prescribed the procedure (Acts 1:8 – "witness").

Although he directed his message specifically toward his disciples, Jesus provides a simple four-step model for strategic planning that a contemporary leader can employ as well. His approach facilitates a fitting conclusion to our brief discussion of the planning component of administration. The four steps are:

Step 1: **Identify the task**, affirming the mission and answering the question, "What are we given to do?" In this step, we address issues such as: the nature of our assignment and whom, where, and how we will serve.

Step 2: **Articulate the objectives**, clarifying the intention and answering the question, "Why are we going to do it?" In this step, we address issues such as: our goal, objectives, aims, and overall strategy.

Step 3: **Describe the process**, envisioning the behaviors and answering the question, "What should we be doing?" In this step, we address and explore issues, ideas, and intentions, and anticipate outcomes.

Step 4: **Prescribe the procedures**, setting the course and answering the question, "How are we going to do it?"

In this step, we address leadership and management while strategizing, calculating, and distributing. Here we create to-do lists and rank the priorities in order to establish scope and sequence for the activities of our strategic plan.

Organizing

The next step in the Administrative Cycle consists of taking these plans and giving them order and structure. So, let us examine the dimensions of a leader's second task - *organizing*. The *American Heritage*° *Dictionary* defines organization as:

> *1a. The act or process of organizing. b. The state or manner of being organized: a high degree of organization. 2. Something that has been organized or made into an <u>ordered</u> whole. 3. Something made up of elements with varied functions that contribute to the whole and to collective functions; an <u>organism</u>. 4. A <u>group</u> of persons organized for a particular purpose; an association: a benevolent organization. 5a. A <u>structure</u> through which individuals cooperate systematically to conduct business. b. The administrative personnel of such a structure (4th ed., 2000).*

Organizing, a verb, may be as simple as the action of grouping and arranging a collection of objects. However, to create an *organization*, a noun, implies the existence of an ordered whole with relationship, coordination, and efficiency in arrangement, which results in a system, group, or structure. It is instructive to note that the verb *organize* is derived from the Latin *organum* – meaning "a tool or an instrument." Organizational activities and the structures they produce can help or hinder, but they will not make or break a leader. They are simply tools to utilize in the fulfillment of the mission.

These definitions provide a glimpse into the breadth of possible interpretations of the nature of an organization and the options an administrator has in utilizing this instrument. Since an organization may be perceived as a system, structure, or group, it would be helpful to briefly explore the underlying aspects and applications of each.

Organization as a *System*

One of a leader's more challenging responsibilities is to assign and arrange people into the most effective systems and efficient conditions for service. Ordering tasks and resources into manageable systems is intended to provide a leader with the handle needed to facilitate the activities of the enterprise. In these activities of organization, the use of the term *systems* is intentional. A few years ago, I became acquainted with a concept I had previously implemented intuitively: *systems dynamics*. Systems thinking requires us to acknowledge that an organization and an organism (some aspects of systems dynamics theory originated in the biological sciences) are composed of interrelated and interconnected components. To affect one component affects the others and the system as a whole. As definition #3 recognizes, an organization contains "elements with varied functions that contribute to the whole and to collective functions."

Systems dynamics describes the function of organizations as receiving inputs, the physical or intellectual raw material, and processing them into outputs or products. To accomplish this requires each part to do its job, efficiently and effectively relating to each other in the AdministraCs referenced in Chapter 1: communication, coordination, and cooperation. This is exactly how the Apostle Paul describes the nature and function of the Body of Christ in 1Corinthians 12-14 and other passages in the New Testament. This body is also called the "household of God" in Ephesians 5:19, and it exhibits all of the characteristics and dynamics of what today would be referred to as a system in an organic state. Christian leaders would be wise to seriously study and implement many of the implications of *systems dynamics*.

Organization as a *Structure*

Structure provides a framework for the system. In other words, an organization is the structure that houses an organism or system. A group therefore exists not for itself but to support the life it contains and the mission for which it has been formed. One of the traditional conflicts in organizational theory occurs in the debate regarding the determination of whether the entity an administrator leads is an organization or an organism. There is a practical problem in distinguishing these terms because most dictionary definitions use each term to define the other. There are, however, some notable distinctions:

- Look at an organism as a system (life substance, it moves, breathes, grows, etc.) with interdependent components.
- Look at an organization as a structure, an arrangement or grouping, of a collection of objects (people, things, or ideas, e.g.,

65

my outlines organize my thoughts), which may be independent or codependent.

The leader, therefore, must determine what kind of organizational structure would best support the organic life and growth of a system. Biblically, every time God intervened in the affairs of humanity to accomplish some task, he organized them by placing them in families. This was true of his intentions when he involved humankind in filling and subduing the earth through the natural family of Adam and Eve. In addition, he accomplished blessing all the nations of the earth through the national family of Israel and fulfilled the Great Commission to reconcile and unite all peoples in him through the spiritual family of the church. He utilized these structures to facilitate communication, coordination, and cooperation with him in the fulfillment of his plans. From the model of Jehovah as both the Father of Israel and the spouse of Israel to that of Paul as both mother and father to the Thessalonian church, we find the family model or metaphor emerging throughout the pages of Scripture.

A number of additional sources have been very instrumental in my understanding of the praxis of ministry that creates family-like environments. In the text *Childhood Education in the Church*, Gene Getz proposes the novel idea of Sunday Schools staffing their classes with husband and wife teams functioning as substitute parents and creating learning groups that "simulate family units" (Getz 1975). Larry Richards notes in his book *A Theology of Christian Education*, "While all Christian education is not to take place in the home, a 'family relationship' or family feeling is to be of concern in every teaching/learning setting" (Richards 1976). When exploring history, we find that the schools of ancient Sumer referred to their teachers as *fathers* and their students as *sons*, and the Hebrew schools were called *houses*. Additionally, I have seen or read about male and female teams working in psychotherapy, community recreation, and day school classrooms that simulate a family's living room. As the distinguished anthropologist Edmund Leach once noted, "It is not the presence of people which is needed, but the obligations of kinship that are wanted" (Leach 1974).

Servant leadership has long been the forte of the family, in which the service is one of nurture, protection, and the development of a child. This service, in fact, is exactly what one expects to find in the administration of a family tree, which in structure is similar to a business organizational chart. The organizational structure of a family, however, anticipates that those on top, the parents, serve those below them, their children and grandchildren.

In the business world, the typical organizational chart implies those on the lower levels serve those who are above them, but Myron Rush reminds us, "The Christian leader is to serve those under him by helping them to reach maximum effectiveness. And the higher up in an organization a person goes, the more he or she is to serve. In fact, the head of the organization is to be totally at the service of those under him (like a slave is to a master)" (Rush 1983). Ken Blanchard has advocated that we turn the organizational pyramid upside down by encouraging those on the bottom to be considered the most important (Hesselbein, Goldsmith, and Beckhard 1996). I propose we do not need to turn anything upside down because the basic structural concept is fine; however, we do need to reverse the flow of service in the administration of our organizations. This is the basis of servant leadership. If servant leadership is the paradigm of the new century, then perhaps the organizational chart should be transformed into a family tree. For over two decades, my philosophy and practice has been to do just that. In Chapter 11, I will address this issue and review some of these illustrations in more depth.

Organization as a *Group*

Organization is only necessary when working with multiples of something; an individual item does not require organization. The big question for administrators is how to approach organizing people. They may function as a system or a structure, but they usually prefer to be perceived as a *group* with all of the dynamics of one.

Group dynamics is a discipline I have enjoyed studying and implementing throughout my ministry career. I have found that the time invested in analyzing a group and then utilizing those findings is more than compensated by the increased effectiveness I experience in my ability to discern and direct the necessary leadership activities.

Dynamics is defined as, "The study of the relationship between motion and the forces affecting motion; the physical, intellectual, or moral forces that produce motion, activity, and change in a given sphere." I also include relational forces in this definition.

In other words, the forces affecting a group's motion include:
- **Physical forces** – size, age, the constitution and permanence of the group, and the location where meetings are conducted
- **Intellectual forces** – purpose, functions, background, and training

- **Relational forces** – organizational and administrative models, communication networks, and personal relationships
- **Moral forces** – values and character of the group, leadership, and spiritual dynamics

The wise leader identifies and utilizes the information extracted from an analysis of these dynamics and how they affect the function of the group. For instance, my wife and I led a small group Bible study for six young married couples, preparing them for a special program in our church's ministry to children. Before the training was complete, four of the couples were no longer a part of the ministry. These couples, however, wanted to continue to be a part of the group, which dramatically altered the purpose for our gatherings and the ultimate reason for our existence. Over time, the meetings took on a different flavor, and ultimately the group disbanded. The relational forces had replaced the intellectual forces as the driving motivation for the dynamics of the group. This group illustrates the application of two of the four forces that affect group life. Further discussion of group dynamics, from a different perspective, will take place in Part III.

The physical force of size also dramatically affects the motion of a group. I was conducting an online college course on organizational behavior when one of the students asked me to identify the differences in leading and teaching large and small groups and to address the disparity in learning styles and preferences. I emailed the class the following response:

> *What is the difference between speaking to large groups of people and speaking to a small group? How can you account for (address) the vast disparity of learning styles and preferences?*
>
> *As a starting point, consider...*
>
> **Content:** *the larger the group the more generic/generalized the subject matter must be. Illustrations should be able to be universally understood. In addition, do not assume everyone in the group is familiar with your favorite author, musician, or hobby.*
>
> **Style:** *in large settings, keep it simple and big – make sure everyone in the back can see, hear, and understand you. Stand up – only Jesus could get away with sitting on a hillside and address a multitude! You can afford to be casual (and sit) with a small group.*
>
> **Methods:** *there are five categories of instructional methods: demonstration, lecture, Socratic, dramatic, and discovery. Use*

lecture and drama for the large group, save discovery and Socratic/discussion for the small (unless you can utilize guided discovery or discussion in sub-groups); avoid Q&A in large groups (see above-they get too specific).

Materials: use big screen AVs and provide handouts/outline guides for people to hear, see, and write (multi-sensory); there are "rules" available for size/distance, etc. for visuals – check the net.

Time: the larger the group the shorter the interest span; last week I had a class of 3 meet around a table and we went for 2 hours uninterrupted – you'd never get away with that in a large group (of Caucasian westerners).

Seating: you can get 3 around a table but not 30 (12 is probably max – I went to a pastor's conference that tried to be "homey" with two dozen pastors in a circle, and just going around to introduce ourselves and tell "something" about us took 3 sessions. Most of us were there for other reasons, and we never got to them!) Start in rows, focused upfront – then if appropriate you can break into groups; but remember in a circle someone's back is always to the front.

"Follow-up": consider having small groups after the presentation to discuss specific aspects and application (I know a church that had elders lead discussions after the preaching service), or producing study guides and application suggestions (distribute after the meeting or as a part of the handouts), or distribute "for further study" notes, articles, texts, websites that the learners can study on their own (now we can do discovery learning). People who "know" their preferred learning style and pace can utilize these.

Competency/skill/training: do not forget the illiterate (I had a man in a class who could not read and was scared I'd call on him to do just that) – the best PowerPoint in the world does them no good. Read the text aloud – tell them to listen/read with their minds, not their eyes. Be sensitive to the techies (I had a man bring a laptop to class – when his battery died, so did his Bible) – they have unique needs.

Lyle Schaller has written a provocative volume entitled *Effective Church Planning,* and he devotes two-thirds of the book to describing the twenty-three ways in which large and small groups differ. I recommend his work to fill in the blanks of my quick survey. Additionally, I recently became acquainted with a great summary of group processes and dynamics from a systems perspective in Stewart L. Tubbs's *A Systems Approach to Small Group Interaction* (Tubbs 2004). I would encourage the review of this excellent work as well.

Putting people and tasks in order is highly relational and inspirational work. It involves not only the product of organization, but also the processes of intuition, discernment, and application of values. To organize in a godly manner equally demands our attention to the relationships that exist between people on the team, and also between the people and the mission. Thus, the selection of workers, colleagues, and staff members is one of the administrator's most critical activities and is worthy of as much, or more, attention than any of the other functions.

Staffing

Most leaders assume that after determining the organization's structure, one proceeds to fill the positions with qualified people to get the work done. In order to facilitate most effectively the intentions of an enterprise, a wise leader recruits, selects, and trains the best people possible to accomplish the mission. Aubrey Malphurs promotes this idea with his concept of "ministry matching" that "starts with the various positions in the ministry organization and matches them to the personal ministry design of the individual" (Malphurs 1995). Thus, the third component of the Administrative Cycle, *staffing*, consists of identifying competent people for positions in the organization.

In my praxis of leadership, however, I frequently reverse the order of organizing and staffing. In the manner of Jesus in John 17, I pray that the Lord would give to me, from out of this world, men and women to whom he desires me to minister. I call these my "John 17 People." After I have established the membership of the team, I then proceed to determine the structure and order the Lord desired when he put this group together. Job design and descriptions can come later, as people assume actual leadership not just positions of responsibility. If leaders focused as much attention on the people as they do upon the position or procedure, many administrative headaches would be avoided. As the sage aptly observed in Proverbs 26:10, "Like an archer who wounds at random is he who hires a fool or any passer-by."

I recently served on a faculty committee to which the members were assigned before its task or any of the responsibilities involved were delineated. In our first two meetings, we clarified not only the undertaking itself, but also the organizational and administrative structure, with the attendant job descriptions we would utilize. Our dean clearly knew whom he wanted to serve on the committee long before a structure was created to facilitate it. He, like me, apparently believed that one structures and organizes in order to accommodate the personnel that are the best candidates to fulfill the mission.

Jim Collins emphasizes this approach in his provocative study and the research that undergirds the *Good to Great* phenomenon, which he wrote about in his bestseller by the same name (Collins 2001). As one of the six outstanding characteristics utilized to identify organizations that make the transition from mediocrity to exceptionality, his recommendation is that one distinguishes "who first, then what." Collins also considers it critical to identify the right people, and he insists that this includes an examination of a candidate's character; one can always train for competence. In Chapter 4, I formally introduce my administrative values and strategies. Among them is one that calls for character over competence over compliance. Based on these two personnel priorities alone, I would highly recommend Collins's work (note also that he completed a monograph addressing the *Good to Great* principles in the social sector, which would include churches and parachurch Christian ministries).

Although the often-recommended procedure of decentralizing the organization virtually requires department heads, it is equally clear that men and women without position can be true leaders. In a church I recently served, the key leaders were not board members but were nonetheless absolutely essential to the ministry. They did not necessarily fit the organization chart, but they did fit the ministry. They served as those "roving leaders" noted by DePree in our discussion of transactive leadership. With that brief introduction to the function of staffing, let us engage in a discussion of some key concepts and then move on to some practical considerations.

Staffing: Key Concepts

The process of recruiting and selecting a staff is, without a doubt, the most vital function in which a leader engages. In his work *The Six Core Values of Sunday School*, Allan Taylor presents an eight-step approach to enlisting volunteer workers, which provides a summary of most of the concepts I promote in this section. Taylor encourages Sunday school leaders to: "1) Explore the Possibilities, 2) Engage the Process, 3) Present Expectations, 4) Examine God's Purpose, 5) Encourage the Prospect, 6) Explain the Potential, 7) Employ a Plan, and 8) Equip the Person" (Taylor 2003). Whether for a salaried or volunteer staff, there are a number of critical considerations and practical steps to which a leader must attend in the selection process. Let us explore the most crucial.

Some Questions to Ask

The first concern we must address is actually a series of questions that focus attention upon the purpose and intention of our staffing efforts. In order to attain and retain a high quality of recruitment, the leader must answer questions such as these:

"For what am I trying to recruit?" What is my vision for the ministry? What kind of programs will it embrace? What kind of commitment is expected (in depth and breadth)? Is the position full or part-time? Regular or substitute?

"What kind of person am I trying to attract?" Is experience necessary? Do I require a specific skill set? What traits am I looking for? What role(s) do I need fulfilled?

"What have I been doing to attract that kind of person to that kind of ministry?" Does it work? If so, why change? If not, why not change?

"Why do I need to recruit?" Is this beginning a new program? Alternatively, am I just starting up the ministry? Is the program experiencing growth and expansion? On the other hand, do I have a recruitment or retention problem?

In answering questions such as these, the recruiter maintains focus and intentionality in the efforts to induce followers to come and join the mission. Reflecting upon these issues and brainstorming their implications provide a framework and foundation for specific recruiting actions to be created.

Some Terms to Consider

In preparing to engage the processes of recruiting and selecting staff, leaders must take into consideration four key concepts as they address the necessary purpose and reason for the recruitment, the kind of person needed, and how staffing has been done in the past.

Selection. Selection is choosing from alternatives (staff), while recruitment is enlisting someone as a worker or member (volunteer) – one chooses leaders and induces followers. Do not be fooled or seduced into thinking that it is imperative to accept everyone who volunteers.

Expectation. Set the standards high, because one can attain only that which is attempted. Yes, it may scare off some candidates – but more often than not, it attracts the high caliber ones.

Retention. Unless the program is starting up or growing out, recruitment means the department or organization is not retaining staff – therefore, spend as much time keeping as recruiting. There appears to be a direct and positive correlation between the amount of time spent in retaining efforts and a reduction in time spent recruiting.

Motivation. Consider why people choose to become involved and then consider what people want when they participate. Motivation not only recruits, it retains. More will be said about this issue later in the chapter.

Understanding the implications in these terms, and acknowledging their impact in the process of staffing, not only helps a leader answer the four questions presented in the previous section, but also lays the foundation for additional considerations.

Character over Competence

Next, consider the administrative strategy I noted previously: character over competence over compliance. Do not appoint someone to leadership simply because they are available and reliable, loyal, and dependable. It may be that their motivations are immature and influenced by personal need or weakness rather than ministry and service. Do not choose a leader just because of aptitude; a truly teachable person can become proficient. Choose the compliant, competent person with trustworthy character. Gary Bredfeldt (2006) calls our attention to the difference between values and virtues, because an individual may exhibit the value of efficiency and still lack virtue. Give me the virtuous person.

I ignored my own rule in a situation a number of years ago and selected for a key staff position based solely on competence. Because of that decision, I suffered the consequences of a disjointed and dysfunctional staff. I pray that I will never make that mistake again. It cost me dearly in terms of relationships, effectiveness, and the long-range stability of the organization.

John 17 People

For our final key concern, let us return to John 17. How did Jesus know the men who the Father gave to him? In Verse 8, Jesus notes, "I gave them the words you gave me and they accepted them… and they believed that you sent me." A John 17 Person does not bring a personal agenda to the team. They know the mission of the leader, and they believe it is a godly declaration. Picture the parable of the sower: the leader spreads the seed (the mission and vision given by God) to whoever will listen, noting those who receive it and allow it to grow and bear fruit. These are the ones who will constitute the staff.

I turn to this natural metaphor when explaining recruitment principles. I recommend that a leader engage in five activities that facilitate the spreading of the message. Inspiring followers, inviting leaders, and identifying John 17 People are facilitated by:

Preparing the Field. Address motivational issues; they not only impact the decision to join, but also if they will stay and tell their friends.

Tilling the Ground. Talk to as many people as possible and use events to recruit. Look for character over competence over compliance. Go slow; it is easier to hire than to fire. To mix the metaphor, do not consistently fish out of the same pond; recruit with diversity in mind.

Sowing the Seed. Cast your vision and announce the opportunities using redundant multi-media. Utilize initial short-term assignment(s) such as retreats, holiday events, etc.

Enriching the Soil. Initiate with a doable assignment. Train, train, train – it raises the bar and provides a natural "selection" process. Remember to commend and correct (Rom. 13; 1Pet. 2).

Looking for Fruit. Generate many ideas – you only use 7% of them, and what worked before may not work now. Do not sell an empty bag. Listen to references.

After answering some preliminary questions, addressing some necessary considerations, laying the appropriate foundation, and praying vigorously that the Lord would reveal the John 17 People of character, a leader is ready to acknowledge and address the practical considerations of the staffing function.

Staffing: Practical Considerations

The process of staffing incorporates three distinct functions: *recruiting*, *selecting*, and *developing*. Each has its own set of principles that provides a leader with the necessary guidance and direction.

Recruiting a Team

The first time I needed to staff a department was in my initial full-time position of directing the children's ministry in a large church. Previously, I served as a camp director and a schoolteacher, but I did minimal recruiting and staffing in those positions. My lack of experience made my first few years very difficult as I stumbled into one trial-and-error experience after another. Then, one year my department coordinators and I decided to require every candidate for a Sunday school teaching position to attend a four-week orientation before they could even visit a classroom. We were amazed; for over a year we never had fewer than nine people in the orientation program, and we did not have to publish one announcement to recruit teachers. Simultaneously, I noticed that nearly eighty-five percent of all the people who volunteered to teach had been encouraged to do so by a friend in the children's ministry.

These two incidents caused me to rethink the entire concept of recruitment. Over the next few years, I concluded that when aggressively and consistently applied within the organization's program, the following simple principles produce all the volunteers I need. I call them the institutional principles of recruitment that work in conjunction with individual motivation. I am convinced that they are the reason 85% of our staffing was actually done for us – in implementing these principles we created an environment that not only attracted volunteers, but also encouraged them to share their experience with friends.

Institutional Principles of Recruitment

1) **Communication:** The first petition is to God. Prayer changes things. Then you speak to the people. They want to be informed, and they want to be asked, so provide information and an invitation.

2) **Organization:** People want to be where it is done right, so provide structure and order.

3) **Fruit:** People want to be where there is something happening, so provide attainable goals.

4) **Family:** People want to be where they belong, so provide opportunities to bond.

5) **Leadership:** People want to be led, not managed, so provide vision and direction.

6) **Commitment:** People want to know you will be there, so provide consistency.

7) **Training:** People want to do what they know how to do, so provide and expect staff development and ministry preparation programs.

Years later, a group of department coordinators were complaining to me that their recruiting efforts were not effective, and they had many assignments left to fill. After listening to their frustrations, I reminded them of these seven principles and quizzed them about how they were applying them in their recruitment programs. After a moment or two of silence, they admitted they were not intentionally focusing on any of them. Therefore, we started with the first principle and prayed together. We then brainstormed for thirty minutes and generated ideas for incorporating *communication, leadership,* and *family* into plans that we could immediately implement: asking people without waiting for them to volunteer, identifying John 17 People after distributing vision flyers, and having a meal with invited candidates. Two weeks later, the positions were filled, and the coordinators learned a valuable lesson.

Whether attempting to recruit volunteer Sunday school teachers, little league coaches, program directors, or employees, these principles "work." A leader can apply them to virtually any recruiting endeavor as a component of a strategic plan and program. Administrators may utilize these principles as a framework for establishing and evaluating the recruitment of any volunteer and paid staff positions that the organization needs to fulfill its mission.

The Recruiting Process

To assist in putting the principles and practices together into a functional strategy, consider the following procedure as a summary guide for direction and stepping through the process.

The Recruiting Process Summarized

Step 1: Ask and Answer a Few Questions...

"For what am I trying to recruit?" "What kind of person am I trying to attract?" "What have I been doing to attract that kind of person to that kind of ministry?" "Why do I need to recruit?"

Step 2: Reflect on Four Critical Concerns...

Selection, Expectation, Retention, and Motivation

Step 3: Acknowledge and Activate Motivational Principles for Individual Issues...

Interest, Preparation, Meaning, Success, Satisfaction, Reinforcement, and Identification

Step 4: Facilitate Motivation (& Retention) Principles for Institutional Issues...

Communication, Organization, Fruit, Family, Leadership, Commitment, and Training

Step 5: Implement Some Practical Suggestions...

Prepare the Field; Till the Ground; Sow the Seed; Enrich the Soil; and Look for Fruit

We will address the personal motivation factors contained in step three in some detail later in this chapter when we discuss the leader's role in directing followers to attend to the mission. Additionally, in reviewing the strategy advocated for recruitment, one may want to adjust some of the concepts and create some specific implementations. The template, however, is valid for any program a leader may need to utilize when recruiting new team members.

As we conclude this discussion of recruitment, it is necessary to acknowledge a couple of cautionary concerns in preparation for our examination of selection. In establishing a team, it is important for a leader to recognize that in some contexts there is no room for error, so it is necessary to be careful – the most important decisions a leader makes are in personnel. One should also remember, "It is easier to hire than it is to fire."

Selecting a Staff

Recruitment is essential, but selection is equally critical. Simply having enough people to fill the required positions does not ensure that they are the right people, as we noted in Collins's observation in *Good to Great* (2001). For that reason, leaders may find it advantageous to over recruit – allowing them the opportunity to select their team.

The Selection Process

Recruitment may provide the personnel resources that are necessary, but the selection process establishes who will actually serve and perform within the ministry. In order to make the selection process more effective and efficient, a leader should consider implementing some critical behaviors and procedures that I have identified as being most beneficial. Adjusting the details for staff or volunteer positions, one can utilize these procedures to identify and select the best candidates from among those who were recruited or have surfaced from within the organization:

The Selection Process Summarized

Step 1: Pre-Screen by providing a FAQs sheet – often the expectations themselves do a good job of attracting quality candidates and eliminating poor ones. At the very least, it sets the bar as high as you want it to be; it provides another communication component for your recruiting plan.

Step 2: Screen by requiring each candidate to submit or sign documents of evidence that they are truly valid candidates – these may include a doctrinal statement, references (that you check), detailed job description affirmation, or background checks, etc.

Step 3: Interview by utilizing a variety of techniques – make sure to adhere to laws and codes and address job specifics by checking with a human resources specialist in your state or locality. Consider requiring a performance interview, where the candidate demonstrates the ability to perform the expected assignment, providing samples or simulating a task.

Step 4: Post-Screen by providing the candidate with an opportunity to ask questions, tour the facility, and to view position- and organization-specific documentation – this often surfaces issues that the interview missed.

Step 5: Select your new staff member, keeping in mind a number of considerations:
- Should I hire from without or develop from within? Am I looking for character or competence? A leader or a manager? Do we need a pioneer or a settler? Am I expecting long-term or a short-term commitment? Does this person really fit our organization and this position?
- Then, when you believe you have your person, do not rush; sleep on it.
- Finally, make it formal, putting it on paper, leaving no room for misinterpretations.

Staff Development and Team Unity

The function of staffing is probably the most important activity in which a leader engages. It involves not only recruiting, selecting, and developing a collection of world-class people, but also uniting them into a team to share together in the fulfillment of the master's mission and vision for the organization. When considering the construction of a staff, therefore, a leader must pay attention to two crucial issues: the development of individual staff members and the establishment of an effective, unified team.

Display 3. On Team Building

On Team Building ...

A strategy with suggested steps for building a team
© *2001 Dr. Michael R. Mitchell*

I. My vision for an organization's members is one of...

- o *Character*: all of the members sharing a value system
- o *Chemistry*: all of the members working together, in the harmonious arrangement of parts
- o *Camaraderie*: all of the members in relationship and unity
- o *Collegiality*: all of the members encouraging and elevating one another into a world-class community.

Collegiality demands open dialogue and debate to "share the power" and stimulate the growth and maturity of both individuals and the organization. To do this requires being open to diverse opinions and doing so in a receptive and accepting manner; therefore, we will...

- ✓ Invite argument, but prohibit the argumentative
- ✓ Embrace dissent, but exclude the dissenter
- ✓ Welcome disagreement, but bar the disagreeable
- ✓ Solicit content, but constrain the contentious

II. A Procedure for Establishing Unity...

For an organization to function effectively, the individual members must submit themselves to a process that binds, blends, and balances their unique contributions into a harmonious whole. The following seven steps are a suggested beginning:

Mental Assent ("one in heart and mind" Acts 4:32):

Step One. Recognition
is... taking the time to acknowledge and become acquainted with each other
&✓ *"I know you–who you are and what you can do."*

Step Two. Reception
is... accepting each other; the mental disposition to assent or approval
&✓ *"I welcome you, and your uniqueness, into my life"*

Practical Acknowledgment ("make every effort" Eph. 4:3):

Step Three. Appreciation
is... letting another person know that you notice and care
&✓ *"I am thankful for you (and want you to know it)!"*

Step Four. Action
is... doing deeds or providing resources to support another person
&✓ *"How can I be of help to you?"*

Personal Involvement ("with" and "among" Mark 3:14, Acts 4:13; IThess 1:5):

Step Five. Participation
is... getting involved; ministry demands proximity
&✓ *"How can I share in your life?"*

Step Six. Contribution
is... using your wisdom, talents, and skills to edify
&✓ *"How can I assist your growth and development?"*

Wholehearted Commitment ("they devoted themselves" Acts 2:42):

Step Seven. Identification
is... a sense of "esprit de corps" (a feeling of pride in belonging to a group and a sense of identification with it)
&✓ *"All I am is yours."*
&✓ *"I am not a part of this group, I am this group!"*

There are a multitude of ways to approach individual personnel development, but the program must address and include at least three critical components: 1) personal growth and maturation, so that the staff has something to say (often implemented through spiritual growth retreats), 2) professional skill development, so that the staff has something to show (often implemented through workshops and seminars), and 3) introduction to the organization and its culture, so that the staff has something to share (often implemented through open houses and orientations). A balanced and well-rounded individual development program also facilitates the establishment of a world-class team.

Camaraderie. Fellowship. Team Building. Esprit de corps! It goes by a number of names; in fact, a special term, *community*, has been coined to combine two key ideas: common + unity, affirming the underlying critical component – the common bond that is essential to successful teams. With a great number of team and group development strategies available, a leader can choose to create a unique program or utilize a published plan. Lyman Coleman's *Serendipity* approach to producing *koinonia* fellowship was one of the first resources I utilized in building my teams, and Lyman graced me with the opportunity to write study questions for Esther and Proverbs in his *Serendipity Bible for Groups* (Serendipity House 1988). I recommend resources like these as a starting point.

In addition to the resources available from publishers, I have created my own strategy for building a team and establishing unity within a group (Display 3). It was the result of two decades of experience in group and team building practice and is a plan that I have found to be very beneficial.

Directing

Directing, the forth function of the Administrative Cycle, is where the rubber meets the road. The hands-on application of ministry skills and techniques directs or guides the enterprise to the fulfillment of its goals and mission. In a very real sense, leadership is directing; hence, our definition of leadership becomes quite notable, especially when contrasted with management. As Steve Jobs, the CEO of Apple Computer, commented in a segment of the *In Search of Excellence* video series (1985),

> *The greatest people are self-managing. They don't need to be managed. Once they know what to do, they will go figure out how to do it, and they don't need to be managed at all. What they need is a common vision, and that's what leadership is. What leadership is – is having a vision, being able to articulate that so that the people around you can understand it, and getting a consensus on a common vision.*

In my philosophy of leadership, the function of *directing* is composed of the three primary activities that Jesus utilized in sending out The Twelve in Matthew 10. He influenced his followers, led them to a common vision, and motivated them to action through instruction, information, and inspiration. In doing so, Jesus provided his administrators with a template to imitate as he:

♦ **Instructed** his disciple-followers as to how he wanted them to go (vv. 5-20): "As you go, preach…," "Be on guard," etc.

♦ **Informed** his disciple-followers of what they needed to know in going (vv. 21-31): "Don't be afraid; you are worth many sparrows."

♦ **Inspired** his disciple-followers with why they should go and obey (vv. 32-42): "Whoever acknowledges me before men, I will also acknowledge him before my Father in heaven."

The leader's function as a teacher, providing information and instruction, will be addressed in some detail in Part II, so I will defer comment on those activities until then. It would be helpful, however, to summarize some of the research on motivation that inspires and the forces that influence a person's decision to move.

Forces that Motivate

What motivates an individual follower or worker to respond positively to the direction and instruction of a leader? For over 100 years, theorists and researchers have been addressing that question. After Frederick Taylor introduced scientific management into the workplace at the turn of the 20th century and Elton Mayo "discovered" the human dimension in the 1920s, science and psychology were wed in the studies of a host of creative thinkers such as Frederick Herzberg and Chris Argyris in the 1950s and 60s. Thus, when Abraham Maslow (1954) conducted a study of healthy, creative people who utilized their talents to fulfill their potential and capabilities, his hierarchy of needs introduced a new realm of motivational understanding. It paved the way for Douglas MacGregor's Theory X and Theory Y in 1960, along with Argyris's corresponding Behavior Patterns A and B. MacGregor's work suggests that leaders have two perspectives from which they can view their followers and employees. One perspective is that they have an inherent dislike for work, in need of coercion and control, and seek security above all (Theory X). The other is that they have a positive view of work, are able to exercise self-direction, and seek responsibility

(Theory Y). Argyris adapted these perceptions into two corresponding patterns of leader behavior called Patterns A and B.

I have learned much from exploring these theories. When coupled with my experience in motivating students to learn, inspiring volunteers to commit to a vision, and encouraging my children to obey, I have identified seven critical forces that appear to motivate individuals. Their specific applications will depend upon many factors, but I have found it profitable to analyze these forces as they influence an individual's decision to move.

Interest. In terms of sequence and impact, an individual asking, "Am I attracted to this?" is the initial force that motivates a disciple-follower. Interest – manifested in simple curiosity and enhanced by an ample attention span – often determines the follower's willingness to engage in an activity. Therefore, identifying what is particularly alluring to an individual and making the enterprise attractive are indispensable weapons in a leader's panoply. Athletes, for example, simply love their sport, so they are willing to participate in the activity at almost any cost and take the time necessary to master the skills. Likewise, when an individual is attracted to a new hobby or avocation, we refer to it as an "interest," accompanied by a willingness to spend time, energy, and money to investigate it. Our followers, in the same way, respond to that which interests and attracts them.

Preparation. An often overlooked but significant motivating force is preparation. Here, the follower asks the simple question, "Am I ready for this?" Immediately after graduating from college, I had the opportunity to be a swimming instructor at a boys' summer camp. One of my greatest joys was teaching non-swimmers how to swim. At the conclusion of each session, I took my students to the deep end for a "graduation ceremony" that consisted of jumping off the diving board and swimming to the side of the pool. They had manifested their training and development in the shallow water, and there was no doubt they could do it. Their emotional and mental preparation, however, was the next barrier. Camper after camper stated, "I'm not ready." Eventually, every swimmer took the plunge and succeeded, but I learned a great lesson for leadership: preparation involves the spiritual, mental, and emotional dispositions as well as the accumulation of a skill set. Our followers must be prepared for their assignments in body, soul, and spirit, and they must be convinced of their preparation and ability to complete the task.

Meaning. Whether or not a follower can sense or identify meaning and value in an activity is often the deal maker or breaker. When the follower can see application and a reason to persevere, the motive and staying power of a vision is enhanced considerably. Why should anyone join another's quest? What makes one's mission, and its accompanying vision, worth a follower's time, energy, and money? As a leader, one needs to ask and answer questions such as these, because the followers will.

Success. "Nothing succeeds like success." No matter how it is defined, success is a force with which to be reckoned. A disciple wants to know, "Will I be able to do it?" It is a challenge to engage in activities and behavior when a person does not feel capable. The leader needs to provide not only the necessary skill training but also the opportunity to experience what John Kotter refers to as "short-term wins" that are easily attainable and motivate followers to attempt the more difficult, long-term changes (Kotter 1996). Achievement, competence, and experience are indispensable allies in the battle to stimulate followers to action. The leader should help followers recognize their abilities (see *preparation*) and utilize them in even small tasks in which they can be successful. As Gary Bredfeldt concisely summarizes, "No matter how much one might want to achieve, without the confidence that success is possible, people just will not try" (Bredfeldt 2006).

Satisfaction. The fifth force acknowledges awareness that the answer to a simple but profound inquiry motivates a follower: "Will it meet my needs?" Satisfaction produced by a fulfilling activity is a powerful force in generating movement and action. People have genuine and positive needs that drive and compel behavior and attitudes; leaders must take these needs seriously and acknowledge the force they contain. Christian leaders, whose Master spent a lifetime meeting people's needs, must decide whether people or programs are more important to them. If the leader cares enough to meet the followers' needs, then the followers may grow to care enough to help fulfill the leader's mission.

Reinforcement. A term popularized by the behaviorists, reinforcement, acknowledges and addresses a simple concern of the follower: "Will I receive something for this?" The fact that rewarded behavior is more likely to be repeated finds biblical support in Romans 13 and 1Peter 2; Paul and Peter both acknowledge that it is a responsibility of governing leaders to "commend those who do right." Granted, conditioning can be manipulative and taken to ungodly extremes, but the concept behind this force is indisputable. People respond to praise and appreciation, whether it is in the form of a personal acknowledgement or a paycheck. Moreover, it is not just the successes that need to be recognized. Knowledge of results or feedback is a proven motivator of learners. They want to know how they did, so we should tell them.

Identification. Although interest and attraction are close in importance, identification is perhaps the most potent force of them all. Followers are motivated to become just like their leader (Luke 6:40). Identification is the ultimate expression of followership, as a disciple imitates and emulates the leader, answering the question, "Will I become who I want to be?" in the affirmative. I am reminded of the impact of leadership when I see my habits and idiosyncrasies duplicated in others, when I hear them utter my catch phrases, and when I observe them prioritizing and valuing the same things I do. My followers, when fully trained, will become just like me. Likewise, after I am fully trained by Jesus, I will become just like him. Harry Chapin's song "The Cat's in the Cradle," affected me greatly. The lyrics reflected the relationship between a father and son from the dad's perspective, and the conclusion was the fact the son became "just like me." As Christian leaders, we have the opportunity to influence and inspire life changes in our followers. Let us make sure we are supplying them with proper models to imitate (1Corinthians 11:1).

Giving attention to these seven forces, and the questions they generate, supports the leader's efforts at influencing the people, i.e., motivating disciple-followers:

1. **Interest** (Am I attracted to this?),
2. **Meaning** (Will it be worthwhile?),
3. **Preparation** (Am I ready for this?),
4. **Success** (Will I be able to do it?),
5. **Satisfaction** (Will it meet my needs?),
6. **Reinforcement** (Will I receive something for it?), and
7. **Identification** (Will I become the person I desire to be?).

The behavior of directing incorporates a variety of skills that the effective leader must grow to master. An abbreviated catalogue of these competencies can be found near the end of Chapter 4. I recommend them as an extension of this discussion.

Controlling

The final component of the Administrative Cycle, *controlling*, has always been personally stressful. Like many others, I conceived control as the policing of an organization and its members. Although I knew and understood the importance of this activity, I avoided it whenever possible.

Hersey, Blanchard, and Johnson, however, define control as the "feedback of results and follow-up to compare accomplishments with plans and to make appropriate adjustments where outcomes have deviated from expectations" (Hersey, Blanchard, and Johnson 2001). Similarly, the Simpson Associates, in referring to the management cycle, acknowledge on their website that, "Organisations define and measure success in many ways: market share, profitability, customer satisfaction, and shareholder value. As they strive for success, organisations engage in a management cycle in which they set plans, monitor performance, explain results, and adapt the plan based on new information" (http://www.simpson-associates.co.uk).

These definitions resonated with me. From this perspective, controlling can and should be truly administrative rather than manipulative or abusive. The administrator is encouraged to promote and facilitate the wise use or stewardship of time and resources, not forcibly manipulate the behavior of individuals.

The Control Panel

As I began to reflect upon how control could be accomplished proactively and positively without punitive and negative implications in an organization, I realized that it contained both passive and active aspects to it. We can further expand these two components into practical stages or steps. Presented in an outline format that I refer to as the "Control Panel," this is my perception of the function of control:

Passive Control

STAGE 1: **Information**: Establish rubrics for effectiveness and efficiency
    Policies
    Procedures

STAGE 2: **Interaction**: Establish processes for communication, coordination, and cooperation
    Observations
    Reports
    Meetings

Active Control

STAGE 3: **Investigation**: Action taken to determine what is happening
    Analysis: "What are we doing?"
    Assessment: "How are we doing?"

STAGE 4: Intervention: Action taken to affect what is or will be happening
    Commendation
    Correction

These four stages move the administrator through a series of actions that establish expectations and then evaluate how well the individual or the institution is progressing in the fulfillment of the mission. In this approach, control is an ongoing function of the administrator rather than an immediate or one-time fix of a troublesome situation or personnel problem. It also focuses upon personal interaction as opposed to intervention that is impersonal and distant.

Control in the Early Church

A biblical illustration of the Control Panel in action can be found by examining how the apostles handled one of the early conflicts among the believers: the integration of Gentiles into a church populated initially by Jews. In what we know as "The Jerusalem Council" in Acts 15, we can observe each of the four stages I have identified.

The problem actually began with a failure of the leaders to provide a Stage 1 rubric, including the necessary policies and procedures, for the incorporation of this new group of believers (vv. 1-5). A meeting, therefore, was held to address the issue (Stage 2 – vv. 6, 7a). Testimony was heard from a number of apostles and ministry leaders to analyze and assess the situation (Stage 3 – vv. 7b-12), and in the end, James intervened by correcting the problem and establishing a rubric to affect future behavior (Stage 4 – vv. 13-21).

It is noteworthy that the leaders then sent a delegation to Antioch with a letter containing a written rubric, which they presented and affirmed in a meeting. After these events, Paul and Barnabas embarked upon a journey to investigate the progress of churches they had planted earlier (vv. 22-36ff), initiating a second cycle of control activities.

Control in Personal Life

Controlling is a critical challenge for a leader, involving not only the positive side of encouragement, motivation, communication, and reward, but also the negative side of correction, conflict, opposition, and rebellion. The following two personal anecdotes will further illustrate this part of administration.

In my youth, I struggled with submission to authority; I was proud, in fact, that I could successfully passively resist and not get caught by those in authority. The Lord, however, did not look kindly upon that attitude, and he set me upon a month-long individual training program to teach me godly and proper submission. He established the rubric, interacted with me, showed me my error, and equipped me with submission skills that put me back in line with his will and direction for my life and ministry.

Another situation involved my learning to live one day at a time after spending so many years depending upon long-range goals to guide me. As I shared in our discussion of the function of planning, I learned to trust the Lord to reveal to me when I was to participate in planning and when I was to simply allow him to do his work in his time.

In both of these situations, the Lord manifested his care and concern for me by exercising control, "making appropriate adjustments where outcomes deviated from expectations" (Hersey, Blanchard, and Johnson 2001), and putting my life back on the appropriate and proper course. In the same way, the Lord's administrators correct and realign the activities and directions of their organizations as necessary and appropriate. The goal of control is to work with our followers so that they will choose to stay on course, fulfill the mission, and implement the vision.

To manage the function of control, a leader must develop the skills of discipline or disciple making, conflict resolution, and the ability to guide people through changes. A leader stays informed and able to guide the necessary adjustments and corrections needed to keep the enterprise on course by keeping close contact with followers, utilizing periodic appraisals and reviews, and staying ahead of the pack. In other words, as Nanus suggests, "the leader is responsible for catalyzing changes in the internal environment – for example in personnel, resources, and facilities – to make the vision achievable in the future" (Nanus 1992). These changes are the intention of control: to ensure progress toward the organization's goals and objectives.

Control in Practice: "AdministraCs"

As was noted in Chapter 1, leaders need managers and managers need leaders. Mutual respect and appreciation for each other's contributions can make the work of these two administrators more effective. In my own ministry, I value what I call the three "AdministraCs": *communication, coordination,* and *cooperation.* They summarize the functional relationship necessary for an organization or group's administrative team to be efficient and effective in assessing feedback and implementing necessary adjustments. The more they work together and cooperate, the more effective they will be at achieving their objectives, while practically implementing control in their ministries.

The following two anecdotes from church life illustrate how the absence of the 3Cs impacts not only the program, but also the personnel. After a successful weekend of training my Sunday school teachers and department coordinators in small group dynamics, I arrived at work the following Monday morning to discover that two other ministry departments in the church had done the same thing that weekend. None of the leaders, including me, had communicated with each other, so we missed an opportunity to coordinate the endeavors and cooperate with each other to give our followers the benefit of each leader's expertise.

In a similar scenario, a leadership-training program that was scheduled for the same weekend as a choir performance forced multiple leaders to choose between two legitimate and effective activities. If the directors had *communicated* with each other, they could have *coordinated* the dates on which the events were scheduled and avoided the conflict. Further, these leaders could have sent teams to support each other's ministry, *cooperating* with each other and increasing the quality of service for both. Simply implementing the 3Cs can greatly increase administrative effectiveness and facilitate control in a proactive and positive manner.

Chapter Summary: By Example

In response to a request to briefly describe my approach to leadership, I generated the following catalogue of personal convictions. These principles summarize how I go about leadership, and they provide a simple expression of most of the concepts that we have addressed in Chapters 1-3:

I attempt to exercise and practice the following guidelines/principles in my leadership:

- *I believe leaders engage in three activities: determining the mission, declaring the mission, and directing the mission.*
  A Christian leader receives his mission and vision from the Lord.
  A Christian leader takes seriously the principles of communication "outlined" in Genesis 11 and John 3:16.
  A Christian leader emulates the example of godly/biblical leaders.
- *Leaders are "mission sensitive" and prioritize accordingly.*
- *Leaders are "systems thinkers" and see the big picture.*

- *Leaders are not afraid to lead but are sensitive to the needs of the followers.*
- *Leaders decentralize their structures and facilitate the exercise of the gifts of the Spirit.*
- *Leaders walk with and among their people (Mark 3:14 & Acts 4:13; 1Thessalonians 1, 2).*
- *Leaders lead by example as well as exhortation, reproducing themselves in their followers.*
- *Leaders listen as much as they talk, do more than they talk, and talk to God regularly.*

Reflection and Response

Self-Check Response Worksheet

Five lessons for leaders were utilized in the introduction to this chapter to illustrate some principled applications extracted from the author's experiences in implementing the administrative functions. If you were to identify and articulate a bulleted list from your own experiences, how would it differ from these?

- Plan your work and work your plan – don't be afraid to be a visionary;
- Structure will help or hinder, but it won't make or break – don't be afraid to be organized;
- Personnel will make you or break you – don't be afraid to be selective;
- Your voice must be heard – don't be afraid to be assertive; and
- Commend and correct as is appropriate – don't be afraid to be encouraging.

Reflect upon your most recent efforts to administrate by influencing both the people and the process. On a notepad describe your attempts; then respond by brainstorming and writing down any ideas, strategies, or plans you may utilize if you decide that you want to do something differently next time.

The last time I attempted to influence the people who follow me, I...

       Inspired them by...
       Informed them of...
       Instructed them to...

The last time I attempted to influence the process of administration, I...

       Planned by...
       Organized by...
       Staffed by...
       Directed by...
       Controlled by...

The next time I attempt to influence the process of administration, I will...

1.
2.
3.
4.
5.

Reflection on Motivation

When attempting to influence people, many leaders question both their understanding of and their ability to motivate their followers. Review the section on the forces that motivate and attempt to construct a strategy for use in the following scenarios.

Consider these to guide and direct your reflection:
Which motivational principle appears to be most impacting? Why?
What do you intend to say and do? What is your backup plan if this fails to motivate?

SCENARIO 1:
You are the church librarian. A volunteer teenage girl is busy doing "something" in the technology section when a member walks in. The girl ignores the person and continues with whatever she is doing. She is the daughter of a close friend and is volunteering to receive service credits at school.

How will you motivate her to attend to her tasks and care for the ministry as you do?

SCENARIO 2:
You recently received a promotion to supervisor of your department. One of your staff has been with the organization twice as long as you and has applied for the supervisor position three times. She appears to have accepted the decision to promote you with grace, but you have your doubts. She is highly skilled and has more expertise than anyone else in the department.

How will you motivate her to perform at her capacity?

SCENARIO 3:

You are the president of a company that just downsized and reduced the workforce by nearly one-third. You've heard rumors that almost one-half of the remaining employees are considering quitting because they are fearful of an increased workload and additional responsibilities.

How will you motivate your remaining employees to stay and perform at a high level?

Four

LEADER COMPETENCIES: *The Tools of the Trade*

Coach Phil Jackson's journal of the 2003-2004 NBA basketball season, referenced in Chapter 1, illustrates the fact that an individual may make a valiant effort to induce and influence followers but still not fulfill the mission; he may exhibit ineffective leadership skills, behave in ways that followers find offensive, or simply fail to communicate. Therefore, the perception of a leader as one who induces and influences followers by determining, declaring, and directing a mission may be an accurate portrayal, but it is nonetheless incomplete. Therefore, to fill the frame and bring it into focus, we must also address the mindset and the skill set necessary to effectively accomplish the mission.

Researchers, scholars, and practitioners have attempted to identify and catalog the most effective attitudes, values, approaches, and techniques available to contemporary leaders. While space prohibits an exhaustive review, in this chapter I will recognize and summarize some of the attitudes and skills that I have observed or found to be most profitable.

Administrative Values and Strategies (A Mindset)

When a decision needs to be made or justified, a follower needs direction, or a strategic plan needs to be instituted or implemented, a leader must have a clear sense of his guiding principles and values. After reflecting upon the challenge of developing such a proactive mindset, I embarked upon a quest to uncover the vital principles and values that would give guidance and direction to the everyday practice of leadership. I wanted to produce a checklist of maxims I could consult and count on in the routine of administration.

Over time, I established such a catalogue and it has evolved to become the mindset that I take into my daily administrative responsibilities. It provides the framework and gives direction to mundane affairs as well as emergency administrative functions, contributing to the coat rack and clothes hangers referred to in the Prologue. My commitment to the principles and values found in Display 4 influences every decision I make or directive I give. Each one has proven to be a "best practice" in the administration of the master's will and in the leading of his people. They enhance the normal routine of my day-to-day administration.

Display 4. Administrative Values and Strategies

Administrative Values and Strategies
By Dr. Michael R. Mitchell © 2002

ORDER (*"the harmonious arrangement of parts"*) IS FACILITATED BY...

Administration Guided by these Priorities...

✔ *Wisdom over Work*
  We will think before we act
✔ *People over Programs*
  We will value education over administration
✔ *Character over Competence over Compliance*
  We will recruit for character and develop competence
✔ *Forests over Fires*
  We will build for the future and not worry over the past or present
✔ *Best over Better over Good*
  We will not be distracted by the good – our goal is the best

Order Facilitated by these Principles...

✔ *Communication*
  Sharing information and life experiences with individuals and departments so as to maximize the facilitation of common knowledge, attitudes, and activities within the organization
✔ *Coordination*
  Aligning vision, direction, and implementation within the organization so as to maximize and conserve time, energy, and resources
✔ *Cooperation*
  Contributing necessary resources to another individual or department so as to maximize the utilization of time, energy, and resources

Behaviors Enhanced by these Practices...

✔ *Establish Foundation before Superstructure*
  We will organize before we implement
✔ *Policy what will be Policed*
  We will only require what we can regulate
✔ *Decentralize Leadership, but Centralize Management*
  We will delegate and transfer leadership whenever possible

and a Staff Characterized by a Partnership *with...*

✔ *Chemistry:*
  all the elements working together, in the harmonious arrangement of parts
✔ *Camaraderie:*
  all the elements in relationship and unity
✔ *Collegiality:*
  all the elements supporting, encouraging, and elevating one another – a world-class staff.

To illustrate how these value-laden strategies affect daily performance, let me share a brief anecdote. A number of years ago, I took on the responsibility to right an organizational ship that was tilting precariously close to capsizing in a storm of disorder, incompetence, and malfeasance. The school was in the throws of a major change of leadership, facing a lawsuit, threatened with closure, and reeling from the remnants of an administrative system that made promises it could not keep. Therefore, it was not uncommon to hear, "What are we going to do about...?" Guided by my "forests over fires" principle, I examined each issue to see if it was about to burst into flames and needed immediate attention, or whether procedures could be created to positively solve the problem by doing something right for the long haul. In other words, I wanted to address the real underlying problem and plant trees to fill the forest, not douse brush fires that would burn out on their own.

In this troubled situation, the temptation was to overreact; people wanted something done immediately. It was my perception, however, that one of the problems the school had was a tendency toward impulsive decision-making and rash actions. One of my values, conversely, is "wisdom over work" and thinking before acting. By slowing down, thinking before we behaved, and "establishing foundation before superstructure," we made our way out of the hole and within three years had reestablished a quality program recognized for excellence among students, families, and the community at large.

A Proactive Mindset

Too many leaders rely upon gimmicks, tricks, and quick fixes to substitute for the hard work of guiding their followers to the fulfillment of the mission. This is especially tempting when facing faulty performance or when challenges and problems, such as those I encountered in the anecdote above, arise. Therefore, after a leader establishes a catalogue of values and strategies, the next logical step is the acquisition of a proactive mindset. An administrator must believe that institutional and individual performance can be improved by simply administrating the organization in a professional, skillful, and aggressive way as a standard operating procedure rather than waiting for problems to arise or faulty performance to hinder the effectiveness of the organization.

In exploring the idea that organizations cannot just hope for success but need to plan for it, Richard Swanson writes in *Analysis for Improving Performance* (1996) that a "standard performance improvement model" for an organization incorporates five phases: analysis, design, development, implementation, and evaluation. While contemplating his proposal, I reflected upon the possibility of a correlation of these five phases with the five functions of administration: planning, organizing, staffing, directing, and controlling (Table 7).

Table 7. Swanson's "Improvement Model" and the Administrative Functions

Performance Improvement Model	Administrative Functions
Step 1: Analysis	*Planning*
Step 2: Design	*Organizing*
Step 3: Development	*Staffing*
Step 4: Implementation	*Directing*
Step 5: Evaluation	*Controlling*

After identifying a positive correlation between the two lists, I came to a liberating conclusion. In implementing an organizational "improvement model," leaders do not need to react to a perceived or assessed problem of faulty performance. Rather, since superior administration facilitates superior performance, they can prevent substandard endeavor by applying effective administrative procedures proactively.

Ruth Brown's "Developing Values in Children" seminar provided me with an exemplary illustration of this assertion in an educational context. In a workshop, she asserted that there are ten attitudes and skills a teacher needs to exhibit when assisting children in their attempts to build personal value systems. Pertinent to this discussion is the observation that eight of the ten points suggested in her lecture were concepts routinely addressed in general teacher-training sessions. In other words, values can be developed in the normal activity of teaching without relying on special programs. This reinforces the notion that teachers as well as leaders can benefit from a proactive rather than a reactive mindset. They do not need performance-enhancing programs for their organizations; they need consistently effective administration and education. As an alternative to looking for programmatic assistance, especially when there is trouble, leaders should be consistently growing in their personal competencies in order to become and function as administrators worthy of following.

A Godly Mindset

One godly application of this proactive mindset is to recognize that a life of love is the context for and frames every biblical discussion of the spiritual gifts. Jesus, Paul, Peter, and James all instructed their disciple-followers to manifest love in their personal and ministerial lives. The reality, however, is that too many of us have experiences that confirm the severe lack of love actually practiced today even by Christian leaders. This deficit is so pronounced that Alexander Strauch wrote *The Christian Leader's Guide to Leading with Love* (2006) to exhort and instruct the contemporary Christian leader in living a life of love (Eph 5:2).

The Apostle Paul suggested another example of a proactive and godly mindset when he warned the Ephesian church to no longer live like the Gentiles do, in the futility of their thinking (4:17). This warning is particularly appropriate in a culture that promotes feel-good decision-making and me-first value systems that drive selfish ambition. The mindset of the Christ-follower is that of love, service, and self-sacrifice; that of his administrators ought to be no different.

Leadership Skills and Behaviors (A Skill Set)

A leader brings to an assignment not only a set of attitudes, perceptions, values, and strategies, but also a package of behaviors and techniques believed to be most effective in inducing and influencing followers. Since there is an abundance of how-to books and resources available for leaders to enrich and enhance their skill sets, my suggestion is to visit local bookstores and libraries to search out those that inform and resonate. Additionally, there are a number of theatrical presentations that dramatize leadership principles; the film *K-19*, for example, is a classic study in the applications of MacGregor's Theory X and Theory Y.

To aid in the process of creating a skill set that is the most beneficial, I will introduce and discuss five diverse strategies, approaches, or practical models for the behavior of leadership. Each set illustrates a unique approach or preferred practices that may provide helpful hints in developing a leader's skill set. We will begin by briefly exploring some vital principles for getting started in a new ministry or leadership opportunity and then move to a brief review of four other sets of leadership behaviors.

Getting a Great Start: a Strategic Approach to the First Few Days

Putting the right foot forward at the beginning of a new ministry or leadership position will make a significant difference in the future effectiveness and success of the endeavor. The activities undertaken in the initial days and weeks, therefore, are crucial as they directly affect the groundwork being laid. The particulars of these days, weeks, or months may differ according to the job, but there are a few key principles that a new staff member needs to follow to make the transition easier and more effective.

They are applicable in any new assignment, whether it is a full or part-time salaried staff position or an opportunity as a volunteer.

The components of Display 5 introduce a basic set of prescriptive principles and practices in which to engage to make the transition to a new job smooth and hopefully effective. Each of these points may require a different amount of time to accomplish, but I have seen every one of them play a crucial role in the initial stages of a new job.

Display 5. Getting a Great Start

Getting a Great Start
By Dr. Michael R. Mitchell © 2008

Preparation.

GET READY: IN BODY, SOUL, AND SPIRIT (REST, DRESS, AND DEVOTION)
Establish priorities early
Practices: Establish and keep your margins – don't burn out. You're in it for the long haul. Let people know up front what's important to you and to what you will give priority.

Orientation

GET TO KNOW: PEOPLE, PLACES, DATES, AND EVENTS
Identify your team (John 17)
Practices: "Submit" yourself to an experienced member who can show you around and introduce you to not only the present but also the past. In one church, I had the privilege of spending three consecutive evenings with a 30-year veteran of the programs of the church – priceless!

Investigation

GET INFORMED: WALK AROUND – BECOME FAMILIAR (READ AND OBSERVE)
Identify institutional values (and history)
Practices: Stop, look, and listen; read everything the organization produces. When interviewing for a new position, I read not only the church newsletter and bulletin, but also annual reports and minutes, etc.

Communication

GET IN TOUCH: LISTEN CAREFULLY, SPEAK CAREFULLY – BE PRECISE
Start sharing your mission & vision
Practices: Attend any meeting that looks like an orientation or introduction. Conduct your own – not only for present members of your department, but also provide orientations for potentials. Share your mission and vision with anyone who will listen.

Participation

GET INVOLVED: BE ACCESSIBLE – HANG AROUND AND GO TO EVERYTHING THE FIRST TIME
Lead! But don't be afraid to follow
Practices: Show your interest in the entire organization – prove yourself to be a team player. "Cross fertilize" people and programs with other departments – it will enrich you both.

Socialization

GET THE T-SHIRT!: LEARN THE LANGUAGE
Start building your team
Practices: Conduct interviews, take people to lunch or dinner, and show up for special events and presentations by other departments. Identify your John 17 people and give them excessive time and attention. If not already done, create and utilize department logos on T-shirts, ball caps, notebooks, and any other paraphernalia you can manage.

Impression

Finally, make good first impressions! Overly prepare for your first business meeting, your first public presentation or message, etc. and build equity. You never know when you might need it!

Laying a strong foundation is one of the most important criteria for success in establishing a ministry or leadership position. To fill out the rest of the leader's initial skill set, consider the following four sets of "best practices" and leadership behaviors. Reflect upon their influence and impact on the three steps of determining, declaring, and directing the leader's mission and vision.

Sir Ernest Shackleton's "Guiding Principles"

It was the summer of 1915, and the great Antarctic explorer Ernest Shackleton was trapped. Ice floes in the frigid Weddell Sea had locked in his ship, the Endurance, for a polar winter so cold that the crew could hear the ice freezing around them.

By September of that year, grinding icebergs had crushed the ship's hull, leaving Shackleton and his men stranded on a vast ice sheet 1,000 miles from the nearest inhabited land...

In a new book, Shackleton's Way: Leadership Lessons from the Great Antarctic Explorer (2001), coauthors Margot Morrell and Stephanie Capparell tease out Shackleton's remarkable leadership methods – strategies the explorer employed for 19 months while leading his crew across treacherous ice, through uncharted waters, and over a murderous mountain to safety. The book examines all of Shackleton's expeditions and includes testimonials from Shack-heads like secretary of the U.S. Navy Richard Danzig; Apollo 13 commander James Lovell; and business leaders from Jaguar, TheStreet.com, and Donaldson, Lufkin, & Jenrette (Hoult 2001).

In the past century, few men or women have inspired both their followers and other leaders as much as Sir Ernest Shackleton, the adventurous explorer of the Antarctic. In their text, *Shackleton's Way: Leadership Lessons from the Great Antarctic Explorer*, Morrell and Capparell capsulize Shackleton's heroic leadership into the following five guiding principles, which form a great transition from the idea of a mindset to the necessity of a skill set. Shackleton's leadership was marked by a consistent application of:

- Optimism
- Communication
- Flexibility
- Strong example
- Encouraging enjoyment

I would strongly suggest further investigation of the life and adventures of Sir Ernest Shackleton. A simple way to start the process would be by viewing the A&E biography of his life available in DVD format. In addition, the Internet provides a variety of sources and resources on the subject.

The Leadership Challenge

While Shackleton's guiding principles frame the way leaders think and work, James M. Kouzes and Barry Z. Posner's book, *The Leadership Challenge*, provides the contemporary administrator with a collection of five "fundamental practices of leaders." *The Leadership Challenge* began as a research project in 1983, when Kouzes, chairman and CEO of TPG/ Learning Systems (a company in The Tom Peters Group), and Posner, professor of organizational behavior at the Leavey School of Business and Administration of Santa Clara University, began to study the time periods that selected leaders designated as periods of achieving their personal best.

In surveys conducted in 1987 and 1995, they identified four qualities as the most important for a leader: honesty, forward-looking, inspiring, and competent. These characteristics are reflected in what Kouzes and Posner suggest are the five practices that encapsulate the essence of outstanding leadership. They further refined these five practices into ten commitments.

1. Challenge the Process

Commitment: Search out challenging opportunities to change, grow, innovate, and improve.

Commitment: Experiment, take risks, and learn from the accompanying mistakes.

2. Inspire a Shared Vision

Commitment: Envision an uplifting and ennobling future.

Commitment: Enlist others in a common vision by appealing to their values, interests, hopes and dreams.

3. Enable Others to Act

Commitment: Foster collaboration by promoting cooperative goals and building trust.

Commitment: Strengthen people by giving power away, providing choice, developing competence, assigning critical tasks, and offering visible support.

4. Model the Way

Commitment: Set the example by behaving in ways consistent with shared values.

Commitment: Achieve small wins that promote consistent progress and build commitment.

5. Encourage the Heart

Commitment: Recognize individual contributions to the success of every project.

Commitment: Celebrate team accomplishments regularly.

The research, which initially utilized surveys received from over thirteen hundred leaders, expanded from 1983-1997 to include data emanating from multiple thousands of managers. These studies provided data and the impetus for the model behind *The Leadership Challenge* and the accompanying evaluation instrument, *The Leadership Practices Inventory*. That instrument has been administered to over ten thousand leaders and fifty thousand of their constituents.

In 2004, an enhanced edition of this work was published for Christian leaders entitled, *Christian Reflections on the Leadership Challenge*. In this text, various guest authors reflect, from a Christian perspective, upon each of the practices. This is a must read.

Situational Leadership

In their famous work *Management of Organizational Behavior: Leading Human Resources*, Paul Hersey, Kenneth Blanchard, and Dewey E. Johnson have identified forty-four "Significant Motivation and Leadership Theories and Models." Spanning a century (from 1911 to the present), these theories and models illustrate one of the theses of this book: there is no commonly agreed upon definition or approach to leadership, thus the need for a metamodel to frame the discussion. If popularity, utilization, and material sales are any indication, however, Hersey and Blanchard's Situational Leadership model may come the closest.

Developed as "a practical model that can be used by managers, salespeople, teachers, or parents to make the moment-by-moment decisions necessary to effectively influence other people, Situational Leadership uses as its basic data the perceptions and observations made by managers... on a day-to-day basis in their own environments." It is this down-to-earth response to real-time circumstances and the recognition of the importance of "the behavior of a leader in relation to followers" that, in part, make this model so attractive (Hersey, Blanchard, and Johnson 2001).

The Situational Leadership model is built around the intersection of the leader's style with the readiness level of the follower(s). Depending upon the willingness and ability of the follower (forming a "Continuum of Follower Readiness" – labeled R1-R4), the leader employs a leadership style (labeled S1-S4) of Telling, Selling, Participating, or Delegating, which is formed by merging two primary behaviors, *task* (spelling out responsibilities) and *relationship* (engaging in communication). Each leadership interaction, then, is a fusion of the perceived readiness level of the follower with the appropriate leadership style, resulting in the leader influencing the follower's behavior. In essence, it is the leader's job and a description of leadership to match style with the perceived readiness level.

Situational Leadership provides a simple and practical model to implement: observe and identify the follower's readiness and respond accordingly. Novice or weak leaders, however, must avoid the temptation to diminish their goals and objectives to accommodate a lower readiness level on the part of followers. When this occurs, the leader becomes the follower. Politicians, for example, may fall prey to the pressure of opinion polls and allow the prevailing preferences of the populace to alter their positions so radically and frequently that it becomes impossible to determine exactly what their mission and vision entails. While Jesus often adjusted his style to the readiness of his followers, he never adjusted his mission or vision to their weaknesses. He would not be deterred from his objective.

Bredfeldt's Competencies of the Leader-Teacher

Gary Bredfeldt's recent book, *Great Leader, Great Teacher*, contributes to our understanding of leadership by emphasizing the teaching role. After synthesizing the eight classic virtues of Aristotle and reviewing the character component of leadership, Bredfeldt addresses the need for competencies and identifies eight "which mark the effective leader. Four of these relate to the teaching aspect of the leader-teacher's calling, and four relate to the leader aspect of that calling. Together they give strength to leadership just as fence posts support and strengthen a fence" (Bredfeldt 2006).

Table 8. Bredfeldt's Eight Basic Competencies of the Leader-Teacher

Leader Competencies	Teacher Competencies
Establish the Team	*Message that is Clear*
Equip the Team	*Methods that Promote Learning*
Empower the Team	*Model the Message*
Encourage the Team	*Minister to People*

I differ with Bredfeldt in the categories delineated, especially the leader competencies. For example, how does one lead if there is no team? At one point in my ministry, I was the pastor of a small house church. When I attempted to recruit leaders for a variety of ministry opportunities, I consistently came up short, and I found myself serving virtually alone. My model makes provision for a leader to determine, declare, and direct when leading individually as well as with a team. Nevertheless, I highly recommend Bredfeldt's work, and I strongly encourage the consideration of his observations as a companion to this study, even though his focus is church ministry exclusively.

The contemporary Christian leader, in a manner similar to an experienced golfer, needs to increase his skill set, by acquiring and honing the use of a bag full of ministry "clubs" to utilize appropriately as the situations unfold. Whether a leader emulates the guiding principles of Shackleton, the practices of Kouzes and Posner, the model of Hersey and Blanchard, the competencies of Bredfeldt, or any of the other theories and models, it is imperative to obtain as many leadership skills and behaviors as possible. As Winston Churchill reportedly observed, there comes "… that special moment when a man is figuratively tapped on the shoulder and offered the chance to do a very special thing, unique to him and fitted to his talents. What a tragedy if that moment finds him unprepared or unqualified for that which would have been his finest hour."

Recommended Skill Set

To summarize and tie together this section on the skill set of a leader, I have compiled a brief catalogue of the competencies a contemporary leader must be able to exercise regularly and consider as essential to his skill set.

Among the multitude of possible leadership activities, an administrator must be capable of:
* Casting a Vision
    Establishing goals and articulating the mission
* Establishing Priorities
    For the leader and the team
* Developing an Organization
    Designing the job(s)
* Selecting a Staff
    Recruiting and developing people
* Working with People
    In groups and leading meetings
* Speaking in Public
* Providing Instruction
* Motivating to Action and Guiding Change
* Solving Problems/resolving conflicts
* Managing Resources

While working on his doctoral thesis project, David Hirschman, a friend and colleague, identified a complementary catalogue of sixteen leadership characteristics. Hirschman's taxonomy is the result of research that he describes in personal correspondence:

> *In a thesis project attempting to identify the transforming leadership characteristics or traits of Dr. Jerry Falwell, various sources were consulted from both the ministry and business worlds, including: Henry Blackaby, John Maxwell, John Noe, Elmer Towns, and Jack Welch. Each of these authors used different terms to identify their characteristics, such as laws, traits, and essentials, and a variety of descriptions were utilized to define the various leadership characteristics/ traits, Nonetheless, an initial table list revealed a catalogue of traits of influential and successful leaders. Based on a detailed examination of each author's characteristics with their corresponding definition, a more comprehensive table cross listing the commonly agreed upon characteristics revealed further areas of agreement between the authors. The results of this second table permitted the identification of leadership characteristics common to all authors and the opportunity to eliminate characteristics where there was little or no agreement.*

> To this reduced list of characteristics/traits were added several items located in a subsequent source, producing a final list of sixteen items used to identify the leadership characteristics/traits of successful leaders.

Augmenting my suggested skill set, and providing a fitting summary conclusion to this brief examination of the components of a recommended mind and skill set, Hirschman's final list included these commonly agreed upon leader characteristics:

Integrity: Respect, credibility
Strong Family Ties: Strong marriages, children, and grandchildren
Ego in Check: Small in their own eyes
Inner Peace: Lack, or control, of stress
Preparation: Willing to prepare, process
High Energy Level: Ability to keep going
Passion: Encounters with God, heart
Vision: Big dreams, no small plans
Victories: Successful track record, rewards
Influence: God's authentication, motivation, positive energy
Communication: Energize others
Decision-Making: Talent to execute
Edge: Navigation, problem solving, tough calls
Timing: Knowing when the time is right
Risk-Taking: Willing to face failure, willing to face fear
Sacrifice: Counting the cost, willing to do what it takes

The Requisites of Leadership (A Godly Man's Model)

In addition to acquiring the necessary mind and skill sets, distinguishing between the *pre-requisites* and *requisites* of leadership can be helpful.

Prerequisites of Leadership

I have found that there are three primary qualities critical for success in leadership: purpose, principles, and passion. The purpose is provided by the mission and vision, the principles to be implemented are the behaviors and skills we have been studying, and the passion is fueled by a sense of call and commission, coupled with a compassion for those who follow and are the recipients of our leadership ministry.

The nature and function of a Christian minister will be explored in more depth in Chapter 12, but for the intention of this chapter, the encouragement of the Apostle Peter will summarize the necessary prerequisite characteristics of a leader:

> *To the elders among you, I appeal as a fellow elder, a witness of Christ's sufferings and one who also will share in the glory to be revealed: Be shepherds of God's flock that is under your care, serving as overseers—not because you must, but because you are **willing**, as God wants you to be; **not greedy** for money, but **eager to serve**; **not lording** it over those entrusted to you, but **being examples** to the flock (1Peter 5:1-3).*

In serving as an overseer, a shepherd of God's flock exhibits five personal characteristics: 1) willing; 2) not greedy for money; 3) eager to serve; 4) not lording it over; and 5) being an example. The necessary passion, purpose, and principles of Christian ministry, especially leadership, could not have been more concisely and convincingly stated.

Requisites of Leadership

The biblical character Joshua is an indefatigable source of inspiration to me as I attempt to administer the call of God in my life. In investigating his life and leadership, I have observed and identified five recurring characteristics that appear to describe the man and his ministry, illustrating the qualities required for an effective leadership mind and skill set. In summary, Joshua was a man of *commitment, power, preparation, hard work,* and *time.* Interestingly, in Warren Bennis and Burt Nanus's classic text *Leaders: The Strategies for Taking Charge,* they identify as critical these same characteristics within the first eight pages of their book (Bennis and Nanus 1985).

The Requisites Exemplified

A brief review of just one of the many incredible adventures of this ancient hero illuminates and illustrates these essentials of successful leadership. Joshua 10 records the story commonly referred to as "The Defense of Gibeon." Even though the Gibeonites tricked Israel into a treaty (Joshua 9), they fulfilled their obligation and came to Gibeon's rescue when five kings attacked the city. In reading the story carefully, the five primary requisites of leadership become apparent. First, we find illustrated the *commitment* Joshua maintained despite the less-than-honorable manner in which the treaty was forged (vv. 6, 7). Leaders stick to their commitments. David could have had Joshua in mind when he described the man who dwells in Jehovah's sanctuary, and lives on his holy hill, as one who "keeps his oath even when it hurts" (Psalm 15:4b). Second, Joshua exhibited a complete dependence upon the might and miraculous work of God, thus we recognize him as a man of *power* (vv. 8, 10-13). As we will see in the next section, it is one thing to have the authority to make a decision; it is another to have the power to implement that decision. In the Lord, Joshua had both. Third and fourth, Joshua did not shy away from the *preparation* (he utilized his best fighting men, v. 7) and *hard work* (they marched all night, v. 9) necessary to accomplish his task. Fifth and finally, Joshua was not afraid to put in the *time* necessary to lead and be successful. In fact, he and his troops, after traveling all night, compacted two days of fighting into one. This story is the context for the miraculous "day the sun stood still," allowing Joshua and his forces to complete their victory (vv. 12-14).

Joshua has provided an excellent and exemplary model for contemporary Christian leaders: he hears from God, speaks to the people, and completes his assignment. In doing so, he plans, organizes, staffs, directs, and controls, all with the leadership requisites of commitment, power, preparation, hard work, and a willingness to take the time necessary to fulfill his mission. I would strongly encourage reading the book of Joshua with a notepad in hand, making observations, taking notes, and then rereading them for devotions.

The Requisite of Power

Time is the currency utilized to pay for the privilege of participation in leadership. *Authority* is one of the essential elements of efficient decision-making, and its influence on responsibility, commitment, and transformative leadership can be profound. *Power*, however, is the key that activates and enables effective leadership; in fact, it is arguably the most critical component of successful administration. It is the ability to "translate intention into reality," as Bennis and Nanus (1985) express it. In their identification and description of the place of power in leadership, they observe:

> *These days power is conspicuous in its absence... there is something missing from all the 'new age' formulations-- one issue which has been systematically neglected without exception:* **POWER, *the basic energy to initiate and sustain action translating intention into reality, the quality without which leaders cannot lead.*** *Just as the economists have painted themselves into a narrowing corner by failing to recognize the limitations and constraints of the free market, so too have*

> *students of organizations avoided the nucleus of leadership.*
> *Without any qualification, we can bluntly state that all of the*
> *current paradigms of organizational life, be they the 'new age'*
> *variety or older brands, have failed to consider power... **power***
> ***is at once the most necessary and most distrusted element***
> ***exigent to human progress...***
>
> *Our concept of power and leadership, then, is modeled on*
> *the Iacocca phenomenon: **power is the basic energy needed***
> ***to initiate and sustain action or, to put it another way,***
> ***the capacity to translate intention into reality and sustain***
> ***it.** Leadership is the wise use of this power: transformative*
> *leadership.*

Power can be described as the personal ability to accomplish a task or the relational capacity to influence others to do so. In essence, while authority is the right to make a decision, power is the capacity to carry it out. Let me illustrate the difference. I was the executive pastor of a large church, and had the authority to make command decisions for virtually every ministry within the organization. I served, however, under a senior pastor who believed in the divide and conquer approach to leadership so that no one could maneuver into a position to usurp a place of influence beyond his established boundaries. To facilitate this strategy, the pastor charged the business manager with controlling information flow, making financial distributions, and determining facility usage, among other responsibilities. In other words, while I had the authority to make decisions, he had the power (in this case, the control of the resources) to implement or impede them.

Authority without power is like a traveler without transportation; power without authority is like a racecar without a driver. Authority, thus, must be partnered with power for a ministry, or any enterprise for that matter, to be effective. Regardless of an individual's position on the orgchart or in the organization's hierarchy, possessing the power to influence is essential for success, and that power must be wielded in a gracious and transformative manner. Teachers, for example, may not hold a position of prominence within the administration of a school, but they can exercise power to change the lives of students every time they gather. It is this power and influence that separates the effective from the ineffectual leader or teacher.

A Taxonomy of Power: PowerPack

Leaders, managers, and teachers can enhance their effectiveness by having a functional familiarity with the research on the sources and forms of power available to them. John French and Bertram Raven (1960) studied the social bases of power and identified five forms of power: Legitimate, Expert, Referent, Reward, and Coercive. Their original taxonomy has been challenged and adjusted over the years (as they and others have added concepts such as information, connection, rhetoric or persuasion, and asset control, etc. to the list), but this seminal work brought attention to power and its effect upon the transformation of disciple-followers and the organizations of which they are a part.

As I considered the French and Raven taxonomy, I recognized the need to adjust their catalogue. I felt, additionally, that a mnemonic device such as an acrostic would make the options easier to recall. As a result of my reflections, I created POWERPACK to identify nine sources of power that a leader can employ in directing disciple-followers in the fulfillment of a mission. In the following concise presentation, I have provided selected illustrations to represent the wide range of possible applications of power available in a leader's toolkit (Position, Ownership, Wisdom, Expertise, Resource, Prestige, Association, Communication, and Kinetic):

Position. Role power is derived from the status of an appointed, selected, or elected administrator. In its application, followers and subordinates are expected to submit and respond with appropriate respect for the position (while respect for the person must be earned). For example, teachers require students to follow their instructions and expect their directives to be obeyed.

Ownership. Permission power is derived from the possession and control of intellectual, organizational, or real property. In its application, the custody of properties gives the leader authority over their use, but permission to employ them empowers the follower. For example, a substitute teacher or an assistant coach can only accomplish assignments for which they have been given the right to make decisions and provided assets they are allowed to utilize.

Wisdom. Principled power is derived from the accumulated repository of tradition, knowledge, and experience. In its application, the leader's capacity to discern "what to do" influences both performance effectiveness and follower response. For example, a member of a congregation will give attention to a pastor's inspired vision and program for church growth and development based upon a record of accomplishment of proven and prudent judgment.

Expertise. Skill power is derived from the acknowledgement of advanced competency in a given field. In its application, the leader's capacity to know "how to do" influences both performance effectiveness and follower response. For example, a trainee respects and responds to a mentor with a demonstrated talent or even a studied knowledge born of observation and successful experience.

Resource. Asset power is derived from the control of tangible supplies such as finances, facility, and equipment along with management tools such as calendars and communication vehicles. In its application, the manipulation of resources facilitates the accomplishment of a task. For example, the administrative assistant who controls the boss's calendar and appointment schedule effectively controls what gets done.

Prestige. Celebrity power is derived from the attraction to famous or well-known public figures. In its application, a follower is willing to take action, even when not directed, because of a desire to emulate a celebrity. For example, a political candidate can attract more volunteers than needed because of a reputation as a legendary community activist.

Association. People power is derived from the connection established between people or organizations. In its application, the capacity to call upon another to accomplish a task is as effective as being able to do it yourself. For example, a camp director tasked with creating a swimming program recruits and selects as director a long-time colleague who is a former lifeguard.

Communication. Exchange power is derived from access to and the ability to share restricted data, information, and knowledge. In its application, the transmission of essential information provides the foundation for every enterprise. For example, the member of an expedition who can accurately read and interpret a map will provide the guidance and direction necessary for a successful journey.

Kinetic. Motive power is derived from the ability to move people or organizations from one location or condition to another, applying pressure primarily by persuasion but also by intimidation or force. In its application, manipulation by conviction, imposition, or even threat (physical, emotional, or social) inspires follower response. For example, a mom makes it clear that her daughter must pass Algebra or she will go to summer school and miss camp.

Power, the ability and energy necessary to make things happen, provides an individual or group with an essential requisite of successful leadership.

Coupled with commitment, preparation, hard work, and time, the necessary ingredients for effective administration, the mission and vision of any enterprise may be fulfilled.

The Priority is People

Leaders must know how to deal with people, individually and in groups. This being the case, it is incumbent upon leaders to acquire people skills. Their effectiveness as leaders will increase exponentially and their followers will benefit greatly. From communication to conflict resolution to supervision and delegation, the leader must always put people before programs and understand his relationship to them.

Realizing people are not isolated but often found in cultural context, the leader must also learn to deal with people in groups. For example, consider the differences in dealing with teenagers when they are alone as opposed to being with a group of peers. Thus a foundational understanding of group dynamics will enable a leader to be much more effective in his instructional and inspirational roles in corporate and organizational settings.

The priority of people-centered ministry will be addressed again, in more detail, in Chapter 12.

In Conclusion

The process of leadership is not complicated. In fact, it is simple, involving just three steps: leaders figure out what they are supposed to do, pass this on to others who will join with them, and oversee the accomplishment of the task. The problem for leaders and their followers is that simple does not necessarily mean easy.

For example, the environment in which today's leader operates affects the ease or difficulty of his task. If someone instructed me to walk across a freeway, it would be a very simple directive to fulfill: put one foot in front of the other and do what I have been doing for years. However, the time of day, the weather, or a host of other conditions make a huge difference in how easy it will be to accomplish. Implementation is as varied as the contexts and the people whom a leader serves, and fulfilling the assignment requires sensitivity, wisdom, nearly inexhaustible energy, and a copious amount of time.

The process of leadership, a metamodel for the principles underlying the proposed behaviors, is the same simple procedure that has been utilized for generations and will continue to be for generations to come. The challenge is to understand and master the various implications and applications of these fundamental principles of leadership and management. In the words of the Psalmist, we are to engage in behaviors and activities that flow from a heart of integrity (a mindset) and skillful hands (a skill set), hiding God's Word in our hearts, that we might not sin (Psalm 78:72 and 119:11).

Reflection and Response

Essential Skills of Administration and Leadership Checklist

1. Reflect upon the text's assertions concerning the necessity of acquiring a mind and skill set.

A suggested catalogue of skills necessary for effective leadership is reproduced below.

2. Rank order each one, according to your perception of their importance to a leader. Use the underlined space before each skill to show your ranking (1-10).

3. Rate yourself, on this simple scale, as to how well you...

* ____ *Cast a Vision*
❑ No problem! ❑ Maybe a little problem ❑ Big problem – Help!

* ____ *Establish Priorities*
❑ No problem! ❑ Maybe a little problem ❑ Big problem – Help!

* ____ *Develop an Organization*
❑ No problem! ❑ Maybe a little problem ❑ Big problem – Help!

* ____ *Select a Staff*
❑ No problem! ❑ Maybe a little problem ❑ Big problem – Help!

* ____ *Work with People*
❑ No problem! ❑ Maybe a little problem ❑ Big problem – Help!

* ____ *Speak in Public*
❑ No problem! ❑ Maybe a little problem ❑ Big problem – Help!

* ____ *Provide Instruction*
❑ No problem! ❑ Maybe a little problem ❑ Big problem – Help!

* ____ *Motivate to Action and Change*
❑ No problem! ❑ Maybe a little problem ❑ Big problem – Help!

* ____ *Solve Problems/Resolve Conflicts*
❑ No problem! ❑ Maybe a little problem ❑ Big problem – Help!

* ____ *Manage Resources*
❑ No problem! ❑ Maybe a little problem ❑ Big problem – Help!

Reflections on Requisites

"Joshua has provided an excellent model for contemporary Christian leaders: he hears from God, speaks to the people, and completes his assignment. In doing so, he plans, organizes, staffs, directs, and controls, all with **commitment, power, preparation, hard work**, and a willingness to take the **time** necessary to fulfill his mission."

On a scale of 1-10, how would you rate your level of…

Commitment _____
Power _____
Preparation _____
Hard work _____
Time _____

Reflections on Power

Reproduced below are the nine sources of power suggested in the text. Review their descriptions, and consider the following for each one:

- **Summarize, in your own words, how each one can be implemented**
- **Provide, from your life and ministry, an example of this power being utilized**
- **Evaluate, biblically and experientially, the strengths and weaknesses of this power**

POSITION POWER
OWNERSHIP POWER
WISDOM POWER
EXPERTISE POWER
RESOURCE POWER
PRESTIGE POWER
ASSOCIATION POWER
COMMUNICATION POWER
KINETIC POWER

- **Reflect upon the following, and explore the application of power**

What other kinds of power would you add to the taxonomy?

Which of the nine powers do you see exercised most frequently?

Which power(s) do you most often utilize (at home, at school, with friends)?

Which of the powers would you exercise in your leadership as you...

Determine your Mission?

Declare your Mission?

Direct your Mission?

Which of the powers would be most effective in your present organization? Why?

- **THINK ABOUT IT**: are there any forms of power that are more appropriate for a Christian leader?

Are there any that should be avoided? Why?

Preamble

to Part II: *On Teaching and Learning*

Leading and teaching share a number of common characteristics and activities. Their purposes, however, are distinct; the leader focuses upon the completion of the work, while the teacher focuses upon the completion of the worker. If we subscribe to the common sense notion that a better-prepared person produces a better product, then teaching must be a critical companion – if not an essential ingredient – to the leader's toolbox. It is inconceivable that a person can lead without being a teacher, so it is to the process of teaching that we now turn our attention.

Although the assertion may be challenged, a commonly accepted dictum acknowledges, "Learning theory generates teaching theory." Therefore, to truly understand, appreciate, and implement the function of teaching, one must have a serviceable comprehension of how people learn. While giving due regard and credit to traditional and secular learning theories and models, our attention in Part II focuses on a pattern established by the wisest man who ever lived. We will explore the implications of this ancient wisdom for contemporary Christian education and its application in leadership venues with the purpose of providing another metamodel – in this case, one that can be utilized in any teaching-learning endeavor.

Foundations

In a manner similar to Part I, we will address three categories of foundations upon which an educational ministry can be built: biblical foundations, theoretical foundations (consisting of teaching-learning theories, educational psychology, and human development), and practical foundations (including an examination of discipline as a prerequisite to learning). All three foundations will be evident throughout Part II, but each of the chapters has its particular and unique emphasis. Chapter 5 will primarily address the theoretical foundations, Chapter 6 will contain the biblical foundations, and Chapter 7 will provide practical foundations.

Distinguishing Terms

Just as we distinguished and clearly defined the administrative components of leadership and management in Part I, Part II considers necessary distinctions in three conceptual dyads with which we need to be familiar as we engage the study of the teaching-learning process. Chapter

8 will discuss the critical role that each of these dyads plays in defining education, but I will briefly present them here.

Training and Teaching

John Milton Gregory's *The Seven Laws of Teaching* introduced me to the distinction between training and teaching, so it is appropriate to allow him to have the first word:

> *As we more carefully study all this, two chief facts become clear: First, this child is but a germ — it has not its destined growth. Second, it is ignorant — without required ideas.*
>
> *On these two facts rest two notions of education. (1) The development of powers. (2) The acquisition of knowledge. The first is an unfolding of the faculties of body and mind to full growth and strength; the second is the furnishing of the mind with the knowledge of things — of the facts and truths known to the human intelligence*
>
> *Each of these two facts — the child's immaturity and its ignorance — might serve as the basis for a science of education...*
>
> *Corresponding to these two forms of educational science we find two branches of the art of education. The one is the art of training; the other the art of teaching. Training is the systematic development and cultivation of the powers of mind and body. Teaching is a systematic inculcation of knowledge...*
>
> *These two great branches of educational art — training and teaching — though separable in thought, are not separable in practice. We can only train by teaching, and we teach best when we train best. Training implies the exercise of the powers to be trained; but the proper exercise of the intellectual powers is found in the acquisition, the elaboration, and the application of knowledge.*
>
> *There is, however, a practical advantage in keeping these two processes of education distinct before the mind (Gregory 2003).*

In light of these distinctions, reflect upon this telling observation by the author of the book of Hebrews:

> But solid food is for the mature, who by constant use have trained themselves to distinguish good from evil (Hebrews 5:14).

In order to receive advanced instruction consisting of solid food, the disciple-follower must first acquire the foundational discernment necessary to comprehend and apprehend the difference between good and evil. Reminded of Gregory's terminology ("the development of powers"), it is interesting to note that the NeXt Bible resource defines *hexis*, the word translated "constant use," as "a power acquired by custom, practice, use."

The distinguishing characteristics and the interdependence of training and teaching can be illustrated with two simple examples. A classic case is learning how to write. Prior to writing a book, developing a chapter, constructing a paragraph, or even inscribing a sentence, the pupil must first have the power to hold a pen or pencil in hand and formulate letters on a piece of paper. Without this capacity, any attempt to teach a student how to write will necessarily fail. There is, however, a dependent interplay between the two: the capacity to hold the pen allows the student the opportunity to learn how to form letters, and this, in turn, produces a new capacity which allows the student the opportunity to learn how to form words. One can readily see that training and teaching are "not separable in practice."

Consider, also, the training and developing of powers essential to learning how to dribble a basketball. After developing the capacity to hold a ball, the youngster needs to learn how to drop and bounce the ball. The achievement of this "power" affords the opportunity to learn how to do it while walking, then running, and ultimately in competition.

Growth and Development

When the prophet Isaiah encouraged his hearers and readers to "lengthen your cords, [and] strengthen your stakes" (Isaiah 54:2), he provided a concise summary of every educator's dream: an increase in the learner's knowledge and understanding that is accompanied by an improvement in the learner's competency or ability to actually practice and apply the lesson. To lengthen the cords symbolizes an increase in size or capacity, while strengthening the stakes represents an increase in stability or maturity.

To put it in other words, *growth* and *development* are equally encouraged and anticipated. Growth involves expansion, whether that increase is in the physical, mental, emotional, social, or even the spiritual dimension. Development involves maturation, whether that increase is in coordination, comprehension, satisfaction, relationships, or a person's walk with God. Growth and development, facilitating an increase in capacity and maturity, are the functional intentions of both teaching and training; neither dyad is competitive, they are complementary.

Theory and Model

Throughout this work, the terms *theory* and *model* are frequently utilized. The distinction between these two critical concepts is rather simple to identify: a *theory describes why* something is the way it is, or why it works or produces something, while a *model describes how* that something works.

In discussing a theory, the answer to the "Why?" question is, "Because." Learning theory addresses what occurs when a student is prepared and responds to instruction. Why does a student learn? Because, as Ted Ward notes, he either acquires knowledge, acquires responses, or constructs knowledge (Wilhoit and Dettoni 1995). In other words, learning theory describes what must occur if someone is to learn.

In discussing a model, the answer to the "How?" question is, "Like this." Learning models address the behaviors and activities that occur as a student is responding to instruction. How does a student learn? If Ward's perception of the options is accurate, a student learns by participating in the processes that facilitate the acquiring of knowledge and responses or constructing knowledge. While the theoretical question of "why" is a legitimate investigative concern, the focus of Part II is a learning model that describes how a student learns, and how a teacher can facilitate that learning.

Additional Terms

Neither teaching nor learning usually stands alone, and since the one virtually determines the other, educators often refer to the teaching-learning process as if it is a single component. We will continue this common practice here. In our metamodel, the teacher supports the process the learner goes through, so it is prudent to use the hyphenated term.

Metamodel

This section is also the appropriate place to address the definition of a metamodel. Since the term *meta* refers to something of a higher order or beyond the present status, I utilize the term *metamodel* to refer to the overarching and encompassing process that includes the independent and functional models related to it. In other words, when referring to a teaching model, there may be a submodel for leading a class discussion or giving a lecture. A metamodel, then, provides the structure in which the individual teaching models or learning theories may be accommodated. For example, a teacher may want to utilize behavioristic or constructivistic concepts. The metamodel provides a convenient framework in which they may be integrated or synthesized into a more complete theory and approach to teaching and learning.

In essence, the goal of Part II is to provide a comprehensive metamodel that can be utilized in any teaching-learning endeavor once the disciple-followers are trained and have developed the necessary capacities to engage new learning. It is this training foundation that we will address first in Chapter 5, followed by an examination of the process used to produce learning in Chapter 6.

PART II
"Come, learn from me"

*"**Come to me**, all you who are weary and burdened, and I will give you rest. Take my yoke upon you **and learn from me**, for I am gentle and humble in heart, and you will find rest for your soul" (Matthew 11:28-30).*

Preview Pane:
Outline and Chapter Synopsis

Chapter 5 – Foundations for Teaching and Learning

The concept of teaching-learning theory is introduced in this chapter. It addresses Bigge and Shermis's notion of an emergent synthesis, including a brief catalogue of the theories and approaches to the teaching-learning process. Based upon the postulation that learning is initiated with parental (or teacher) discipline, sometimes referred to as training, a three-step procedure for discipline, extracted from the biblical illustration of the heavenly father "child-training" believers (Hebrews 12, quoting Proverbs 3), is presented.

Chapter 6 – A Metamodel for Teaching and Learning

This chapter addresses the five stages of the Proverbs 2 Metamodel for Teaching and Learning, providing biblical, scholarly, and anecdotal evidence and support of the model. As the centerpiece of the study, the precepts of teaching, leading, communicating, and transforming lives are integrated. It concludes with an example of a professional application of the model for both teacher and learner. The questions, "How does a student learn, and what can I do to help?" are answered.

Chapter 7 – A Model for Teaching

This chapter provides an historical and biblical illustration of the teaching-learning metamodel at work. It also explores the case study and criteria for success provided by the Old Testament priest, scribe, and scholar, Ezra.

Five
Foundations for Teaching and Learning

> *Now when he saw the crowds, he went up on a mountainside and sat down. His disciples came to him, and he began to teach them saying:*
> *"Blessed are the poor in spirit,*
> *for theirs is the kingdom of heaven.*
> *Blessed are those who mourn,*
> *for they will be comforted.*
> *Blessed are the meek,*
> *for they will inherit the earth.*
> *Blessed are those who hunger and thirst for righteousness,*
> *for they will be filled..."*
> *When Jesus had finished saying these things, the crowds were amazed at his teaching, because he taught as one who had authority, and not as their teachers of the law (Matthew 5:1, 2; 7:28, 29).*

Those in attendance that day had no idea that the simple homily they heard would be recorded and generally recognized 2000 years later as one of the greatest sermons ever preached. I once heard a pastor preach this sermon by simply reading the text of Matthew 5-7. That was it – no exegesis, no commentary, no suggested application – he just read what Jesus said. No higher praise could be expected or given.

Biblical Foundations for Teaching and Learning

The Sermon on the Mount in Matthew 5-7, the encounters with Nicodemus and the woman at the well in John 3 and 4, the healing of a man by the pool in John 5, and the feeding of the multitudes in John 6, provide telling examples of the Master's method of teaching. In these four chapters of John alone, we find that he engaged people right where they were, utilized Socratic methods, demonstrated his message, and insisted that people respond in some way to his lesson. If we add to this list dramatic methods such as the Last Supper, lectures such as the Olivet Discourse, and a willingness to lay down his life for his disciples, we acknowledge that he was, indeed, a master teacher. The sheer volume of material that has been written about him by Christian and secular authors alike confirms this assessment.

Herman Harrell Horne, in his classic *Teaching Techniques of Jesus* (1971), describes the qualifications of a "world-teacher" modeled after Jesus. Horne suggests that the Master's ministry incorporated these five characteristics:

- A vision that encompasses the world
- Knowledge of the heart of man
- Mastery of the subject taught
- Aptness in teaching
- A life that embodies the teaching

A brief examination of the previous biblical passages will acknowledge and affirm his powerful and persuasive pedagogy. In addition to the example Jesus provided, the rest of the Scriptures also include instructive illustrations and practical models to imitate and emulate. The examples of the Old Testament prophets and the New Testament apostles, especially as recounted in the Acts or referenced in the Epistles, are cases in point. Paul's personal memoirs, as recorded in 1 Thessalonians 1-3, also provide ample demonstrations of what we would now refer to as "biblical models."

This work will actually center on an ancient model extracted from Proverbs 2, which we will address and expound upon in Chapter 6. Therefore, we will leave these introductory paragraphs with the affirmation that there are biblical foundations for education and move on to the other foundations for teaching and learning that we will identify in this chapter. Let us begin with a brief look at three theoretical foundations.

Theoretical Foundations for Teaching and Learning

In their text *Learning Theories for Teachers* (1999), Morris Bigge and S. Samuel Shermis propose that an educator chooses to perceive and regard learning and related theories from one of three perspectives. The experience of three friends illustrates their thesis.

The Sunday morning church service had just concluded, and three friends made plans to have lunch together. Since they could not agree upon a choice of restaurant, they decided to go to a buffet cafeteria. Sally, a vegetarian, chose a salad and a plate full of vegetables. Bill, who will eat anything, had a meal consisting of beef, turkey, chicken, a side of potatoes, a small salad, and a bowl of string beans. He could not decide what to have for dessert, and his indecisiveness resulted in his selection of both cake and pie. Jack was on a diet, which had developed from reading three books and a magazine purchased at a health food store. From the menu, he selected items that conformed to the specifications of his carefully crafted personal diet plan.

The first perspective, like Sally, is to draw from one source exclusively. The second, more like Bill, is to draw from a variety of learning sources in an eclectic compromise. Finally, in line with Jack's personal diet plan, a teacher may create an emergent synthesis by blending and uniting a number of approaches into a new and personally developed understanding of the teaching-learning process.

Bigge and Shermis indicate, rather strongly, that choosing the first option and sticking exclusively to a single theory significantly restricts an educator. They also believe an eclectic compromise is inferior all around because of its unstable foundation. They recommend that an educator draw from a variety of sources and create a personalized theory that is new and emerges from a synthesis of the diverse elements (Bigge and Shermis 1999).

Regardless of which of the three approaches they take, educators select or synthesize their personal conviction based upon theoretical and experimental research. Because of this scholarly activity, a wide range and variety of teaching-learning and other education-related theories and models exist. Together they provide a vast reservoir of resources for the practice of education. In this section, I will introduce three of the theoretical foundations for teaching and learning that can be extracted from this pool: 1) teaching-learning theories, 2) educational psychology, and 3) human development. My intention is to "connect the dots" and show how the critical components of each of these foundations lead us to the thesis of this chapter: preparation is necessary to ready the pupil for learning.

Teaching-Learning Theories

I recently spent some time examining two sets of texts that addressed the teaching-learning process. The first was an older set, a few volumes of which I had studied in my undergraduate program; the second consisted of the latest editions of the eminently popular and frequently utilized educational psychology texts by Robert Slavin (2006) and Anita Woolfolk (2006), as well as the Bigge and Shermis text (1999). My intention was simple: I wanted to compare the categories that these scholars utilized to catalog teaching-learning theories. I had observed in my studies that researchers have identified over fifty different theories as valid and functional understandings of how learning occurs, and I wanted to see how they addressed and handled them today in comparison to a generation ago. In essence, I was investigating which, if any, had stood the test of time. What I discovered confirmed a perception that will unfold as we progress through this chapter.

A Brief Review

The first of the older works that I perused was Daniel Barlow's masterful study of teaching and learning from a Christian perspective, *Educational Psychology: The Teaching-Learning Process* (Barlow 1985). Bigge and Shermis have joined him in placing learning theories into three categories: 1) those focusing on cognition, 2) those emphasizing behavior, and 3) those with humanistic assumptions and leanings. Both of these sources more or less imitate the catalogue of theories found in Robert Biehler's standard *Psychology Applied to Teaching* (Biehler 1978) that also organizes learning theories into cognitive, behavioral, and humanistic approaches.

Bigge and Shermis indicate the theories in these categories are all scientifically-based and rooted in the research of Piaget, Vygotsky, Erikson, Kohlberg, Skinner, and Bruner, to name a few. They also point out that the philosophically based theories, such as mental discipline (held by Augustine and Calvin among others), have slowly yet perceptively declined in the support they receive from educational theorists and researchers (Bigge and Shermis 1999).

I found it interesting to observe that in another older work, Herbert J. Klausmeier and William Goodwin (1966) took a different approach and restricted their catalogue to "four theories with relevance to school learning," which limited their usefulness in non-traditional or informal learning settings, including church, home, business, or recreation. These four theories included purposive learning, conditioning, imitation and observation, and meaningful reception learning. Later in their text, however, they also discussed processing information, skill acquisition, and attitude development, placing their observations and perceptions within the scope of the cognitive, behavior, and humanist approaches.

Ronald Habermas and Klaus Issler (1992) take a more recent and Christian approach to the theories proffered by Klausmeier and Goodwin. Their catalogue contains three avenues of learning, again correlating closely with the cognitive, behavioral, and humanistic schools: the information-processing family, conditioned learning, and the social learning family.

A Current Perspective

The catalogues have changed little over the years. Constructivist theories have joined the cognitive and behavioral theories and have extended the humanist perceptions and tendencies. Slavin and Woolfolk articulate this current perception. In three separate chapters, Slavin addresses: 1) behavioral theories of learning, 2) information processing and cognitive theories of learning, and 3) student-centered and constructivist approaches to instruction. Woolfolk affirms the catalogue, and identifies behavioral, cognitive, and social cognitive and constructivist views of learning. In common language, a priority is given to the mental, behavioral, and socio-emotional aspects of learning, respectively. As we will see, this would be anticipated in an educational psychology that takes its nature seriously.

Educational Psychology

The home in which all of these theories reside is referred to as *educational psychology*. This discipline addresses the principles of psychology that may be applied to the teaching-learning process and related educational activities. As simple as that process may appear, it is fraught with difficulties due to the lack of a clear and consistent understanding of what constitutes the discipline of psychology. Since a significant amount of educational theory is built and dependent upon conceptions that emanate from this field of study, it is valuable to spend a few moments exploring and contemplating the implications and applications it generates.

We must begin at the beginning, when God created human beings in his own image (Genesis 1:26, 27). I adhere to the conviction asserted in Chapter 2 that humans were created as tripartite beings constituted of body, soul, and spirit, thus mirroring the trinitarian makeup of the Godhead (see 1 Thessalonians 5:23). In Romans 8:5-10, the Apostle Paul makes reference to all three components and lends credence to this interpretation when he informs us that the flesh and the spirit wage battle for control of the mind, with the victor producing a carnal or spiritual man. To put it simply, I affirm humankind's trinitarian constitution as a component of God's image. I assert that this conception enables us to comprehend the dynamics and consequences (e.g., communication and worship) of the educational process we are investigating.

Scholars vary in their opinions and debate as to whether the immaterial component of humanity should be called the soul, mind, or heart. Regardless of the designation, this inner element of humankind consists of a triad of functions commonly known as cognition, emotion, and volition (see Chapter 6 for further explication and application).

Utilizing the term *soul*, which is my preference, John Drakeford makes the following observation in an older seminal work, *Psychology: In Search of a Soul*:

> *Words are like children. They grow and in the process change, until at last in full development it is sometimes difficult to find any resemblance to their earlier meanings. Psychology is a good example. It is derived from two Greek words: psyche, meaning "soul," and logos, meaning "word." Thus, it literally means "the study of the soul," In their observations of personality the Greeks were concerned about the soul, often seen as the breath of life. Observers had noted that at death breathing stopped, and all communication with the individual was cut off. When the last breath was drawn it was felt that the essential element of man had fled from his body. Therefore, the study of the soul was the major task of these prescientific students of personality.*
>
> *Passing time brought a change in the concept. Psychology had been a part of the over-all discipline of philosophy, but the two branches of study gradually diverged into separate pathways with psychology borrowing more of its methods and techniques from the developing scientific fields. Experimental methods, statistical procedures, and laboratory techniques became increasingly important. Previously, sharply-drawn distinctions between body and soul were abandoned, and it was no longer thought necessary to give attention to the soul. The word "soul" lost its place in the psychologist's vocabulary, as he left to the theologian the task of clarifying the troublesome word (Drakeford 1964).*

Drakeford bemoaned the loss of psychology's interest in the soul. Educational psychology's recently renewed attention to the cognitive and affective domains has resurrected this interest, even if partially and inadvertently. The result is that educational psychology has returned to its roots and restored the perception that the activity of the soul is worthy of attention and study. Identifying the three components or functions of the soul and their involvement in the teaching-learning process should not be problematic for the Christian educator. In fact, they should be a focus of our scholarly and pragmatic attention.

The Discipler's Model

A review of William R. Yount's Discipler's Model would be beneficial at this point of our study. The model is "a seven-fold approach to Christian teaching... that provides a useful framework for the study of educational psychology," and can be found in his work *Created to Learn* (Yount 1996). It is one man's attempt to form a truly emergent synthesis for Christian education today.

Components of the Model

Two stones provide the foundation upon which "The Discipler's Model" is established. The first is *Biblical Content* and refers, as would be suspected, to the Christian educator's firm reliance upon the Word of God as his primary source of knowledge, understanding, and wisdom. The second foundation is *Student Needs*. Decades ago, C. B. Eavey was fond of saying that the starting point of learning is student need (Eavey 1940), and most contemporary Christian educators would agree.

Upon this foundation stand three pillars, which represent *Thinking, Feeling, and Doing*. The "Christian Teacher's Triad" is built upon these pillars and forms the primary vehicle through which an emergent synthesis is developed. Yount postulates that a teacher's responsibility is to "help learners think," and by knowing and understanding cognitive learning theories a teacher will be much better prepared to do so. A teacher is also responsible to "help learners respond and value," and applying some of the humanist or constructivist attitudes and approaches may assist a mentor in this process. Finally, a teacher is to "help learners do," and the behavioral understandings of learning theory can be of tremendous assistance in this endeavor.

The capstone of the model is *Maturation* and growth in Christ – evidenced in a changed life and the ability to apply biblical principles. The ministry of the *Holy Spirit* circles and encompasses the entire model and reminds us of the spiritual dimensions of our task as well as the role the Godhead plays in our efforts.

Critique of the Model

The value and applicability of Yount's work is unmistakable. It now provides the focus and the structural framework for the second edition of the text, *The Teaching Ministry of the Church* (Yount 2008). It has universal appeal, and I have employed it in a number of courses on the ministry of teaching.

In addition to providing a primer in educational psychology, Yount's work makes two significant contributions pertinent to our study. The first consists of his integration of the three psychological functions, and connecting them to the Christian educator's goals of knowing, loving, and obeying God in service. By helping the student learn how to think, respond, value, and do, Yount solidly anchors his educational psychology in the soul. Second, he, like Slavin and Woolfolk, introduces and addresses human development as separate from, yet essential to, the teaching-learning process. Both of these contributions provide support and affirmation for contentions that will be made in Chapters 5 and 6.

I find, however, two critical omissions that limit the effectiveness of his work. Missing in his model is any reference to the work or activity of the physical body and its senses. Christian education cannot take place without the senses or the function of the brain. Yount's model gives no hint as to the vehicle(s) used to supply the data for the thinking, feeling, and doing pillars to utilize as fuel to fire up the changes needed to take place in a learner's life. Later in the text, he does address the behaviorist approach to learning, which is a physiologically rather than psychologically based theory, but the model itself does not incorporate it.

The second omission is any reference to non-biblical sources for the message(s) to be transmitted. This may be an adequate model for those who focus exclusively on biblical studies, but the omission is noteworthy for all other forms of Christian education. For example, a Christian liberal arts curriculum for a school or college, materials for home or outdoor educators, or even a church-sponsored literacy program would all take advantage of non-biblical curricular supplies. Granted, the Christian educator depends upon revelatory bases, but it is necessary to acknowledge that there are manifold vehicles of his revelation; the Lord speaks through creation, our constitution, his work in human affairs, and to our hearts. These are all valid sources for an educator's message, and they need to be seriously explored and considered in a congruent and consistent manner. Although these two weaknesses, coupled with a lack of a structured procedural sequence, have motivated me to look elsewhere for a comprehensive metamodel, Yount has performed an admirable service for the Christian education community. His attempt to create an emergent synthesis enables the Christian educator to give attention to and integrate the three dominant schools or categories of learning theories in a comprehensive model. When that attention is isolated and exclusively focused upon the individual components of the soul, the result is three independent and disjointed schools of thought: cognition, humanism or constructivism, and behaviorism. When coalesced into an integrated and inspired emergent synthesis, the result is an effective and psychologically sound theory of learning.

In summary review, educational psychology, in search of a soul, is a central component of a biblically-based, creation-oriented approach to the teaching-learning process that integrates and coordinates the functions and activities of all three of the inner states of a human being: thinking, feeling, and deciding. As we progress through the rest of this book (especially in Chapters 6 and 8), it will be apparent that the principles and practices resulting from such a perception impact the goals set, the processes utilized, the anticipated products produced, and how the people served are viewed.

These theories and functions, however, do not operate in isolation or independence. In fact, they are dependent upon the outcomes of human development. Therefore, the remainder of this chapter will be devoted to an examination of the thesis that the developed and trained capacity of the learner is a necessary prerequisite to learning.

Human Development

In recent educational psychology texts, such as those by Robert Slavin (2006), John Santrock (2000), and Anita Woolfolk (2006), the development of a student in physical, cognitive, and socio-emotional domains is addressed separately from learning theories. In a similar manner, this chapter will address, independently from the teaching-learning process, the activities of training and discipline that foster human development. This approach suggests that a foundational and necessary preparation for learning occurs in the formation and development of a student's essential capacities or powers.

Although significant research has addressed other aspects of human development, including the physical, mental, emotional, and social, Ted Ward (1995) reminds Christian educators that they must also be concerned with spiritual development. Spiritual formation, faith development, and spiritual direction are certainly critical components of a truly Christian education. Prominent Christian authors such as Richard Foster and Dallas Willard have brought the idea and concepts of spiritual formation to the forefront of Christian reflection and response, by way of the spiritual disciplines. In doing so, they offer an exemplary model for the implementation of the thesis that preparation is an essential component of education. Willard summarizes their proposition: the mature spiritual life, as in physical athletic competition, is not formed in the heat of the battle but in the daily exercise of the disciplines that equip an individual for such encounters (Willard 1988). As athletes and artists prepare before they perform, so also do Christians undergo discipline to become disciples. Likewise, students undergo developmental preparation and training in order to receive teaching. Thus, human development theories join teaching-learning and educational psychology as theoretical foundations of education. We will now focus our attention upon some of the practical pillars.

Practical Foundations for Teaching and Learning

John Milton Gregory clearly points out that in implementing the seven laws of teaching, "order is a condition precedent to good teaching."

> *These rules, and the laws which they outline and pre-suppose, underlie and govern all successful teaching... No one who will thoroughly master and use them need fail as a teacher, provided he will also maintain the good order which is necessary to give them free and undisturbed action. Disorder, noise, and confusion may hinder and prevent the results desired, just as the constant disturbance of some chemical elements forbids the formation of the compounds which the laws of chemistry would otherwise produce. Good order is a condition precedent to good teaching (Gregory 2003).*

Observations made during a year of substitute teaching for a local school district by my wife, Sharyn, confirmed Gregory's assertion, "Good order is a condition precedent to good teaching." One of her most telling assessments was that, "These kids need to learn how to listen; they lack the basic skills of paying attention and establishing any order or organization." She noticed that the highest achieving classes still sit in rows and exercise personal discipline in the control and utilization of their senses.

Simultaneous with her work in the public schools, Sharyn also taught an English course to junior high, home-educated students. While a small handful of these students were able to write with proficiency, she found the majority of students came into junior high unprepared to write effectively. Sorrowfully, I have found the same to be true of high school and university students as well. In our present system, students often pass from grade to grade without attaining the requisite skills for the next level. So, the teacher is confronted with an unsatisfactory dilemma: either stop, retrace their steps, and retrain the students, with the possibility of discouraging the already proficient ones, or force unequipped students onward into material and skills for which they are not yet prepared.

Among the countless stories, anecdotes, and reflections emerging from these venues, we recognized a common thread running through every class, grade, and subject. The law of apperception, which states that all learning is based upon previously acquired knowledge or skill, is essentially universal, unaffected by demographics or socio-economic status. When joined with the classroom order suggested by Gregory, previous experience provides the foundation necessary for learning to occur.

Anecdotal evidence, spiritual formation theory, and developmental research thus emerge as a triad of testimonies to affirm a simple axiom: the prerequisite for any learning experience is this foundational and preparatory development – whether physical, intellectual, emotional, or even spiritual – which produces "readiness" in the learner.

Educative Discipline: a Prerequisite

An alternate label for certain aspects of this development, and the acquisition of the preparation necessary for teaching to produce learning, is *training*. Training is often facilitated by a number of sources, including parents, teachers, tutors, or coaches who *discipline* with the goal of a student acquiring the self-discipline necessary for lifelong learning and the ability to select worthy personal goals. In other words, as we noticed in the Hebrews 5:14 text quoted in the Preamble, having been developed, trained, and disciplined, the student is expected to come to the teaching-learning experience with the background necessary to achieve and attain all the knowledge, attitude, or aptitude that is available to him. To state it succinctly, discipline is a prerequisite to learning.

To be obedient, ordered, organized, structured, and self-controlled are common expectations for a disciplined person. In this perception of discipline, a parent, teacher, tutor or mentor reprimands, corrects, and redirects the pupil. Perceived primarily as correction for misbehavior or as an attempt to establish an ordered regimen, discipline is a response to an out of alignment lifestyle or behavior. Consequently, it is reactive rather than proactive, corrective rather than educative, and far too often punitive in its pursuit of the elusive expectations.

Based upon biblical and etymological considerations, I would like to add a proactive dimension to the conception of discipline. In fact, I believe it is more appropriate to primarily perceive discipline as an educative modality rather than a corrective modality. After all, studying a subject is referred to as mastering a discipline, and the student is referred to biblically as a disciple, (from the Latin *disciplus*, a learner), and both of these practices are perceived in a positive manner. I prefer, therefore, to think of the prerequisite preparation stage of discipline in that light. A disciple-follower, who has been prepared in the process of discipline, is a ready learner.

Discipline: What Is It?

Nine positions, nine innings, one player. Major League Baseball player Bert Campaneris of the then Kansas City Athletics was the first player in the modern era to accomplish the feat of playing every position in a single game. In doing so, Campaneris redefined the term *utility player*. Utility players are valuable ingredients in the composition of a team's roster. Their versatility allows coaches to use and insert them in places and situations where many other single dimension players would not be able to perform. The education team has such a utility member on its roster, and it goes by the designation *discipline*. Able to function in both the proactive mode that includes training and teaching and in the reactive mode that includes correction and restoration, discipline plays many positions and adjusts to many different situations and scenarios.

One of the most frequently quoted and foundational texts for our study of discipline is found in Hebrews 12:5, 6, referencing and translating Proverbs 3:11, 12. The term for *discipline* utilized by the author indicates a person being child-trained (*paideia*, the root for the English "pedagogy"). The NeXt Bible's definition of *paideia* acknowledges its utilitarian nature, and assists us in our comprehension of the term; it includes:

1) The whole training and education of children (which relates to the cultivation of mind and morals, and employs for this purpose now commands and admonitions, now reproof and punishment) It also includes the training and care of the body

2) Whatever in adults also cultivates the **soul,** *esp. by* **correcting** *mistakes and curbing passions*

2a) **Instruction** *which aims at increasing virtue*

2b) Tutorage, i.e. education or training; by implication, disciplinary correction; chastening, chastisement, instruction, nurture

In light of our present investigations, it is instructive to observe that this definition incorporates some of the critical terms that we have observed so far: soul, correction, instruction, and training. Apparently, usage determines its specific definition, so it would be helpful to explore two other verses from Hebrews 12 that indicate possible application.

In verse 11, the author states, "No discipline (*paideia*) seems pleasant at the time, but painful. Later on, however, it produces a harvest of righteousness and peace for those who have been trained (*gumnazo*) by it." *Gumnazo* refers to a vigorous training and exercise of either the body or the mind, but its first and primary usage was apparently to prepare athletes for participating in the games, just as Campaneris had to prepare himself in order to succeed in baseball. Earlier in Hebrews 5:14, the author observes, "Solid food is for the mature, who by constant use (*hexis*) have trained (*gumnazo*) themselves to distinguish good from evil." As noted previously, the term *hexis*, translated here "constant use," indicates a routine or a "power acquired by custom, practice, use, or habit."

In other words, discipline is the process of preparing and equipping a disciple-follower for the learning to come through the acquisition of the necessary prerequisite competencies ("powers") facilitated by obedience, order, organization, and control. It is apparent, especially in the context we are addressing, that an appropriate synonym for a function of discipline would be *training*. This brings us full circle and back to the previous conclusion: we must train students so that they are equipped with the necessary competencies to proceed with a new lesson to be learned.

What It Is Not

Whether perceived and implemented in its educative mode as a proactive strategy for preparation or in its corrective mode as a reactive response, there are a number of common misperceptions concerning discipline that we must dispel. We will address three of them.

The first is that discipline is by nature manipulative and coercive, shaping an individual into the image of an artificial caricature. To the contrary, its purpose is to provide opportunities for individuals to become everything for which they were created. The second common misperception is that discipline is simply rectifying misbehavior in children. It should be obvious from our brief introduction that correction is but one component of the process. The third misconception is closely related: the terms *discipline* and *punishment* are often used interchangeably. In reality, they are antithetical; while discipline is primarily educative and corrective, punishment is primarily a retribution for an actual or perceived wrong. Since discipline has a corrective mode, the role and place of punishment needs to be addressed.

On Punishment

The Apostle Paul, in 1Corinthians 11:32, informs the church that the *padeia* (child training) discipline of the Lord is actually intended to avoid punishment:

> *When we are judged by the Lord, we are being disciplined*
> *so that we will not be condemned with the world.*

Our responsibility is not to punish people for their sins; God does that, and he provided the sacrifice of his son as a foundation for forgiveness. Whether or not an individual chooses to accept that forgiveness is between that person and God. It is our privilege to disciple them into wholeness, perfection, and restoration to uprightness, as we will observe in Chapter 8. To help distinguish between discipline and punishment, I have generated a table that illustrates the distinctions between the two.

Table 9. Discipline vs. Punishment

	Discipline	**Punishment**
Scriptures	*Proverbs 3:11,12* *Hebrews 12:5-10* *Revelation 3:19* *Jeremiah 10:24*	*Isaiah 13:9-11* *Matthew 25:46* *II Thessalonians 1:7-9* *Jeremiah 10:25*
Purpose	To promote holiness and assist in struggle against sin Prune a tree to bear fruit Train for correction	To judge and inflict penalty for offense Cut down tree for no fruit Penalize for sin
Focus	Future - correct behavior *correction*	Past - misdeeds *penalty*
Attitude of Parent	*Love- Delight, Concern*	*Hostility- Anger, Frustration*
Resulting Emotion of Child	Security- Consistency	Fear and Guilt- Inconsistency
Resulting Behavior of Child	*Long-term conformity*	*Short-term conformity*

The Purposes of Discipline

Discipline may not be punitive, but it is corrective and restorative in its reactive mode. Even though God provided forgiveness for sins through the cross, the Hebrews 12 passage indicates he assists his children in their struggle against sin. In doing so, he has three distinct aims in mind: to share in his holiness, to produce a harvest of righteousness, and peace (vv. 10, 11). In its proactive mode, discipline nurtures and develops, preparing and training the student. In either mode, the process is basically the same; therefore, the essential concern is answering the question, "How can a teacher (or parent, et al) facilitate this training? What is the process of discipline?"

Discipline: How to Do It

There are, of course, many strategies and models for the discipline process available to teachers, leaders, and parents. The problem is that most of them focus upon a specific venue or age group and the availability of certain resources or skills, thus limiting their range of effectiveness. They also have a tendency to focus upon one of the dimensions or modes, reactive or proactive, again restricting their effectiveness. What we need is a model that works for everyone, everywhere, and facilitates both preparation and correction. The contemporary Christian educator requires an approach that is simple, sound, and seasoned.

We turn, therefore, to the wisdom of God's Word to guide and inspire us in the task of making disciple-followers and exercising discipline as we prepare our students for a lifetime of living and learning. Although the terms and concepts behind the idea of discipline are scattered throughout the Bible, our attention is drawn to two sections: Solomon's Proverbs and Hebrews 12 (Table 10).

Table 10. Biblical Terms for Discipline

Old Testament Terms from Proverbs (Hebrew)	New Testament Terms from Hebrews (Greek)
Yakahh: *to reason, instruct, reprove, convince* *(a primarily verbal function)*	**Paideia:** *the training of a child ("pedagogy")*
Yawsar: *to chastise, with a blow or with words*	**Elegcho:** *to rebuke (speak strongly); convince (verbal)*
Mosayraw *corporal, bodily pain (a purely physical act)* *A Hebrew noun for a "desert"*	**Mastigoo:** *a scourge, physical beating, plagues, ulcers* *(a purely physical act)*

Whether in the heavenly Father's care for his loved children, the natural father's interaction with his sons, or a boss's communication with employees, we find a number of interesting implications:

1) Discipline involves giving direction and providing instruction, often verbal, sometimes harsh and corrective;

2) Discipline involves inspiration, aggressively and somewhat simultaneously encouraging and convicting;

3) Discipline involves intervention, both verbally and physically, intending to correct and restore.

These three components – instruction, inspiration, and intervention – remind me of Paul's declaration that "you know that we dealt with each of you as a father deals with his own children, *encouraging, comforting* and *urging* you to live lives worthy of God, who calls you into his kingdom and glory" (1Thessalonians 2:11, 12). They also remind me of the three functions of direction exercised by the leaders we studied in Part I: inspiring, informing, and instructing. Once again, we observe the interconnected relationships of teaching, leading, and parenting; we are making disciple-followers in each role. A self-disciplined parent or teacher applies these components and characteristics in a context of love, consistency, and relationship, and implements them with correction in mind, not punishment.

While the Proverbs and Hebrews texts provide hints and clues, three other sections of Scripture in the Gospel of John and the Epistle to the Romans illuminate the sequence of steps utilized by God himself, providing us with a biblical metamodel, displayed in Table 11.

Table 11. God's Model for "Discipline"

Passage / Process	John 17:6-8, 20	Romans 1:16-24, 26, 28		Romans 2:18-20
A First Step	Words are given	The Gospel is Proclaimed		A Standard is set: his Will
The Second Step	They received them	Belief	Rejection (suppressing the truth)	Instruction is given: the Law
The Third Step	They kept the Word: now they know, believe, and share	Salvation	Wrath of God	The Results were an Approval or Correction

Carefully examine the strategy presented before moving on to the next section. Notice, in the Romans 1 passage, that the reactive and proactive modes are both evidenced in the response to the proclamation of the Gospel, affirming that the model is appropriate for training in both dimensions.

The Discipline Model

We will begin our exploration of the process of discipline that trains and prepares students for learning by detailing the procedure and conclude by illustrating ways in which the discipline model can be employed in specific teaching-learning experiences at home, church, and school. To translate the biblical terms and the behaviors they anticipate into a model procedure, I assert good discipline involves the application of three simple, although not always easy, steps. The child training referred to in Hebrews 12 occurs in three generally sequential phases:

1. Providing thorough instruction,
2. Requiring intentional response, and
3. Ensuring appropriate consequences.

Step 1: Thorough instruction is conveyed.

Good teaching is the foundation for every educational or leadership activity, so it should come as no surprise that communication is the hinge upon which effective discipline swings.

We are all familiar with the question "How many times do I have to tell you?" This frequently uttered frustration is evidence that communication consists of more than sending a message; it is ensuring the message is received and understood. We must pay attention to our message (the words we say) and the methods we use (how we say them) to make sure we are communicating effectively. The point here, of course, is we cannot expect pupils to do something or be prepared to learn something new, if we do not first provide them with the necessary information in a comprehensive and effective manner.

I introduced and briefly explored the process of communication in Chapter 2. We will investigate the processes of teaching and learning in detail in Chapters 6 and 10. We can summarize those sections, however, quite simply. I would suggest a review of my model for the communication process (Display 2) and Myron Rush's six-step strategy for communication that puts into words the concepts presented in my graphic approach (Rush 1983). Rush's six steps include:

1. *Develop a clear concept of the idea or feeling to be communicated*
2. *Choose the right words and actions to convey the idea or feeling*
3. *Become aware of the surrounding communication barriers and work at minimizing them*
4. *The receiver must absorb the transmitted information by listening to the words and observing the actions*

5. *The receiver must translate the words and actions*
6. *The receiver must develop correct ideas and feelings*

Although more detail on the subject of instruction is necessary and will be presented as Part II progresses, we can conclude with this summary statement: the first step in effective discipline is thorough instruction with meaningful communication.

Step 2: An opportunity to respond is provided.

Once our pupils have received and understood our instruction, we must give them the opportunity to choose to respond. This is a challenge for educators who expect and demand unquestioning obedience from a student. Personally, I would prefer my students to stop, consider, reflect, and then own their decision. As we saw in the leadership section, authority promotes responsibility, which in turn generates commitment. We need to allow our charges the time to genuinely consider our instruction and its impact for their lives.

If the teacher understands the three primary influences upon choice in a person's life, this step in the process is enhanced. By acknowledging and supporting these influences, we can provide guidance for our students' decision-making processes:

- **Perception of Reality** *i.e., that which one perceives to be true. Our behavior is determined by our perception of reality, which is formed primarily in experiences.*
- **Value System** *i.e., that which one holds in highest esteem. Our choices are determined by what is of value and importance to us, which is formed primarily in relationships.*
- **The Will** *i.e., the element of the soul that brings together reality (intellect), values (emotions), and all sensory input to sort out and make a choice.*

When parents, teachers, pastors, and even friends intend to minister to an individual who is about to make critical life choices, they must become aware of and affect the perceived worldview to which the person adheres. It is critical to recognize that a person's *perception* of reality and the corresponding values is the determining factor in the process of choosing and deciding. A belief that something is true will directly influence one's choices, even if it is not really true. For example, if teenagers are convinced that an immoral or unlawful behavior is acceptable because everyone is doing it, then that will direct their course of action. A person's perception of life and a preference for how it is to be lived, not the objective truth of a matter, influences choice.

In the teaching-learning setting, the choices a pupil makes concerning the practice and application of the lessons learned directly impact readiness and the ability to move forward with new learning. Before proceeding to the next step of the process, I would like to enhance this discussion by calling attention to five conditions that influence the learners' choices as they make decisions (Display 6). In parentheses under each condition listed, I have included a possible reason for a person's poor or inappropriate choice. These suggestions may assist in determining the rationale behind the choices and illuminate the issues that a teacher must address in disciple-making efforts.

Display 6. Conditions that Influence Choice
(if poor choice, look for...)

- **Heredity** -what you have been "given"
  (sin nature: an individual is neither a blank slate nor an inherently good person)
- **Maturity** -what you have done with it
  (immaturity: a capacity to perform/respond is simply not present)
- **Ability** -what you can do
  (mistake: an attempt, albeit a poor one, was made)
- **Information** -what you know
  (incomplete instruction or "failure": the individual did not really know what, or how, to do)
- **Environment** -where you are
  (inadequate context: an individual has not been exposed to a positive milieu)

These conditions provide the context in which the decision-making process unfolds and thus have profound impact upon the choices a learner makes. It is incumbent upon the educator to give guidance and direction to the experiences our students encounter, the people with whom they associate, and the thoughts and feelings they experience in our care. These influences inform and shape our disciples. Therefore, the curricular plan or program of a school, church, or any educational agency must be perceived in the broadest possible terms, because every experience or exposure a student encounters is truly educative.

In addition to considering these conditions, it is also beneficial to review the seven forces that motivate presented in Chapter 3. Motive wields a powerful influence upon choice. The leader-teacher, in the same manner as the learner, holds certain values and ascribes to certain perceptions of people. These influence and affect not only the teacher's selection of curriculum, but also the treatment, communication, discipline, and leadership of the class or group.

Step 3: A consequence is received.

The third step of our discipline model occurs after a student makes a choice and reaches a decision. Based on the results of those actions, the teacher ensures that the student receives the appropriate consequence.

The philosophy behind this step also has a scientific basis: every action has a reaction, and every decision a person makes has a real-life, real-time consequence to it. The Holy Scriptures are also abundantly clear on this point: a man will "eat the fruit of [his] ways" (Proverbs 1:31) and he "reaps what he sows" (Galatians 6:7). Therefore, "God will give to each person according to what he has done" (Romans 2:6). The consequences for our choices, behaviors, and thoughts are consistent: "There will be trouble and distress for every human being who does evil… but glory, honor and peace for everyone who does good… For God does not show favoritism" (Romans 2:9, 10). Granted, this passage has ultimate ends in mind, but the principle is valid for the present as well (see 1Timothy 4:8).

Categories of Consequences

Both Paul and Peter, in Romans 13:3, 4 and 1Peter 2:14, refer to the role of human authorities in administering two categories of consequences:

> *Everyone must submit himself to the governing authorities, for there is no authority except that which God has established. Consequently… rulers hold no terror for those who do right, but for those who do wrong. Do you want to be free from fear of the one in authority? Then **do what is right and he will commend you**. For he is God's servant to do you good. But **if you do wrong, be afraid**, for he does not bear the sword for nothing. He is God's servant, an agent of wrath to bring punishment on the wrongdoer (Romans 13:1-4).*

> *Submit yourselves for the Lord's sake to every authority instituted among men: whether to the king, as the supreme authority, or to governors, who are sent by him to **punish those who do wrong and to commend those who do right** (1Peter 2:13, 14).*

"Governing authorities," whether rulers, teachers, employers, or parents, are commissioned by God to ensure that the appropriate result of the choices and behaviors of their disciple-followers is administrated and implemented. These passages indicate that their actions fall within and execute the intentions and goals of two classes of consequence: *commendation* for those who do right and *correction* for those who do wrong. As the example of the Heavenly Father reveals, they must be administered appropriately and consistently:

> God *"will give to each person according to what he has done." To those who by persistence in doing good seek glory, honor and immortality, he will give eternal life. But for those who are self-seeking and who reject the truth and follow evil, there will be wrath and anger. There will be trouble and distress for every human being who does evil: first for the Jew, then for the Gentile; but glory, honor and peace for everyone who does good: first for the Jew, then for the Gentile. For God does not show favoritism (Romans 2:6-11).*

If a person follows evil, suffering is the result; if a person does well, honor is bestowed. There is no favoritism on his part; his most loved children will suffer if they do wrong. As teachers and leaders, we cannot afford to be inconsistent or play favorites. Consistency, however, does not demand equality, although it does require fair treatment. For example, consider Jesus' story about the laborers who debated fair and equal treatment in pay (Matthew 20). Fairness to a student takes into consideration the conditions, the motive behind the behavior, and the circumstances. When my daughter was seven, she complained that I was not treating her the same way as her older brother and stated, "This is not fair." I told her, "I will treat you that way when you are a fourteen year-old boy." Although overstated and facetious, she was not her brother, and it was not fair to treat her as such. She certainly was not asking for his chores, his expectations, or his discipline; she only wanted the benefits.

With these introductory texts and thoughts in mind, let us consider the two categories of consequences.

Commendation

It is a cardinal tenet of behaviorism, but it has its roots in Romans 13: human beings are more likely to repeat a behavior if they are reinforced by reward, compensation, or commendation. In Chapter 3, we even identified reinforcement as one of the seven primary motivating forces. When a disciple-follower makes a good decision, responding well to instruction and direction, it is our responsibility to commend the behavior and bless the individual. We all have stories to tell about how simple words of thanks, congratulations, or encouragement have spurred us on to love and good deeds (Hebrews 10:24).

The passages we have examined place equal emphasis upon responding to good, right behaviors and choices as well as poor ones. Far too often, however, teachers ignore the ones who are doing well and deserving of praise because their focus is upon correcting bad behavior. Commendation may not come easy for some. It is, however, a generally positive and pleasurable experience that does not demand much thought or planning. On the other hand, most people perceive correction as a negative, distasteful activity and a rather demanding process. Therefore, when correction is necessary to discipline poor choices and improper behavior, I recommend the following strategy.

Corrective Discipline

The strategy I utilize consists of five components. These are not necessarily steps to be followed in a sequential fashion; they are tools to be used in a manner reminiscent of artists creatively utilizing the brushes and techniques at their disposal. When conducting corrective discipline, I engage five reactive procedures:

1. Confrontation

Ecclesiastes 8:11 warns, "When the sentence for a crime is not quickly carried out, the hearts of the people are filled with schemes to do wrong." When a person responds improperly, we must immediately confront it and address the issue. Ignoring the behavior may extinguish it in accordance with behaviorist principles, but the root problem will still exist.

Confrontation must take place. Failure to do so may lead others in the group to assume that the teacher or leader either does not really care about the behavior or that it is not important enough to address. Paul writes about this very issue in Romans 2:4-6; God's kindness, tolerance, and patience is designed to lead to repentance not to the perception that he does not care or that the behavior is acceptable. I have even stated to a habitually disruptive student, "You have left 2:4 and are now entering 2:6," meaning that my kindness, tolerance, and patience have come to an end and you will now receive the consequence of your attitude or action.

2. Counsel

In another of Paul's letters, the apostle states his intention to deal "with each of you as a father deals with his own children, *encouraging, comforting* and *urging* you to live lives worthy of God, who calls you into his kingdom and glory" (1Thessalonians 2:11, 12). In this component of the corrective discipline process, I engage in four behaviors as I counsel, encourage, comfort, and urge my disciples:

1. **REASON** (*yawkahh*)
   Discuss & Discover - your response depends on why the individual did it
2. **REBUKE** (*yawsar*) + (*elegcho*)
   Many people respond right here, and the discipline process is concluded
3. **REINSTRUCT**
   It may have been a mistake or poor instruction that can be rectified
4. **REFER TO THE LORD**
   It was against Him the sin occurred; don't take it personally (usually)
   Take the entire matter to him- Pray

Consistent with Paul's practice, I have found that after confronting a wayward disciple, I frequently do not need to go beyond the first two steps of corrective activity. If the confrontation and follow up counsel have produced the desired response, and there is genuine repentance with a change of heart and behavior, I thank the Lord, bless the student, and move on. If repentance and change are not evident, then I must determine whether additional corrective intervention is necessary. It is at this point that the implementation of consequences is appropriate.

3. Consequence

In the administration of consequences, the disciplinarian may utilize two types of commendation and correction: *natural* and *logical*. Although addressed in this discussion of corrective discipline, it is important to realize that these consequences are equally valid as commendations, so I will supply illustrations for both types.

Natural Consequences

Natural consequences are the direct results of a choice and its corresponding behavior. They are the manifestations of the decision to "let nature take her course." For example, we diet and lose weight, ignore our friends and they quit calling, or go out unprepared into cold weather and end up sick. When a student takes the time and makes the necessary effort to study hard, a good grade is a natural consequence. The natural consequence when a person jumps off a roof may be a broken leg, but this same person could also enjoy the consequence of no pain or injury when choosing to use a ladder to get down.

In other words, life usually provides its own consequences, appropriate and consistent with the choice or behavioral response. It is usually not very difficult for a leader, teacher, or parent to find a consequence that is a natural result of an individual's decision, choice, or behavior. Sometimes the best discipline is to let nature take its course. One of the jobs of a teacher, leader, or parent is to determine when to let the process unfold and not interfere.

Logical Consequences

There are circumstances and situations, however, when the natural is not forthcoming or obvious. In those cases, we resort to "logical" consequences. As a school principal, I frequently dealt with situations that required the corrective and reactive dimension of discipline. For example, there were students who had vandalized property, gossiped about another student, or cheated on a test. I found myself challenged to identify how to "naturally" discipline in a corrective mode, so I opted for consequences that appeared to be "logical." For instance, when students defaced property, they cleaned it up; when they vandalized, they paid for the repair; when they disrupted class and took a teacher's time, they "replaced" it with a required detention. Many times, I engaged both the victims and perpetrators in discussion about appropriate consequences, soliciting their perceptions and suggestions, so that they would own the decision. I have invested many hours considering the appropriate logical consequence for a behavior, because a student's discipline should do more than just bring retribution. I want the discipline and discipleship to be both meaningful and productive in the student's life. Therefore, I apply a consequence that is as closely aligned to the behavior as possible, avoiding an "illogical" consequence that it not related to the "offense." The goal is correction, not simply punishment.

The following illustration, also in the school context, demonstrates discipline from the educative and proactive mode. One of the most powerful proactive discipline experiences is participation in student government, where students are not only engaged in leading their classmates, but they are also receiving preparation for future opportunities in their jobs, churches, and homes. In my efforts to disciple these students, I trained them to be leaders, creating a student government workshop designed for their level and utilizing their present experiences and activities. As we progressed through their terms of office, I made certain that they acknowledged and held themselves accountable for the decisions and choices that they made as leaders. Many times the consequences were obviously natural, but others required my exercising creativity and wisdom to discern an appropriate logical consequence that would prepare them for a similar experience in "real life." The process of discipline, whether proactive or reactive, educative or corrective, requires that a leader-teacher oversee the necessity for a student to receive an appropriate consequence, whether natural or logical, for the choices that they make.

In simple summary, the teacher has the responsibility to commend students who have done right and correct those who have not. The implementation of appropriate consequences avoids power struggles with students, teaches responsibility, and ultimately prepares the student for the next lesson as well as a lifetime of learning.

In order to facilitate these principles, in practice I adhere to three guidelines:

1. Make certain that the student realizes the connection between the choices made and the consequences received
2. Provide an opportunity for reinstruction and cooling off
3. Administer the consequences so there is discomfort, not harm - not to punish, but to teach that bad choices bring "pain" in life

Although the circumstances may differ, there are obvious implications and applications of this approach for church life, home life, and even the mundane of everyday life. Following these guidelines has allowed me to graciously, but insistently, discipline young ministers with much potential but little experience and wisdom. For example, Charlie was the most effective youth minister with whom I have ever had the privilege to serve.

He was the template we utilized in recruiting, and the rubric that set the standard and benchmark for assessing success. The only chink in his armor was an inability to say, "No." Despite the strength and resilience of youth, he eventually burned out and requested a leave of absence to recuperate. After three months, he pronounced himself revitalized and ready to resume his duties. Natural consequences had taken their toll, and they threatened to permanently sideline a valuable teammate, so I intervened by implementing a logical response: I restricted the number of venues in which he could participate. He resisted, of course, but I stood my ground: "We did it your way before; this time we do it mine." Taking on limited responsibilities, Charlie returned to effective ministry, exemplifying not only reactive discipline but also proactive preparation and training for a lifetime.

4. Coventry

There is, in reality, a fourth guideline for logical consequences. Its nature is so distinct, however, that I consider it a fourth component of corrective discipline. It is the concept of *coventry* – the separation or removal of an unrepentant or belligerent student.

The term comes from the city of Coventry in England. Royalist prisoners of war incarcerated there during the English Civil War (1642-51) were apparently the first to be "sent to Coventry." In the United Kingdom, according to the *Encarta World English Dictionary*, this means, "to refuse to speak to or associate with somebody as a punishment or mark of disapproval."

The concept also has biblical underpinnings. In passages such as Romans 16:17, Philippians 3:17, and 1Corinthians 5:13, we find the church "marking" the disobedient and separating them from the body or the family. In other words, the offender is isolated and separated from the group as a consequence for combative or radically unacceptable behavior.

The traditional "go to your room," "wait for me in the hall," and the tersely stated "you are not welcome here anymore," are comments parents and teachers often make to offending children and students. These type of statements reflect this principle: if an individual is not willing to abide by the guidelines established for the class, family, or business, the offender is not welcome to remain in the venue. Churches excommunicate, the armed services dishonorably discharge, schools expel students, and businesses terminate employment. Dismissal is a logical consequence for rebellious and "antisocial" behavior.

5. Conciliation

This separation, however, does not need to be permanent. Forgiveness and restoration reside at the foundation of all ministries, including discipline. Foreseen in the ministry of reconciliation between men is the ultimate goal of the reconciliation of God and man. Therefore, my primary goal is also my fifth component.

The Apostle Paul, in Romans 12:18, encourages us, "If it is possible, as far as it depends on you, live at peace with everyone." The implication within this statement is that some simply will not be willing to be at peace, so the application of consequences may need to be supplemented with intervention. I have had the privilege of knowing, during the course of my ministry, two lawyers who spend a significant amount of their time participating in the ministry of formal reconciliation. They choose to devote their skills this way because of their conviction that resolving matters in this fashion is more profitable for everyone involved than contentious disputations or even court proceedings. This is their way of fulfilling the biblical injunction to avoid court and affirm unity among the members of the household of God. They provide an exemplary illustration of the ministry of conciliation. Every minister would do well to become proficient in the skills necessary to restore personal relations as well as correct inappropriate behaviors back to their original and upright condition.

Some Sample Practices of Educative Discipline

Discipline, as it contributes to development and training, is exercised when an educator provides for *communication, choice,* and *consequence(s)*. As the Scriptures reveal, this is how God child trains his heavenly sons and daughters. Without implying comprehensiveness or exclusivity, the following simple examples show how we may implement each of the steps of an educative and proactive discipline model.

Train to teach and teach to train. This is a debate reminiscent of the chicken or the egg controversy. We are focusing on training and developing capacities, but it is helpful to realize that teaching often provides the new capacity for another lesson. Consider, first, the way in which a teacher trains and prepares a student to acquire a physical skill such as riding a bike, swimming, or skiing. The instructor fills the first stage with training and teaching by providing information, examples, and practical opportunities to increase balance, muscular coordination, and strength. In order to do so, the student must make the right choices to eat properly, exercise, sleep, and practice. The consequences of these choices become readily evident:

the student should have the strength, coordination, balance, and necessary foundation to learn the skill. If so, the teacher may engage the student in the instruction and application of the components necessary to acquire the competency to perform. If not, the learning of the skill must wait until the student is prepared for the task.

In preparing to learn an academic subject such as writing, reading, or math, the foundations of identifying letters and words, counting, and other necessary skills must be laid. The student must choose to take the time to be exposed to good books, counting games, and practical experience. As Robert Slavin (2006) puts it, "teachers need to ensure that students have mastered prerequisite skills and to link information that is already in their minds to the information you are about to present." The consequence, as with learning a skill, is readily evident: the student can read a book, solve a problem, or write a complete sentence. If not, the teacher utilizes this experience as another layer of the preparatory work necessary to learn the lesson at a later time.

Finally, let us take a brief look at preparing to learn spiritual lessons, as in Sunday school or church. The initial Bible teaching, illustrations, testimonies, and practical Christian living experiences are all founded upon the assumption that the disciple-followers can read, listen, understand discerningly, and generally receive instruction. Assuming these capacities, learners then have to choose to attend and present themselves to the opportunities offered. If the necessary competencies are in place, and the disciples have chosen to receive instruction, the expectation is that the learning will occur and lives will be changed.

From Theory to Model

Life is rife with teaching and learning opportunities. In fact, after a student has developed the essential capacities and skills through the process of discipline, the adventure of learning begins. Everyone has participated in lessons as a learner or a teacher, and exploring these personal experiences makes one wonder whether there is a universal framework for an understanding of the teaching-learning process. The thesis of the next chapter is that such a pattern does exist. Functioning as a blueprint or guide, it contains a prescribed sequence that is present in every teaching-learning endeavor. In developing this thesis, we will explore ancient biblical wisdom for contemporary Christian education and make the transition from learning theory to a teaching-learning model, shifting from *why* to *how*.

In Proverbs 2, in preparing his sons for their princely responsibilities, King Solomon presents a five stage metamodel for the teaching and learning process. In it, he anticipates the necessary human development, expects psychological involvement, and provides for the integration of the various learning theories. His foundations are solid. From our current perspective, it provides the biblical foundation upon which the believing educator can depend. Therefore, it is with some excitement and anticipation that we turn our attention to Solomon and his sons.

Reflection and Response

Discipline Response Worksheet

1. You have an approach to disciple making (discipline) that is uniquely your own. List, in "brainstorm" fashion, those insights you gained from this chapter that affect your style. (For example, *"I have to give better first instruction"* or *"I'm not allowing enough time for my students to make personal choices."*)

2. Based on your "insights" what specific things can you do to be a more effective disciplinarian/disciple-maker? (For example, *"After an instruction I will have at least two students repeat [feedback] the instruction in their own words"* or *"I will remember to commend as often as I correct."*)

3. Choose one of these changes to be implemented immediately and specify your plans.

4. Review each of the three steps for discipline/disciple making and brainstorm three specific "prescriptions" for each.

Step 1: Communication
(*"I will be sure to involve at least two senses every time I communicate [e.g., hearing AND seeing]."*)

Step 2: Choice

Step 3: Consequence

5. Using a role-play script, chart, outline, or other visual device, describe or illustrate a discipline situation in which your prescriptions are utilized in each step.

6. Consider these cases; how would you respond, given the principles provided in this chapter?

You are teaching a third-grade Sunday school class with fifteen students and your partner has stepped out of the room. In the middle of the Bible story portion of your lesson Jamie screams words at Sarah that sound like swearing while she is pulling on her hair. You instruct her to stop, but she does not...

Or

You are leading an adult home group with three married couples and five singles. In the prayer request time one of the singles becomes offended when she thinks one of the requests violates a confidence. She harshly rebukes one of the married men, whose wife reaches over and slaps her...

Reflecting on Developmental Tasks

Two of the more popular and enduring results of developmental theory have come from the work of Robert Havighurst – developmental tasks and teachable moments. Havighurst summarized both concepts in his brief discussion Developmental Tasks and Education *(1972). While each was groundbreaking in the field, they both add a dimension to the proposition presented in Chapter 5: disciplined development prepares a student for learning. As you read Havighurst's summary statements, reflect upon the impacts and consequences for Christian education.*

"As the individual grows, he finds himself possessed of new physical and psychological resources. The infant's legs grow larger and stronger, enabling him to walk. The child's nervous system grows more complex, enabling him to reason more subtly and to understand the complexities of subjects such as arithmetic. The individual also finds himself facing new demands and expectations from the society around him. The infant is expected to learn to talk, the child to learn to subtract and divide.

These inner and outer forces contrive to set for the individual a series of developmental tasks which must be mastered if he is to be a successful human being..."

"The Teachable Moment

Thus, some of the developmental tasks may be located at the ages of special sensitivity for learning them. When the body is ripe, and society requires, and the self is ready to achieve, a certain task, the teachable moment has come. Efforts at teaching, which would have been largely wasted if they had come earlier, give gratifying results when they come at the teachable moment, when the task should be learned. For example, the best times to teach reading, the care of children, and adjustment to retirement from one's job can be discovered by studying human development, and finding out when conditions are most favorable for learning these tasks."

1. What "tasks" are necessary "to be a successful human being" in the spiritual realm?

2. What "conditions are most favorable for learning these tasks"?

3. What development must occur for these conditions to become manifest?

4. What can you do to facilitate the discipline necessary to make this development possible?

Six
A Metamodel for Teaching and Learning

The young prince, lying quietly in bed, receives a kiss on his cheek and proceeds to ponder the words he has just heard from his father – words that have fueled his dreams and fostered a vision.

> *Lay hold of my words with all your heart; keep my commands and you will live. Get wisdom, get understanding; do not forget my words or swerve from them. Do not forsake wisdom, and she will protect you; love her, and she will watch over you. Wisdom is supreme; therefore get wisdom. Though it cost all you have, get understanding (Proverbs 4:4-7).*

Years pass, and after the death of his father the prince is anointed king. In a dream, on the night of his coronation, God offers him the opportunity to "ask for whatever you want me to give you."

His request was not a manifestation of a lust for wealth, success, or other forms of personal prosperity. On the contrary, yet not surprisingly, his request was a manifestation of the learning inspired by parental influence: "So give your servant a discerning heart to govern your people and to distinguish between right and wrong."

God's response was equally profound and impacting: "God gave Solomon wisdom and very great insight, and a breadth of understanding as measureless as the sand on the seashore" (1Kings 3:5,9; 4:29).

Again, years pass and the king has sons of his own. In what we now know as Chapter 2 of the biblical book of Proverbs, King Solomon weaves an expression of his God-given wisdom into a beautifully crafted lesson that reveals a sequence of activities designed to equip his sons with the knowledge, attitudes, and skills necessary for their princely and kingly roles to come. In reprising the pattern his own parents employed in teaching him, he prepares his offspring for a lifetime of leading and learning.

The Proverbs 2 Metamodel for Teaching and Learning

I contend that the strategy he employs contains transferrable ancient wisdom that informs contemporary education, and provides a template for the teaching and learning processes. In doing so, he transmits a message that still resonates with parents and children, teachers and students, and leaders and followers nearly 3000 years later:

> 1 My son, if you **Accept my words** and store up my commands within you,
>
> 2a **Turning your ear** to wisdom and
>
> 2b **Applying your heart** to understanding, 3 and if you call out for insight and cry aloud for understanding, 4 and if you look for it as for silver and search for it as for hidden treasure,
>
> 5 **Then you will understand** the fear of the LORD and find the knowledge of God. 6 For the LORD gives wisdom, and from his mouth come knowledge and understanding. 7 He holds victory in store for the upright, he is a shield to those whose walk is blameless, 8 for he guards the course of the just and protects the way of his faithful ones.
>
> 9 Then you will understand what is right and just and fair—every good path. 10 For wisdom will enter your heart, and knowledge will be pleasant to your soul. 11 Discretion will protect you, and understanding will guard you. 12 Wisdom will save …
>
> 20 **Thus you will walk** in the ways of good men and keep to the paths of the righteous.

Although it is certainly possible that the stages of the teaching-learning process may appear randomly or out of sequence in unique circumstances, the intentionality and word choice Solomon applies (if>then>thus) seems to infer specificity to the order in which they are implemented. Therefore, based upon the selection of terms and the sequence in which Solomon presents them, we can identify and extract a pattern for the steps or stages that encompass the instructional experience.

- First (v.1), the pupil must choose to participate in the learning and **"accept my words."** The tutor obtains the student's attention and motivates the individual to learn.
  Exploring interests, to hold attention.
- Second (v. 2a), the learner engages in **"turning your ear"** – the process of receiving the intended message. Utilizing a variety of methods and materials, the teacher stimulates the senses.
  Exciting senses, to penetrate the soul.

- Third (v. 2b), the student participates in critically reflective listening, thinking, emoting, and making choices by "**applying your heart.**" The instructor will not be satisfied with hearing, but will inspire the individual to study intently and master the content. *Expanding knowledge, to promote wisdom.*
- Fourth (vv. 5, 9), the scholar will "**then ... understand**" – raising the learning levels beyond knowledge to understanding and wisdom (vv. 5, 6, 9, 10, 12). Never content with lower levels of learning, the mentor utilizes probing questions and stimulating exercises and experiences to encourage growth. *Extending limits, to reach potential.*
- Fifth (v. 20), the educated follower experiences life change and "**walk[s] in the ways of good men.**" Learning has occurred when the disciple is a "doer of the word." *Exploring applications, to enrich lives.*

In implementing and following these stages, a change in what a learner knows, feels, or is able to perform occurs. *Learning* implies a person is different after the experience. By promoting and facilitating these stages, the teacher affects a change in the competence of the learner. *Teaching* thus implies that a student has learned something. Therefore, by extracting from Solomon's wisdom the nature and essence of learning, a preliminary, biblically based, and experientially verified definition is possible:

Learning is the process that produces change within a person. Incorporating both sensory and psychological components, this process produces alterations such as: the acquisition of new information, skills, and behaviors; adjusted or confirmed attitudes and values; and the resulting emotional and volitional responses. In short, learning produces change, a becoming something new.

Table 12, "The Proverbs 2 Metamodel for the Teaching-Learning Process," was created to connect the pattern in the Proverbs passage with the learning process, identify the responsibilities of both the teacher and the student, and provide a brief acknowledgement of the potential correlations between the model and educational psychology.

Table 12. The Proverbs 2 Metamodel for the Teaching-Learning Process

Scripture (Proverbs 2)	Stage (Steps of the Learning Process)	Definition	The Student is Accountable to...	The Teacher is Responsible for...	(Potential) Ed Psych Correlations
Hebrews 12 (cf. Proverbs 3)	*A Pre-Requisite:* DISCIPLINE	A Preparation for Learning	*Submit to Discipline*	Training	Development Theories
Proverbs 2:1 "Accept my words"	*Stage I:* DECISION	The Preliminary Aspect to Learning	*Attend with Interest*	Motivating	Motivation Theories Behaviorism
Proverbs 2:2a "Turn your ear"	*Stage II:* EXPOSURE	The Physical Aspect of Learning	*Receive the Message*	Communicating	Brain-Based Learning & Info Processing
Proverbs 2:2b-4 "Apply your heart"	*Stage III:* PROCESS	The Psychological Aspect of Learning	*Study the Material*	Inspiring	Cognitive & Humanistic Theories
Proverbs 2:5-19 "Then you will understand"	*Stage IV:* ACHIEVEMENT	The Psychometric Aspect of Learning	*Learn a Lesson*	Elevating	Constructivist Theories
Proverbs 2:20 "Thus you will walk..."	*Stage V:* APPLICATION	The Practical Aspect of Learning	*Experience a Change*	Activating	Behaviorist Theories

In this chapter, we will investigate each of the five stages of the teaching-learning process. In doing so, we will address the biblical and educational psychology foundation for each stage and explore the potential implications and applications. Chapter 7, then, includes illustrations of the practical implementation of this metamodel by the nation Israel and one of its scribes and teachers, Ezra. Further on, in Chapter 10, we will also explore the connections between this process and the creation of a lesson plan for teaching and learning that implements the stages through the appropriate use of methods and media.

The explication and comprehension of these stages emanates from an exploration of the Hebrew text. When accompanied by critically reflective thinking upon personal educational experiences, the basis for contemporary educational practice emerges. David Suiter, a Hebrew scholar, contributor to the *Anchor Bible Dictionary*, and reference librarian for Regis University in Denver, Colorado, investigated the Hebrew language utilized in this passage. I asked him to assess whether or not I could interpret and apply the text as directly as it appears. In response, he indicated in written correspondence that the Hebrew text is "straight forward" and can be taken as it is stated. He also noted, "There is no symbolism or poetic styling that needs to be taken into consideration." Solomon was "calling it as he saw it." He appears to have chosen specific words to communicate some unambiguous concepts and truths to his son and, by extension, to us (Suiter 2000).

Although built upon solid scholarship, the exposition presented in this chapter is primarily practical. The arguments, therefore, will be comparatively brief and selectively annotated. For further research on this passage, or education in the wisdom literature in general, I would suggest commencing with works such as Daniel Estes's *Hear My Son: Teaching and Learning in Proverbs 1-9* (1997) or Charles Melchert's *Wise Teaching: Biblical Wisdom and Educational Ministry* (1998) and other more academically inclined texts. Although I encountered Estes's book very late in my personal research, it confirmed virtually every one of my critical contentions. Melchert and Estes both outline their expositions in a manner consistent with the questions I address in Part III, and each of these authors affirm and attest the observations made there.

I acknowledge that some may challenge this study with the same question Estes poses, "Can one with validity elevate its content from description to prescription?" (Estes 1997). In other words, can I confidently assert that Solomon is doing more than conversing with his sons and that he is influencing educators for all time? Is it possible for this ancient wisdom to be translated into effective contemporary education? Aside from the fact that I would not have written this chapter without believing it to be so, I offer three justifications for implementing Solomon's wisdom today: theology demands it, Solomon's life asserts it, and praxis confirms it. As a pastor-teacher, I regularly and frequently stand before others with a conviction that God's Word is as valid today as when it was penned. I believe in the authoritative, inspired Scriptures. They declare that Solomon was the wisest man who ever lived; therefore, we can take him seriously. Finally, this pattern has been corroborated by personal and practical experience; when this prototype is implemented, people learn.

These convictions undergird the following exposition of Proverbs 2 as a metamodel for the teaching-learning process.

Stage I: "If you accept my words" (v. 1)

The nature of the word "accepting" is not meant in the sense that learners need to agree with every statement the teacher makes, but there needs to be an internalization of the material suggested. Kuhn and Dean (2004) use the term interiorization to describe this reception. In their description of the general natures of both Vygotsky and Piaget they submit

> that this action should be included as a part of the metacognitive
> development of students (Forrest 2008).

Solomon begins at the beginning. His word choice reflects an understanding that the learning process commences when a self-disciplined disciple-follower "seizes" the opportunity to learn and "lays hold" of the privilege in front of him. *The Theological Wordbook of the Old Testament* gives these very meanings to the Hebrew word translated "accept" in this verse (Harris 1980). The king recognized that a student is responsible for his own learning and must choose to learn before the process can truly get under way.

A number of scholars and researchers have come to the same conclusion. Robert Gagne has suggested in his "Events of Instruction" that the first step for a teacher is "gaining [the] attention" of the pupil (Gagne and Briggs 1974). This echoes Gregory's *Law of the Learner*, which states "the learner must attend with interest to the material to be learned" (Gregory 2003), and enriches Estes's observation, "The learner must begin with an attentive spirit" (Estes 1997). Ruth Beechick notes that her success in teaching handicapped children to read was predicated upon the fact her students "wanted to learn" (Beechick 1982). A local TV station for a series of programs on student achievement interviewed Ed Salazar, a Denver Public Schools teacher in 1990. In his concluding remarks Salazar stated, "If you want to learn, you will, if you don't, you won't." Expressed in another way, John Westerhoff notes, "There is no true learning if someone is not searching."

Viewing this from the instructor's perspective yields the recognition that the learner's mindset and motive is far more potent than the instructor's intention: "How often do we engage in teaching and preaching with the conviction that there is something that someone else needs to know? We go about our task faithfully, but we have unsatisfactory results. Few, if any, learn what someone else wants them to know, care about, or do" (Westerhoff 1994). All the theory, best practices, and school reform efforts cannot replace this simple acknowledgement.

Solomon himself affirmed this truth in Proverbs 17:16 (The Living Bible), "It is useless to provide tuition to educate a rebel who has no heart for the truth." This verse, in fact, played a prominent role in my counsel to the mother of a teenage girl who simply would not apply herself at school. The student enrolled at our Christian high school, but she seldom attended and never did any of her assignments. After the mother had tried and failed at every attempt to motivate her daughter, she came to me and stated, "I'm not paying another dime of tuition for this girl!" The woman was surprised as I quoted Solomon's words to her. After a brief conversation, we disenrolled her daughter, recognizing this young adult had to make her own decision to learn. We could not make it for her.

The following success story also illustrates this point. Terry, as I will call him, was a typical middle-school boy, but he was out of shape and not very athletic when he came out for our school basketball team. He loved the activity and being with his friends. He hated, however, the workouts I put him through, and at the end of each day, he would direct his frustration at me, stating, "I don't like this. I quit. I'm telling my mother." Then the next day he would be back for more. This went on for most of the season until the family moved, and I did not hear from them for a year. We had the opportunity to reunite while I was attending a conference in the community where they had moved. When Terry found out I was in town, he made a special effort to locate and invite me to his school the next day. He had made the school's intramural all-star team and wanted me to watch his game. Of course, I went and enjoyed every minute. Despite all of his previous grumbling and griping, he made the decision to learn the game and became successful.

Accept my words

The examples of these two teens demonstrate Stage I behavior from both the positive and negative sides. Both made decisions based upon factors in their lives that moved them in a particular direction. It is valuable, therefore, for a teacher to have a working acquaintance with the forces that influence movement (i.e., motivation theory) and the decision-making process that affects a student's behavior.

St. Augustine, as noted in the leadership section, observed in his work *On Christian Teaching,*

> *The interpreter and teacher of the divine scriptures, the defender of the true faith and vanquisher of error, must communicate what is good and eradicate what is bad, and in this process of speaking must win over the antagonistic, rouse the apathetic, and make clear to those who are not conversant with the matter under discussion what they should expect. When he finds them favourable, interested, and receptive, or has made them so by his own efforts, then there are other goals to be achieved, as the particular case demands (Augustine 1997).*

This leads us to the question: how does one make them "favourable, interested, and receptive"? Years ago, I read an article on motivation in a management journal. The first three pages described all of the methods that managers employed to motivate workers for two previous decades; none of them had proven universally successful. Likewise, library shelves are lined with texts specifically geared to motivating students, and educational psychology texts provide significant space to motivation theories. Yet, with all of this available information, we still see many unmotivated students. We usually call them lazy. Although this presents a discouraging picture, we cannot just give up on our efforts or our students.

We need to take another look at how we motivate our students to learn and reexamine how we attempt to stimulate our disciples. We can start by making sure we are exploring the right concept. The core issue is learning, not just performing tasks such as "doing school work" or "writing lessons." Learning involves change, growth, and becoming something or somebody different in knowledge, attitude, or skill, than existed before the learning took place. We may be able to force a student to do an activity, but unless that behavior produces change, what value is it? We are all familiar with the unspoken attitude, "You can make me stand up on the outside, but I'm sitting down on the inside, and as soon as you are gone, I'm sitting down."

Since learning is a self-process that produces change in a person's life, students must pursue their own learning. We cannot learn or change for them. They must process this experience for themselves. We cannot pour it in and make it stay. Each pupil must be a participant. As A. W. Tozer has stated, "What the learner contributes to the learning process is fully as important as anything contributed by the teacher" (Tozer 1996). Simply inspiring pupils to behave, perform, or do something is inadequate. Teachers should desire change in their students' lives that is transforming and permanent.

The Teacher's Contribution: Motivation

We can narrow the concern for motivating students to two considerations: the issues that stimulate change in learners' lives and the factors that will cause learners to pursue the study of a lesson that will make them different from who they are now.

C. B. Eavey states, "The pupil is interested and engages in effort only as he has a purpose or motive; consequently adequate and proper motivation is the key to effective learning." Eavey also points out, "Since all learning results from the activity of the learner and since all activity has a cause, the teacher needs an understanding of the forces that act upon life to produce activity" (Eavey 1940). Motivation, therefore, is as integral to this discussion as it was in leadership, so a brief refresher is in order. The *Webster's Third New International Dictionary, Unabridged* defines *motivate* as "to provide with a motive," and a *motive* as "something within a person (as need, idea, organic state, or emotion) that incites him to action." Notice the words "within a person." Motives are of the inner man; therefore, students are motivated internally and we must focus our motivation efforts to that end. External forces may influence the action, but the nature of motivation is intrinsic. In other words, an activity of the soul stimulates movement.

As previously discussed in Part I in the *inspiration* aspect of a leader's behavior, there are seven major motivational forces that induce action and influence the disciple-follower's decision or choice to learn.

A student will attend to lessons stimulated by:

1. **Interest** (Am I attracted to this?),
2. **Meaning** (Will it be worthwhile?),
3. **Preparation** (Am I ready for this?),
4. **Success** (Will I be able to do it?),
5. **Satisfaction** (Will it meet my needs?),
6. **Reinforcement** (Will I receive something for it?), and
7. **Identification** (Will I become the person I desire to be?).

Identification as a motivational force is gaining in recognition, although a colleague with research interest in the Proverbs 2 metamodel (Forrest 2008) has noted that:

> Exploring the implications that interpersonal relationships have on the motivation of learning is increasing in popularity among mainstream researchers. The innate difficulty in this task is that in spite of the ways that researchers are able to glimpse the many ways "by which interpersonal relations and academic motivation affect each other... the theoretical and empirical variation in the field makes attempts to synthesize these understandings difficult" (Anderman and Kaplan 2008).

Nevertheless, in a February 1997 edition of *Education Week*, an article on teens' attitudes toward teachers stated that a relationship with a teacher was "the most important variable in whether they learn or not." In a similar vein, Augustine acknowledges the learner may not need further information, but may need to be "moved rather than instructed" (Augustine 1997).

It would also be helpful at this point to review the three primary influences upon choice and the "Conditions that Influence Choice" (Display 6) that were explored in Chapter 5. Understanding the forces and conditions that influence a person's behavior can obviously affect the approach taken with our students.

The Learner's Responsibility: Attention

While a teacher may influence the decision, it is the student's ultimate responsibility to choose to "attend with interest to the material to be learned." Thus, when Gregory observed, "The mind attends to that which makes the greatest appeal to the senses," he also noted that the learner engages in one of three levels of attention. He labels these, in sequence, as "passive," "active," and "secondary passive" attention and describes them thus:

> *One may let one's mind flit from this object to that, following each passing stimulus for a moment or two until something else "catches the attention." Or one may hold oneself resolutely to a certain object and still be "aware" that other objects are tempting one in other directions. Or one may become so completely absorbed in a given object that all other objects are practically nonexistent so far as consciousness is concerned (Gregory 1972).*

I experienced all three of these levels while conducting a study of 1John as a young, part-time youth minister for the church in which I grew up. It began one evening during this study, when everyone's attention and interest was waning as the conversation drifted on whim. Then, one participant suggested a very controversial interpretation of the confession sentence in 1:9. Suddenly, we all became actively engaged in discussion and debate. We did not reach consensus, so the next afternoon I decided to further pursue the subject. I remember starting my study about 1:00 p.m. and the next thing I knew, three hours had passed. I had been completely absorbed and carried away with my exploration of the text, and "all other objects [were] practically nonexistent so far as consciousness [was] concerned." I discovered after three hours of searching the Scriptures, doing context and word studies, and trying out various interpretations that I was energized and satisfied. I had also memorized the entire chapter without even trying.

An objective of every teacher is to engage students in "secondary passive" attention. An educator, therefore, will do whatever is necessary to attract and gain the acceptance of the student and keep the focus upon the lesson to be learned. In commenting upon the need for a teacher to be interesting and attention grabbing, Howard Hendricks once observed:

> *Jesus was far too unpredictable to ever be boring. It's so painful to go into many of our churches and Sunday school classes and Bible study groups – they're so predictable you can fall asleep, wake up ten minutes later, and find them exactly where you expect them to be. It's like what the Bishop from England said: "You know, wherever the apostle Paul went, they had a riot or a revival. Wherever I go, they serve tea." And what do they do where you go? (Wilkinson 1992).*

Driving down a street in our town, I passed a large electronic message board erected in front of a megachurch in my neighborhood. Advertising their services, the message began: "No one said church should be boring." Regardless of what one may believe about megachurches, seeker-sensitive services, and modern technology, it has to be granted: this church takes Stage I of the model seriously. They want to attract attention, inspire interest, and motivate the masses to accept their words.

Accept *my words*

In addition to motivational issues, the first verse of Proverbs 2 also includes a reference to the content of the message to which the student is to pay attention and that which he is to "seize." Solomon instructs his sons to accept "my words." Seen in the light of the declaration of the *Shema*, as described in Deuteronomy 6, the words of the law were indeed in Solomon's heart, and he was compelled to impress them upon his sons. Perceptions of life, codified in the law, were understood and lived by the teacher. His desire and intention was to transmit these messages from his heart and life to his offspring, so that they would understand the meaning and apply the precepts.

Constructivism

There is no hint in Proverbs 2 or Deuteronomy 6 that the student is to create his own reality from experience, critically reflect upon it, and construct knowledge, as suggested in the more extreme constructivist theories and other contemporary and progressive educational philosophies.

It is critical, however, for Christian educators to have a working knowledge and understanding of the theory of constructivism because it is such a dominant force in education today.

Elizabeth Murphy summarizes one view of constructivistic thought thus:

> How we perceive knowledge and the process of coming to know provides the basis for educational practice. If we believe that learners passively receive information, then priority in instruction will be on knowledge transmission. If, on the other hand, we believe that learners actively construct knowledge in their attempts to make sense of their world, then learning will likely emphasize the development of meaning and understanding. Constructivists generally claim that knowledge is not discovered and that the ideas teachers teach do not correspond to an objective reality (Murphy 1997).

As with any philosophy or theory, the definitions of terms are critical. In Murphy's second sentence, for example, she couples passively receiving information with transmitting knowledge. The assumption, therefore, must be that information and knowledge are synonymous. Most practitioners, and certainly most scholars, would challenge this perception. Identifying and analyzing the differences between *data, information, knowledge,* and *meaning* are beyond the scope of this book, but some distinctions are necessary. Data and information can be thought of as the canisters containing the raw materials, while knowledge and meaning (or understanding) can be perceived as the products to be produced.

Although Murphy does not define knowledge, the inference is that it deals with "coming to know." Determining what can be known, and how, resides within the domain of epistemology, and later in the article Murphy does address the epistemological impacts of constructivism. As one of its philosophical tenets, constructivism rejects the ability to know an objective reality and indeed denies its existence. What a person "knows" must be constructed from within, not received from without. Therefore, since objective reality does not exist, the learner cannot accept the words of the instructor as authoritative, and all the teacher can do is offer a personally subjective interpretation of experience. Kevin Ryan and James Cooper summarize this position when they definitively declare, "we know knowledge is not transmitted but constructed" (2001). Robert Slavin, however, suggests, "The term *direct instruction* is used to describe lessons in which the teacher transmits information directly to students," and that it is "particularly appropriate for teaching a well-defined body of information or skills all students must master (Gersten, Taylor, & Graves, 1999, Gunter, Estes, and Schwab, 2003). It is held to be less appropriate when deep conceptual change is an objective or when exploration, discovery, and open-ended objectives are the object of instruction. However, recent research has supported the idea that direct instruction can be more efficient than discovery in conceptual development as well" (Slavin 2006).

According to another more moderate and prominent version of the theory of constructivism, learners construct not knowledge but a personal understanding of a lesson instead. If Ryan and Cooper are assuming the distinction between information and knowledge that Murphy ignored, their statement is foundational to the more conservative approach that retains the objectivity of the information but allows for student application. Many educators therefore speak of constructing *meaning* rather than *knowledge*. Writing in *Christian Perspectives in Education*, William Robertson defines constructivism as

> a learning strategy that builds upon students' existing knowledge, beliefs, and skills (Brooks and Brooks, 1993). Within a constructivist approach, as students encounter new information, they work to synthesize new understandings based on their current experiences and their prior learning. In other words, the constructivist approach to learning states that learners of all ages build new ideas on top of their personal conceptual understandings (Eisenkraft, 2003). In this process, students and teachers experience common activities, while applying and building on prior knowledge. Learners construct meaning while continually assessing their understandings of concepts (Robertson 2008)

If *meaning* is interpreted as that which the student accepts and understands for himself, hence making his own meaning, then the student is expected to explore the variety of possible comprehensions and interpretations of the message and choose which one he will accept. Thus, in this theory, what may be true for the learner may not be true for others. The meaning of the message to a student may not be what the author or speaker intended it to mean, but it still has value and impact in the learner's life. On the other hand, if *meaning* refers to that which the originator of the message proposed to say, i.e., its literal denotation, then a student can and should receive, discover, and discern the sense of that message. The veracity and validity of the meaning exists in the author's argument, not in the student's interpretation.

Christianity and Constructivism

To balance the concerns and cautions that are no doubt obvious to a Christian, I acknowledge that numerous Christian educators find constructivism to be a positive dynamic with exceptional motivational power. In fact, one of my current colleagues is a Christian constructivist, and Robertson declares Jesus to be the greatest constructivist educator ever in noting that

> *The teaching methods utilized by Jesus Christ as recorded in the New Testament Gospel of Matthew demonstrated the use of a constructivist methodology as a pedagogical approach. Jesus continually challenged his disciples and followers through the use of experiences, parables, and questions in order to relate the context of His eternal message to their practical and daily lives. In this way, He centered His instruction on developing conceptually correct understandings that had to be discovered and personalized by the learner (Robertson 2008).*

In citing Roth, Robertson also notes, "Learners search for evidence and reason, recognize and reflect upon assumptions, discover implications and consequences, and extrapolate from what is really known versus merely believed (Roth, 1989)." This understanding of learning, he postulates, underscored Jesus' approach to teaching. It implies that Jesus focused upon the personal and interactive work of the student and was not dependent upon any transmissive activity or ability of an instructor. Although the second half of this perception can be challenged, it is patent that Jesus was interactive with his disciples and forced them to come to grips with "His eternal message" in a personal and pragmatic way.

In applying this concept to the principle of accepting the teacher's words, we note that when the student constructs understanding, and assigns meaning and application from knowledge, we are solidly within the constraints of "accept my words." It is also appropriate to state that when an attempt is made to construct knowledge from the hard data and information the learner has received, it is an act of "accept[ing] my words." The biblical educator, however, must take offense and reject the radical interpretation of constructivism that expects the student to construct his own information and then call it knowledge.

It is incumbent upon the Christian educator to have a clear understanding of the impacts of constructivism upon the philosophical underpinnings of pedagogy. The implications for metaphysics, epistemology, and axiology are staggering. Theologically, the doctrine of revelation is a critical concern for Christian educators as they reflect upon and establish their theories and models for teaching and learning. Therefore, the biblical notion of *receive* is critical. A student receives and accepts the message of the teacher and then determines the meaning intended, the purpose of the transmission, and the potential value of its application. Hence, it would be beneficial for the instructor who believes in the validity and value of the transmission of knowledge and truth to conduct a word study of the biblical use of the term *receive* in texts such as these:

> *I tell you the truth, anyone who will not **receive** the kingdom of God like a little child will never enter it (Mark 10:15);*
>
> *A man can **receive** only what is given him from heaven (John 3:27);*
>
> *No one takes it from me, but I lay it down of my own accord. I have authority to lay it down and authority to take it up again. This command I **received** from my Father (John 10:18);*
>
> *He was in the assembly in the desert, with the angel who spoke to him on Mount Sinai, and with our fathers; and he **received** living words to pass on to us (Acts 7:38);*
>
> *Therefore, get rid of all moral filth and the evil that is so prevalent and humbly **accept (receive)** the word planted in you, which can save you (James 1:21); and finally,*
>
> *Now the Bereans were of more noble character than the Thessalonians, for they **received** the message with great eagerness and examined the Scriptures every day to see if what Paul said was true (Acts 17:11).*

From the biblical perspective, there is a body of knowledge, a reality, and a factual basis upon which all of life rests, and Solomon wants to communicate this to his son. The son must then determine its meaning, i.e., application, for his own life. Whatever else we may say about curriculum, learning theories, or knowledge itself, we must agree with the biblical writers that the revelation of God's truth is the foundation from which all learning must proceed.

Sources of a Message

Before exploring Stage II of the teaching-learning metamodel, I want to briefly address the question of how a teacher accesses this revelation of God's truth and determines the message or lesson to deliver to the student. What are the potential sources of the lesson presented for investigation and life application? From where do "my words" originate?

As we will see in some detail in Part III, the instructor selects from the content base of God's revealed reality messages for the student to receive. Just as a leader does in determining a mission, the teacher chooses the message for a lesson from four available sources: tradition, observation, participation, and inspiration.

Tradition, or the living words of the community, is constituted by the messages/lessons embedded in and extracted from the historical "stuff" that societies codify in their texts and contain in their treasures to describe and perpetuate their culture: experience and tradition, transmitted in both oral and written expressions. For the classroom educator, this is the textbooks, testimonies, and other resources utilized in a given lesson. For the Sunday school teacher or small group leader in a church ministry or program, this is the Bible and the historical records handed down through the generations.

Observation of the experiences and life needs of the pupil, or the raw "stuff" that every individual brings to the educational experience to be refined and cultured, also assists the instructor in determining the message. These lessons are embedded in and extracted from the life experiences of the students as the teacher witnesses and interprets them. A wise instructor will verify these perceptions before constructing the curricular plan.

Participation refers to the messages/lessons embedded in and extracted from the life experiences and activities of the teacher. It is the refined "stuff" that each educator brings to the experience to share with others: the life experiences of the teacher as they inform and influence the lessons to be learned. This "life message" of the teacher will receive significant attention in Part III because of its impact upon the curricular or lesson plan.

Inspiration refers to the messages/lessons embedded in and extracted from divine disclosure, or the instruction and direction of the Holy Spirit. This is the anointed "stuff" that the teacher receives from above and transmits here below. It can be, and often is, perceived of as intuition or "insight" – an innate sense of what is necessary to communicate to the student: the immediate direction and prescription of the Holy Spirit as the teacher seeks guidance from the divine source.

As we bring our study of Stage I to a close, it is interesting to note that two of Gregory's seven laws, the *Law of the Teacher* and the *Law of the Learner*, find their underpinnings in this Scriptural foundation. Gregory believes the learner must "attend with interest to the material to be learned," and the teacher "must know that which he would teach" (Gregory 1972). These two laws are condensed in the first stage of the teaching-learning process as the learner chooses to "accept (and attend to with interest) my words (which have been personally experienced and affirmed)." Solomon recognized these principles over 3,000 years ago, and through the education of his own son, he has passed this wisdom on to us today.

Stage II: "Turning your ear" (v. 2a)

The mind attends to that which makes the greatest appeal to the senses (Gregory 1972).

We do not have any knowledge or experience that is totally free of involvement with our bodies (Willard 1988).

Once a student has chosen to accept the message of the mentor, turning the ear and engaging the senses to receive the transmitted material is the next step. "Turning" means to pay attention and to heed, while the "ear" is "a part of the body subject to symbolic action," indicating it is the "organ" that receives the messages (Harris 1980). Suiter suggests that the ear represents all of the senses that are stimulated by the media that the instructor utilizes to transmit "my words" (Suiter 2000). *The Theological Wordbook of the Old Testament* notes "the ear can perhaps best be studied under three headings: as an organ of hearing, as a part of the body subject to symbolic actions, and as a sign of responsiveness and understanding. These usages are frequently interrelated [and] most references to the 'ear' or 'hearing' involve a response from the hearer. To hear, or to incline the ear, means to pay close attention" (Harris 1980).

James, the brother of Jesus and pastor of the Jerusalem Church, uses a fascinating analogy in the first chapter of his epistle that illustrates each of these aspects. He encourages his listeners to remove the "filthiness" that blocks their ability to receive and respond to the word implanted within them (James 1:21). William Barkley reports that medical doctors also used this Greek word as a term for "ear wax." In other words, James is instructing his flock to get the wax out of their ears so they may hear and understand the message. Similarly, the Apostle John acknowledges the role of the senses when he reminds his readers, "That which we have heard, which we have seen with our eyes, which we have looked at and our hands have touched – this we proclaim concerning the Word of life" (1John 1:1).

The New Testament contains many anecdotes concerning people who physically touched Jesus and whose lives were changed because of it. Thomas challenged Jesus to let him touch Him to confirm the veracity of the resurrection. The Scriptures also contain, in both testaments, the record of the use of feasts and festivals, prophets who creatively presented their messages, and the command to participate in the Eucharist. All of these ministry activities involve a variety of the senses.

Regardless of whether the learner is actively participating or passively receiving instruction, the senses are engaged and the ear is turned toward the message being presented. While the instructive commands to "Sit still and listen" and "Pay attention" may seem old-fashioned in this day of pupil-centered instruction, the underlying ancient wisdom is still applicable. In fact, research in educational psychology, especially within the information-processing model of learning, has impressed upon educators the realization that "information that is to be remembered must first reach a person's senses, then be attended to and transferred from the sensory register to the working memory, then be processed again for transfer to long-term memory" (Slavin 2006). Alan B. Stover (2004), in a thesis concerning online education, summarizes some of the research conducted on multi-sensory modalities. His work would be an excellent starting point for an investigation of the physical aspect of learning.

Two Components of the Physical Dimension

This physical aspect of learning is comprised of external and internal components, each of which is crucial to the effectiveness and success of the learning process.

The External Component

The most visible component of the physical dimension is composed of the five senses. The impact they have on learning has abundant confirmation and available evidence in the physical and psychological sciences. The information-processing theory of learning, for example, is built upon the idea of receptors receiving stimuli from the environment via the senses and creating neural impulses. Neuroscience and brain-based theories also anticipate the entire physiology of an individual being involved. Hence, the adage "the senses are the gateway to the soul" has been confirmed scientifically and has biblical support.

I find it particularly interesting that one of the biblical Greek words for "learn" is *manthano*, a term the translators of the Septuagint utilized to translate at least three distinct Hebrew verbs. *Manthano* is utilized for learning that is facilitated by seeing, hearing, reading, writing, and eating in the presence of the Lord. It is found in Exodus 2:4 and Deuteronomy 4:10; 5:1; 14:23; and 17:19, where these activities produce learning that follows the Law and reveres the Lord, providing yet another indication that leading and teaching are interconnected. We noted in Part I the role of the physical body in all communication efforts. Here we find it essential to the teaching-learning process.

That the involvement of the senses is critical to the learning process is also illustrated by the *Webster's Third New International Dictionary, Unabridged* definition of the word *know*: "to apprehend immediately with the mind or with the senses." The concept of knowledge, therefore, includes empirical material as well as that derived from inference or interpretation. Since a human being is physically exposed to almost 3000 messages a day, the senses provide the means to receive adequate empirical material for an individual to consider, reflect upon, and *learn*.

The Eyes Have it

"Jenkins' Ear" was the name of a CompuServe online forum for educators I visited frequently in the 1990s. The title of this discussion board came from the consideration of a series of unfortunate circumstances, events, and warring responses involving England, Spain, and even the American colonies in the early 1700s. These actions were due to a misunderstanding related to the severing of the ear of a British shipmaster, Robert Jenkins. Inspired by this historical incident, the site's intention was to promote and facilitate the free and effective exchange of information, which is vital to the education enterprise. The effort demands commendation, but the effect was curious: none of the participants in this forum utilized their ear. They only used their eyes to read the posted articles and discussions.

While the ear in Proverbs 2 may represent all of the senses, our modern, technology-driven culture invests an enormous amount of its resources attacking the sense of sight. Our modern, western literary society focuses a vast array of time, energy, and money attending to those who will read or see the information. The fact that this book is read rather than listened to affirms the contemporary assumption. We cannot, however, ignore those who are unable to read for a variety of reasons including ineffective education, physical impairments, or simply hindered in the opportunity to learn. They deserve our attention as well.

He Who Has Ears

When Solomon encouraged his son to turn his ear, he was no doubt aware, as current scholarship attests, that ninety percent of the ancient world was illiterate (Melchert 1998). "Listen, my son" or similar statements alluding to the necessity of listening occur over a half-dozen times in the first nine chapters of the Proverbs, and the personification of Wisdom speaks, not writes, to the masses. Indeed, the primary forms of education and the common tools of public communication were speaking and singing stories, utilizing pneumonic devices such as alliteration, and repeating those stories in a variety of settings such as walking in the countryside, working in the fields, eating meals, sitting at the campfire, and being tucked into bed.

Generations later, the Master was telling stories, giving verbal instruction, and using parables as memory devices to engage his listeners; in fact, Jesus never instructed his followers to read or study, only to follow, listen, and imitate his life. When he healed the blind, Jesus did not provide them with a book to read. He gave them a verbal command to follow. It is amazing that we do not imitate Jesus' approach more closely in an age when educators are encouraged to compensate for a variety of styles and preferences in learning. After all, as noted in Part I, when the technology fails, all that is left is what is memorized in the mind and hidden in the heart (Psalm 119:11).

In order to be a great and global, truly world-class educator, one must not presume every student is literate or educated enough to receive the message solely by reading or studying, an assumption too often found in the formal schooling paradigms utilized in our classrooms and churches. As we prepare for global ministry, our arsenal of academic weapons must include the ability to emulate the Master and verbalize our message in a manner that is efficient and effective. It should, however, also include a strategy that gives attention to literacy and the ability to hear from God through a diligent, daily investigation of the Scriptures, following the example of the Bereans (Acts 17:11).

The Internal Component

There is, in addition to the senses, an inner aspect of the physical dimension of learning – the brain. In a recent review of the learning theories Christian educators supported, I was surprised to discover that in over two dozen books on Christian education, C. B. Eavey's *Principles of Teaching for Christian Teachers*, written over a half-century ago, was one of only two with any material on the brain (Eavey 1940). The other was Ruth Beechick's short but provocative *A Biblical Psychology of Learning* (Beechick 1982; the latest edition is entitled *Heart and Mind*). Her integration of biblical and psychological data, along with her exploration of the role of the heart and learning, was virtually groundbreaking for Christian education.

In this context, it is important to note the conclusions of Donald O. Hebb, one of the first researchers to do extensive work on the brain's role in learning. He suggests that cell assemblies and phase sequences determine much of the learning a student "acquires" (Hergenhahn 1988). It is also interesting to note that dendrites, the extensions of nerve cells that make up 80% of the cell, stretch, grow, and expand when confronted with new learning of any kind. However, when the information comes in the same old way, they retract and "go to sleep." The senses need to be stimulated in new ways and different forms for learning to continue and mature, i.e., to make meaning out of the random bits of information received through the senses and processed in the brain, forming knowledge. We cannot overemphasize the role and impact of the physical component of learning, especially the contributions of the senses and the brain.

Highlights of Brain Research

As I investigated the role and activity of the brain in learning, I discovered three highlights to consider when reflecting upon the physical aspect of learning. The first consists of some fascinating research indicating that just as the rest of the physical body needs to be warmed up before exercising, the brain also should be warmed, stretched, and prepared for learning. The most intriguing aspect of this research, especially for Christian educators and pastors, is that the best way to accomplish this preparation is through music.

Warm it Up

An article in a March 1997 issue of the periodical *Education Week* states, "Researchers from the University of California-Irvine and the University of Wisconsin-Oshkosh found that piano training was better than computer training at enhancing children's spatial-temporal skills – their ability, in other words, to form mental images from physical objects or to see patterns in space and time." The article suggests exposing preschoolers to music is a better preparation for math than exposing them to computers. The same article also makes the observation that "This latest study builds on Mr. Shaw's theory that the connecting cell patterns formed in the brain for certain higher-order thinking skills are identical to the patterns of notes in certain complex styles of music." Finally, the connection between the outer dimension of the senses with the inner work of the brain was noted in the impact of visual and musical art forms upon increased intelligence and rising standardized test scores:

> *The researchers said a handful of schools across the country are also testing possible links between music and intelligence on their own. In one such study, 1st graders who took part in a special music and visual arts program at The Music School in Providence, R.I., saw their reading and math skills increase dramatically. A report on that study was published last May in the journal* Nature.

In his classic work, *The Republic* (Book VII, 401-D), Plato opines, "Musical training is a more potent instrument than any other, because rhythm and harmony find their way into the inward places of the soul." Teachers who begin class with songs are right in tune (pun intended) with the latest research on brain-based learning. I now appreciate my church history professor in seminary who began each day with a hymn or even "Jingle Bells" on a snowy day.

Trinity College and Seminary's *Orientation to Self-Directed Learning* (1997) supports this idea and proposes a novel study habit by advocating that listening to music actually warms up and prepares the brain for learning:

> *Music can be used to prepare your brain for learning. The music must have between 55-70 beats per minute to synchronize your pulse and heart rate. The best music for this type of exercise is either music of the late Baroque period, 1700-1750 (J. S. Bach, Antonio Vivaldi, or G. F. Handel), or music of the classical period, 1775-1825 (W. A. Mozart, F. J. Haydn, L. V. Beethoven).*

When I presented this concept to a worship leader, he challenged the beat count, but affirmed the concept in principle. Anecdotal evidence suggests that many students find their concentration enhanced if they listen to music while they study.

Use it or Lose it

Jack Maguire summarizes the second highlight in *The Care and Feeding of the Brain* (1990). Although reviewers have labeled his text as uneven and misleading at points, Maguire understands that "One article of popular wisdom about the brain's intelligence is inarguably true. Use it or lose it." This research also indicates a verification of the point made in the last section – dendrites actually grow and increase in number the more the brain is used and the more variety it encounters; when confronted with a lack of variety or boredom, they decrease. Although it is not a human comparison, studies now show that old rats interacting with new toys evidence incredible brain growth. When I entered my doctoral program, three students in my cohort were fifty years of age or older. The speed of learning may diminish with age, but the quantity and quality do not. Use it or lose it at any age. Stimulate the brain, expose it to rousing long-term intellectual challenges, and experience the product of growth.

Cool it Down

The final highlight is the increasing evidence emanating from research that the brain needs a cool down period after intellectual exercise similar to the need for other muscles to recuperate after physical activity.

Trinity's manual suggests,

> *After you have stayed on task and have completed your planned learning session, listen to music again that employs adagio, larghetto, and largo movements. While listening to the music, allow what you have learned to "find a slot" and get integrated and processed. Let your mind interact and react to what you have heard and read. If it is not distracting, talk aloud to yourself about what you have just learned and how you think and feel about it. Keep a notepad close by so you can jot down any creative ideas or concepts that come to you during this time (1997).*

Current educational research suggests a simple pattern: warm up with music, study the lesson, and then, also aided by music, cool down and respond.

As a pastor, I have seen the effect of the neglect of this pattern in worship services. In most conservative, evangelical assemblies, music plays an integral part in preparing worshippers to hear from God in the sermon. Seldom, though, is it utilized to confirm, fix, and reflect upon that message. Therefore, numerous parishioners observe that the final hymn serves as an unanswerable call to worship and response. This is one of the reasons I utilize an order of service that commences with music ministry, where we speak *about* God to one another in hymns and songs. We follow this with an exposition of the Word, and conclude the service with worship, where we sing and speak *to* God with our acknowledgement, adoration, and service in active response. This order recognizes the value of music and its impact on learning and simultaneously facilitates the first three steps of Solomon's model (ready>receive>respond).

It is clearly beyond the scope of this work to explore in depth the role or responsibility of the ear, eye, brain, or any of the other physical aspects of learning. It is within the scope to establish and affirm the activity of the senses as a significant component of the learning process. Stage II's physical aspect of learning provides the foundation for the psychological aspect of Solomon's next observation and recommended step, in which a learner processes in the soul the source material and information that has been received through the senses.

The Spirit as an Internal Component

Before we engage that discussion, however, it is essential to acknowledge that because human beings are constituted of more than flesh and blood, the necessary data and information may also be received via the spirit. In the passage we are studying, Proverbs 2, Solomon himself makes reference to the fact that after the student turns the ear, it is the Lord who "gives wisdom and from his mouth come knowledge and understanding" (Proverbs 2:6). The apostle Paul also affirms this perception in his first letter to the Corinthian church:

> We do, however, *speak a message of wisdom among the mature, but not the wisdom of this age or of the rulers of this age, who are coming to nothing. No, we speak of God's secret wisdom, a wisdom that has been hidden and that God destined for our glory before time began. None of the rulers of this age understood it, for if they had, they would not have crucified the Lord of glory. However, as it is written: "No eye has seen, no ear has heard, no mind has conceived what God has prepared for those who love him"*—but God has revealed it to us by his Spirit (1Corinthians 2:6-10).

Since some messages are transmitted and received by spiritual means rather than physical, it is incumbent upon the Christian educator to not only acknowledge and allow such transmissions, but also to facilitate them. Because we are commissioned to make disciples who worship Jesus, we must go beyond the physical dimension of the senses and address the psychological dimension of a person's soul, where the intellect, emotions, and decision-making aspects of our being reside and worship is generated. Christian leaders and teachers must do more than gain attention (Stage I) and stimulate the senses (Stage II); they must help their disciple-followers process the message in the inner man, whether it is called the soul, the spirit, or the heart (Stage III). Paul Spears and Steven Loomis affirm this in their work *Education for Human Flourishing: A Christian Perspective*:

> *Educators need to understand this holistic nature of humans. Since one of the basic ways humans gain information about reality is from the outside world, it is important to understand the interconnectedness of the body and the mind. External stimuli play an important role in how information is obtained. Experiences like physical touch inform our existence; but describing touch as merely sensory contact with data transfer from neurons to the brain underreports the complexity of essential human properties, which include mental properties (Spears and Loomis 2009).*

Therefore, after the student has received the messages, whether via the senses or the spirit, the learner is then ready to advance to Stage III of the metamodel for learning extracted from Proverbs 2.

Stage III: "Applying your heart" (v. 2b)

> *Knowledge acquisition can be conceptualized as intentional changes in the semantic and propositional network of the learning mind (Imhof 2001).*

"You've been told; so maybe it's time that you learned," are the opening lyrics to the Eric Clapton song *I Can't Stand It.* Jesse Niremberg wrote in *Getting Through to People,* "When you are trying to influence someone's thinking your responsibility does not end with putting your ideas into words. You can't just say to yourself, 'Well, I've done my share in putting my thoughts in clear, well-organized, sensible terms. It's up to him to grasp it.' If your communicating goes only as far as verbalizing your ideas, you'll not be getting through" (Niremberg 1967). These musings summarize the essence of Stage III: learning is more than just receiving a message through the senses.

The senses and the brain are certainly critical components in the learning process. However, as C. B. Eavey noted over a half century ago, learning also includes "consciousness" that cannot be explained simply by the functions of neurons, dendrites, and synapses (Eavey 1940). In fact, the literature often refers to an act of the *will* when describing the "synaptic leap." A miracle occurs within a man that cannot be explained by simple physiological means. Thus, Solomon reminds his son that after turning his ear and responding physically to the message, he must apply his heart as well. As summarized by Spears and Loomis: "The combination of our rational capacities and the grace given to us through the revelation of God enables us to be educated" (Spears and Loomis 2009).

On the Heart

In *Naming the Elephant: Worldview as a Concept*, James Sire (2004) asserts that a worldview is a matter of the heart and identifies biblical support for the variety of *soulish* experiences referred to as functions of the heart:

> *Today we think of the heart as the seat of the emotions (especially tender, sympathetic emotions) and perhaps the will. But it rarely includes the mind. The biblical concept, however, includes the notions of wisdom (Prov. 2:10), emotion (Ex. 4:14; Jn. 14:1), desire and will (I Chron. 29:18), spirituality (Acts 8:21), and intellect (Rom, 1:21). In short, and in biblical terms, the heart is "the central defining element of the human person... It is from this heart that all one's thoughts and actions proceed."*

This conception of the heart as the center of man's inner being is affirmed in the *Theological Wordbook of the Old Testament* (Harris 1980):

> *In its abstract meanings, "heart" became the richest biblical term for the totality of man's inner or immaterial nature. In biblical literature it is the most frequently used term for man's immaterial personality functions as well as the most inclusive term for them since, in the Bible, virtually every immaterial function of man is attributed to the heart."*

Similarly, K. A. Farmer notes, "The 'heart/mind' represents the place within the human body where both rational and emotional decisions are made" (Farmer 1991). *Heart* refers, therefore, to "the inner or immaterial nature in general or to one of the three traditional personality functions of man: emotion, thought, or will" (Harris 1980).

When the biblical Daniel told the king of his dream, he referred to it being in both his "head" and his "heart" (Daniel 2:28, 30). In other words, *heart* may very well be a synonym for *soul* and thus the psychology, i.e., the study of the soul, which focuses on education must consider the heart seriously. This is the very nature of Beechick's work, although she includes an emphasis upon the role of the physical heart.

A brief concordant study in the New International Version of the Bible reveals that the words *heart, soul,* and *mind* occur 878 times, and the words *think, meditate, consider,* and *understand* are utilized 660 times. These findings reveal a significant amount of attention paid to the inner workings of a human being. As an example, in a passage referenced frequently in this volume, Paul warned the Romans about not allowing their fleshly sin nature to rule in place of the Spirit. He reminded them that the result was an impact upon their minds; if they were of the flesh, they became fleshly-minded, but if they were of the Spirit, they became spiritually minded (Romans 8:5ff). The apostle also warned them not to be conformed to the world but to have transformed and renewed minds (12:1, 2), and he exhorted the Ephesians (4:17) not to be engaged in the futile thinking of the Gentiles. In other words, the Scriptures indicate that while the senses and the (human) spirit receive the messages, it is the soul that processes them by making choices and determining what will be done with them.

Applying the Heart

The Hebrew term translated *apply* in Proverbs 2:2 denotes a "stretching out" or "extending" (Harris 1980). "Applying the heart," therefore, connotes extending and engaging the mind in critical thinking and analysis, the activity of logically processing and reacting to information or data in a sophisticated manner. In this sense, Jesus utilized *manthano* to encourage his disciples to "go and learn what this means" (Matthew 9:13). He wanted them to participate in that inner work that sets real learning apart from the "I'm going through the motions but nothing's happening" activity of many students. In other words, the learner must do something with the message received, and it is the function of the teacher to inspire it.

Estes postulates from his study of Proverbs 1-9 that the "role of the learner" correlates with four of the five categories Krathwohl utilized in his taxonomy of educational objectives for the affective domain: the learner receives, responds to, values, and assimilates wisdom; the only category he did not address was organizing (Estes 1997). Thus, the cognitive, affective, and volitional dimensions are equally addressed in an effectual and biblical model for the teaching-learning process. In fact, these three traditional functions of the soul coordinate with and correspond closely to the three goals of Christian education (to know, love, and grow in the Lord), the three dominant categories of learning theory (cognitive, humanist, and behavioral), and the three components of worship (acknowledgement, adoration, and action/service). It is no wonder that humanists reject so harshly the behaviorist's approach to learning, which denies any work in the inner states of an individual and focuses solely upon bodily responses and behaviors generated by conditioning.

A classic example of applying the heart occurred when my son was being home educated in the sixth grade, and I was his math instructor. We would read the lesson, discuss it, and then do the practice assignments. One day after the reading, I asked him to explain the concept of the lesson, and he just responded with that all-too-familiar blank look often observed on students' faces. I called to his attention that he must "read with the mind, not just the eyes," and we started again. Two days later, I caught him reading with that glazed look and asked him if he was reading with his mind. He admitted that he was not and started over. This became a verbal cue, and we utilized it regularly. Then came the day when in the middle of his reading he said, "Dad, I have to start over, I've been reading with my eyes and not my mind." A *eureka* moment for a sixth grader; he realized that to truly learn he had to "apply his heart."

A Simple Strategy

Most educators are aware that seeing words does not equal reading, hearing words does not equal listening, and seeing symbols or movement does not equal observing. In an attempt to overcome these inconsistencies and facilitate the work of the heart in the educational process, many educators have created and promote the use of various learning strategies. One of the more famous, the SQ3R study method (Robinson 1946) has been revised to the PQ4R method (Thomas and Robinson 1972) which encourages learners to Preview, Question, Read, Reflect, Recite, and Review.

Regardless of the method, however, it appears all of the strategies can be reduced to three simple ideas: 1) stimulate higher level thinking by asking numerous questions and expecting the student to read with the mind and not just the eyes, 2) stir the emotions, and 3) expect change to occur in the learner's life and behavior. The Bible instructs us to "consider how we may spur one another on toward love and good deeds" (Hebrews 10:24). This is also the goal of the Christian teacher and prepares the way for the next stage in the process of helping students learn and grow. In summary, Gregory said it best: "True teaching, then, is not that which gives knowledge, but that which stimulates pupils to gain it" (Gregory 1972).

These three strategic ideas acknowledge the total involvement of the inner man. If the biblical term *heart* is truly a synonym for the soul, the Christian educator should encourage students to "renew their minds" (Romans 12:2), "think about such things" (Philippians 4:8), "love the truth" (2 Thessalonians 2:10), and "choose you this day..." (Joshua 24:15).

That the intellect and will are active in learning is virtually axiomatic, but before leaving our discussion of this stage, I would like to reflect upon the role of emotions in learning. A conscientious and sensitive educator takes a concern for the place of emotions seriously and responds to disciple-followers appropriately.

A Note on Emotional Responses

Larry Richards shares the following anecdote as a reminder that the emotions play a significant role in Christian education and ministry:

> A pastor friend of mine made a perceptive comment recently. Speaking of classroom training for the ministry, he noted that it is essentially "intellectual-spiritual." That is, the biblical view of life is studied to be presented primarily in an intellectual framework in sermons and teaching. But the ministry itself, he said, is essentially "emotional-spiritual." The biblical portrait of reality has to be communicated and grasped where people live; communicated as life to life so that it can be felt as well as understood (Richards 1972).

Whether a disciple-follower is responding to the instruction of a teacher or the direction of a leader, it is important to acknowledge an important truth of the communication process. Simply stated, the catalogue of soulish functions labeled "cognition, affection, and volition" is not proposing, or implying, a sequence of activities: first thinking, then feeling, and finally deciding. In fact, emotional responses often precede the thought work that follows. I remember a time when I stood in front of a group of parents at a family camp and taught them about training children from Proverbs 22:6. I thought my study had been well received and beneficial, until a woman walked up to me, looked straight into my eyes, and addressed me intensely for fifteen minutes. She adamantly stated her opinions, beginning her phrases with words like, "I don't agree with you... I don't think... You're not right...." I could hardly get a word of response into the conversation. Finally, I was able to respond and said, "Ma'am I'm sorry you feel this way. I genuinely feel bad that I set off this reaction in your heart. But this is what I believe the scripture teaches, and I'm sorry but I cannot teach otherwise. It's what I believe the book says, and it is what I need to share." We continued for a moment more, and she finally walked away upset.

Within six months of this encounter, that woman evidently came to agree with the material I had presented and became one of the biggest supporters of my ministry. During this time, I was serving as the principal of the school that was connected with the church, and she became the head of our parent-teacher group. In the years we worked together, she was one of my most vocal cheerleaders. Although we never discussed her change of heart, I believe if I had responded to her emotions and her anger by backing down, taking it personally, or even rejecting her, I would have lost her completely and missed the blessing she became to my life.

Although dealing with negative emotional responses can prove difficult, I am far more concerned about students who yawn their way through a session with no reaction. They are not paying any attention, and I have probably lost them. I would much rather have an upset woman or man walk out on my class or my practices than have someone bored and leave unaffected with a quick "Thanks Dr. Mike, that was okay, and I'll see you around." That kind of neutral response concerns me because I am not sure if these people have been reached or understood the message. Like Hendricks, I want a revival or a riot. I want to see some stirring up and movement in peoples' souls. When that kind of soulish and affective response is evident, it is much easier to proceed to Stage IV and the cognitive levels of learning anticipated at that stage.

Stage IV: "Then you will understand" (v. 5)

One of the two summative points describing the educational theories of constructivism is that "learning is an active process" and "true understanding here can involve a major shift in thinking."

The application to educational learning theories "grew from Piaget's ideas and posits that when you tell students about an idea, they will unconsciously compare what you say with all the rest of their knowledge and experiences" (Colburn 2007).

David Suiter (2000), echoing the consensus of scholarship regarding the wisdom literature of the Proverbs, suggests that in Verse 5 the *"then"* sets off the consequences of the *ifs"* that have preceded it. *If* the student has accepted the words, turned his ear, and applied his heart, *then* there should be some discernible outcome from the process. In other words, at this point Solomon is suggesting his son should attain some level of learning. This outcome has been identified in the previous verses as attaining *knowledge* and *understanding* which prepare his son and student for *wisdom* to be manifest in the daily affairs of his life.

The background idea to the Hebrew word translated *understand* indicates Solomon was concerned that his son be a discerning individual. In fact, this is the identical word used to describe the request Solomon himself made in his prayer for wisdom in 1Kings 3:9. He wanted his son to know the difference between right and wrong, good and evil, and between simply knowing something and being able to use it in his life. The Apostle Paul had a similar concern for the Colossian church when he prayed they would be filled with "wisdom and understanding" (Colossians 1:10). The Greek word translated *understanding* means the ability to see the relationship between two things. In that case, he apparently meant the relationship between the words they had received and the life they were to live. After receiving his words, Solomon wanted his son to know how to use them to change his life and give him wisdom in dealing with wicked men, prostitutes, and a host of other evil forces.

Raising the Level of Learning: a Progression

To proceed from *knowledge* to *understanding* to *wisdom* is Solomon's intention for the educational process (Proverbs 2:5-9). It is the forerunner and foundation of the taxonomies of educational objectives and levels of learning proposed by secular researchers like Benjamin Bloom (1956) and the Christian concerns of scholars like Lawrence O. Richards (1970). Richards proposes five levels of learning in his text *Creative Bible Teaching*: Rote, Recognition, Restatement, Relation, and Realization.

Christian educators cannot be content with transmitting information alone. They must also be concerned with stimulating more advanced levels of thought and behavior, as John Westerhoff, mirroring Bloom, has summarized:

> *No one can force another to learn. We can, through one or another positive or negative manipulative means, get someone to repeat what we say or do what we did, that is, pass a test.*

But that does not mean that the other learned it. The lowest level of knowledge is repeating back what someone has said. Comprehension follows, but that requires that someone can put what one has heard into one's own words. Only then can anyone use what has been heard for some purpose.

Having learned to apply what one has heard to some task, one is then ready to analyze what was heard, that is, to discover how that position was reached and compare and contrast it with other positions. Only then is it possible for someone to develop one's own position based on available information. Then comes the highest form of knowledge, the ability to make a judgment on a particular proposition's or conclusion's truth or value. Most people never learn to do that, because that ability is dependent on mastering all the other levels of knowledge. Instead, believing that they are making value judgments, they offer only uninformed, passionate opinions that have little value and cannot be argued or reconciled (Westerhoff 1994).

Some Examples

My daughter is a bright student with a keen mind, and she has always been a fast learner. At three years of age, she was reading a book with her mother, when her brother came into the room. Grabbing his attention, my wife said, "Michael, listen to Carrie, she can read." Her brother, who was seven years older, stated, "She can't read, she's just got that memorized." To which Carrie responded, "Unh uh; watch. I can even do it with my eyes closed." Promptly covering her eyes, she "read" the story to her brother. Larry Richards calls rote learning "memory without meaning." Carrie certainly did not know what "memorized" meant and though she may have had a clue about the story's meaning, she obviously did not know how to read it. As entertaining as it was, this was not a significant level of learning, and we would not have been content with her remaining at that level.

Another example that illuminates the concern for a higher level of learning occurred while I was watching the rehearsal for a kindergarten graduation ceremony. As part of the program, the teacher asked a series of Bible questions and the students provided the pre-arranged answers. I was enjoying these young scholars and their performances when the teacher asked the profound question, "Why did God ask Abraham to sacrifice Isaac?" A little boy in the front row provided the answer, "Because God was testing him!" After the applause, they moved on to the next question.

When the practice session ended, the students sat down in the sanctuary. During this pause, I walked over to the group and asked the boy what it meant that God was testing Abraham. The "blank look" syndrome struck again. "It means he was testing him," came the reply. I inquired further by asking, "But can you tell me what that means? What is a 'test'?" At that point, three other kindergartners jumped in with the same answer. I finally gave up, smiled, congratulated the group, and walked away. Apparently, the teacher was content with a very low level of cognitive functioning and never addressed the true meaning of the story.

I witnessed the same phenomenon one night while helping my son study for a geography test in fifth grade. Everything was fine until he had to define the lines of longitude and latitude. He got the basic answers right, but when I asked him to discuss the lines in more detail the blank look appeared. Therefore, I pulled out a globe and began a discourse on the meaning and purpose of the lines. My son was able to tolerate this for a time but finally declared in exasperation, "Dad, I don't have to know all this. I just have to memorize the definitions." His teacher expected nothing more; I found this very disheartening, and it became one of the reasons he was home schooled in sixth grade.

Some Suggestions

"Then you will understand" is not only the wishes of a caring father; it is the natural result of truly knowing and the precursor to wisdom. Referring again to Paul's prayer in Colossians 1, it is pertinent to note his prayer follows and appears to be a direct result of an acknowledgement that they *learned (manthano)* of the Gospel from Epaphras. The acknowledgement of the Gospel is simply the precipitation of a process that increases the learner's level of Christian growth and maturation. It is true that Paul could not pray for a superior knowledge or wisdom until the foundation was laid, but his intention was that his disciples progressed beyond simply receiving and believing the facts to an acquisition of understanding.

To provide teachers with some guidance in this process of stimulating higher levels of thought and learning, I offer these six suggestions:

1. Set High Standards, and expect them to be met;
2. Communicate Experience, not just information;
3. "Create" Tensions, with problems to solve or needs to meet;
4. Vary Your Methods, addressing the many styles and preferences in learning;

5. Expect (demand) Application, and use a plan that helps; and finally,
6. Test for correction and direction for future learning.

Suggestion #6 reminds the Christian educator of the necessity to engage in some form of assessment to evaluate a student's learning in order to prepare for the next level of scholarship. The New Testament, in particular, is filled with references to "test," "approve," and "correct," and clearly intimates that although we are not wise to compare ourselves with one another (2Corinthians 10:12), we ought to be constantly measuring ourselves against the rubric of God's approval (2Corinthians 10:18). Knowing this standard and having a biblically based theory and understanding of the evaluation process is a vital component of every educator's arsenal. We will give further attention, therefore, to this process in Chapter 10.

Stage V: "Walk in the ways of good men" (v. 20)

> *Behavioral objectives… communicate teaching and learning plans, and they serve as guides for evaluation and documentation of the learner's success or failure… their purpose [is] to describe the behaviors that can be expected at the completion of the learning activity (DeSilets 2007).*

Elevating and evaluating a student's learning is a worthy goal, but it is still not enough. The sage informs us that to complete the learning process, a pupil must put the words into practice. Solomon concludes his educational model with an expectation of a change in behavior and life application; hence, the definition of learning proposed earlier. His behavioral objective was for his son to walk in the ways of good men and avoid the snares of the wicked by keeping fast to the paths and lifestyle of the righteous. Verse 9 (Stage IV) observes that the process of learning will produce an understanding "of what is right and just and fair – every good path." This learning, however, is not complete until that understanding is converted into life change and behavior "modification," with the student actually walking the path of the righteous. To be a "doer of the Word," thus, is the primary objective and test of the teaching-learning process.

It should come as no surprise, then, that the Scriptures pay close attention to the necessity of life change; to put it in Pauline terms, we are to "live a life worthy of our calling" (Ephesians 4:1). Although there are numerous texts that focus on this theme, e.g., Philippians 4:9 and James

1:22, et al, the three concluding paragraphs of what is commonly called the Sermon on the Mount provide the ultimate expression of the need to not only hear the word but to do it. The Master skillfully leads his learners to this conclusion in three steps. He commences by getting their attention with a warning.

> *Watch out for false prophets. They come to you in sheep's clothing, but inwardly they are ferocious wolves. By their fruit you will recognize them. Do people pick grapes from thornbushes, or figs from thistles? Likewise every good tree bears good fruit, but a bad tree bears bad fruit. A good tree cannot bear bad fruit, and a bad tree cannot bear good fruit. Every tree that does not bear good fruit is cut down and thrown into the fire. Thus, by their fruit you will recognize them (Matthew 7:15-20).*

In the investigation of prophets, we simply become live fruit inspectors. True prophets produce true fruit; false prophets produce false fruit. Jesus, however, does not stop there. He observes that sometimes even false prophets appear to produce true fruit. He clearly declares that they will not fool the Father or the Son, but the implication is that they may fool the populace:

> *Not everyone who says to me, 'Lord, Lord,' will enter the kingdom of heaven, but only he who does the will of my Father who is in heaven. Many will say to me on that day, "Lord, Lord, did we not prophesy in your name, and in your name drive out demons and perform many miracles?" Then I will tell them plainly, "I never knew you. Away from me, you evildoers!" (Matthew 7:21-23).*

Whether prophet, leader, or teacher, it is critical that there be some other identifiable characteristic that sets the true apart from the false. Jesus insists and illustrates that this characteristic is simply doing the will of the Father. The problem is identifying and distinguishing his will. The false prophet, apparently, interprets this as superficial activity of a religious nature. Jesus, apparently, does not. His focus is upon being a "doer of the word and not a hearer only," as we shall see in the final of the three paragraphs:

> *Therefore everyone who hears these words of mine and puts them into practice is like a wise man who built his house on the rock. The rain came down, the streams rose, and the*

> winds blew and beat against that house; yet it did not fall,
> because it had its foundation on the rock. But everyone who
> hears these words of mine and does not put them into practice
> is like a foolish man who built his house on sand. The rain
> came down, the streams rose, and the winds blew and beat
> against that house, and it fell with a great crash."
>
> When Jesus had finished saying these things, the crowds
> were amazed at his teaching, because he taught as one who
> had authority, and not as their teachers of the law (Matthew
> 7:24-29).

The true prophet is known, thus, by the behavior of his life, and the disciple-follower who builds his house upon the solid rock is the one who not only hears the word, but also puts it into practice. I can think of neither a clearer expression of the Master's intention for his disciples nor a more precise way to illustrate Stage V of Solomon's teaching-learning metamodel.

The Evidence of Learning

We find the assertion that *change*, along with the resulting behavior, is the evidence of learning in nearly every secular or Christian educational psychology book. Gagne once wrote that performance in and of itself, however, is not enough. "It is necessary to show that there has been a *change* in performance" in order for an activity to have been considered *learned* (Gagne 1977). In other words, simple repetition is not satisfactory; improvement is expected. To be transformed into the image of Christ must be more than just a slogan. Being a doer of the word demands more than lip service, it must be demonstrated in living service and worship (Romans 12:1, 2). The educational enterprise reaches its ultimate goal when there is evidence of an increase in knowledge, understanding, and wisdom that influences both attitudes and behavior – in other words, life change.

Dallas Willard, in explaining the purpose of his provocative *The Spirit of the Disciplines: Understanding How God Changes Lives*, states, "While I write to teach, to add to our knowledge, my ultimate aim is to change our *practice* radically" (Willard 1988). I applaud his desire for his readers to experience the disciplines and their effects, but I challenge the notion that teaching is simply adding to knowledge. To truly teach, one must elevate the levels of learning (e.g., from knowledge to understanding to wisdom) and generate life changes in the pupils. That Willard desires a radical "change in practice" is commendable, but to divorce it from the teaching process is regrettable. Instructors cannot be allowed to believe they have finished their work when they have transmitted information, added to knowledge, or even stimulated reflective thought, critical thinking, or affective response.

Terry, my contentious and rebellious teenage basketball player, was proud of his change in performance. My son came to understand lines of latitude and longitude, and he recently completed a Master of Arts in English to complement his previously attained Master of Divinity degree. My daughter has completed law school, and she is a published journalist. These young people are walking in the ways of good men, and I trust the kindergartner now knows about a test of faith, and I pray our Proverbs 17:16 young woman is now worthy of the cost of tuition. The Christian educator must not be content until his students have changed and become something different than they were previously.

In summary, we need to consider and reflect upon the observations of the Lord and his Son in Ezekiel 33:31, 32; Matthew 5:19, 23:3; and especially Luke 8:21 where Jesus declares that, "My mother and brothers are those who hear God's word and put it into practice." If these are the perceptions and intentions of the godhead, the human educator must bear them in mind as well.

Putting it All Together

The teaching-learning metamodel we have been exploring was first presented publicly to a conference of home educators. Along with the discipline model, I was able to share this biblical approach with moms and dads who took the formal education of their children personally and seriously. Later, in megachurch settings, I trained Sunday school teachers, camp counselors, and group leaders with Proverbs 2 as a foundation. Then, finally, a few years ago, I conducted in-service training programs, utilizing a necessarily de-biblicized form of the chart and model, to challenge and guide public school teachers in an academically-rigorous, content-rich, college prep curriculum. As a high school math teacher, I taught my algebra classes how to learn before I commenced teaching. In other words, Solomon's wisdom and educational perception has made the rounds and been a critical component of nearly every teacher or leadership training program I have conducted for the past twenty years.

Along the way, I had a very encouraging encounter while serving as the principal of a private Christian school. During a fall pre-service session, I surveyed the metamodel of Proverbs 2 with the faculty and engaged them in an interactive workshop to explore the implications and applications of the concepts, stages, and sequence presented (see the Reflection and Response section at the end of this chapter for just such an exercise). The discussion was lively and fruitful, but by the end of the day, everyone was tired and wanted to go home.

Display 7. A Student-Teacher Agreement

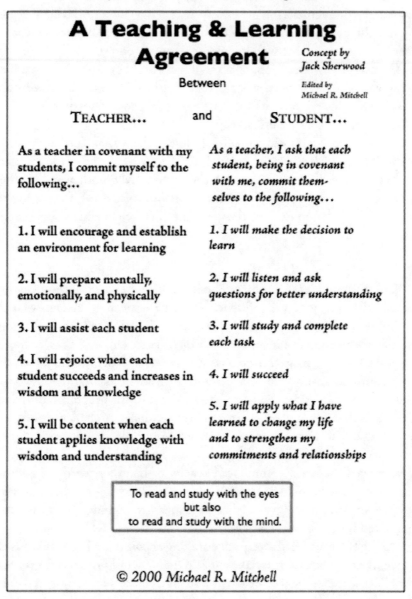

A Teaching & Learning Agreement

Concept by Jack Sherwood

Between

Edited by Michael R. Mitchell

TEACHER... and STUDENT...

As a teacher in covenant with my students, I commit myself to the following...

As a teacher, I ask that each student, being in covenant with me, commit themselves to the following...

1. I will encourage and establish an environment for learning

2. I will prepare mentally, emotionally, and physically

3. I will assist each student

4. I will rejoice when each student succeeds and increases in wisdom and knowledge

5. I will be content when each student applies knowledge with wisdom and understanding

1. I will make the decision to learn

2. I will listen and ask questions for better understanding

3. I will study and complete each task

4. I will succeed

5. I will apply what I have learned to change my life and to strengthen my commitments and relationships

To read and study with the eyes but also to read and study with the mind.

© 2000 Michael R. Mitchell

The next morning, one of the science teachers, Mr. Jack Sherwood, showed me a "Teacher-Student Agreement," in essence a contract, that he created after the prior day's session. He was intending to distribute the agreement on the first day of school and have the students, their parents, and himself sign it. It was a blessing to see at least one person actually made it to Stage V of the learning process and not only realized the implications for his work, but also took steps to implement the stages in his classroom. He had experienced an attitude and behavior change himself, as he prepared to minister to his students.

Although the original conception and design were Jack's, I made a few editorial adjustments when I utilized the agreement in my own courses (Display 7). I cannot think of a better way to conclude and summarize our discussion of the stages of the teaching-learning process than to view this edited version of one man's attempt to reach Stage V.

In Summary and Review

I have proposed in Part II that teachers, through instruction and inspiration, influence students to attain personal growth and development by facilitating the five stages of learning that produce maturation and life change. In summary conclusion, I want to present a simple review of the stages of the metamodel by utilizing a visual display memory device that uses the fingers on the hand. It has proven valuable as a retention tool to many of the students in my classes and training programs. For instance, a rookie junior high English teacher used to hold his hand up and review each of the stages as he created his daily lesson plans. A missions administrator who took a course in which I shared Solomon and this hand display walked up to me in a store nine months after the class and held up his hand stating, "I still remember!" Both of these men utilized the following visual device as a handy way to review and apply the five stages:

- "Thumb" usage indicates approval or a desire to hitch a ride. Most education is "mediated," i.e., you allow another to assist you down the road; but a learner must choose to climb aboard and go for the ride: Stage I ("accept my words").
- "Index finger" points the way; a learner receives instructions via the senses and follows directions in order to acquire all the information needed: Stage II ("turning your ear").
- "Middle finger" signage often indicates some emotional response (in sign language, every sign for an emotion involves the use of the middle finger); learning is more than knowledge,

195

it is also a reaction and response of the "inner states": Stage III ("applying your heart").

- **"Ring finger"** indicates achievement (right hand) and commitment (left hand); a learner follows through and realizes some higher level of accomplishment or relationship: Stage IV ("then you will understand").
- **"Pinky finger"** is often utilized as a sign of refinement or attainment; a learner's life is different, and more mature, than it was before: Stage V ("thus you will walk").

To conclude this chapter's brief introduction to a biblical understanding of the teaching-learning process, I would like to resubmit the following definition of learning. It should be fraught with fresh meaning and implications:

> *Learning is the process that produces change within a person. Incorporating both sensory and psychological components, this process produces alterations such as: the acquisition of new information, skills, and behaviors; adjusted or confirmed attitudes and values; and the resulting emotional and volitional responses. In short, learning produces change, a becoming something new.*

In Chapter 7, we will investigate an ancient example of the Israelites implementing this learning definition while utilizing the metamodel in a national celebration. We will follow that, and conclude Part II, with a brief examination of some of the implications for contemporary Christian teachers and learners.

Reflection and Response

Teaching-Learning Response Worksheet

After reviewing the contents of Chapter 6 and Table 12,
respond to the following for each of the five stages of the metamodel.

1. **Summarize** this stage and its key concepts, using your own words, in three sentences or less.

2. What **key words** (or phrases) would you use to describe the activity of the *teacher* in this stage?

3. What **key words** (or phrases) would you use to describe the activity of the *learner* in this stage?

4. Create a list of "**Dos and Don'ts**" for both teacher and learner as they engage this stage:

Teacher Do:	Don't:
1.	1.
2.	2.
3.	3.
4.	4.
5.	5.

Learner Do:	Don't:
1.	1.
2.	2.
3.	3.
4.	4.
5.	5.

5. Illustrate (in narrative, script, or drawing) **a successful interchange** between teacher and learner in this stage.

Reflections on Critical Thinking

*Stage III of the Proverbs 2 Teaching-Learning Metamodel recognizes
and affirms the role of the mind and the process of critical thinking. Many
educators today believe that the fostering of critical thinking skills is one
of the most significant contributions a teacher can make in the life of a
learner. It would, therefore, be advisable for an educator to be thoroughly
conversant with the concepts and practices of critical thinking. Listed
below are four foundations for and four activities of critical thinking.*

*Read and reflect upon these foundations and activities, considering
practical ways and means in which they may be applied and implemented
in teaching-learning endeavors.*

FOUNDATIONS for critical thinking are those essential building blocks upon which the process may proceed.

1. Knowledge. The more profusely read (and observant) and profoundly experienced the learner-thinker is, the more background information is available that allows interaction with the subject at hand.

2. Wisdom. Born of the emergent synthesis of knowledge and experience, wisdom allows a learner-thinker to assess both the argument and its possible implications.

3. Values. That which one holds in high esteem provides the framework and the foundation from which evaluation proceeds. Having a clearly articulated value system allows a learner-thinker to interact with an argument from what may be considered a moral perspective.

4. Rubric. As a result of the learner-thinker's knowledge, wisdom, and values, a standard by which judgments may be made can be forged. A rubric for both the content and process provides the foundational basis for ultimate evaluation and conclusion.

ACTIVITIES of critical thinking are these essential components; they constitute the processes to be undertaken:

1. Analysis. Consisting of three steps – inspection, interpretation, and inference – the analysis stage includes gathering evidence and identifying patterns and relationships; comprehending and expressing meaning; and forming conjectures and hypotheses.

2. Argument. The argument stage presents evidence in ordered fashion, to buttress the hypothesis.

3. Assessment. Validation of the evidence and the logic of the argument is the purpose of assessment.

4. Action. In conviction and commitment, people learn something and live something.

Seven

A Model for Teaching

The Israelite nation was in shambles. In the sixth century B.C., the capitol lay in ruins, all the quality young people had been taken captive and transported to a foreign land, and morale was at an all-time low. Into this despair, however, the Lord sent the people of Israel a series of capable leaders to restore them to their promised land. The first seven chapters of the book of Nehemiah recount one phase of this remarkable renaissance. Then, in the eighth chapter, after an heroic and historic rebuilding effort under Nehemiah's guidance, the people of the city of Jerusalem call Ezra to bring forth the Word of the Lord and instruct them in the ways of Jehovah. When a heretofore unknown makes an appearance on stage, it causes one to wonder why. Therefore, I did a little research.

Ezra was a scribe, priest, scholar, and teacher. History indicates that he was a student of the scriptures while in exile. Ezra was also a collector, having established the first edition of the canon, and a writer of scriptures himself. Tradition ascribes to him the Chronicles, the book of Ezra, and Psalm 119. He was also a priest of Aaron's family, and the king gave him an appropriate gift of money for the temple offerings and sacrifices. Ezra's greatest contributions, however, came as an educator. He was the organizer of the Great Synagogue, the forerunner to the Sanhedrin, and he was a teacher of the Hebrew Scriptures in Aramaic, the common language of the people.

When the worship center was the Temple, ritual was the focus. When the synagogues were central, as in the exile, reason and instruction were focal, hence the need for a teacher. The Israelite community in exile thus called for Ezra to come, bring out the Book of the Law, and lead the people in a celebration and consecration of their labors. The Book of the Law that Ezra was "told to bring" was the record that the Lord instructed Moses to write before he died and which Joshua was to meditate upon, and not depart from, as he led the Israelites to inherit the land (see Deuteronomy 31:9, 26 and cf. Joshua 1:8).

A Model Man

Historical record is only one component of the answer to the question, "Why Ezra?" Another key emerges in careful reflection upon the book that bears his name. Although the narrative of the events does dominate the account, we discover in Chapter 7 something special about this man – "the hand of the LORD his God was on him" (7:6). The phrase is repeated a few verses later, but this time with explanation: "...*the good hand of his God was on him. For Ezra had devoted himself to the study and observance of the Law of the LORD, and to teaching its decrees and laws in Israel*" (Ezra 7:9b, 10). What enabled this man to experience so much favor and the good hand of God upon him? The text reveals the source. God's hand was on him because he regularly participated in or devoted himself to three specific activities: 1) studying, 2) observing, and 3) teaching. These three pursuits are the foundation upon which any effective educational ministry should be based. They encompass the components of the well-balanced life of a scholar, practitioner, and professor. A teacher would do well to examine and emulate this model and participate in what I call "the Ezra Experience."

He devoted himself...

Devotions are all too often perceived as a quick Scripture reading, maybe a short prayer, and a "Thanks, God, I'll see you later." To be truly devoted to something, however, demands dedication, commitment, persistence, and perseverance. In short, it is hard work. When Ezra devoted himself to the study of the Law, it was more than just a casual passing glance. He would not understand the present practice of going to church on Sunday, sitting in the pew, hearing the words, and then going home with nothing changed in one's life.

1. To Studying

> *Study to shew thyself approved unto God, a workman that needeth not to be ashamed, rightly dividing the word of truth* (2 *Timothy* 2:15 *KJV*).

To get a good grip on the experience of Ezra, we need to examine what the idea of *study* meant to him. First, note that he *devoted* himself to his study. He was not easily distracted or diverted from his task. A devotion to study implies quality as well as quantity of time spent in mastery of the material. Second, Ezra devoted himself to studying the *Law of the* Lord. His focus was upon the revealed Word of God. He apparently did not spend a lot of time studying what others said in commentaries, the new and improved theologies of his day, or the false gods of the surrounding nations. Third, he spent his time *studying* the text, not just being exposed to it. Superficial reading or perusing the Scriptures may have given him an acquaintance with the law, but not a mastery of it. This is critical, because until an individual knows something, he cannot teach it or communicate it, as we discussed in Chapter 2.

Godly instructors, thus, need to personally study and know or experience the truth before they engage in communicating it to others. John Milton Gregory's *The Seven Laws of Teaching* affirms this in describing the law of the teacher: "The law which limits and describes him is this: *the teacher must know that which he would teach*." This would appear to be self evident, but an investigation of some of its implications would be profitable. To enrich our understanding of this observation, we need to consider some admonitions from both biblical and human sources. The following passages reflect and reaffirm two simple truths: individuals can only teach what they know and they only truly know what they have experienced.

The *Shema* (Deuteronomy 6:4-9) is one of the most notable and poignant passages in the Old Testament Law; the love of the one and only true God is both the corner and capstone of the Hebrew faith. That this is to be "pressed" upon the children of the community is critical. As Donald Joy once noted, "Christian faith is never more than one generation from extinction" (Joy 1975). Nevertheless, the hinge upon which this process swings is that the commands are to be "upon [the] hearts" of the parents and other adults within the community (6:6). Before parents and teachers can communicate the lessons of the Law to the children, they must know it themselves.

In his letter to the church in Rome, Paul reveals a personal conviction:

> I will not venture to speak of anything except what Christ has accomplished through me in leading the Gentiles to obey God by what I have said and done – by the power of signs and miracles, through the power of the Spirit (Romans (15:18-19).

Paul did not dare preach about anything other than that which he had come to know and personally experience in Christ.

The Apostle John also expresses the importance of knowing one's message:

> That which was from the beginning, which we have heard, which we have seen with our eyes, which we've looked at and our hands have touched – this we proclaim concerning the

> *word of life. The life appeared, we have seen it and testified to it, and we proclaimed to you the eternal life, which was with the Father and has appeared to us. We proclaim to you what we have seen and heard, so that you may have fellowship with us (1John 1:1-3).*

The only message John was willing to testify to and proclaim was the one he knew from experience – that which he had touched, handled, and seen with his own eyes. I once did a cursory examination of every biblical term translated *knowledge* in Hebrew and Greek, Old and New Testament, and found something incredible. They all, at some point in their etymology, referred to and denoted that knowledge was acquired through personal experience; knowledge demanded personal participation and apprehension of the truth. This same refrain is noted in non-biblical writings as well. J. M. Gregory and C. B. Eavey both endorse and provide applications of these observations in their texts, *The Seven Laws of Teaching* and *Principles of Teaching for Christian Teachers*, respectively. These applications provide an inspiring conclusion to this section:

> *To experience imperfectly is to know imperfectly is to teach imperfectly.*
>
> *That teacher will be cold and lifeless who only half knows the subject he would teach. But one fired with enthusiasm, will unconsciously inspire his pupil with his own interest (Gregory 1972).*
>
> and
>
> *A teacher is one who has gone the way over which he is leading his pupils.*
>
> *What is true and central in his life because he has experienced it is imparted to others (Eavey 1940).*

2. To Observing

> *Whatever you have learned or received or heard from me, or seen in me – **put it into practice**. And the God of peace will be with you (Philippians 4:9).*

The result of study is putting into practice what one has learned. If the teacher's desire is for his life or the lives of the students to be peaceful, built on rock, and free of deception, then he should be as devoted as Ezra to the study and the observance of "the Law of the LORD."

Based on our discussion in Chapter 6, it should come as no surprise that the Hebrew term translated *observing* refers to doing, practicing, and applying, rather than simply and passively seeing or hearing. In current usage, the English term *observe* also implies more than sight. It connotes respect, honor, and a willingness to abide by implied as well as stated intentions. We observe, for example, laws and holidays by doing something – obeying, celebrating, and participating. Ezra not only studied the Law, he came to know it by observing or practicing it.

The old English term *taecean* was one of the first English words for "teach" and meant, "to show how to do" (Moran 1997). In other words, the original perception of teaching rested upon the concept of skill transference. This concept implies that the teacher knows how to perform the particular skill and suggests a moral obligation to pass it on to others. Gabriel Moran addressed this theme in his provocative tome *Show How: the Act of Teaching* (1997). The text also includes a section on the relationship between religion and teaching. The moral dilemma inherent in education and religion as a transmission imposed upon another is especially noted.

It was George Bernard Shaw who stated the now infamous, "He who can, does; he who cannot, teaches." He may not have been able to foresee the consequences of his dictum, but my daughter caught the absurdity. As was the case with her brother, Carrie spent a portion of her compulsory education experience in home school. We were preparing the curricular plan for her eighth grade year, when she expressed her desire to learn to speak French. Since neither my wife nor I speak the language, we searched for program materials to assist us. Unable to find an appropriate curriculum, we tried to steer our daughter in a different direction, but Carrie was persistent in her desires. She came to me complaining, "Mom won't teach me French." Assuming I could end this quickly, I retorted, "Carrie, it's because she doesn't know the language." Undaunted, she declared, "Those who can, do; those who can't, teach!" Paraphrasing Shaw, she stated the obvious absurdity with a pixyish grin and a twinkle in her eye; we both burst into laughter.

Thankfully, the counter observation of Alexander Pope enriched our culture: "Let such teach others who themselves excel." I think this may be where Steve Jobs, the CEO of Apple, got the idea that a person should only work for people from whom something can be learned. Kevin Ryan and James Cooper also explored this view in their 2001 work, *Those Who Can, Teach*. In the May 1995 issue of *Downbeat* magazine, Dave Helland also addresses this concept in an interesting article entitled, "Those Who Can

Play, Teach." Helland examines the increase of professional jazz musicians teaching and heading departments in college music programs. Whether in the work force or classroom, our society desperately needs people who are great at what they do to teach others.

I would like to confirm and clarify this point by reexamining two familiar biblical references. Each of these passages gives affirmation to the premise Gregory articulated: to teach demands not only providing abstract knowledge but also promoting practical application.

We will commence with the book of James, the first chapter (vv. 22-25). James implores his readers:

> Do not merely listen to the word, and so deceive yourselves. Do what it says. Anyone who listens to the word but does not do what it says is like a man who looks at his face in a mirror and, after looking at himself, goes away and immediately forgets what he looks like. But the man who looks intently into the perfect law that gives freedom, and continues to do this, not forgetting what he has heard, but doing it—he will be blessed in what he does.

In order to avoid self-deception and the willful neglect that hinders a reception of blessing, one must not merely listen but one must also respond in obedience and personal application of the Word. An example of this blessing can be noted as we reconsider the words of Jesus that conclude the Sermon on the Mount (Matthew 7:24-27):

> Therefore, whoever hears these words of mine and puts them into practice is like a wise man who built his house on the rock, and when the rains came his house stood firm because it was built on a solid foundation. But everyone who hears these words of mine and does not put them into practice is like the foolish man who built his house on sand.

Jesus himself describes the difference between the wise man who experiences the blessing of building his house on rock and the foolish one who builds his house on sand. What separates them is not in the hearing of his words, because they both do that. The difference is in putting those words into practice.

Two Corollaries

Situations may arise that present a challenge to the proposition that those who can, teach. One example of this occurred when I accepted my first children's ministry position before having children or even being married. It was simply unrealistic to assume and futile to anticipate that I had much to say to parents, but it was expected of me nonetheless. In order to make the proposition valid in such circumstances, there must be some exceptions. I can think of two, but I prefer to see them as corollaries as opposed to contradictions.

The first corollary is actually a realization: "I am not in this alone." I have at my disposal and can utilize the resources of the entire community – in my case, other teachers and parents. If I do not have knowledge in a particular subject area my students need, I will recruit someone else to teach them. School systems encourage and support field trips, guest speakers, and outside projects for their students. The Sunday school teacher, home educator, small group leader, and pastor should do likewise. As I was growing up, it was a common occurrence for our little church to have a testimony time in which people shared their real-life lessons and experiences with others. Sometimes the best a teacher can do is step aside and allow a more knowledgeable expert to instruct the pupils.

For years, Tom Lasorda and Tom Landry were on top of the baseball and football worlds, winning a number of World Series and Super Bowl titles with the Los Angeles Dodgers and the Dallas Cowboys, respectively. At first glance, they were exceptions to Gregory's law and Ezra's experience; they were not highly skilled athletes and had only limited competence and experience to share with their players. They were good leaders, however, and provided their teams with outstanding Hall of Fame credentialed assistant coaches, who actually taught the players how to play. When these assistants were recruited to head coaching positions of their own, the Dodgers and Cowboys ceased to win world championships. Rather than contradict the rule, these teams and coaches proved it: the teacher-leader has to know and experience the lessons before they can be passed on to others. The case of basketball coach John Wooden, an All-American guard in college, further affirms this law. Coach Wooden, known as a premier teacher of basketball, was on the floor every day instructing his athletes, who in turn went on to win ten national championships. He had already "gone the way over which he was leading" his charges (Eavey 1940); those who can play, coach.

The second and possibly more crucial corollary is that sometimes the most important information we can teach our students is how to study, learn, or discover it for themselves. This actually enhances the role of the teacher, because learning how to learn may set the student on a course to supersede the capacities of the teacher. In other words, if it is true that one teaches what one knows then in this case what is known is how to learn, and this is the knowledge that is taught.

3. To Teaching

> *Anyone who breaks one of the least of these commandments and teaches others to do the same will be called least in the kingdom of heaven, but whoever* practices *and* **teaches** *these commands will be called great in the kingdom of heaven (Matthew 5:19).*

Ezra was not only a scholar and a practitioner; he was a professor as well. After he studied the Law and applied it to his life, he took the responsibility to pass it on to others. A picture hanging in my office illustrates this commitment to the ministry of teaching. An embroidered work was given to me by a parishioner of the small Kansas church I pastored a number of years ago. It is a rendition of a little boy standing on a stool and leaning over a crate, which is his pulpit, teaching one little mouse. The caption under the scene reads, "Preach the truth no matter what." This piece of art also reflects very accurately my commitment to teaching. I must teach no matter who is in the audience, how many are present, or where I am. At a large church I served, the senior pastor made it very clear that he would not waste his time doing a Bible study for less than fifty people. I consider that a violation of the trust placed upon us by the shepherd who lived the example of leaving the ninety-nine to secure the one. Would this pastor have not stopped for the blind man, Zaccheus, or Nicodemus? Teachers teach. They cannot do otherwise.

Gregory's Law of the Teacher, that he must know what he would teach, has a corollary attached. Gregory also notes, "What a teacher knows he must teach." I interpret that to include two aspects: 1) a teacher must teach out of obligation; i.e., with a responsibility to the community, and 2) a teacher must teach by nature; i.e., the messages pour forth from the life of the mentor.

Ezra fulfilled both of these aspects as he ministered the word of the Lord. How he taught is an example of the very strategy we have been studying. Whether or not he consciously followed the Proverbs 2 model, we may never know. The fact that he did, even if intuitively, is instructive and provides a case study for us to examine.

Biblical Implementation of the Proverbs 2 Model

The book of Nehemiah provides an excellent example of an application of the thesis of this book: to truly co-labor with the Lord in administrating his will requires the merging and blending of both leading and teaching. In 1:1-2:17, we find Nehemiah determining his mission; in 2:17, 18, he declares his mission; and from 2:18b to the end of Chapter 7, he is directing the implementation of the mission (see Table 4). Then, in Nehemiah 8, as the Israelites celebrate their accomplishments, we find recorded a teaching-learning event that is significant because Ezra follows Solomon's model, in sequence, while teaching the Israelites the Word of the Lord. The first time I noticed this correlation, I printed out the text and with five different colored highlighters marked the key words and phrases that were appropriate to each stage. It was visually compelling and graphically revealed the correspondence with the five stages described in the Proverbs 2 Teaching-Learning Metamodel (see Table 12).

The Ezra Experience: the Model Illustrated

In the first three verses of Nehemiah 8, we find the people choosing to learn and accepting the words of the Lord. They gathered in the square, told Ezra to bring out the book, and listened attentively. Stage I was thus successfully navigated; a motivated and responsive class was prepared to learn, and a predetermined curriculum was agreed upon.

In the next three verses, we find Ezra standing on a high platform so that everyone could see him, opening the book, and reading it from daybreak until noon. The people stood up, "turned their ears," stomped their feet, raised their hands, fell to their knees, and involved nearly every sense in the learning experience. To say they were into it would be an understatement. Every portion of their being was involved. Stage II was clearly implemented.

Verses 8 and 9 indicate Stage III was then engaged. The Israelites "applied their hearts" and sought for understanding from the Levites and scribes in attendance, who "made it clear" and "gave the meaning." This allowed the Israelites to understand the lesson and have that message touch their emotions, producing mourning, tears, and repentance.

In the next paragraph (vv. 9-11), Nehemiah and the Levites guide the learners into a Stage IV experience of elevating their learning levels from knowledge and understanding to wisdom. The leaders provided the people with two possible applications to consider: 1) to receive "the joy of the LORD" and not grieve and mourn, for it was a sacred and holy day and 2) to enjoy the fruit of their labors and to literally have a feast and share it with others. In other words, they not only heard and understood the words, they also considered their meaning and the applications in their personal lives and community.

Finally, in the twelfth verse we see that after having understood the words, the people did go "away to eat and drink, to send portions of food and to celebrate with great joy." They became doers of the Word and applied it in practical ways, fulfilling Stage V – completing the process and experiencing change.

That, however, was only the beginning. As recorded in the next paragraph (Verses 13-18), the cycle was repeated the following day in a "discovery learning" experience that revealed the Law's command to "live in booths during the feast of the seventh month." After assembling, hearing the word, receiving understanding, and seeing its implications, they went out and applied what they heard in the life of their community and personal homes, celebrating in a way that had not been known since the days of Joshua. Of course, the question must be asked, "Was it sustainable, or just a camp-like mountaintop experience?" According to the text, it was continuing three weeks later in Chapter 9. Too often, we are inappropriately satisfied when our students remember the lesson three days later.

As stated previously, when the Lord first revealed this passage to me, I was astonished at the correlation between this historical event and the model Solomon proposed. Ancient Jews were separated in time, space, and national ethos from their most famous king. Nonetheless, they still applied his words to their educational enterprises; we should do no less.

A Prophetic Pronouncement: the Model Affirmed

An additional biblical affirmation of the Proverbs 2 Teaching-Learning Metamodel can be found in an examination of the following passages from the prophecy of Isaiah and the Gospel of John. Considering the possible implications for preaching and teaching ministries, a reflection upon the original message from the Lord to Isaiah, and how John applies it, is in order:

> Then I heard the voice of the Lord saying, "Whom shall I send? And who will go for us?" And I said, "Here am I. Send me!"

> He said, "Go and tell this people: 'Be ever hearing, but never understanding; be ever seeing, but never perceiving.'
> Make the heart of this people calloused; make their ears dull and close their eyes. Otherwise they might see with their eyes, **hear with their ears, understand with their hearts,** and **turn** and be **healed**" (Isaiah 6:8-10).

> Even after Jesus had done all these miraculous signs in their presence, they still would not believe in him. This was to fulfill the word of Isaiah the prophet:
> "Lord, who has believed our message and to whom has the arm of the Lord been revealed?"
> For this reason they could not believe, because, as Isaiah says elsewhere:
> "He has blinded their eyes and deadened their hearts, so they can neither see with their eyes, nor understand with their hearts, nor turn—and I would heal them." Isaiah said this because he saw Jesus' glory and spoke about him (John 12:37-41).

Utilizing a quotation from Isaiah 6, John reveals the reason why many of Jesus' followers did not believe in him despite witnessing many miraculous signs (see John 11-14). In his explanation, the apostle recounts the observation of the Lord to his prophet that people hear with their ears, understand with their hearts, repent or turn, and receive healing. With this declaration, the Lord acknowledges to his messenger the sequence of steps that people go through when they are confronted with his word. Both the prophet and the apostle affirm the assertion that even the gospel message is processed by utilizing the same stages of the learning sequence that we studied in Proverbs 2 and saw illustrated in Nehemiah 8. We, likewise, can apply this pattern in educational endeavors and inspire our disciple-followers (Stage I) to hear (Stage II), understand (Stage III), turn (Stage IV), and receive the healing of God's word (Stage V).

Implications for Teaching and Learning

The Proverbs 2 Metamodel for the Teaching-Learning Process contains a number of implications for contemporary educators as they create their own emergent synthesis from the options available to them. The most obvious is that Solomon's model implies that teaching and learning are two sides of the same coin – in fact, it can be asserted that there is no teaching without learning. Hebrew scholars who note that two common terms for teach and learn in the Old Testament stem from the same root, *lamad*, affirm this perception. *The Theological Wordbook of the Old Testament* observes that, "While Greek uses two different words for 'to learn' (manthano) and 'to teach' (didasko), each having its own content, goal, and methods, Hebrew uses the same root for both words because all learning and teaching is ultimately to be found in fear of the Lord" (Harris 1980). The practical ramifications of this metamodel provide simultaneous direction for both the teacher and the learner as they approach and encounter the teaching-learning experience (see Table 12 and the columns "the teacher is responsible for…" and "the learner is accountable to…").

Implications for Learning

Solomon reminds us that students must choose to learn and be motivated to receive the transmitted message. His observation indicates that knowledge is revealed and received, thus limiting but not eliminating our reliance upon constructivist theories. His approach, however, clearly expects students to be active participants in the process. They are not to be passive spectators, and improvement – not just movement – is an expected outcome of learning. Finally, some elevation of learning levels is demanded in each educational encounter. No one is allowed to remain as they are; transformation is the goal of Solomon's model and Christian education.

It is noteworthy that learning often occurs in social and communal settings. After all, Solomon was preparing a future king to lead his people, and the illustration in Nehemiah 8 of the teaching-learning process was a community affair. The Christian life was never designed to be lived alone, and Christian education was never designed to be isolated. The frequent use of the Greek term *allelon*, often translated "one another," in the New Testament reminds us of the need for community, fellowship, and group learning. Thus, the Christian teacher must always consider the social dynamic of learning as well as the individual.

To put it simply, the student is accountable for five distinct *essential activities of the learner*:
1) Attend with interest,
2) Receive the message,
3) Study the material,
4) Learn a lesson, and
5) Effect a change.

In the implementation of these activities, learning occurs.

Implications for Teaching

Most teachers could use a reminder of a few essential attitudes and behaviors. The first implication for teachers is the recollection that to truly have taught a lesson demands that a student has learned something. Simply transmitting information does not ensure student learning. A teacher must facilitate the learning process within a student. Therefore, as stated earlier, since understanding how people learn determines the way we teach, learning theory generates teaching theory.

The second implication is that in order to teach, it is critical to have something to say. In Romans 15, Paul told the church he would only speak those things that he had personally experienced and knew because of his relationship with Jesus Christ. Teachers need to truly know and master their material, i.e., "my words."

Next, the Apostle John gave great emphasis to the need to touch, handle, and personally experience the truth. The Christian teacher gives great priority and attention to stimulating the senses of the students, using as many media tools as are available and appropriate for the class and individual students.

The teacher also needs to teach the students how to think and apply their hearts. It has been said that the greatest outcome of education is the ability to think, and Solomon would have probably agreed. Paul warned the Ephesian church to live not as the Gentiles do, "in the futility of their thinking" (Ephesians 4:17). This is one of the greatest challenges in the church today, since the mindset and worldviews of secular humanism and postmodernism are so prevalent.

Thinking, however, must produce more than a superficial idea or two. The teacher must determine if the student engages in critically reflective thinking and assesses the process through an appropriate evaluation system. Ultimately, that evaluation should reveal a significant change in the student that facilitates participation in the life and lifestyle of the teacher. After all, it was Jesus, the master teacher, who once stated, "Everyone who is fully trained will be like his teacher" (Luke 6:40).

To put it simply, an instructor is responsible for five distinct *essential activities of the teacher:*
1) Motivating,
2) Communicating,
3) Inspiring,
4) Elevating, and
5) Activating.

In the implementation of these activities, teaching occurs.

Reflection and Response

Ezra Experience Reflection

If you practiced the "Ezra Experience" seriously, how would it affect your life, your study and preparation, and how you present your lessons?

Jot down, on a notepad, some of your "brainstorming" by completing the following sentences.

If I took this model seriously,
I would probably stop doing...

I would probably start doing...

I can see that my study time would have to be more...

I can see that my life would have to be more...

My lessons would probably begin to...

My expectations of my students would begin to...

My students would actually begin to...

I would not be satisfied with my teaching unless...

Preamble

TO PART III: *On the Structure of the Discipline*

> *"Come, follow me,"* Jesus said, *"and I will make you fishers of men"* (Matthew 4:19).

> *"Come to me, all you who are weary and burdened, and I will give you rest. Take my yoke upon you and learn from me, for I am gentle and humble in heart, and you will find rest for your souls. For my yoke is easy and my burden is light"* (Matthew 11:28-30).

Instructions couched in the language of invitation were employed in Parts I and II of this book to introduce two critical concepts: leading and learning. Before we begin our exploration of Part III, let us briefly reflect upon what we have discovered about the processes of leadership and education.

Looking Back

Whether we deduce that a teacher leads or a leader teaches, we come to the same conclusion: educators and administrators have something to say, say it, and then make something happen in the lives of their disciple-followers. How to facilitate these processes has been the central focus of our study, and we can summarize our discoveries in a compacted review of the principles and practices addressed in each section.

Compacting Part I

In Part I, we explored the implications of the assertion that a leader induces and influences people to come and follow while engaging in three behaviors: determining, declaring, and directing a mission. We then acknowledged that in fulfilling the mission the leader implements a strategic plan and influences the people through instruction, information, and inspiration. We also examined how leaders and managers influence the process through the administrative functions of planning, organizing, staffing, directing, and controlling.

To provide a précis, *leadership* is the ministry of standing before people with a clear mission and attendant vision, effectively conveying the messages and efficiently supervising the actions needed to fulfill that mission.

Management, on the other hand, is the utilization and manipulation of the resources necessary to keep the enterprise on course and actively engaged in progress toward its objectives. In more concise terms, *leadership* is "an aspect of administration in which others are influenced to come, follow, and contribute to the accomplishment of a mission."

Compacting Part II

In Part II, we investigated a teaching-learning metamodel based upon the wisdom of Solomon found in Proverbs 2. This metamodel offers a biblically based emergent synthesis that provides direction and guidance for both the teacher and the learner. It also provides a framework for the integration of the theories and practices extracted from educational psychology. In fact, the student of educational psychology finds in this metamodel, and in the host of examples and illustrations offered (especially those of Solomon in Chapter 6 and Ezra in Chapter 7), a convenient "hanger" upon which to place the findings and applications from a variety of theories.

The best and biblical components of behaviorism, humanism, constructivism, motivation theory, and cognitive approaches to the teaching-learning process can be integrated and implemented in the appropriate stages (see Table 12). For example, Stage I is enhanced by an understanding of certain elements of motivation theory and behaviorism. Stage II is enriched by a comprehension and application of sensory-based learning styles along with brain-based and information processing theories. Stage III is supported by appropriate cognitive and Christian humanist understandings, as well as psychology-based learning styles. Finally, Stages IV and V are facilitated by the utilization of some of the biblically supported concepts of behaviorism and constructivism. Educational psychology, and the theories it supports, finds in its search for a soul a resting place in the Proverbs 2 Teaching-Learning Metamodel.

Comparing Parts I & II

In the prologue that introduced this work, I observed that teaching and leading have a number of components in common. Both attempt to influence others, depend upon effective communication, and utilize modeling and imitation as key methodologies. If we add that they both start with a mission and a message to share and conclude with a change of behavior and performance, we understand why our Master is simultaneously referred to as leader and teacher. He provides for us the template that balances and integrates both functions in effective educational ministry and leadership service.

Table 13 outlines the connections and parallels between the metamodels for each function, including a possible integration with the discipline/disciple-making process. It would be a profitable exercise to consider and reflect upon the implications for ministry. For example, how much leadership occurs in a teacher-training program, and how much teaching takes place in a staff meeting? In what ways can a leader facilitate discipleship in either?

Table 13. A Comparison of the Teaching and Leading Metamodels

Learning	Discipling	Leading
I: *Accept my words*		Determine
II: *Turn your ear*	Communication	Declare
III: *Apply your heart*	Choice	
IV: *Then you will understand*	Consequence	
V: *Walk in the ways*		Direct

Whether Jesus is the *master* or the *rabbi*, whether his invitation is to "Come, follow me" or "Come…and learn from me," the result is the same: people's lives are changed forever as they are transformed and become like their teacher (Luke 6:40). To follow and learn of Jesus is the only way to become competent and equipped enough to lead and teach others.

This is exactly the intention of Jesus. After we come, follow, and learn from him, he commissions us in his authority to "Go, make disciples." It is to this command that we will turn our attention in Part III, as we explore the five essential activities that the Christian educator utilizes to complete the mission of the Master.

Looking In

In a manner similar to the use of hangers to sort and store clothing, we will create a conceptual closet with hangers for the mind and skill sets we will attain… This framework can also be employed as a filter to help us winnow out the perilous and unprofitable influences encountered in the journey of living, learning, and leading. The result will be an "academic screen door" that allows in the breezes of fresh air but keeps out pests

> *and irritating bugs. The tighter the weave of the mesh, derived*
> *from study and experience, the more effective the filter will be.*

With these words from the Prologue, I echo the sentiment of scholars such as Frank Ryan, who recommends, "studying a particular subject from the standpoint of its basic structure so that as new information becomes available and as older ideas become obsolete, they can more readily fit into the structure of the discipline being studied" (Chadwick 1982). Ron Chadwick extends this thought by defining and describing the composition of the structure of a discipline:

> *There is much talk today in the field of education about the structure of a discipline. But what do we mean by this? The structure of a discipline consists, at least in part, of the body of imposed conceptions (concepts) which define the investigated subject matter of that discipline and control its inquiry. The **structure of any discipline is composed of the basic concepts or principles without which you would not have that discipline or which, when put together, form the basic, unchanging framework for that discipline.***
>
> *Ralph Tyler states that the structure of a discipline deals with five basic areas: (1) the **questions** it deals with; (2) the kind of answers it seeks; (3) the concepts it uses to analyze the field; (4) the methods it uses to obtain data; and (5) the way it organizes its inquiries and findings. This, he says, becomes the means of analyzing the structure of a particular discipline (Chadwick 1982).*

Exploring the Structure of the Discipline

Education that is Christian, i.e., making disciples who worship Jesus, is the particular discipline we are analyzing in this volume. In doing so, we are exploring the dual processes of *leading* people to Jesus and *teaching* them to walk in his ways.

The manner in which disciples are made, and how these processes are implemented and applied, is the subject of a host of books. What makes this one different is my insistence that when making disciple-followers, the methods utilized find their focus and direction in the answers to the who, what, where, when, how, and why inquiries delineated in the Prologue. In addressing these questions, we are identifying the structure of the discipline, as Tyler suggests in the noted quotation.

I found that while analyzing that structure, I simultaneously discovered an interpretive framework to support the entire enterprise of ministry. Seymour and Miller describe this concept:

> In the human sciences, considerable attention has been given to the way persons come to experience and define reality. A conviction emerging from this research is that human beings construct models, paradigms, and myths which serve as **interpretive frameworks to help them limit, organize, and act** upon impressions. In short, these models, constructed from personal life stories and understandings of reality taught by the culture, provide lenses through which the world is focused, and define patterns, experiences, and facts to which individuals must respond.
>
> On the basis of (this) research, it has become clear that the uncovering and analysis of interpretive frameworks are of utmost importance because these frameworks and the metaphors they employ define the way reality is structured (Seymour and Miller 1982).

Viewed from a philosophical perspective, we observe that as people develop their interpretive frameworks, they simultaneously formulate a perception of life and living known as a worldview. This perspective in turn frames and provides footing for a distinct approach to education, commonly referred to as a philosophy of education.

Toward a Philosophy of Christian Education

A philosophy of education can be considered from two discrete perspectives. The first is the application of philosophical concerns, such as metaphysics, epistemology, and axiology, to educational practice. The second is the identification of the philosophical foundations and the formulation of "a statement of the **essential basic principles** which when put together provide the rudder to guide and govern the educational aims and the total curriculum or program" (Chadwick 1982). George Knight attempted to integrate both approaches in his book *Philosophy and Education* (1998), and I will pay attention to both in this work. Applying the concepts of philosophy to education will be addressed by way of a graphic overview provided in an appendix. Identifying the essential basic principles is utilized here in Part III as we explore the five questions.

In establishing these essential principles we accomplish at least three major tasks: 1) We establish the parameters of a really good, really global approach to education and leadership that can be utilized and implemented anywhere, with anyone. 2) We create a philosophical filter that, like a screen door, allows in only profitable elements and restricts the inappropriate. The tighter the grid, the more efficient the filter – allowing, as Frank Ryan suggested previously, both the free flow of new ideas and the disposal of the obsolete. 3) We formulate the primary components of a rubric to ascertain whether or not we are being successful in our disciple making. Put simply, we devise a checklist to both guide our planning and assess our efforts.

Looking Forward

In essence, the exposition that is contained in the next five chapters is one man's attempt to identify the interpretive framework that gives structure to the disciplines of (Christian) education and leadership. By addressing five critical inquiries, the essential basic principles that provide a philosophy of ministry emerge to give direction and distinctiveness to the educative process.

Foundations for Ministry

As I mentioned in the Prologue, the exploration of the five questions originated in my quest for an understanding of Christian education and evolved into an examination of the foundations for any ministry endeavor. Although I will continue to frame the inquiries in their original language (e.g., "What is education?" as opposed to "What is ministry?"), the answers have implications and applications for any attempt to induce and influence others to follow Jesus.

A Different Design

With that preface to the content and contour of the next five chapters, I want to acknowledge two slight variations in format for Chapters 8-12. The first is that after a brief introduction, each chapter will consist of two major sections: "Concerns Critical to the Inquiry" and "Activities Essential to an Application." In these two segments, I will introduce the essential basic principles that constitute the structure of the discipline and explore some of the enriching ramifications for practical implementation.

Principal Principles

The second variation is that at the end of each of the five chapters I will identify three Principal Principles that underlie the investigation and serve as summary conclusions. These fifteen observations were formulated as a result of an exercise in cataloging and condensing my convictions for an Introduction to Christian Education course I taught in a Bible institute. I designed them as a simple and easy way to outline, and hopefully remember, the key concepts from each segment of the study. Two decades later, I still believe they accomplish that purpose. I recommend a serious consideration of the principles embedded in them – along with the included Prime Characteristics and Essential Activities – and how they summarize and inform this study. They may be conceived as the first pegs to be attached to the theoretical sorting and storing rack we are constructing.

Factors that Frame

In addition to these alterations within the chapters, I have included in Appendix A a graphic depiction of the five lines of inquiry that define, describe, and direct the philosophy of Christian education, or discipleship ministries, presented in Part III. Consisting of the "Factors that Frame the Investigation" and concisely identifying the necessary Biblical Foundations, Theological Pre-Suppositions, Philosophical Concerns, Scientific Considerations, and Educational Assumptions and Praxis for each of the five questions, each component of the graphic contains a representative sample of the issues and concerns that inform the investigation. Although no attempt has been made to be exhaustive in scope or depth, I have tried to acknowledge the critical components I addressed in my personal research. Most of these issues can be explored in a comprehensive manner by exposure to the sources catalogued in the Works Cited Reference List in Appendix B. I recommend, especially, the above-noted text by Knight, Pazmiño's *Foundational Issues in Christian Education* (1997), and Estep, Anthony, and Allison's *A Theology for Christian Education* (2008).

With this preamble preparing the way, let us commence Part III of our educational journey. We will begin by addressing the definitive inquiry: what is (Christian) education?

PART III
"Go, make disciples"

*Then Jesus came to them and said, "All authority in heaven and on earth has been given to me. Therefore **go** and **make disciples** of all nations, baptizing them in the name of the Father and of the Son and of the Holy Spirit, and teaching them to obey everything I have commanded you" (Matthew 28:18-20).*

Preview Pane:
Outline and Chapter Synopsis

Chapter 8 – What Is (Christian) Education?
"What is education?" and "What makes it Christian?" are the driving and definitive inquiries addressed in this chapter. A functional and original definition of education is presented and explained, and an investigation of the people, purposes, processes, and products that make it Christian is undertaken.

Chapter 9 – What Is the Content of Education?
How an educator chooses lessons and the forms they may take are the central concerns of this chapter. Highlighted is a functional outline and strategy for individual and institutional curricular and program planning.

Chapter 10 – What Are the Processes of Education?
How do people learn? How do I teach? What do I need to know about methods? Are there any plans I can follow? These practical concerns are the focus of this chapter. Building upon the teaching-learning model presented in Part II, along with eight biblical observations, this chapter recommends an appropriate lesson plan format and methods for implementing it.

Chapter 11 – What Is the Context of Education?
How do I best group students for learning? What kind of an organizational structure should I utilize? In attending to questions such as these, the family metaphor for educational organization is introduced and recommended.

Chapter 12 – Who Are the People Involved in Education?
The Godhead, the individual, teachers, leaders, and family members are all involved in the educational process. This chapter explores their functions and some of the critical and guiding principles affecting relationships and ministry contexts.

Eight
What Is (Christian) Education?

As a highly decorated veteran of over thirty years in public education, my father-in-law was the logical choice to contact when I was ruminating over the definition of *teaching*. His response to my inquiry was as stunning as it was simple: "Teaching is creating an environment in which a student just might learn." For nearly thirty years, I have had a love-hate relationship with that definition and approach to education. I love it because I believe teaching is creative, bordering on an art form, and I have always believed that the environment is a critical piece of the education puzzle, frequently being referred to as the hidden curriculum. I dislike it because I am not sure a teacher has taught unless someone has learned, and simply creating an environment feels too passive.

When I began asking the question, "What is (Christian) education?" and its attendant concern, "What is teaching?" I was being strongly influenced by three distinct, but related, forces: 1) church renewal and the passionate authors of the 1960s and 1970s; 2) reformed theology and its approach to education; and 3) although I did not know it by name then, the socialization approach to education. The common component in each of these influences was an emphasis upon *community*. My exposure to and relationship with Lyman Coleman and Serendipity House only served to reinforce a growing conviction that environment mattered, and helping people to experience *koinonia* and the unity it facilitated was a legitimate goal for Christian educators. In fact, one of my early attempts at an answer to the question "What is…" was articulated as "the process of developing and communicating a Christian culture."

Little did I realize that my journey would take me full circle, and I would do my doctoral research and dissertation on the perceived socialization of Christian home-educated students. In researching socialization, ritual, and the proponents of such an approach to education (e.g., Bushnell, Groome, and Richards), I came face-to-face, again, with the community component of the educational enterprise. I am still reflecting upon the impact of creating an environment for learning, whether known as context, culture, or community. My father-in-law's perception that a teacher creates an environment landed in very fertile soil, and the love component of my relationship with this definition took root.

On the other hand, I also had to contend with the "hate" component of my reaction. The fertile soil that produces the wheat of community also supports the chaff of focusing on the group to promote corporate success and leaving personal needs and maturation issues unattended. I mentioned in Part I my disdain for individuals and service industries that have abandoned their true call to serve people for the sake of the bottom line and the supposed good of the company. Jesus did not ignore an individual for the sake of his mission. After all, people were his mission. To put it simply, an approach to education or a definition of teaching that does not place a primary emphasis and focus on personal growth and development is incompatible with "Christian" education.

Personal experiences along the way contributed to this paradoxical notion of accommodating community without sacrificing individuality. One of those was a season of ministry in conservative charismatic churches and movements. I was highly impressed by the emphasis upon the gifts of the Spirit for each individual, but I was also dismayed at the lack of concern for the common good and the expectation that the community and all of its members would benefit (1Corinthians 12:7).

To illustrate this tension, a woman in a church I once served stated that her gift was a private matter between her and God. She had no conception of using her gift for others in the Body of Christ. When a prominent leader, however, encouraged emerging charismatics to try out their gifts on others with the encouragement, "Don't worry if you make a mistake; you'll be forgiven and learn from it," thus promoting the maturation of the community and its leadership, my heart went out to those individuals who were being experimented upon. They were spiritual guinea pigs and the victims of incompetent spiritual practices. Stated succinctly, it is essential to recognize that the community is composed of individuals, some of whom are hurting and in need of ministry beyond the growth of the group. As a consequence of this perception, I now approach educational opportunities from the perspective that touching individual lives first is the key to truly bring increase and maturation to the community and its culture. I know there are some theopolitical implications in that last statement, but that is for another book.

A definition of teaching and the description of education must spotlight the student while simultaneously addressing the community and culture of which the learner is a part. I conclude, therefore, that the idea of education must include both personal and communal dimensions. That, however, only serves to introduce the subject. To fully comprehend the concept requires that we dig a little deeper.

Concerns Critical to the Inquiry

By conviction, training, and experience, I am an educator, a Christian educator. When people ask me what I do, I am tempted to answer, "Educate!" That, however, begs the question for most; they want to know in what activities I engage and why they matter. After all, it is obvious that people can learn without formal instruction, and more than one student has a story to tell about a teacher who discouraged rather than stimulated their pursuit of learning. What I do and why I do it is a critical concern because it justifies and validates the reason for my existence and why God calls anyone to this ministry.

Education: What Is It?

We shall commence our exploration of the first of the five questions that frame and give structure to the discipline with an investigation of two concerns critical to our inquiry: what is education, and what makes it Christian?

Since uncovering the *what* is meaningless without understanding the *why*, we will address the biblical foundation for educational ministry first. In doing so, we will mine the data for some clues that may assist us in formulating a definition of education.

The Biblical Mandate

The sacred Scriptures provide a plethora of data in the form of both principles and practices that inform our exploration of education. A number of Christian educators before me have investigated, cataloged, and then codified their research under titles that encompass the teaching techniques of Jesus, explorations of wisdom literature, and training disciples, to name a few.

In addition to these complete works, one can also pursue individual studies of key concepts and words. Some of the most interesting references of this type are found in Ron Chadwick's *Teaching and Learning*, which contains a two-page table of "Bible Words for the Teaching-Learning Process," an accompanying five-page explanatory appendix, and a summary catalogue, "The Study of the 72 References to *Preaching* in the New Testament" (Chadwick 1982). Chadwick and the others have provided a wonderful service by bringing together this vast collection of biblical selections.

These references, however, only acknowledge that education does take place in the biblical context. What informs this study and provides the contemporary Christian educator with impetus and inspiration are the suggestions and directions that form a mandate to implement. For example, the Israelite nation has long accepted the challenge to teach their children the *Shema*, the Christian community has received the commission to make disciples, and all of humankind has assumed an educative imperative in the charge to subdue the earth. Progress cannot be made if every generation must discover afresh the advances their predecessors made.

Toward a Definition of Education: Crucial Components

Suffice it to say we have received a biblical mandate to transmit knowledge and educate – to go make disciples. What then are the crucial components and impacting principles that inform and give direction to this imperative? It is to these inquiries we now turn our attention.

Scriptural Indications

Let us begin by reflecting upon four representative passages and consider what they indicate concerning an understanding of education:

> *Ecclesiastes 7:29: This only have I found: God made mankind upright, but men have gone in search of many schemes.*

> *2 Timothy 3:16, 17: All Scripture is God-breathed and is useful for teaching, rebuking, correcting and training in righteousness, so that the man of God may be thoroughly equipped for every good work.*

> *Colossians 1:28: We proclaim him, admonishing and teaching everyone with all wisdom, so that we may present everyone perfect in Christ.*

> *Ephesians 4:16-18: From him the whole body...grows and builds itself up in love, as each part does its work. So I tell you this, and insist on it in the Lord, that you must no longer live as the Gentiles do, in the futility of their thinking. They are darkened in their understanding and separated from the life of God because of the ignorance that is in them due to the hardening of their hearts.*

A cursory examination of these and other Scriptures reveal a number of salient features for a comprehension and description of education:

- The product is intended to be corrective
- The process is instructional
- The process is inspirational
- The process is individual and relational
- The product is intended to be completion

Advancing beyond this initial description, we will explore other indications and then extrapolate a tentative, but suggestive, definition of education. Our next step will be to examine the theoretical basis for that definition; therefore, the following section contains a scholarly perspective that might demand a slower and more thoughtful read.

Scholarly Indications

Educational psychologists currently perceive learners as *passive, active,* or *interactive* regarding their contact with the environment. Based, primarily, on the distinctions between these conceptions, Bigge and Shermis identify and differentiate three families of learning theories. Passive theories of the "behaviorist family" describe human learning as a component of the psychological characteristics that are the product of environmental forces. Active theories of the "mind substance family" describe human learning as a component of the psychological nature that is the product of internal forces. In this family of theories, the environment simply serves as a context for the processes of natural unfoldment. Interactive theories of the "cognitive family" describe human learning as an attempt to make sense of the physical and social environment, as the psychological nature emerges from these connections (Bigge and Shermis 1999). Utilizing language that we encountered in Chapter 5, the interactionist (or cognitive) family of theories is an emergent synthesis, incorporating the strengths of each of the others. As we shall see, this synthesis has a biblical as well as a theoretical foundation, and articulates a well-balanced approach to the educational enterprise.

In our attempt to define education, the distinction between passive and active learning is of particular interest. One of the notable differences between them is that passive learning involves accepting another's transmitted content, while active learning involves reflecting upon one's own constructed knowledge. Simply put, to facilitate learning, passive theories depend upon external influences while active theories depend upon internal influences. We can anticipate some of the implications of this and other differences by considering the resemblance to a distinction writers make. When composing a document, authors distinguish between passive and active voice, which is analogous to the way educators distinguish between passive and active learning theories when preparing to teach.

In writing, a passive construction occurs in a sentence when the object of an action takes the place of the subject. For example, when stating that, "A lesson was learned by Jack," the author employs the passive voice, placing the primary emphasis upon the object, "lesson," rather than the subject, "Jack." Theories that perceive learners as passive similarly concentrate their attention upon the lesson, and the learner's responsibility to accept transmitted knowledge and objective meaning is emphasized.

On the other hand, in writing, an active construction occurs when the subject performing the action is the center of attention. When stating that, "Jack learned a lesson," the author employs the active voice, placing the primary emphasis upon the subject, "Jack," rather than the object, "lesson." Theories that perceive the learner as active similarly concentrate their attention upon the learner, and the responsibility to construct knowledge or personal meaning of the lesson is emphasized.

Chadwick affirms this distinction; however, he asserts that the essence of education is a synthesis of both the transmission of culture-critical content, often simply referred to as "putting in" (a passive approach), and the nurture of creator-imbued characteristics and powers, or "drawing out" (an active approach):

> *The etymology of the word education provides additional insight as to the nature of the process.*
>
> *Generally, the idea obtains that the word education comes from the Latin term educere, which is of the third conjugation and means "to lead out." Education is thought of, therefore, in terms of drawing out the powers inherent in the person and developing them. In other words, it carries the idea of expression. The idea is good as applied to education, but unfortunately, it is not involved in the word itself. For were the word derived from the third conjugation, it would have to be "eduction" instead of "education."*
>
> *Looking a little further, we find that if the word is from the first conjugation then the form is educare. This term, however, has a very different meaning. Instead of signifying "to lead or draw out," it means "to nourish or nurture." This carries*

the idea of supplying food or sustenance rather than drawing out or exercising. It is the "impressional" rather than the "expressional" idea. From this viewpoint education consists in supplying ideas or inspiration more than securing responses.

A full conception of the educational process, however, requires both ideas. First, there is an infilling process which includes the inculcation of ideas and the forming of ideals. Second, there is a drawing out aspect which includes the activity side. In other words, a complete process of education includes both impression and expression—nourishing and exercise (Chadwick 1982).

Slavin also addresses both of these dimensions when he suggests that teachers utilize "direct instruction as well as discussion, cooperative learning, and other constructivist techniques." He observes that "these methods are often posed as different philosophies, and the ideological wars over which is best go on incessantly (see Berg & Clough, 1990/91, Hunter, 1990/91; Joyce, Weil, & Calhoun, 2004, Presley et al., 2003). Yet few experienced teachers would deny that teachers must be able to use all of them and must know when to use each," and that they "should be seen not as representing two sharply conflicting philosophies of education, but as complementary approaches to be used at different times for different purposes" (Slavin 2006). Thus, most passive theories acknowledge that learners also identify and "construct" personal and practical applications of the lesson, as they "actively" listen, observe, and in other ways participate in the learning experience.

Solomon likewise acknowledges the same balance in Proverbs 2:1, 2 (KJV) as he encourages, "*My son, if thou wilt receive my words, and ... apply thine heart to understanding.*" In other words, in joining Bigge and Shermis, along with Chadwick and Slavin, a biblical approach recognizes both passive and active components in an emergent synthesis. A teacher, therefore, is confronted with the challenge of exchanging data believed to be universal truth while also facilitating the opportunity for students to explore and express that truth as they perceive and experience it in life. As discussed previously, these processes occur within both individual and institutional contexts.

Merging the Dimensions of Education

Considering the evidence we have examined so far – personal and communal contexts along with passive and active aspects – education can be understood as a conjunction of two axes of continuums: Individual/Corporate and Transmission/Reflection. The intersection of these dimensions of education produces four quadrants of activity. Display 8 demonstrates this, with sample behaviors extracted from religious ministries for each quadrant.

Display 8. The Dimensions of Education

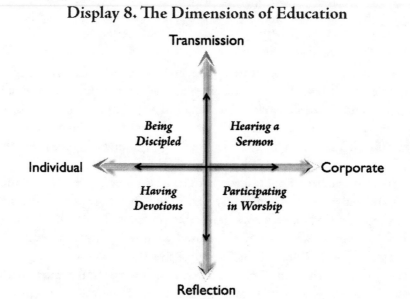

Since formal schooling is the most dominant form of education practiced today, it may prove beneficial to explore some teacher and student behaviors that exemplify each of the quadrants. The Sunday school teacher who tells a story to six third-graders engages the Transmission-Corporate dimension, while answering a specific question or sharing with a child after class demonstrates Transmission-Individual activity. The two Reflection quadrants can be illustrated by personal prayer and working on worksheets as individuals or by a group creating a role play in response to the lessons learned in class that day.

Reference to some common practices of educators and leaders as they perform the everyday activities of their ministries can also easily exemplify these dimensions. Consider the following behaviors and how they illustrate each of the respective quadrants:

- *Personal Tutoring and Job Descriptions* are examples of the **Transmissive/Individual** function
- *Preaching and Vision Casting* illustrate **Transmissive/Corporate** behaviors
- *Conducting Services and Workshops* are representative of **Corporate/Reflective** practices
- *Counseling and Personal Goal Setting* are samples of **Individual/Reflective** concerns

One can readily see that all four dimensions are frequently utilized to create a well-rounded and balanced educational experience for students. They also provide a framework for curricular preference options, including learning styles and inclinations, which will be explored in detail in Chapter 10.

Proposing a Definition of Education

Proceeding from what we have discovered, yet anticipating further explication, I define education as follows: *Education is the creative process of utilizing external and internal forces to facilitate the functions of teaching and training in promoting and attaining growth and development, enabling complete individuals to comprehend, contemplate, and contribute to their community and culture.*

People learn and grow because of all of the educational activities we have identified and illustrated in this volume; therefore, it would be inappropriate to select one axis or one quadrant as descriptive or definitive of the educational endeavor. In acknowledging the diversity of educational experience, an identification and analysis of the impacting principles that inform and give direction to the discipline not only helps define and describe the educational process, it also assists in determining prescriptive practices.

Exploring a Description of Education: Impacting Principles

My proposed definition anticipates transmissive and reflective delivery systems intended to nourish and exercise, both personally and corporately. It also contains notions and conceptions that, in order to be fully appreciated, need to be expanded and clarified. These impacting principles will be examined in the next few pages, where I will identify and describe the implications and applications of this definition.

Education is the <u>Creative</u> process

While at lunch one day with Daniel, a friend of mine, education became the topic of conversation. At one point in the discussion, I offered the observation that teaching was an art – a suggestion he quickly refuted. Daniel was and always will be an engineer. He was also a manager within the department where he worked. This dual role generated within him the conviction that the manager's greatest tool was the computer and that management was a science not an art. As we talked, I was reminded of two books I had read on teaching and learning. My college mentor had given me Gilbert Highet's text, *The Art of Teaching* (1957), and I had been stirred by the author's conviction that teaching could not be reduced to formulas and mechanical techniques. Highet explained this perspective in the book's introduction:

> [*This book*] *is called The Art of Teaching because I believe that teaching is an art, not a science. It seems to me very dangerous to apply the aims and methods of science to human beings as individuals, although a statistical principle can often be used to explain their behavior in large groups and a scientific diagnosis of their physical structure is always valuable. But a "scientific" relationship between human beings is bound to be inadequate and perhaps distorted. Of course it is necessary for any teacher to be orderly in planning his work and precise in his dealing with facts. But that does not make his teaching "scientific." Teaching involves emotions, which cannot be systematically appraised and employed, and human values, which are quite outside the grasp of science. A "scientifically" brought-up child would be a pitiable monster. A "scientific" marriage would be only a thin and crippled version of a true marriage. A "scientific" friendship would be as cold as a chess problem. "Scientific" teaching, even of scientific subjects, will be inadequate as long as both teachers and pupils are human beings. Teaching is not like inducing a chemical reaction; it is much more like painting a picture or making a piece of music, or on a lower level like planting a garden or writing a friendly letter. You must throw your heart into it, you must realize that it cannot all be done by formulas, or you will spoil your work, and your pupils, and yourself* (Highet 1957).

A few years later, however, while I was engaged in a serious study of educational psychology, I encountered Robert Biehler's counter proposal:

> *Some educators (e.g., Highet, 1957) argue that teaching is an art that cannot be taught in a scientific way, and they even maintain that a scientific approach may interfere with effective teaching. This text is based on a diametrically opposed point of view: Scientific information can be of particular value to future teachers…and the suggestion is offered that you strive to act as a teacher-theorist even as you function as a teacher-artisan, or teacher-practitioner (Biehler 1978).*

In reflecting upon these apparently conflicting perceptions, I came to the personal conclusion that the answer is virtually paradoxical: a teacher creatively utilizes scientifically based skills and techniques to produce a work of academic art in an individual's life.

A painter acquires skill in a craft that requires a variety of brushes and strokes; a musician masters the mathematical science that underlies the tones and tunes he creates; and the sculptor attains an ability to manipulate the tools that allow him to reveal the images hidden in metal and stone. In the same way, a teacher draws upon tools, techniques, and personal dexterity honed in countless hours of practice, including scrutiny of and experimentation with a wide variety of instructional implements and methodologies. The "tricks of the trade" are usually well established and universally applied devices founded upon painstaking research and some painful experiences. Thus, science provides the foundation, and enables the skill set, upon which an "artistic" education may be established.

Education is the creative <u>Process</u>

As with artisans, educators cannot simply snap their fingers and instantly produce a product. Inquire of any instructor or trainer and they will quickly affirm that teaching is hard work. *Work* because it demands the exertion of much energy, and *hard* because it seems to encounter obstacles at every turn. If, however, it were *easy play* it would still require a series and sequence of steps and procedures to generate its intended outcome, the learning of a lesson.

Education as Process and Product

The term *process* implies that procedures are implemented and steps are taken. These activities are the practices that, when creatively applied, do produce a product. Nonetheless, I have often encouraged teachers, ministers, and leaders to recognize that making progress is a valid indicator in evaluating success. In other words, I look to see if there is improvement, growth, or even minimal movement in the right direction. Specific failures are much more readily accepted and addressed when it is obvious that general progress is being made and positive steps are being taken. Hence, I often utilize the phrase "process over product" to emphasize the priority of progress.

Being "in process," therefore, is a very positive statement. It implies that someone or something is working and advancement is evident. Since we will more fully address the processes of educational activity in Chapter 10, it is sufficient at this time to acknowledge that an educator should be as concerned with the growing of the student as with the measuring of the student's growth.

Education as Cycle of Event and Process

The adult education movement of the mid-twentieth century taught us much about the differences between the way adults and children learn. Central among these distinctions was the observation that a crisis event, such as a birth, a death, a new job, a marriage, a divorce, or even a novel experience was more often than not the motivator that moved an adult to pursue a new learning opportunity. For example, I learned to live one day at a time as the event of my schedule change altered my perception and understanding of planning. The experience of the police officer who failed to communicate precipitated a process that changed his perception of the behaviors of leadership. To put it simply, for adults, *event precipitates process.*

Children, on the other hand, receive instruction and engage in learning in order to prepare for life. Whether it is a skill learned in the kitchen under the tutelage of their mother, a technique acquired from the Little League coach or dance instructor, or the formal preparation received in the school setting, youngsters are constantly getting ready for something. This truth was brought home to me while sitting in a junior high class. The teacher had just assigned homework for the night, when from the back of the room came a fellow student's voice, "Why do we have to learn this?" The startled teacher's reply was, "Because you will need this in high school." Without missing a beat, the student retorted, "When are you going to stop preparing us and start teaching us something?" Neither the teacher nor the class knew how to respond; thankfully, the bell rang and we scattered. The point, however, was made. To put it simply, for children, *process prepares for the event,* and even young adults do not want to be treated as children.

As an introduction to this conception of education as a cycle of events and processes, consider how life begins with an event, conception, which is then supported by a nine-month process. The event of birth then precipitates another series of processes, growth and development. This sequence – event then process – continues in early childhood until approximately the age of five, at about the time compulsory education or schooling begins. At that point, we find the sequence reversing itself, and students are now processed educationally and prepared for the events of life. This continues until adolescence, the onset of young adulthood, at which time the sequence again reverses itself and events precipitate the process of education. In other words, each learner continually finds himself at a point along a developmental continuum.

In summary, infants learn through events that precipitate a process. For example, they learn from experience, "Ouch! Oh, I'd better not touch the stove when it's hot." Grade school children learn through the process of preparing for events. For example, they learn that turning on the stove is the first step in cooking; this is similar to my campers learning to swim, and thus being prepared to jump off the board. Finally, adults learn through a process precipitated by events. Now in the kitchen, we find comments such as, "Ooooh, I like that. I think I'll learn how to prepare it."

To put it simply, children learn to live while adults live to learn.

Education is the creative process of utilizing the functions of <u>Teaching and Training</u>

Facilitating the acquisition and formation of powers and capacities, collaborated with the communicating of knowledge and experience, form the complementary dyad known as training and teaching, respectively. A teacher cannot teach without training, and training is dependent upon teaching. They are interdependent educational processes, equally essential to the promotion of the primary goals of education – growth and development. These complementary, yet distinct, functions of education are critical to the process and were addressed in the Preamble to Part II and in some depth in Chapter 5.

Education is the creative process of <u>Promoting</u>

We had spent a morning in pre-service orientation, and the faculty had dutifully given their attention to the virtually mindless details of school administration. After lunch I decided it was time to shake things up a bit, so we participated in a forced choice event where I asked them to agree or disagree with my proposed definition of education. Those who agreed went to one side of the room and those who disagreed formed a group on the other side. We quickly identified the battleground: those who disagreed believed that education should not or could not be promoted. We were equally swift to acknowledge that the debate centered on semantics and definition. No one wanted education perceived as something to be marketed, and most agreed that what I had in mind was the idea of motivation. Well, yes and no.

A quick look at a dictionary reveals three primary definitions of *promote*: to advance something or someone (such as in rank); to support or encourage; or to advertise. The debate that day focused on advertising, but I was making the case that education involved supporting and encouraging students so that they may advance in their knowledge, understanding, or skill. Learning a specific concept in isolation may require little outside influence or motivation, but to truly become educated demands the efforts of an instructor and the community at large to support, encourage, and advance the pupil's attainment of growth and development. In other words, most learning is mediated, and that medium is often another person who promotes the process.

Education is the creative process of promoting and <u>Attaining</u>

Process without product, however, is nothing more than spinning wheels that never make contact with the ground; no progress or advancement is achieved. To be truly educated, one must have accomplished or achieved something, and reached some intended goal or state of growth. This is the simple explanation of *attaining*.

In Part II, as we explored the teaching-learning process, I advocated for the thesis that learning produces an alteration – the student experiences a change in what is known, felt, or is able to be performed – that extends or enriches previous capacities. In order for true learning and effective education to take place, some change must occur in the learner's life. While the question of what that something consists is probably a curricular concern, we can summarize the expectations in two words: growth and development.

Education is the creative process of promoting and attaining <u>Growth and Development</u>

As noted in the Preamble to Part II, when the prophet Isaiah encouraged his hearers and readers to "lengthen your cords, [and] strengthen your stakes" (Isaiah 54:2), he provided a concise summary of every educator's dream: an increase in the learner's knowledge and understanding that is accompanied by an improvement in the learner's competency or capacity. To lengthen the cords symbolizes an increase in capacity, while strengthening the stakes represents an increase in stability or maturity. In other words, growth and development are facilitated.

Coaching junior high boys' basketball provided me with some excellent experience and, as I have noted before, some interesting anecdotes. During my time as a coach, I frequently noticed the disparity between the physical size and the coordination of my players. The tallest, biggest, or strongest boys were frequently the least coordinated. The figurative picture of a gangly, awkward teenage boy was often true. Their cords were long but their stakes were not strong; their skill development had not caught up with their physical growth.

As noted previously, many current theorists believe some level of development is a necessary prerequisite to any form of learning. Therefore, the study of human development is an important endeavor for anyone involved in the care and nurture of others. Consideration of the physical, mental, emotional, social, and especially spiritual aspects of a person may well provide a key to future learning.

Education in the Third Dimension

Maturity (development) must always accompany an increase in capacity (growth), whether this increase is in knowledge that demands wisdom, physical growth that demands coordination, or spirituality that demands holiness. This is true of human beings, and it is equally true for the organizations they frequent, such as churches, schools, or businesses where increasing numbers require escalating administration, especially management. Maturation psychology and growth management are, therefore, additional resources worthy of exploration and investigation for educators and leaders alike.

Display 8 was utilized earlier as a graphic attempt to represent the interplay between the functions of transmission and reflection with the dimensions of individual and corporate education. I would now like to add a third axis to that display – one that represents a continuum of the aspects of growth and development – in order to complete the array of components involved in education. Three-dimensional education acknowledges the interplay and impact upon teaching and training of three intersecting ingredients perceived as continuums (Display 9):

- Transmissive and Reflective activities,
- Individual and Corporate contexts,
- Growth and Development aspects of the process.

Display 9. Three-Dimension Education

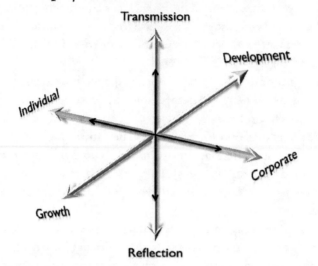

We must appreciate each of the dimensions and not err by minimizing or diminishing the necessary preparation and planning that should go into balancing all three in an effective educational experience. Since this three-dimensional representation is valid for virtually every educational activity and opportunity, illustrations and applications should not be hard to find. In fact, they exist in every venue and version of education. For example, while attending weekend events or even church services, it would be beneficial for leaders and teachers to spend some time observing and reflecting upon the educational activity that they perceive to be going on in the hearts and lives of the participants as they proceed through the experience.

The first to be noticed would no doubt be the Individual-Corporate dynamic. The up front leader, of course, has the aggregate audience and overall program in view, while a burned-out young administrative assistant has a more personal agenda to be addressed. On the Transmissive – Reflective continuum, small group leaders, with usually less than an hour to teach and train, find themselves more often than not in transmissive modes, while the attendees are hoping for the opportunity to have their questions answered and the time to reflect upon personal applications of the information provided. Add to this mix, from the Growth-Development axis, the inexperienced first-timer coerced into joining the team that plans and prepares the orientation reception, and we have a three-dimensional look at the components of educational practice. Corporate concerns intermingle with individual needs; lecture methods clash with contemplative contexts; and novices are encouraged to run before they can walk.

I have planned and participated in countless numbers of these events because they offer a variety and balance of educational experiences. With appropriate planning and foresight, these meetings can be beneficial for all the participants. For example, the traditional lecture or keynote address (Transmission-Corporate-Growth) can be balanced and enriched by breakout sessions that explore the implications and applications of the critical concepts presented (Reflection-Corporate-Development). A panel discussion may also provide the opportunity to expand upon or even challenge concepts and ideas presented in the general sessions (Transmission-Corporate-Growth). A lengthy lunchtime may be utilized to facilitate the opportunity for individuals or small groups to consider and meditate upon the material encountered that morning (Reflection-Individual or Corporate). Books, take-home materials, and resources can be distributed for further individual study (Transmission-Individual-Growth), and a provocative film may be shown to stimulate consideration of possible applications of the issues addressed over the weekend (Reflection-Corporate-Development).

Attempting an Answer: What is Education?

In summary, let us revisit my definition of education: *Education is the creative process of utilizing external and internal forces to facilitate the functions of teaching and training in promoting and attaining growth and development, enabling complete individuals to comprehend, contemplate, and contribute to their community and culture.* This process anticipates both personal and corporate maturation, operates in both transmissive and reflective content distribution modes, and facilitates an increase in both capacity and maturity.

Nurture that promotes personal maturation, spiritual formation, scholastic success, and contribution to the community is a well-balanced education that includes, but goes beyond, technical or vocational training. It inspires the soul to articulate itself in academic achievement, creative expressions, and interpersonal skills such as communication.

Education: What Makes It Christian?

When Jesus proclaimed the simple goal of being perfect as our Heavenly Father is perfect, he raised the bar and declared that the standards pagans meet are inadequate for his disciples (Matthew 5). A true Christian education demands that both teacher and learner are committed to a process of producing excellence in academic achievement, professional competence, and personal maturation. This process must produce disciples who worship Jesus and proclaim him to the world, utilizing knowledge and competencies acquired in the processes of reconciliation, restoration, correction, and perfection.

Thus, a Christian education engages learners in acquiring the mind and skill sets necessary for an increasingly mature understanding of the Creator, the created order, and themselves as created in the image of God, while also discovering their contribution and place in God's kingdom, as well as their community.

Toward a Christian Education

During my second year as a church educator, I was standing outside a private Christian school classroom sharing an afternoon break and listening to a teacher complain about some unsatisfactory elements of his day. An initially friendly, pleasant, and simple conversation instantly turned provocative and reflective. Growing increasingly weary of hearing how difficult his life in school education was, I retorted, "You ought to be in Christian education!" To which he responded, "I thought I was!" I, of course, was referring to the education programs of a church (*Christian* education), while he was thinking of compulsory education in his school (Christian *education*).

Two years later, I found myself serving as the principal of that school in addition to my church responsibilities. The programmatic distinctions we were making that day suddenly became subservient to a more encompassing distinction: what makes any education Christian? By then, our church educational program had grown to include camps, clubs, community recreation, ministry training, parent training, and a seven-day a week nursery service. The school had developed a day care component, competitive athletics, and an expansive music program in addition to its emerging academic curriculum. This expansion of our program made me wonder what distinguished all of these activities as Christian education. What made us different from the public school (or, e.g., community outdoor education programs or day-care centers)? What made our Sunday school truly Christian? To focus my concerns and challenge the staff, I presented them with a simple vision: "To be a Christian school, not just a school with Christians in it."

Definitive Components

The challenge we faced was to first identify the components of an education that is truly Christian. In examining Scripture, reading texts and commentaries, reflecting upon personal experiences, and trusting the elusive illumination of inspiration, it became apparent that a vibrant Christian education demanded a theology of personhood, a clear and biblical understanding of our objectives, a practice of pedagogy that imitates the Master's, and results in individuals within the community who acknowledge the Lord, adore him, and act in his service. The application and implementation of the principles discovered in this process became the driving forces behind every decision, plan, and project undertaken. To this day, I still believe that there are four critical components of a thoroughly Christian education: godly and biblical people, purposes, products, and processes.

People

"God created man in his own image" (Genesis 1:27). There can be no better place to begin a discussion of people than "in the beginning." For an education to be Christian, our view and perception of humanity must be rooted in an anthropology that has a *creation* foundation and an *image* orientation, with a theology anchored in the conviction of a personal and sovereign God.

The people who are involved in educational ministry will receive a fuller treatment in Chapter 12. I will briefly address, however, the critical ideas of *God*, *created*, and *image* and the impact they have in this discussion.

The Lord of Education

The entire Godhead is involved in the process and product of discipleship ministry and this is no more clearly stated than in 1Corinthians 12:4-6:

> *There are different kinds of gifts, but the same Spirit. There are different kinds of service, but the same Lord. There are different kinds of working, but the same God works all of them in all men.*

In these verses, we find all three members of the Godhead personally and sovereignly engaged in, and giving direction to, the ministries that occur within the Body of Christ. The Holy Spirit distributes and empowers the gifts; the Lord Jesus determines and directs where and how they will be exercised; and the Father takes responsibility for the outcomes and consequences. This last observation is based upon the wordplay and interaction between the terms *working* and *works*, with the latter signifying the results. What an encouragement for the Christian educator – both the novice volunteer and the seasoned professional depend upon the same source: the present and active involvement of the entire Godhead.

Our theology and the praxis of a truly Christian education are vitally connected to the persons of the Godhead. Psalm 139 indicates that this involvement is more than a superficial management of God's business dealings with man. It is primarily the manifestation of a caring and loving Creator who is in touch with his creation. This fact leads to a brief discussion of the crown of that creation, humanity.

The Crown of Creation

The creation-evolution debate has raged for a century and shows little evidence of subsiding. That dispute will not be engaged here. I simply affirm a conviction that God created the entire universe, including human beings. The primary implication inferred from this position is that educators and other ministers share the responsibility to treat every person with the same care and concern as the Heavenly Father. We cannot refuse to give a cup of cold water, whether it is material, spiritual, or educational. We cannot embrace the attitude of the pastor of a megachurch, referred to in Chapter 7, who refused to conduct a Bible study for a group of less than fifty people. Consider how Nicodemus, Zaccheus, or Lazarus would have felt had Jesus shared this attitude toward people. Education ministers cannot give anything less than their best when they stand before God's people in leadership or education. They are serving him while ministering to others (Matthew 25:40).

The Image of God

The image issue has been the subject of discussion and deliberation for much longer than the creation controversy. There are a few themes within that debate, however, that are pertinent to contemporary Christian education. The first is the conviction that since the nature and constitution of God is trinitarian, it would be logical to assume that man's constitution would be likewise. The importance of this perception, and some of its implications, has been addressed in some detail in previous sections, and will underlie critical components in two of the questions still to be examined in Part III. It is an essential element of the philosophy of Christian education espoused in this work.

A second theme is actually an affirmation concerning the image of God in man, and consists of the recognition that the Lord independently and responsibly makes choices and exercises a will. He created humankind in his image to do likewise. The existence of individual will suggests that we cannot make choices and decisions for our disciple-followers any more than God makes them for us. Our students must make their own, and we must encourage and allow them to do so. We have already noticed the impact of this conception upon the discipline and teaching-learning processes.

There is obviously more to say about the practical impact of being created in God's image upon such issues as creativity, sensitivity to beauty, intentionality, and our distinctiveness from animals, but for the purpose of this study, we will reflect upon one more related theme. While humankind is created in the image of God and has the capacity for choice, all human beings are also conceived in sin (Psalm 51:5). Both pupils and instructors are sinners, and their predispositions have been perverted in the fall. If we anticipate it being otherwise, we will be disappointed and frustrated. An education that is Christian must acknowledge and address this. Thus, one of the primary purposes and goals of making disciple-followers is the regeneration and restoration of fallen men, women, young people, and children.

Purposes

While serving as the principal of a charter school, the yearbook editor asked me to submit a reflection on my expectations and anticipations for students who received a diploma from our high school. In this piece, I identified eight characteristics I wanted to observe in our graduates, and it became the catalyst for a document containing fifteen expectations I came to refer to as *The Marks of Maturity*, representing the standards and anticipated outcomes of a successful secondary education.

While compiling this set of expectations, I had two nagging inquiries: what would it take to make this list "Christian," and does the Bible provide a similar list for maturity in Christ? Although I spent a brief season attempting to make the catalogue Christian, that project was relegated to the shelf after I completed my assignment in secondary education. I did, however, find "lists" of expected attitudes and behaviors in Psalms, Galatians, and Colossians, describing the individual who ascends the holy hill of God, the fruit of the Spirit in a believer's life, and the clothing of Christ's which should adorn his followers. I am still intrigued by the purpose principles I have found dotted throughout the New Testament. It makes sense to me that evidences of maturity in the student are, in essence, evidences of the fulfillment of purposes.

In education, goals and objectives dictate curricular decisions while providing direction and intention to the process. It is appropriate, therefore, to identify our purposes prior to investigating the process activities utilized to accomplish them. So, what are the purposes and intended outcomes of Christian education?

Based upon the explicit directive of Jesus in Matthew 28 and the implicit instruction of multiple texts, the overarching and ultimate goal of Christian education is producing *disciples who worship Jesus.* Disciple making is an all-encompassing educational endeavor, as Spiros Zodhiates observes in *The Hebrew-Greek Key Study Bible:*

> In the Lord's Great Commission (Matthew 28:19, 20), the command is not to go, baptize, or teach, but to make disciples (matheteusate). "Discipling," therefore, is a more comprehensive term than "teaching" (didasko [1315]), involving a commitment of the will as well as an exercise of the intellect. Baptizing (evangelism) and teaching (education) are primary elements of the discipling process (Zodhiates 1984).

This goal can be concentrated and condensed into four objectives that in combination paint a fairly comprehensive picture of the intentions implied in making a disciple through evangelism and education. We will briefly consider each of them: *reconciliation, perfection, restoration,* and *correction.*

Reconciliation

Any endeavor claiming to be Christian must acknowledge and address the gulf that exists between sinful persons and a sinless God. One of the objectives of discipleship ministries, therefore, is the *reconciliation* of these two estranged parties.

> So from now on we regard no one from a worldly point of view. Though we once regarded Christ in this way, we do so no longer. Therefore, if anyone is in Christ, he is a new creation; the old has gone, the new has come! All this is from God, who reconciled us to himself through Christ and gave us the ministry of reconciliation: that God was reconciling the world to himself in Christ, not counting men's sins against them. And he has committed to us the message of reconciliation. We are therefore Christ's ambassadors, as though God were making his appeal through us. We implore you on Christ's behalf: Be reconciled to

God. God made him who had no sin to be sin for us, so that in
him we might become the righteousness of God (2Corinthians
5:16-21).

As Habermas and Issler suggested in their 1992 work *Teaching for
Reconciliation*, this is the foundation of the educational endeavor. It consists
of the two pillars Zodhiates described as evangelism and education. This
dual nature of reconciliation is acknowledged in a number of Scriptural
texts as summarized and condensed in Table 14.

Table 14. The Dimensions of Reconciliation

The Great Commission: Matt 28:16-20	Evangelism Baptism	Education Teach them…
Reconciliation: 2Cor 5:16-21	Position in Christ (vv. 16, 17) Back to God	Practice of Christ (vv. 9, 10, 15, 17) Perfect/complete
Regeneration: John 3:3	A New Life Eph 2:9, et al	A New Life Style Eph 2:19ff, 4:1ff & 5:1ff, Matt 5:48, Col 2:6, 1Thess 2:12, 4:1

Perfection

Once an individual has been reconciled with God, experiencing both an
introduction into new life and instruction in a new lifestyle, participation in
the *perfection* process commences, involving the two objectives of *restoration*
and *correction*. The rubric of perfection is the established expectation of the
man or woman of God engaged in making disciples. When Jesus instructed
his followers to "be perfect, therefore, as your Heavenly Father is perfect"
(Matthew 5:48) and Paul advised the believers in Corinth to "aim for
perfection" (2Corinthians 13:11), they were establishing the benchmark
against which all educational endeavors must be measured.

One of the perceived obstacles in aiming for and attaining perfection is
the legitimate fear that it is an expectation beyond any reasonable prospect,
because no human is capable of God-like perfection. However, a simple word
study, examining the denotation and connotations of the text and context
of these two passages elicits hope and peace rather than fear and trembling.
The term *perfect* is the English translation of a word used to describe the
attainment of an aim, the completion of the work, or the setting out for a
definite border, and can also be translated *purpose* or *result*. It implies the

attainment of a goal; hence, we aim for perfection and become as God-like as is humanly possible. This achievement allows us to reflect, at least partially, his image. In the products of education section, we will see that the completed man is the consequence of an education that is Christian, not a straw man to be pulled down.

Given the nature of the introductory comments to this chapter, it is no surprise that this perfection/completion can be fulfilled in two dimensions: individual and corporate. The individual dimension manifests itself when a person grows in wisdom, stature, and favor with God and man, as illustrated in the life of Jesus (Luke 2:52). This is alternately referred to as maturation. The corporate dimension entails a purposeful education ministry, which will be making sustained progress toward the establishment of a Christian culture inside the societal boundaries that it serves. Since, by definition, a culture is composed of at least four critical behaviors and the resulting manifestations, we should be observing growth in the Christian community's:

- *Construction of a Christian worldview*
- *Conduct of a Christ-like life style*
- *Continuance of the God-ordained institutions*
- *Creation of expressions of reflection and response*

Restoration

Restoration is an integral part of the perfection process and another critical objective in Christian ministry. Consider first the words of the Preacher in Ecclesiastes 7:29, "This only have I found: God made mankind upright, but men have gone in search of many schemes." Consequently, the Apostle Paul had to exhort the Galatians, "Brothers, if someone is caught in a sin, you who are spiritual should *restore* him gently. But watch yourself, or you also may be tempted" (Galatians 6:1). Likewise, the Lord himself will reclaim and restore those who have fallen: "And the God of all grace, who called you to his eternal glory in Christ, after you have suffered a little while, will himself *restore* you and make you strong, firm and steadfast" (1Peter 5:10). God created humankind perfect, complete, good, and in his image, accomplishing all he aimed to do. It is his intention that his image be restored in humankind and that it reflects that image in response to him.

Correction

How restoration is enabled is, in part, a function of the final objective of Christian ministry: *correction*. When an individual stumbles and falls, the courteous and most appropriate response is to offer a hand of help to enable that person to again stand straight. When humanity fell in its rebellion and sin, God offered the life of his son and the hands of his followers to lift men and women again to right standing before him. This idea of restoring to the perpendicular (a "right" angle), straightening again, or in moral terms, rectifying a wrong, is at the heart of the Greek word Paul uses in 2Timothy 3:16 for *correction*: "All Scripture is inspired by God and profitable for teaching, for reproof, for correction, for training in righteousness." Although this passage refers to the preparation of a man of God, a similar concept, utilizing a different word, is also implied in Paul's admonition to Timothy regarding the "correction" of his opponents (2Timothy 2:25).

When a reconciled disciple has been brought back to right standing before God in Christ, that is only the beginning. This new life must take on a new lifestyle in keeping with the nature of the life received and implanted. Perfection, in all of its dimensions and aspects, is the only acceptable manifestation of God's life; however, it is not so easily attained. Hence, the Christian educator and minister must be sensitive and alert to the opportunities to extend a hand to a fallen companion and restore, through correction, that brother or sister to an upright life and lifestyle before the Father.

We turn our attention, then, to the components of that restored life.

Products

Watching a young basketball player noticeably improve his skills, my children excel at academics, and parishioners mature in Jesus are all examples of the success stories we long for as ministers and educators. There is nothing more satisfying and encouraging to a parent, pastor, coach, teacher, or trainer than to see disciples learning, growing, changing, and performing as they have been instructed. These are evidences that the processes work and our purposes can indeed be fulfilled, producing a discernable "product": a complete individual, ready to serve both the Lord and the community. In order to make these intended outcomes simple and memorable, I employ the descriptive terms *perfected person* and *prepared person*.

The Perfected Person, Complete in Jesus, Colossians 1:28

Education, whether referred to as teaching, leading, or making disciple-followers, transforms an individual into something different than he was previously. For the Christian educator, this includes a refurbishing or restoration of the image of God in Christ; the newborn child in God's household (Ephesians 5:19) begins to take on or reacquire the likeness of God in being and lifestyle. In Colossians 1:28, the apostle describes it this way: "We proclaim him, admonishing and teaching everyone with all wisdom, so that we may present everyone *perfect* in Christ."

The question we must ask, then, is, "What are the characteristics of a person who is perfected in Christ?" How do we know if someone has been made complete? The comprehensive answer falls within the domain of the theologian, but in layman's terms, it begins with the simple acknowledgement of personal reconciliation of God and man in Christ. Larry Richards referred to this as "evangelism as education" (Richards 1975). Once a disciple-follower receives forgiveness and new life, a positional perfection is imparted and right standing before the Father is accomplished. The old has passed away and all has become new (2Corinthians 5:17). Education that is Christian commences, therefore, with the restoration of right standing between an individual and God.

As surely as this positional perfection is available, a striving toward practical perfection is assumed. After explaining the great love of God that "made us alive with Christ even when we were dead in transgressions" and "brought [us] near through the blood of Christ," Paul encouraged the believers at Ephesus, "I urge you to live a life worthy of the calling you have received" (Ephesians 2:5; 2:13; 4:1). This calling consists of membership in the household of God (Ephesians 2:19) and, after receiving Christ's name and new life, it anticipates maturation into his lifestyle as well. In Ephesians 4-6, the apostle describes this "perfect" lifestyle and the four marks of maturity that identify a "complete" person in Christ.

Ephesians 4-6: The Marks of Maturity

The first mark identified by Paul is to "make every effort to keep the unity of the spirit in the bond of peace" (4:3). Despite the diversity of gifts and distinctiveness of applications, there is one God and Father working in the one body and through the one Spirit (4:4, 6). "How good and pleasant it is when brothers live together in unity!" (Psalm 133:1). This community, and the resultant *koinonia*, is the first mark of maturity in the family of God, and it justifies the time and energy spent in team building activities such as those discussed in Chapter 3.

The second mark of a perfected person in Christ is right thinking. "So I tell you this, and insist on it in the Lord, that you must no longer live as the Gentiles do, in the futility of their thinking" (4:17). The expected mindset of a believer contains the realization of the necessity to "put off" behaviors such as lying, anger, stealing, and unwholesome speech (4:20-32).

It then produces a person who is "made new in the attitude of your mind; and to put on the new self, created to be like God in true righteousness and holiness" (4:23, 24). Paul affirms this expectation in Romans 12:2, where he encourages believers to be transformed by the renewing of their minds and no longer follow the pattern of this world.

In Part II, we discussed how critical the involvement of the soul or heart was to the teaching-learning process. Helping a follower to think and reflect biblically and critically is one of the primary objectives of a truly Christian education. This kind of mental processing will protect us from the futile thinking of the world, which tempts us to call good evil and evil good, and generates a pattern of reflection that leads to the third characteristic of a perfected person: imitating God (5:1).

The third mark of maturity, "Be imitators of God, therefore..." implies a wholehearted and thorough conversion of the lifestyle to emulate the Father himself. To simplify what this entails, Paul guides his readers through four directives that encapsulate all that it means to imitate the Father:

1. A life of **Love** (vv. 1-7)
2. A life of **Light** (vv. 8-14)
3. A life of **Wisdom** (vv. 15-20)
4. A life of **Submission** (vv. 21 - 6:9)

None of these, however, are possible without the presence and powerful work of the Holy Spirit, so Paul concludes this section of Scripture with the fourth mark of a perfected person: the individual is filled with the Spirit and "strong in the Lord and in his mighty power" (6:10). Taking on the entire panoply of God's armor, the perfected person stands his ground against the enemy and stands firm prepared to do battle on Christ's behalf (6:10-18). The "Perfected Person, Complete in Christ" now becomes the *prepared person.*

The Prepared Person, Ready for Service, Ephesians 4:12

To introduce this segment, I would like to revisit the story told in the Prologue. Despite years of church ministry experiences, a number of formal and informal educational leadership opportunities, and a degree in Christian education from a prestigious program, I felt nonetheless woefully unprepared for my first full time church ministry position. I did have some tools in my belt, and my formal education did provide a foundation. I understood many aspects of the teaching-learning process, and I had been exposed to multiple competent and contemporary models. I was not, however, aware that there was a teaching-learning metamodel rooted in the wisdom literature, that Jesus and Moses provided examples of exemplary administrative concepts and procedures, or that there was a unified and consistent "structure of the discipline" I could investigate and implement in my ministry.

Like so many others before and after me, I was called to an undertaking for which I was only partially prepared. God, however, utilizes the weak and foolish to accomplish his plans, so he has commissioned his pastors and leaders "to prepare God's people for works of service, so that the Body of Christ may be built up" and fully equipped (Ephesians 4:12). It is for this reason that very early in my career I became convinced that making disciples demanded attention to ministry training and leadership development. I could exercise my gifts personally, but I was also expected to help others exercise theirs and prepare them for the works of service to which they had been called and commissioned.

The obvious question, therefore, is, "How can a human educator accomplish this in the life of a disciple-follower?" The answer is the simplistic, "God's work must be done God's way." Discovering God's way and how Christian education is actually accomplished are the issues to which we now turn our attention as we explore the final component of an education that is Christian.

Processes

The processes of an education that is Christian will be explored in further detail in Chapter 10, and Parts I and II provide an exposition of leadership processes and the teaching-learning endeavor. In the following discussion, I will focus on two sections of Scripture that illustrate the truly critical components of an effective relationship between a student disciple and a mentor master.

Ministry Demands Proximity

In the 1970s, one of my favorite sections of the magazine *Christianity Today* was a regular feature entitled "Eutychus and his Kin," a poignant, pithy, and penetrating column that explored contemporary and occasionally contentious concerns in the Christian community. One that particularly caught my attention was a satire on how "quality time" could be advantageous in the church today. Based on a popular premise that effective parenting can be measured by the quality rather than the quantity of time spent with a child, the article surmised that a church service could be more effective and efficient with a high quality ten-minute sermon and a thirty-second prayer.

The implied argument was evident: nothing can replace time with another person.

Day schools, including the ones I served, generally require their faculty to participate in "duty" responsibilities before school, during recesses, at lunch, and after school. In one Christian school, however, we had an effective and revenue-generating day care and outdoor education program that allowed us to hire playground staff to perform these traditional duties. This freed our faculty to spend time with the students; teachers were assigned MOMs – Moments of Ministry – where they were expected to be with and among the students. They ate lunch, played jacks, organized soccer leagues, jumped rope, and sat on the curbs with their charges, conversing and participating in their lives.

The idea was simple: teachers were to get to know their students in real-life situations. They were to watch and listen as the students communicated, calculated, reasoned, and related to one another. Faculty members were to learn about their students' lives, including their backgrounds and the condition of their souls. They were to listen to their charges as they related their stories, needs, fears, and hopes.

The impact of proximity upon a teacher's success with students should be obvious. It provides an effective means of assessing how well they are truly learning their lessons and, as we will see in the next chapter, provides clues as to the next message to be addressed in their curriculum. It also can mitigate embarrassment. A family in my church told me the story of a student at a Christian school who was honored as "Disciple of the Year," a very prestigious award in their elementary program. The pronouncement came as a surprise to many of the girl's classmates who knew her as a liar, cheat, and obnoxious young girl. This provoked the obvious question: how could this happen? The answer was actually simple. The teacher never left her classroom, never went to the playground, and never saw her students outside of the highly regimented and ordered classroom she demanded. This "disciple" mastered the ability to adapt to this regime and endeared herself to the teacher while isolating herself from all her classmates. The teacher only saw the polished classroom demeanor, while the students witnessed her profane playground deportment. Time spent with and among her students could have revealed this condition and motivated the teacher to attend to the obvious hypocrisy the rest of the class observed and experienced.

Two worthy models to imitate, Jesus and Paul, both illustrated a commitment to this critical principle, which is condensed to the axiomatic "ministry demands proximity." When Jesus was ready to commence his public ministry and choose his staff, he "went up on a mountainside and called to him those he wanted... that they might be with him" (Mark 3:13, 14). Most sermons on this passage reflect primarily upon the intended results of this commission, to preach and drive out demons (vv. 14b, 15). I focus, however, on the process Jesus utilized: he called them to be *with* him. Why? It may have taken three years to come to fruition, but consider the observation made about Peter and John by the rulers, elders, and teachers after they had questioned them: "they were astonished and they took note that these men had been *with* Jesus" (Acts 4:5-13). The time that Jesus spent with these men produced amazing results.

Note also Paul's autobiographical description of his ministry to the Thessalonian church:

> *"You know how we lived among you for your sake."*
> *"We were gentle among you..."*
> *"You are witnesses...of how holy...we were among you..."*
> 1 Thessalonians 1:5; 2:7; and 2:10

One cannot be *with* people without being *among* them. Ministry demands proximity. Therefore, a necessary follow-up question must be addressed: what do leaders do when in proximity to their disciples? What are the necessary processes for a ministry of discipleship to be effective when the teacher is with and among the students?

Ministry Deploys Process

Stories and practical applications of truth from life experiences can contribute to an understanding of the many concepts we are studying, but in this case, the brief anecdote recounted by Paul in 1Thessalonians 1:4-8 is sufficient to describe the activities of ministry:

> *For we know, brothers loved by God, that he has chosen you, because our gospel came to you not simply with words, but also with power, with the Holy Spirit and with deep conviction. You know how we lived among you for your sake. You became imitators of us and of the Lord; in spite of severe suffering, you welcomed the message with the joy given by the Holy Spirit. And so you became a model to all the believers in Macedonia and Achaia. The Lord's message rang out from you not only in Macedonia and Achaia-your faith in God has become known everywhere.*

When the Apostle Paul lived among them (v. 5), he declared the gospel, provided them an example to follow, and motivated them to put their faith into practice. In his letter to the Philippians, he summarizes this strategy thus: "Whatever you have learned or received or heard from me, or seen in me – put it into practice" (4:9). These processes will be explored in detail in Chapter 10, but even in this brief look at these verses, Paul makes it clear that he spent time with those to whom he ministered.

After Peter and John had been with Jesus, they astonished the elders and forced them to reconsider their perceptions of Jesus and his disciples. After being exposed to the ministry processes of the Apostle Paul, the faith of the saints in Thessalonica became known everywhere. Christian education, it appears, accomplishes its purpose when believers are thoroughly equipped to minister to others and to their culture at large.

In summary, the processes of effective Christian education are: spending time with and among people; sharing life messages and models; and motivating disciple-followers to do likewise. All effective education incorporates these basic behaviors.

Activities Essential to an Application

Educators, cognizant of the theoretical foundations underlying their practice, comprehend that their successes and failures correlate positively with the quantity and quality of their skill sets. They understand that they must be prepared and equipped with enough ability to implement their theories. Thus, an important balance exists between theory and practice. In other words, it is not enough to know why something is being done; it is also necessary to know how to do it.

As we discussed in the Prologue, the "Essential Activities of Education" constitute the basic skill set necessary to implement the principles extracted from an examination of the five questions. In review, the five activities that we will address in Part III are:

1. Make a Disciple who Worships Jesus
2. Construct a Curricular Plan
3. Prepare a Plan for Teaching and Learning
4. Establish an Environment for Education
5. Have a Heart for and Serve People

The critical inquiry we have investigated in this chapter, "What Is Christian Education?" is answered in the declaration of our purpose and our desired product: "Make a Disciple who Worships Jesus." This phrase also identifies the two components of the essential activity in which educators who strive to be Christian must engage and energize in their student followers: facilitating discipleship and promoting worship.

Disciple-follower: the Perfected Person, Complete in Christ

Three sets of biblical concepts express the necessary and critical components inherent in the constitution of "a disciple who worships Jesus": new birth and lifestyle, positional and practical sanctification, and evangelism and edification (see and compare Table 14). Therefore, the essential activity includes the transmission of the life of Jesus Christ to another and the nurture of this disciple-follower into the disciplined lifestyle that accompanies regeneration. In educational terms, we have identified these concepts as *training*, "the development of capacities," and *teaching*, "the communication of experience" (Gregory 1972). Training, as we have seen, is often synonymous with discipline. Since *discipline* has its root in the word *disciple* and is thus an educative process, the procedure for making disciples is the activity of discipline.

The processes and procedures for effective discipline are explored throughout this work (see Chapters 5, 6, and 10), so a detailed review of those sections is recommended. Let it suffice to say that discipline is exercised as an essential activity of education when the mentor facilitates *communication, choice,* and *consequence(s)* in the disciple-making process.

Worshipper: the Prepared Person, Competent to Serve

Christian education is more than a disciple-follower attaining Christ's life and likeness. The intended result of disciple making is a lifetime and lifestyle of worship, so understanding and practicing it is patently an essential activity of education. When I first began to study worship in the early years of my ministry, there were only a small handful of books readily available on the subject, and the commencement of the intense debates about worship styles was still at least a decade away.

It was during this time that I conducted a weekend retreat focused on the study of worship with the staff and faculty of a children's ministry. Our time together yielded an understanding of, and an experience of, worship that none of us had previously known. After that retreat, and the spiritual growth and development it facilitated, I knew worship was a critical practice for disciple-followers of Jesus as it completes the discipleship process.

In the years since, I have studied, practiced, and taught worship in workshops and seminars for worship leaders and church congregations. Not being a talented musician, my focus has been upon the practice of worshipping the Lord from an educational rather than a musical perspective, although my wife and I have led many worship services with my guitar and her piano accompanying the songs. Music is frequently a central component of worship, and it should be, based upon the findings we discovered in Chapter 6. This element is, however, far from being the only legitimate expression of our soul's response to the Lord.

To conclude this chapter on the definition and description of Christian education, I will briefly summarize my perception of worship and its correlation with the education enterprise.

Toward a Definition of Worship

Among the many definitions of worship that have been proposed, I adhere to that submitted by W. E. Vine in his *Complete Expository Dictionary of Old and New Testament Words* (1996):

> *Worship is the direct **acknowledgment** to God, of his nature, attributes, ways and claims, whether by the outgoing of the heart in **praise** and thanksgiving, or by **deed** done in such acknowledgment.*

At first, I reacted negatively to this definition, but during a month of extensive study and discussion with colleagues, I found myself drawn to it repeatedly. In time, I began to realize that Vine's perception was not just good theology but a rephrasing of the instructions found in Hebrews 13:15, 16:

> *Through Jesus, therefore, let us continually offer to God a sacrifice of **praise** – the fruit of lips that **confess** his name. And do not forget to **do good** and to share with others, for with such sacrifices God is pleased.*

Vine succinctly summarizes some very critical components of this passage and supports a theology of worship that provides definite implications for a disciple maker.

Observations: Implications and Applications

The most notable implication from these texts is that the act of worship engages the worshipper in a response to the functions of the soul. When it was announced that she was to be the earthly mother of Jesus, Mary declared that her "soul magnifies the Lord" (Luke 1:46). She described worship in a very personal and practical manner: her intellectual, emotional, and volitional dimensions were actively engaged, in essence forming a psychology of worship. She set a standard and provided a benchmark by which effective worship is to be manifest and measured.

As these activities of the soul are evidenced in outward observance, we find ourselves experiencing worship with expressions of *acknowledgement, adoration,* and the *action*s of service. Although the text of Hebrews 13:15 can be translated "confessing his name," some versions translate it "acknowledging," and I prefer that translation choice.

The first and perhaps most significant application we can make concerning worship is that it is directed to and expressed for God. It is neither self-centered nor self-satisfying, it is acknowledging and glorifying God. The battles over style, atmosphere, and culture appropriateness are manifestly human-focused, not Father-focused. "Worship" services that satisfy the flesh, or even evangelize the soul, are missing the point. Worship is a direct acknowledgment *to* God, not words, songs, dances, or Power Point presentations *about* him. As a pastor I directed my worship leaders to distinguish between music ministry, when we "speak to one another in psalms, hymns, and spiritual songs," (Ephesians 5:19) and worship, when we speak to God. I also directed them to acquire a catalogue of "to songs" that we would sing to him. We also reworded choruses about him; for example, "he is my rock" became "you are my rock."

Acknowledgement is, however, only one of a triad of expressions in the worship of God. The second application we can make is to recognize that acknowledging his name must be accompanied by both adoration and action. To be truly of the Spirit, worship must also include the experience and expression of the emotions as well as the exercise of the will.

To adore, through offering praise and thanksgiving, is an expression of the emotions, which conservatives and evangelicals far too often fear. Richards notes,

> But praise is more than acknowledgment. It is also an expression of delight. It is reveling in the God who has shown himself to us. It is expressing the love that wells up with us. Praise takes first place in the vocabulary of worship as God comes first in the life and thoughts of believers (Richards 1976).

Worship, though, cannot be restricted or minimized to contain only words, whether spoken or sung, whether in acknowledgement or adoration. Worshippers must also act in service to Christ. A transformed life, produced by a renewed mind, manifests itself in the ultimate act of worship – sacrificial ministry to God and his people, especially "the least of these" (Romans 12:1, 2 and Matthew 25:40). In other words, the educator's insistence that a lesson is not complete until the student has become a doer of the word finds its ultimate fulfillment in worshipful service rendered to the Lord.

Worship and Education

The third application we can infer from the definition and description offered by Vine and the author of Hebrews is the connection with the educative process. Worship is a response to God that is generated by a confession or acknowledgement that was incited by a stimulus. In other words, God speaks or acts, and we respond to his initiative. In terms with which we are familiar from Part II: God has a message to declare (Stage I of the teaching-learning process), he communicates it to us (Stage II), and we respond in acknowledgement, adoration, and/or action (Stage III) with our soul magnifying and glorifying him. When a student grows in knowing, loving, and obeying or serving his Master (Stage IV), the inevitable manifestation will be a disciple who worships Jesus (Stage V).

An examination of this connection between education/discipleship and worship is enhanced by the following observation from the provocative work *Education for Human Flourishing: a Christian Perspective* (Spears and Loomis 2009):

> *Moral education, particularly within monotheism and especially within Christianity, has among its chief ends the attentive* **recognition** *of God's existence, the necessity of orienting one's being toward a loving* **relationship** *with God, and alignment with God's eternal, divine and natural* **laws**, *including those that require treating other persons with dignity and justice (Isaiah 1; Micah 68).*

Here we find three goals of an education that is moral: recognition, relationship, and responsiveness to God's laws. In meeting these goals, we acknowledge, adore, and act in service to the Lord. The connection between education and worship is patent. Discipleship prepares for worship, and conversely, worship is the product of discipleship.

It has been distressing to me to observe what appears to be an increasingly intentional disregard of the place of education in the worship experiences and practices in church and Christian school ministry. People often perceive of education as cold and lifeless while the worship experience is warm and full of life. This is an unfortunate perception, as there is nothing more academically complementary or aesthetically compelling than a disciple who worships.

Therefore, worship as an educated response to the Lord contains an implied application for the construction of worship services in settings such as churches or Christian school chapels. In Chapter 6, I recommend that worship follow and be in response to the Word taught or preached. Not only is this a logical and practical treatment of our discoveries, it also has the support of at least three other Christian educators:

> *According to the Bible, worship is not a prerequisite for Bible study, but rather the converse would be true. We read in passages such as Isaiah 6, Matthew 28:16-20, and John 4 that the Word of God properly understood causes a response of worship of God. Bible study as an end in itself will produce spiritual stagnation. To study the Word and see God reveal Himself and then respond in worship will produce spiritual stimulation or motivation for service. We are saved to serve, not sit, soak, and sour; for the motivating or propelling force for service comes as a result of worship (Chadwick 1982).*

> *I happen to have the crazy idea that preaching should precede rather than follow the worship service. Preaching should be followed by sharing, application, prayer, and other worship responses. We should prepare our people for change (Hendricks in Barna 1997).*

> *Praise in both the NT and the OT is essentially the response of the believer to God's self-revelation. God shows us His attributes... The believer recognizes and acknowledges... (Richards 1976).*

In review, the salient points of this section on worship include the recognition that worship is a consequence of discipleship. It engages all three elements of the soul in acknowledgment *to* God, not *about* him, and it engenders adoration and active service.

The teaching and preaching ministries of our churches, schools, agencies, and even homes would be enhanced greatly if the simple principles and prescriptions of this chapter drove our educational, disciple making, and worship experiences. "Go make disciples who worship Jesus" must be more than a catchy slogan, motto, or branding theme. It is the mission that impels the discipline of Christian education.

The Principal Principles

In conclusion and summary, discipleship ministries operate most effectively within the structure and guidelines provided by the principal principles I acknowledge in the Preamble to Part III. The first three provide a response to our initial inquiry, "What Is (Christian) Education?"

Principal Principles:

In succinct review, Christian education:

1. makes disciples who worship Jesus, fulfilling the Great Commission: (Communication, Choice, Consequence).

Hebrews 12; Matthew 28

2. promotes and attains growth and development, fostering personal maturation.

Luke 2:52; John 14, 16; Ephesians 2

3. employs biblically based elements, enabling a Spirit-inspired education.

1 Thessalonians 2

Prime Characteristic: Christian education is Christ-centered.

(Centered: "to give a central focus or basis — the point, area, person, or thing that is most important or pivotal in relation to an indicated activity, interest, or condition. The source from which something originates.")

It is Christ that makes education Christian. His pre-eminence in all things is the focus of Christian education. Therefore, the goal of education ministry is to lead people to discover the life and lifestyle of Jesus Christ.

Essential Activity:

Make a Disciple who Worships Jesus

Reflection and Response

Reflections on the Terms

The primary intention of this chapter was to define the term "education" and to describe the conditions under which it could be called "Christian."

After reflecting upon the content of this chapter, how would you...

1. **Define education?**
2. **Describe Christian education?**
3. **Defend your perceptions?**
4. **Determine whether or not you have been effective as a Christian educator?**

Reactions to the Text

The following statements have been taken directly from the text. Review and reflect upon the assertions presented, and for each one write out a short response affirming or challenging it.
Include in each response the reasons for your position.

** *"Teaching is creating an environment in which a student just might learn."*

** "Education is the creative process of utilizing external and internal forces to facilitate the functions of teaching and training in promoting and attaining growth and development, enabling complete individuals to comprehend, contemplate, and contribute to their community and culture."

** *"Maturity (development) must always accompany an increase in capacity (growth), whether this increase is in knowledge that demands wisdom, physical growth that demands coordination, or spirituality that demands holiness."*

** "Ministry demands proximity."

** *"Based upon the explicit directive of Jesus in Matthew 28, and the implicit instruction of multiple texts, I understand the overarching and ultimate goal of Christian education is to be making disciples who worship Jesus."*

** "The first, and perhaps most significant, application we can make concerning worship is that it is to, and for, God... The battles over style, atmosphere, and culture appropriateness are manifestly human-focused not Father-focused. 'Worship' services that satisfy the flesh, or even evangelize the soul, are missing the point – worship is a direct acknowledgment *to* God, not words, songs, dances, or Power Point presentations *about* him."

** *"I happen to have the crazy idea that preaching should precede rather than follow the worship service. Preaching should be followed by sharing, application, prayer, and other worship responses... We should prepare our people for change"* (Hendricks in Barna 1997).

Reflections on Worship

The following passage has been taken directly from the Gospel of John and represents the Master's concise perception of worship. Review and reflect upon the assertions presented, and for each one write out a short application response.

JOHN 4:19-24:

"Sir," the woman said, "I can see that you are a prophet. Our fathers worshiped on this mountain, but you Jews claim that the place where we must worship is in Jerusalem."

Jesus declared, "Believe me, woman, a time is coming when you will worship the Father neither on this mountain nor in Jerusalem. You Samaritans worship what you do not know; we worship what we do know, for salvation is from the Jews. Yet a time is coming and has now come when the true worshipers will worship the Father in spirit and truth, for they are the kind of worshipers the Father seeks. God is spirit, and his worshipers must worship in spirit and in truth.

THE PRACTICE OF WORSHIP...
Involves the Holy Spirit
- Worship the Father (the Spirit reveals what God is like and what he would "like.")
- In spirit
- In truth

Reflect and respond: In what ways is your spirit involved when you worship?

Reflect and respond: How would you know if worship was "in spirit" or "in truth"? What evidences would there be?

Involves the Body of the Believer *in three ways...*
- Assume a posture
- Engage in activity
- Accomplish a service

Reflect and respond: In what ways are your senses involved when you worship?

Involves the Soul of the Believer *in three ways...*
- Instruct the intellect and *Acknowledge*
- Inspire the emotions and *Adore*
- Involve the will and *Act in Service*

Reflect and respond: In what ways is your soul involved when you worship?

Reflect and respond: In what ways would your responses differ if you were worshipping with children? Young adults?

Reflect and respond: In what ways would your responses differ if you were worshipping at a school? At a camp?

Nine
What Is the Content of Education?

Athletic coaches formulate game plans for their teams, corporate officers construct business plans for their companies, and pastors develop ministry plans that they believe will accomplish a specific goal in their congregation or parish. Administrators in virtually every venue routinely design strategies for communicating and implementing their organization's mission and vision. In a church, this strategic activity is generally referred to as creating a *program*, while in schools it is known as constructing a *curricular plan*, but the terms are virtually interchangeable. In fact, one of the definitions of the word *program* in the *Merriam-Webster Dictionary* is, "a plan or system under which action may be taken toward a goal."

Upon assuming my duties as the principal of a public charter high school, it was immediately apparent that revamping and revitalizing the curricular plan needed to be at the top of my pressing priorities list. I began this reconstruction project by assembling a task force of faculty members who participated in an extraordinary undertaking that exemplifies the hard work and attention to detail that is essential to the creation and implementation of such a plan of action. Their labor also illuminates, and provides a template for, the central concern of this chapter – identifying the content of education.

The task force began its work by formulating a simple four-stage strategy for the development of our plan. In the initial stage, we identified and acknowledged our goals and expectations. In this case, they took the form of a description of an anticipated graduate of our school; in other words, we delineated the characteristics and competencies an individual receiving our diploma should exhibit. The result was the completed *Marks of Maturity* document I referred to previously in the "Purposes of Christian Education" section of Chapter 8.

In the second stage, we cataloged the knowledge base, mindset, and skill set that would facilitate the production of such a person. This taxonomy formed the frame and gave direction to the plan to be established. The third stage, then, involved determining what courses, texts, teachers, and activities the students would need to be exposed to and experience in order to accomplish these goals and facilitate the acquisition of these skills.

Finally, in the fourth stage, we arranged these components into a scope and sequence chart followed by a master schedule of offerings for each academic term. The faculty in the science department astounded me at this point in the process. I have had the privilege of witnessing a number of spectacular and extraordinary educational efforts, but this one resides near the top of the list. These teachers were not performing or presenting before a board of directors, a gathering of parents, or even a class of students, but their energy and expertise was evident to me as I entered their room. I observed two five-foot tables placed end-to-end and littered with nearly one hundred 3 x 5 index cards. The secondary science teachers had labeled these cards with every topic covered in biology from grades seven through twelve and were arranging them in rows and columns to create a scope and sequence "chart," aligning what was to be taught in each grade, each semester. Their attention to detail and creative methods to insure success were exemplary. Their Herculean effort exceeded my wildest expectations.

When this phase was completed, the entire faculty, not only the science teachers, had a curricular plan and an outline of what we believed our students needed to know and would be able to accomplish by the time they graduated. For this particular school, we addressed and responded to the second question of the five we have identified as determining the structure of the discipline, "What Is the Content of Education?"

In this chapter, we will attend to the principles and practices that enable us to answer that question for any educational organization, whether a church, school, camp, club, or family. We will investigate exactly how we, as parents, educators and leaders, can construct such a program or curricular plan to communicate the substances that produce disciple-followers – well-trained followers and well-educated students. Creating such a program or plan, as we will see, imitates the model established by the Heavenly Father who lays out a course over which his disciplined children race (Hebrews 12:1-3).

As in Chapter 8, we will commence our study with an examination of the critical concerns that drive our inquiry. An exploration of the essential activities necessary for an application of these principles will follow. In conclusion, there will be a summary of the cardinal points of the chapter and a review of the "Principal Principles" that encapsulate the foundations upon which our investigation is based.

Concerns Critical to the Inquiry

...it is worth pondering a New Yorker lament about what is lost in the brave, new "audience-driven" preaching of the day:

"The preacher, instead of looking out upon the world, looks out upon public opinion, trying to find out what the public would like to hear. Then he tries his best to duplicate that, and bring his finished product into a marketplace in which others are trying to do the same. The public, turning to our culture to find out about the world, discovers there is nothing but its own reflection. The unexamined world, meanwhile, drifts blindly into the future" (Guiness 1993).

While attacking the megachurch's flirtation with modernity, Os Guiness provides the Christian educator with a provocative introduction to the concerns of content and curriculum. Utilizing a quotation regarding preachers, he suggests that it is inappropriate for communicators to determine their message simply by "find[ing] out what the public would like to hear." He implies, and later states, that there is more to education than perpetuating a reflection of the public's perception of the world.

For Christian educators, the source of the messages we transmit is transparent. Although I am not a radical dualist, who sees a great gulf fixed between the spiritual world and that of the natural, I do acknowledge a world that God alone comprehends, a world that he created perfect and exists as he knows and intends it to be. The substance of that world is partially hidden from us due to the fall of man and the ultimately incomprehensible nature of God. It has, however, been revealed by the Spirit (cf. 1Corinthians 2:9, 10) and forms the content of the messages that God wishes us to receive.

Addressing Some Preliminary Concepts

Educators often use terms such as *content, curriculum,* and *lesson* interchangeably. While the effect of this practice upon communication is normally negligible, it is still profitable to distinguish between shades of meaning and their impact upon our understanding of the educative endeavor.

Examining Important Terms

For this discussion of educational content, we will examine the definition and implications of five important terms: *content, curriculum, message, teaching methods,* and *learning activities.*

Content

When we ask the *content* question, we are inquiring about "Something contained, as in a receptacle. The subject matter of a written work" (*The American Heritage Dictionary of the English Language,* 4th ed.). Some authorities also contend that it applies to "substance" and "meaning." Therefore, the content of education consists of the subject matter and materials that give substance to our endeavors and are contained in our lessons' messages. For the Christian educator, this also includes the substance of the spiritual realm as well. In fact, the intersection of these two planes promotes worship in spirit and in truth, facilitating Christian education in its complete and full-orbed expression. Stated simply, the Lord reveals the world as he created, knows, and intends it to be, and these messages provide the container from which we extract the content of specific lessons for our students. The Lord's creation and revelation contain all that we need to know, experience, and teach.

> *The heavens declare the glory of God; the skies proclaim the work of his hands.*
>
> *Day after day they pour forth speech; night after night they display knowledge.*
>
> *There is no speech or language where their voice is not heard (Psalm 19:1, 2).*

At a junior camp, the blaze of the campfire was warm, comforting, and enlightening. The glow and glare of artificial light was nowhere to be seen. I encouraged, therefore, the entire camp of children and their counselors to stop, look, and listen. I wanted them to stop talking or thinking about tomorrow, look all around, at the sky, the stars, the trees, the mountain splendor, and listen to the Lord. After five minutes of silent meditation and reflection, I asked them to share their ponderings. Slowly, but with growing enthusiasm, campers and counselors alike opened their hearts and shared the secrets of their devotional time with the Lord and his handiwork. Through the world he created, the works he performed, and the words he has directly spoken to humankind – both through his Spirit and in the inspired writings of men – the Lord has communicated all that is necessary for life and living. These campers caught a glimpse of that divine revelation and the messages it contains.

Narrowing the Options

Content, therefore, consists of all the matter, materials, substance, and even meanings available to an educator to communicate and transmit to students. For the Christian educator, however, not all content is appropriate for nurturing the life and lifestyle of Jesus. In fact, there are forces and influences that are diametrically opposed to Christianity. For example, eighty years ago, Charles Francis Potter (1930) observed that, "Education is the most powerful ally of Humanism, and every American public school is a school of Humanism. What can the theistic Sunday Schools, meeting for an hour once a week, and teaching only a fraction of the children, do to stem the tide of a five-day program of humanistic teaching?" Although humanism can be defined, described, and developed from a number of perspectives, including some that incorporate a religious, if not Christian, component, the form Potter refers to is patently anti-Christian.

Five decades later, the Council for Democratic and Secular Humanism acknowledged that,

> *Of special concern to secularists is the fact that the media (particularly in the United States) are inordinately dominated by a pro religious bias. The views of preachers, faith healers, and religious hucksters go largely unchallenged, and the secular outlook is not given an opportunity for a fair hearing. We believe that television directors and producers have an obligation to redress the balance and revise their programming. Indeed, there is a broader task that all those who believe in democratic secular humanist values will recognize, namely, the need to embark upon a long term program of public education and enlightenment concerning the relevance of the secular outlook to the human condition (Kurtz 1980).*

In this light, note the observation made by John Childs in his provocative *Education and Morals*:

> *No human group would ever bother to found and maintain a system of schools were it not concerned to make of its children something other than they would become if left to themselves and their surroundings... Moreover, in order to develop the preferred and chosen patterns of behavior, it is*

necessary to hinder other and incompatible kinds of growth (Childs 1950).

The sage must have had this idea in mind when he penned the oft-quoted, "Train up a child…" text (Proverbs 22:6). The term translated *train* comes from a root word that literally means to restrict, funnel, or choke off. The root of the translated term *child* means rowdy, tumultuous, and busy. This verse, then, paints a word picture of a large funnel sweeping across a desert and restricting, narrowing, and directing the course of a blowing, tumbling tumbleweed. That tumbleweed, tossed about in many directions by the wind, is the child. The training or funneling of a young child's life provides the necessary direction and guidance in the way he should go. Many negative exposures and experiences are winnowed out in the process, and the youngster is protected from their influence.

My wife and I taught our children to critically analyze everything they hear, from sermons to advertisements, and to be alert to foolish messages and messengers. In the same way, whether in day school, home school, or church school, a teacher selects content messages deemed appropriate to the goals of a truly Christian education, restricting and protecting the students from inappropriate content and subject matter.

Instructive, therefore, are the words of wisdom in Proverbs 14:7: "Go from the presence of a foolish man when you do not perceive in him the lips of knowledge." No wonder Moses warned the Israelites, "Do not inquire after other gods" (Deuteronomy 12:30), and the Psalmist would allow no evil thing or man before his eyes (Psalm 101:3, 4). New Testament perceptions also enhance these Old Testament warnings. For example, the Apostle Paul states that it is "shameful to even mention what the disobedient do in secret" (Ephesians 5:12).

Curriculum

Let us run with perseverance the race marked out for us (Hebrews 12:1).

It seems that the word "learn" comes from a prehistoric German word, liznojan. It was inherited from an Indo-European word, leis, which meant "to track." Thus the word originally had the connotation of gaining experience by following a track (Hull 1995).

The term curriculum itself comes from the Latin currere
referring to "a course" or "a running" (Marlow 1994).

From the content contained in the creative and redemptive works of
God and revealed to humankind, the educator chooses certain substances
or subject matters to transmit to the learner. After narrowing the choices,
an instructor selects the exposures and experiences he wishes his students
to encounter. These become a course of study, a carefully laid out plan to
which the student gives attention during the race to the goal.

While *content* refers to the universe of messages available to the
educator, *curriculum* refers to the actual messages chosen to transmit to
the student. As we shall see, these messages may be in the form of exposures
to texts and teachers, or they may be experiences with the environment
and life situations. The sum of these exposures and experiences forms the
curriculum. In fact, "Curriculum has come to mean the sum of all learning
experiences resulting from a curriculum plan, directed toward learning
objectives" (Colson 1969).

Expanding the Opportunities

While acknowledging that the content must be restricted in order to
fulfill specific goals, it is also true that the curricular plan must be expanded
to include all of the activities in which a student is engaged. In this approach,
there is nothing extra. Every activity is educational and integral to the
curriculum. Every encounter with a student is rife with the opportunity
to produce something new, and is thus educative and curricular. For this
reason, I choose to refer to these experiences as co-curricular rather than
extra curricular activities. This is why I utilize anecdotes from many life
experiences including camps, sports, and classrooms; every experience of a
student should be perceived as part of the course raced toward the goal of
a disciple who worships Jesus.

Since the Christian life was never designed to be lived alone, and the
corporate maturation of our community is one of our goals, the race may
be perceived of as a "relay" with the strongest runners first and last. It is
commenced and anchored by Jesus, the Alpha and Omega, the author
and finisher of our faith, and the middle legs are run by each of us. As we
develop curricular plans that are truly Christian, we must constantly remind
ourselves of the need for *koinonia* fellowship, mutual ministry, and the value
of the group dynamic in education, merging the individual dimension with
the corporate. For example, in the high school curriculum plan discussed

earlier, three of the marks of maturity we sought to attain in our graduates addressed interpersonal communication and self-confidence.

Co-curricular Activities

We decided that one of the guidelines for our after-school activities was that the programs were to be instructive in all areas of the students' lives. In other words, the content of our program went beyond what we communicated through textbooks and formal classroom instruction. Thus, when I went to a varsity boys' basketball game, I was disheartened to watch the members of the team lower their heads and look to the ground as they were introduced to the crowd, the opposing coaches and players, and even the referees. After the game was over, I went to the head coach and asked him to address this with his players.

The coach accepted the responsibility to guide his charges in areas of personal growth and maturation as well as in basketball competence as he expanded the opportunities for development within the program. I was pleased to observe that when this team went to the state championship and the introductions included all twelve members of the team, all but one kept their heads held high, extended their hands, and actually acknowledged the opponent's existence. They even shook hands and exchanged greetings with the referees.

This same holistic attitude and approach to the curriculum plan is evident when a Bible teacher takes the time to minister to the whole person and not solely the cognitive functions, such as comprehending the lesson. Another application occurs, for instance, when a teacher finds out why a student is downcast and follows up with personal counsel and prayer or participates in the joyful times of a student's life with blessing and encouragement. The curricular plan is also implemented when a preschool Sunday school teacher stops after class and counsels a parent troubled with discipline issues at home as well as when a pastor decides to break a month-long series of theologically-driven sermons in order to address a recent tragedy within the community.

Co-curricular Guidelines

To gain the most benefit from these co-curricular opportunities, the following three guiding principles are essential: instruction, inclusion, and participation.

Instruction. Every co-curricular activity must produce some form of learning, growth, or development within the student. The basketball program, for example, was part of a concept that we referred to as "recreational skills for life." Therefore, even if an athlete neither was a starter nor participated very frequently within the interscholastic contests themselves, the student still had the opportunity to learn the game and develop a personal capacity for lifelong recreation, fitness, and health.

In a familial example, my two children were encouraged to participate in two physical activities every school year, at any level, in any program, in order to satisfy the needs of physical activity, health, and emotional release. One day, not too long ago, after my daughter finished playing a game of softball with her coworkers, she thanked me for instilling in her the discipline and appreciation for lifelong fitness and recreation skills for life. I have the same desire for all my students.

Inclusion. The principle of inclusion can be implemented by requiring that every student who wants to participate in an activity be allowed to do so. To revamp our school's curricular plan, the sports program found ways to keep rather than cut players, the theater department created more roles on and off the stage, the yearbook staff added more jobs, and in student government everyone who wanted to serve was provided an opportunity. We had to be creative and very flexible in order to fulfill this guideline. In order to create new opportunities for student participation, the faculty had to go above and beyond the call of duty. For example, the head coach created an additional intramural league to accommodate all of the students that were interested in our program. He also created a C team, which was not common in our division, and he had to find other schools that would be willing to play at odd hours and in less than optimum conditions. In the fine arts program, the drama teacher worked with student directors, costume designers, set constructors, and advertisers, to name just a few of the activities formed to enable more student involvement. Likewise, when creating a musical, the music department incorporated a choir into the script so that anyone who wanted to sing would have the chance to do so. To put it simply, we went out of our way to be inclusive.

Participation. Simply allowing students to be members of a team, band, or production is not enough – we must encourage them to be actively engaged. An experience I had while watching my daughter play volleyball in high school framed the motive behind this third guideline. I watched her coach ignore a young teammate for an entire season; this girl never played in the games, and the coach seldom used her in any of the practices or scrimmages. As I arrived daily to pick up Carrie from practice, I would see this young athlete in the corner either bumping volleyballs off the gym wall or sitting alone watching the practice. The disappointment and discouragement on her face increased daily until she finally gave up.

Later that year, long after volleyball season was over, my daughter and I attended a theatrical production at the school. During the play, I noticed the performance of one particular actress who seemed to be a cut above all of the others. I was astonished to realize that it was the same young woman who had been neglected in volleyball. She had found her niche, and someone had obviously encouraged her to do so. It brought a smile to my face and a small tear to my eye. I was so thankful that someone in that school had been willing to let her participate and excel.

Using the language of the teaching-learning metamodel in Part II, the volleyball program barely brought her to a Stage II exposure, while the theater engaged her in a Stage V experience. I have shared this story with the directors of many co-curricular activities, and it has made a difference in how they approach their programs, implementing the metamodel in co-curricular as well as curricular venues.

Message

The word *message* is derived from the term *missive*, referring to something sent, such as a letter. Choosing from all of the substances available, the teacher selects the messages appropriate for the student and the lesson to be presented and then delivers these messages. It is neither the delivery system nor the presenter that matters, but the idea that something is being sent to a learner or disciple-follower.

Hebrews 12 indicates that God as our Father-Teacher lays out a course for us to run. To do so, he chooses specific messages from all of the content available to him in order to communicate with his disciple-followers. Human teachers, likewise, choose from all the messages available and select those that are appropriate to send, based upon the unique lesson, situation, and students they are presently teaching. Through exposure to and experience with the ones employed, the student explores and explicates the lesson.

Teaching Methods and Learning Activities

In order to facilitate the presentation and comprehension of the session's selected message, the teacher determines and utilizes instructional methods and materials. The intention is to physically engage the student with these methods in order to stimulate the soulish activities of learning: thinking, feeling, and choosing.

Early in my career as the pastor of a large children's ministry, I investigated many published, ready-made curricular resources to determine an effective curricular plan for the Sunday school. One plan from Gospel Light Publications emphasized a component called the BLAs or "Bible Learning Activities." I was thrilled to see a wide range of engaging and stimulating games, songs, student work sheets, and suggestions for puppets, dramatic skits, and role-plays. I do not recall, however, any instructions or guidance concerning what these activities were designed to accomplish in the life of the learner.

Very little information or resources were offered concerning how to raise learning levels, deal with students' reactions, assist in good decision-making, or apply the acquired truths in their lives at home, school, or even church. It appeared that the authors of the curriculum assumed that teaching methods were virtually synonymous with learning activities.

Methods of teaching, however, do not ensure activities of learning. While the teacher may control the methods and materials to be utilized, the student determines whether or not learning will actually take place. Combining these elements in order to facilitate the teaching-learning process is manifest in what is commonly referred to as a lesson plan. There will be a more detailed discussion of this topic in the next chapter.

Exploring Impacting Principles

In addition to defining and examining the previous five terms, there are four additional concepts to address that have a tremendous effect upon our understanding and implementation of curriculum. We have already identified the first as the paradoxical process that involves both narrowing and expanding the parameters of a curricular plan. The Christian educator restricts the messages to which a student is exposed and experiences while at the same time recognizing that every contact with content is curricular. We dare not ignore what appears to be peripheral and insignificant. Every exposure is impacting.

Preach What you Practice

David Cook, the President of International Bible College, adroitly captured and summarized the second impacting principle when he utilized a catchy quip at a commencement ceremony. He challenged the graduates by observing that, "Jesus didn't practice what he preached, he preached what he practiced." The apostles John (1John 1) and Paul (Romans 15) both referred to the need to have experience with the truths being taught, and Luke summarized it well in his introduction to the book of Acts, declaring that what Jesus "began to do and to teach" (Acts 1:1) was the foundation of his ministry and the source of power in his efforts to make disciples. Cook stated the obvious: in constructing his curriculum, he transmits that which he has personally practiced and experienced in life. In making that observation, Cook summarized the concepts and scriptures we referred to in our discussion of the Ezra Experience.

It must be noted, however, that preachers and teachers can fall prey to the temptation to alter their message, or even reinterpret their text, based on their experience. I have personally witnessed preachers distort what appeared to be a clear biblical teaching because of their family life or a personal peccadillo. The contemporary researcher, communicator, and educator must recognize, acknowledge, and make the necessary provisions for protection and precision while creating a curriculum. They must take seriously the fact that their lives and personal experiences become critical components of the messages they transmit.

Practice Provides Preparation

The third foundational principle is that the "practice" that is preached also provides the groundwork essential to personal development and the preparation for future ministry. I identified this principle after reflecting upon an experience that impacted and transformed my life and understanding of curricular planning. The incident occurred on a vacation trip to Hawaii, during a tour that took me to the governor's mansion.

While strolling about the grounds at the mansion, our group stopped to rest under an unusual tree with branches and limbs spread over such a vast expanse that an entire picnic area, complete with chairs and tables, was located under it. Our guide informed us that this was a Banyan tree. What made the tree so unique, though, was not the size or width of the limbs, but that the branches grew out from the tree and then turned down to the ground to take root. The result of this natural phenomenon produced not just an umbrella effect, but also a functional tent. As I rested under that tree, I experienced a dramatic sensation that there was something special all around me, and I needed to reflect upon its significance.

After time spent in reflection, consideration, and meditation upon a wide variety of possible interpretations, I was impressed by a number of applications: 1) just as the original gardener had to prepare the plot years in advance for the ultimate size, shape, and arrangement of the tree, so the formation of my life would take some time and preparation by God for everywhere he desired me to take root and grow; 2) just as the trunk of the tree was pointing upwards, so also was the direction of my life to point to and give glory to God; 3) just as the tree's branches are rooted in earthly soil, so also do the outcroppings of my life take root in the daily affairs of others and the direction of my ministry branches out in many directions – I am a minister and ordained to touch other people's lives; and 4) just as the gardener must till, fertilize, and prepare the soil, so also does the Lord discipline and nurture my life "soil" for the present and future plans he has for me. The Master utilizes jobs I had once despised, people who had irritated me, painful encounters I endured, and lessons I had learned from both study and experience to prepare my life for his service.

Since that day, I have told the Banyan Tree Story many times to countless individuals and groups, often with an accompanying graphic that can provide a compelling and encouraging visual reminder. The need to allow the Gardener to till, fertilize, and prepare lives for wherever the branches of ministry are to take root is a message that every disciple-follower of Jesus Christ must consider and heed. It also informs my understanding of God's perception of curricular planning and the laying out the course of my life. Once again, I must acknowledge that every exposure and experience is curricular. The Apostle Paul may have had this in mind when he penned, "And we know that in all things God works for the good of those who love him..." (Romans 8:28).

Organizing Principles: Scope and Sequence

Finally, the fourth impacting principle in curricular design is the recognition that after the curriculum has been determined it must be organized into some form of structured framework. Selection of the simultaneously restricted and enhanced content determines curriculum *scope*, but the related issue of *sequence* requires some additional coordinating principles.

Curriculum specialists commonly use one of the following approaches as an organizing principle for curricular activity:

- *Chronology (e.g., historical studies);*
- *Complexity (e.g., simple concepts lead to more complicated ones, as in math);*
- *Theory or Thesis (e.g., literature);*
- *Pedagogy (e.g., moving from personal experience to more remote events, or from concrete to abstract; event-process cycle).*

It is comparatively easy to recognize the organizing structure in scholarly and professional studies, but a similar rationale should be applied to "arranging biblical studies into an effective instructional sequence" (Oliva 1982). Whether preacher, Sunday school teacher, small group Bible study leader, or Christian day or home school instructor, an educator must seriously consider the framework used to organize in light of both the content to be presented and the learner to receive it.

In summary, four impacting principles provide assistance and guidance in curricular selection: narrow and broaden the curricular offerings, preach what you practice, prepare the soil for learning, and identify the organizing principles. It would be helpful, however, to dig a little deeper into the origins and sources from which the educator's message is selected.

Addressing Some Practical Considerations

David Kurtz, a former student in one of my seminary education courses, submitted the following description of the process utilized in the selection of materials for a small group ministry in his church. His story helps to illustrate some of the problems and difficulties involved in curriculum construction and lesson selection, and it provides some hints concerning how a teacher determines a lesson's message:

> *The education team felt that there should be a Bible-based course, i.e. a book of the Bible or a biblical topic. The team looked through many different curriculums on Biblical books, looking for a class that would appeal to the congregation. After much research, a study on First and Second Thessalonians was determined to be the class to start with, because the curriculum fit the format as well as the topic was "discussion-friendly."*
>
> *The second one was going to be a study of a Christian book of some sort. For the past few years, some men of the church have met on Friday mornings, and have worked through books, written by authors like Oz Guinness and Steve Farrar. Since Max Lucado lends itself to easy reading and discussion, "Come Thirsty" was picked to fill the second slot.*
>
> *Finally, it was decided that the third class would be a "wild card." I struggled with what would be a good course to offer that would be different from the other two classes, but would be interesting. While at the local Christian bookstore, picking up books for the other courses, I was able to find a DVD study on being a Christian in the workplace, and after studying the material, it was selected to fill the last spot (Kurtz 2006).*

The Sources from Which the Message is Extracted

Deciding what, whom, and when to teach are the perennial concerns of practitioners and theoreticians. In an attempt to distill the research and prescriptions for healthy curricula, I address two critical concerns: the sources of an educator's message and the forms these messages take as they are transmitted to a learner. Each of these issues consists of four components that facilitate narrowing the options and expanding the opportunities, respectively.

The sources of a message are found in tradition, observation, participation, and inspiration. These sources are defined and described in Display 10 as we continue the discussion commenced in Chapter 2.

Display 10. Sources from Which an Educator's Message is Extracted

The Sources of a Communicator's Message

By Dr. Michael R. Mitchell © 2007

Tradition:
the messages/lessons embedded in and extracted from the "heritage of the race" (J.M. Gregory, 1888)

> **Description:** The living words of the community
> The historical "stuff" that societies codify in their texts and contain in their treasures to describe and perpetuate their culture (the "content" of socialization)
>
> **Scripture:** 2 Peter 1:16-19; 1 Corinthians 1:18-25; cf. Romans & Ephesians
>
> **Prescription:** So know the Word, and teach it regularly (systematically)

Observation:
the messages/lessons embedded in and extracted from the learning activities of the student

> **Description:** The life needs of the pupil
> The raw "stuff" that every individual brings to the educational experience to be refined and cultured
>
> **Scripture:** 2 Peter 1:12; 1 Corinthians 1:26-31; cf. Galatians
>
> **Prescription:** So listen to and observe your student(s); cf. the epistles to churches and individuals

Participation:
the messages/lessons embedded in and extracted from the life experiences of the teacher

> **Description:** The life message of the teacher
> The refined "stuff" that each educator brings to the experience to share with others
>
> **Scripture:** 2 Peter 1:18; 1 Corinthians 2:1-5; Romans 15:18; cf. 1Thessalonians 2
>
> **Prescription:** So teach what you know (preach what you practice).

Inspiration:
the messages/lessons embedded in and extracted from the instruction and direction of the Holy Spirit

> **Description:** The leading of the Lord
> The anointed "stuff" that the teacher receives from above to transmit here below; often perceived of as intuition or "insight" – an innate sense of what is necessary to communicate to the student
>
> **Scripture:** 2 Peter 1:21; 1 Corinthians 2:6-16; cf. Acts 16:6-10
>
> **Prescription:** So "keep in step with the Spirit" (Galatians 5:25) and listen to his voice

I have observed that this idea of sources of a message has been difficult for some students in training classes and seminary courses to grasp. For some, it is helpful to consider these four sources as a well from which they may draw to lay out the course the students will race. For others, perceiving the sources as "origins" is beneficial. Regardless of how they are perceived, I propose that over time an educator must:

- Allow the influence of all four sources
- Ensure the messages are congruent and support each other
- Utilize the decision-making process and consider the influences upon choice

After examining Display 10, which provides the "theory" and biblical support to summarize the sources, the following anecdotes will illustrate an application of each. We will then observe a demonstration of how they affect choosing a story to tell children in Sunday school, clubs, or even at home.

Tradition. One of the more challenging ministries that my wife and I have experienced was being the pastor of a small church in Michigan. While taking a personal retreat to recharge and reflect upon God's intention for my ministry, the Lord's direction was impressed upon my heart: "Teach my word regularly and frequently." It was patent to me that I was to extract messages for my ministry to the church from the Bible as my primary and first source of teaching. I was to give attention to the "codified text" that had been handed down from the prophets to the apostles and is still profitable for instruction and correction.

Observation. One afternoon early in my ministry at a large church in California, a Sunday school teacher in our children's ministry knocked on my door looking for some help. She informed me that out of a class of fifteen third-grade students, seven of them had experienced death or dying in their immediate or extended families within the past month, and she wanted to know how to approach her pupils. After some time of discussing the situations, her students' knowledge and experience levels, and what she was presently doing in her studies, we agreed upon a plan to create a primary level study of a Christian view of death and dying.

The culminating experience included a visit to a convalescent hospital where the students could converse with people who may be approaching death. When we looked at the calendar, we realized that the field trip was to occur on the weekend of Palm Sunday and would be preparing her students for the celebration of the resurrection the following week. This provided an excellent way to complete this study of the Christian view of the subject. The actions of this Sunday school teacher provide a good illustration of *observation*; by paying attention to her students, she was able to devise a curricular plan tailor-made for her class.

Although many texts have been written on the subject (D. Campbell Wyckoff's classic *Theory and Design of Christian Education Curriculum* probably being the best known), few give adequate attention to the roles of the learner and the Holy Spirit in the development of the "course" over which the learner will run. This young teacher's example offers a healthy correction to that oversight.

Participation. One of the impacting principles that I discussed earlier in this chapter revolved around the story of the Banyan tree. This was a classic example of how *participation* in life actually provided a message to share with others as well as a lesson to experience. It has become an essential component of my life message and an integral element of my curricular plan.

Inspiration. After finishing a Bible study in the Psalms with the congregants of the church in Michigan, I was contemplating the direction of my curricular plan and the next message that the Lord had for the congregation. As I was reflecting upon the choice and decision that was before me, the Lord impressed me to "Teach my people about the Holy Spirit." Without thinking, I wittily responded, "I don't know about the Holy Spirit." I then commenced a month-long research process that provided the necessary messages to share. It was very encouraging to be guided not only to teach the Bible regularly and frequently, but also to be given specific and divine direction as to the next content to present.

To Illustrate Further

The scenario of a Sunday school teacher selecting a story to tell children illustrates these principles and their implementation in a typical educational activity. Storytelling is one of the oldest forms of communication and education. It has been utilized around campfires for community socialization and celebration, by parents for morals development, and by businesses in their efforts to transmit values and culture to their employees and customers. More than a century ago, John Milton Gregory called the educator's attention to the necessity of transmitting what he referred to as "the heritage of the race" (Gregory 1888). Passed from generation to generation, in a variety of settings, people have effectively transmitted and retained the traditions, values, and worldview of the community.

Reflect, therefore, upon the guidelines for choosing a story extracted from Scottie May, Catherine Stonehouse, Beth Posterski, and Linda Cannell's *Children Matter: Celebrating Their Place in the Church, Family, and Community* (2005). Although their work refers primarily to children's ministry within the church, I believe their observations have some universal value. Notice how each of the sources of a message is employed in story selection.

Concerning **observation**, and drawing a message from a student's present life experiences, they note:

> *Telling a story begins with deciding what story to tell. Obviously we will choose stories with the listeners in mind. Who are the children? How old are they? What stories do they already know? Are they dealing with a particular crisis in their lives?*

They also acknowledge **participation**, or the life experiences of the teacher, in their comments:

> *Telling a story is always a process of interpretation and selection. We bring our own experience, our own history, and our own spin on things when we tell stories. When we consider which stories to tell, we tend to first think of some of our own favorites.*

The role of **tradition** and the need for a secure foundation in the selection of stories is reflected in their recommendation that Bible stories find a central place in teaching:

> *We need to come back again to the Scriptures and discover the stories that we have passed over or never noticed before. Of course the Bible is a big book. It takes a lifetime — at least — to master all the stories that we find there. But we can help our children make a start on the journey, set them on the way of discovering God's story for themselves. This journey will be enhanced if we set out to give children an overview of the full Bible story.*

Although not referencing the Holy Spirit directly, his imprint would be evident in this final aspect of the selection process, providing **inspiration**:

> *Ask yourself, with whom will the children identify in this story? Using this question as a guide will affect the choice of story, the telling of the story, and the response to it. … Identification with a story creates space for the listeners to learn from the*

*characters' experience as if they had actually participated in
the story — which they have, imaginatively.*

To Purchase or Not to Purchase

One of the most common questions and concerns confronting a
Christian educator is that of whether or not to use prepackaged published
curricular materials for use in classes, clubs, camps, or any other organized
teaching venue.

While the practice of purchasing prepared materials is widespread,
some churches choose to spend their curricular budgets on teaching
aids and resource supplies that their faculty can employ in constructing
personalized lessons, rather than acquiring packaged materials from a
national or denominational publisher. In this type of situation, the director
may believe that the local team can develop a more relevant curriculum, as
the familiarity and proximity to the children can contribute to the creation
of a curricular plan that is more tailored to their specific needs. If, for
example, a particular concentration of study is more appropriate at a certain
time of year, the changes in schedule and direction can easily be made
without confusion or inconvenience. In certain cases, this may be critical,
as flexibility might be essential to the leadership team of the church.

Each organization should choose the type of curricular resources
that will be most effective for its program. Personally and professionally,
I neither consistently encourage nor discourage the use of published
materials. Rather, I recommend the educator address a number of simple
questions to help determine whether or not it would be appropriate for the
educational setting.

The decision to purchase packaged curricular resources is dependent
upon an educator's answers to questions such as these:

- Are you expected to stick to a scope and sequence chart
  provided by your leadership?
- Are you a veteran teacher, knowing what to do, or are you a
  rookie in need of help?
- Will these materials be consistent with the philosophy of
  teaching you employ?
- Are alternate materials available for the lesson to be taught?
- What method(s) will you be employing? How can published
  materials support or augment it?

The education administrator must also consider the available facilities and resources, the impact upon budget, the amount of training necessary to implement the materials, and the horizontal and vertical alignment of a department's plan with others in the ministry. This last issue addresses the correlation of content with other departments immediately above and below.

Establishing the course over which the student will run to accomplish the educational goals involves selecting the messages appropriate for the present course, unit, or lesson from the available possibilities. Acknowledging and utilizing the available sources or origins of these enables the teacher to facilitate this process. To summarize, the wise Christian teacher takes into consideration:

1. Experience and tradition, transmitted in both oral and written expressions, such as textbooks and in the case of Christian education, the Bible;
2. Life experiences of the students as they are witnessed and interpreted by the teacher;
3. Life experiences of the teacher as they confirm and impact the lessons to be learned; and
4. Immediate direction and prescription of the Holy Spirit as the teacher seeks guidance from the divine source.

The Forms in Which the Message May Be Manifest

In establishing a curricular plan, the instructor must also acknowledge and address the fact that a selected message may manifest itself in as many as four different forms. In the same way that H_2O is one "substance" but can take a variety of forms (as water, ice, or gas), an educator's message may be experienced as: 1) the lesson's *subject matter*, 2) the class *environment*, 3) the students' *life (experiences)*, and 4) the example of the *teacher (model)*. These are not distinct and unique messages, but expressions of the chosen curricular content. In other words, each one is simply a means by which the original intent is revealed and exhibited.

Since some messages are better expressed in one manner over another, identifying and utilizing the most appropriate form will increase the likelihood of the lesson being received accurately. For example, when individuals cool a drink with ice, or cook an egg with boiling water, they are appropriately employing one of the forms of H_2O. In the same way, teachers are more effective when they make use of the most fitting form of the specific curricular message. Additionally, as we will see in Chapter 10, by utilizing a variety of curricular message forms and instructional methods, a teacher can differentiate instruction and facilitate student diversity in learning style preferences.

Display 11. The Forms of an Educator's Message

The Forms of a Communicator's Message

By Dr. Michael R. Mitchell © 2007

Subject Matter
- A *replacement* for reality
- What will you "say" (or show, or direct them to learn)?
  The messages we normally refer to as "content" – often dictating the substance of a lesson
  Examine the lesson: What's the point? What is its contribution to the curricular plan?
  What are your objectives? What is the irreducible minimum content?
- Jesus: We proclaim him! (Col 1:28)
  Eph 4:20: "to know Christ"
- The "control factor" in education

Environment
- A *framework* for reality
- What will you say with your facility, tone, and relationship?
  The messages frequently referred to as the "hidden curriculum" – often dictating the response to the lesson
  Establish the environment: Is it inviting? Is it stimulating? Is it collegial?
- Jesus: in him we live and move and have our being (Acts 17:28)
  Eph 4:20 "taught in him"
  Acts 17:28; Context speaks messages
- The family model speaks messages, too!

Life (experiences)
- A *participation* in reality
- What will your student(s) do to experience/practice this truth?
  The messages embedded in what the student actually experiences – often dictating the perception of the truth of the lesson
  Expect participation and interaction: what will you have them do?
- Jesus: I am the way, truth, life (John 14:6)
  Eph 4:22 "you were taught to put off/put on"

Teacher (model)
- A *representation* of reality
- What will you do to demonstrate this truth?
  The messages the instructor exhibits – often illustrating (and illuminating) the lesson
  Original term for teach "taecean" meant "to show how to do" (cf. Moran, 1997, p. 37, 38)
  Examine yourself: Are you who you want your students to become?
- Jesus: an example that you should follow (1 Peter 2:21)
  Eph 4:20 "heard of him"
  (John 14:6; cf. Hebrews 1:2, 3 "God spoke "in son")
- Abraham and family, Timothy's family (Luke 6:40)
  Falsehood passed on (4 generations of liars)
  Faith passed on (3 generations of biblical students)

Diversity may enhance it, but for a message to be truly heard and trusted, these forms must be in balance and congruence with each other. For example, a Sunday school teacher can say every member of the class is loved, but if favorites are selected and some students are ignored, what is really being said? A preacher can preach ethical living and yet be found to be financially immoral; which message will the congregants hear? A mother can say, "You're forgiven" and then scream at her daughter; what message is she actually sending? A coach can tell his team that everyone will have equal opportunity, but when his son plays every down, what will the other players really think? The receivers of these messages do not know what to believe because the modes of transmission are incongruent and sending conflicting signals. That is why we call them "mixed messages."

The material in Display 11 defines and describes the four forms that can be utilized to transmit a message. They are illustrated and explained through the use of biblical example and practical encouragement – in both the display and in the sample illustrations following.

To Illustrate Biblically

Observing and reflecting upon Paul's ministry to the Thessalonians can identify and illustrate the variety of forms that he applied to his message (1Thessalonians 2:6-14). Evidences of the four forms in which a message can be conveyed are highlighted in bold.

> *As apostles of Christ we could have been a burden to you, but **we were gentle among you, like a mother** caring for her little children. We **loved** you so much that we were delighted to share with you not only the **gospel of Go**d but our lives as well, because you had become so dear to us...* (Subject matter and environment)
>
> *You are **witnesses**... of how holy, righteous and blameless we were **among** you who believed. For you know that we dealt with each of you as a father deals with his own children, encouraging, comforting and urging you to live lives worthy of God, who calls you into his kingdom and glory.* (Teacher model)
>
> *And we thank God because, when you received the **word** of God... you accepted it not as the word of men, but as it actually is, the word of God... For you, brothers, became **imitators** of God's churches in Judea: You **suffered** from your own countrymen the same things those churches suffered from the Jews,* (Life experience)

The 3-Legged Stool

Further evidence that curricular content can take many different forms is readily observable in a brief note that I distribute to students in both my residential and online courses. In explaining how I present course content, I utilize the metaphor of a three-legged stool to describe the variety of delivery and learning experiences over which a student will race.

What is the 3-Legged Stool?

> *The 3-Legged Stool is a metaphor for the three primary content delivery systems employed in this program. The first leg consists of the textbooks utilized in a given course. Since a text is virtually a printed lecture, it is a convenient and efficient means to dispense information. It is assumed that the student will read, comprehend, and utilize this acquired knowledge in graded learning activities and class discussions. Questions concerning and challenges to textbook material are certainly welcome in class to clarify and confirm student learning. The second leg represents the subject matter addressed during class sessions. Whether presented in lecture, discussion, or media format this material is considered as critical to the course as the textbook information. Since this additional material is not often found in a text (but still copyrighted by the professor or guest), the student is expected to give attention, and to do so with interest. It is anticipated that this material, likewise, will be referenced in course assignments. Finally, the third leg represents the data discovered and mined during personal research and preparation for the graded learning activities submitted for course credit. It is expected that the student will consult other works, online sources, journals, and even interviews, etc. to fulfill the assignments. During this experience additional information not found in the texts or course materials will be uncovered. The student, therefore, should recognize that all three "legs" are considered equally viable and critical to success not only in the course but also in preparation for further study and life application.*

Descriptive Guidelines for Curricular Components

As a bridge to the next section on the application of the principles of curriculum construction, consider these descriptive guidelines. They incorporate virtually all of the critical concepts we have encountered so far. To be Christian, a curricular plan must incorporate components that are:

✓ Christ-centered
  o 1Peter 2:21; 2Peter 1:3-10; Philippians 3:8-10

- ✓ Bible-based
  - ○ 1Corinthians 2:9-13; Romans 1:16ff
- ✓ Pupil-experienced
  - ○ Matthew 7:24; James 1
- ✓ Others-related
  - ○ 1Corinthians 12, Hebrews 10:24, 25
- ✓ Family-focused
  - ○ 1Thessalonians 2
- ✓ Socially-applied
  - ○ Romans 12:18, Chapter 13, 15:2; 1Peter 2, 3; James 1:27
- ✓ Evangelistically-concerned
  - ○ Matthew 28:19, 20

Activities Essential to an Application

What exposures and experiences facilitate a student's mature reception of Christ's abundant life and lifestyle? The answer to this simple restatement of the content question includes the observation that the essential activity of this aspect of Christian education is to "Construct a Curricular Plan." We will begin our examination of this essential activity with a brief review.

Reflecting the "classic" definition of *curriculum*, which emanates from the Latin term for "a course of running," Hebrews 12 indicates that God as our Father-Teacher lays out a track for us to race over. In establishing this course of study, he chooses to communicate, from all of the content messages available, the ones appropriate for the lesson being explored at that time. Similarly, the human teacher extracts, from the appropriate source(s), all the messages that have been revealed to be the ones necessary for the unique lesson, situation, and students being taught. Through exposure to and experience with the forms of the message encountered, the student races over the course toward the goal of discipleship.

Determining a Curriculum: Some Necessary Distinctions

Accurately defining and describing not only the word *curriculum* but also the concepts underlying it are difficult tasks. Failing to distinguish between curriculum and a curricular plan is a common practice that compounds the problem. The greatest distinction between the two is this: teachers construct a plan or program, but learners confront the curriculum. Laying out the track establishes the curricular plan, but running over the course is when the curriculum is truly experienced. Although educators use the term to describe everything from narrowly perceived published resources to the broadly considered co-curricular perspective presented in this chapter, the curriculum is what actually occurs in the teaching-learning process.

In order to identify some of the primary distinctions between these two terms and the concepts and applications they embody, I have created Table 15. It provides a simple and convenient way to address and analyze some of their differences. My intention is not to place them in competition or contrast with each other, as they indeed are complementary. My purpose is to stimulate thought about, reflection upon, and consideration of the implications for teaching and the preparation of the essential messages to be delivered.

Table 15. Curricular Plan and Curriculum Compared

Curricular Plan	Description	Curriculum
Adjective	Nature	*Noun*
Prescription	Intention	*Description*
Goal	Outcome	*Objective*
Institution	Location	*Classroom*
Administration	Authority	*Faculty*
Teacher	Focus	*Pupil*
Anticipation	Experience	*Fulfillment*
Preparation	Involvement	*Participation*

Another distinction educators must not ignore is the difference between the curricular plan of the institution and that of the instructor. From the vantage point of an administrator, the curricular plan is global, but the curriculum that a student experiences is local. From the perspective of an instructor, the plan may be local, but each lesson is individual. Thus, while administrators may think in terms of the scope and sequence of courses, teachers think in scope and sequences of lessons and individual studies. While administrators may think in terms of organizational policies such as attendance, discipline, or as in the case of a day school, academic honesty and testing, teachers think in terms of seating arrangements, rules for communication, and whether or not to use a PowerPoint presentation. Additionally, we must also consider the diversity experienced by coaches, music teachers, small group leaders, and even pastors as they stand before their congregations to preach. The distinction between the perception of those who primarily lead people and those who primarily manage organizations is palpable.

A concluding observation to this discussion concerns those situations in which the administration fails or chooses not to provide a curricular plan for the organization. For example, consider what happens when the only tools provided a third grade Sunday school teacher are a commentary and a box of markers for the white board; the only instructions a small group leader receives is to discuss the pastor's sermon; or the recently appointed training coordinator is told to start providing classes before the department and the program have been established. These are not just fanciful illustrations; they happen frequently in churches, schools, and businesses. When such a scenario occurs, the instructor faces the responsibility not only of leading the pupils in a successful educational endeavor, but also of constructing an appropriate plan as well. As a pastor once informed me, "Give the people language, or they will make up their own." The students, after all, will be exposed to and experience something. They will hear lectures, observe demonstrations, interact with other students, and watch the teacher; they will race over a course, whether it has been planned or not.

The student, teacher, and department or organization all benefit when the curriculum is intentional rather than accidental. Planning for the experiences the students will encounter as they race over the course created for them is the essential activity required to implement the principles we have discovered in this chapter. Let us now, then, discuss and explore a recommended approach to curricular planning.

A Suggested Approach to Curricular Planning

In the introduction to this chapter, I shared the story of the development of a curricular plan for a high school. The steps we took in that process are transferrable, at least in principle, to any educational endeavor in church, school, home, or business.

A Quick Look Back

It would be beneficial to review the steps the school took and then establish a sequence of behaviors that any educator may imitate and emulate, whether planning for formal classroom instruction or the variety of informal venues in which learning takes place. The four stages of our project, which are very similar to the four steps of "The Master's Plan" we explored in Chapter 3, included:

1. Establish goals and expectations

Step number one in developing the curricular plan is establishing both institutional and individual goals and expectations. Reviewing the distinctions between educational goals, objectives, and aims, therefore, is a beneficial contribution to the content question. The ultimate *goal* of Christian education is to produce disciples of Jesus who worship him, and the Christian educator has all of the content messages available to choose from in order to do so. Since goals focus upon the result of the educative process, it is more common to find them in curricular plans established for institutions and organizations.

One of the *objectives* and evidences of Christian discipleship is the formulation of a Christian worldview, so the Christian educator narrows the options and expands the opportunities in the selection of the appropriate exposures and experiences necessary to produce such a view. Since objectives are commonly perceived of as sub goals, or steps along the way to accomplish the ultimate goal, they are more rightly within the purview of a learning group and, therefore, established by the instructor or leader.

Finally, as was illustrated earlier, one of the components of the Christian worldview, for example, is a biblical perception of death and dying. The Christian educator *aims* for such an understanding in the pupils by providing teaching methods to facilitate activities that promote and produce learning.

In each of these progressive illustrations, we see that the goal, objective, or aim is facilitated by content or curricular choices and the selection of appropriate messages necessary for fulfilling our educational intentions.

2. Identify the knowledge base, mindset, and skill set necessary to fulfill the expectations

Step number two in the process addresses two primary purposes. The first is to provide a functional rubric that enables the educator to determine whether the goals and expectations have been met. The second is to provide a practical framework for content and curricular message selection. The educator does not go to the four sources and randomly pick lessons that appear to be interesting or "cutting edge" simply for convenience or attraction; the sources can only be rightly utilized when the intention for their use has been identified.

To illustrate, let me reproduce the knowledge base, mindset, and skill set our high school expected of our graduates. They influenced everything we taught and practiced:

✓ An Essential **Core Knowledge** consisting of:

An attainment of the state and district Model Content Standards

A fulfillment of the graduation requirements

✓ An Effective **Skill Set** consisting of:

The ability to...	With the skills of...
Think critically	*Written communication*
Solve problems	*Oral communication*
Do independent research	*Lifelong learning*
Express one's self artistically	*Personal recreation and fitness*

Which will be manifest in the "Marks of Maturity"

✓ An Engaging **Mindset** preparing for:

Responsible citizenship within the community, armed with the ability to discern right from wrong and to be successful in college and life beyond

Any organization, group, team, or even individuals can think through their goals and expectations and generate a catalogue of anticipated content that would be necessary to fulfill those goals. It is this second step in developing a curricular plan that provides the foundation for step three, which is where curricular planning transitions from theory to practice.

3. Determine the resources needed to accomplish these goals and acquire these skills

When the third grade Sunday school teacher, whose students had been experiencing death and dying, approached me for help, we had a pretty good idea of what we wanted to accomplish and the messages it would take to do so. The biggest question we had that day was whether we could find resources and materials that were both age-appropriate and theologically sound.

She had some investigation to do. Of course, her research began with the Scriptures, but it included visits to the library and bookstores. She also interviewed experts and informed lay people. She searched for visual resources, stories to tell, anecdotes to share, and guest speakers to invite.

After an instructor accumulates the necessary resources, they have to be arranged and ordered to present them to the students in the most effective and efficient manner possible. Hence, the concluding step.

4. Arrange these components into a scope and sequence chart and a master schedule of offerings

Finally, an educator must facilitate with efficiency and effectiveness the selection and implementation of an intentional scope and sequence for the instructional exposures and experiences. This is the step where the distinction between institutional and individual curricular plans is most prominent. The school administrator, faculty forum, or task force focuses its attention upon course offerings, academic policies, and mundane matters such as class length, bell schedules, and lunch times. The education pastor likewise reviews the possibility of purchasing packaged curricular supplies, arranging the appropriate size room and equipment for each class, and wondering whether or not he can recruit the kind of people to teach that are really disciple makers and not just slot fillers. Administrators simply have different perspectives and priorities than instructors; they think corporately.

Teachers, on the other hand, focus on methods and specific content issues rather than big themes; for example, they structure and sequence units of lessons rather than entire courses. Coaches focus their attention upon the dozen games on their team schedule, not the one hundred that concern league officials. Dance instructors and music teachers focus upon the specific performances of their charges and design a plan to produce excellence; their attention is on their pupils, not on the other participants and attendees at the recital. No matter what the subject area, the focus of the instructor's concentration is a particular discipline or activity rather than the larger picture; they think individually.

A Nicely-Ordered Procedure

Mark Smith has summarized an approach to curricular construction that places emphasis upon the product of learning rather than the activity of teaching. In quoting Ralph Tyler and Hilda Taba, he recognizes the same basic concerns addressed by the charter school, but expands them into seven steps that produce a "nicely-ordered procedure" that either a leader or a teacher may implement.

Ralph W. Tyler has made a lasting impression on curriculum theory and practice. His theory was based on four fundamental questions:

1. What educational purposes should the school seek to attain?

2. What educational experiences can be provided that are likely to attain these purposes?

3. How can these educational experiences be effectively organized?

4. How can we determine whether these purposes are being attained? (Tyler 1949: 1)

"We can see how these concerns translate into a nicely-ordered procedure:

Step 1: Diagnosis of need

Step 2: Formulation of objectives

Step 3: Selection of content

Step 4: Organization of content

Step 5: Selection of learning experiences

Step 6: Organization of learning experiences

Step 7: Determination of what to evaluate and of the ways and means of doing it. (Taba 1962)

The attraction of this way of approaching curriculum theory and practice is that it is systematic and has considerable organizing power. Central to the approach is the formulation of behavioural objectives – providing a clear notion of outcome so that content and method may be organized and the results evaluated (Smith 2000).

A Brief Look Forward: A Suggested Approach

Tyler's four questions correlate closely to the four stages implemented by the high school, and Taba's corresponding seven-step procedure for contemplating and constructing a curricular plan incorporates most of the issues and principles we have dealt with in this chapter. In fact, with the addition of some suggestive questions, I recommend and utilize Taba's work as a template for a worksheet that a leadership team may use to guide and direct their curricular efforts. Located on the Reflection and Response page, I have reproduced the worksheet in outline form to provide a series of sequential steps that an educator can revisit at any time as new direction unfolds and the vision's focus is sharpened. Informed by the answers to pertinent questions, an instructor or administrator can follow these steps to construct a curricular plan or program for any educational endeavor. The process of creating such a plan will progress down a creative and fluid path that proceeds from the more or less theoretical to the intensely practical.

This procedure aids the educator in conceiving and constructing the course of exposures and experiences over which the student races to the goal line of learning and experiencing a life change. To illustrate how this works practically, we will first look at a biblical example of curriculum development (Acts 2:42-47) and then explore a contemporary application to close out this segment.

A Biblical Illustration

They devoted themselves to the apostles' teaching and to the fellowship, to the breaking of bread and to prayer. Everyone was filled with awe, and many wonders and miraculous signs were done by the apostles. All the believers were together and had everything in common. Selling their possessions and goods, they gave to anyone as he had need. Every day they continued to meet together in the temple courts. They broke bread in their homes and ate together with glad and sincere hearts, praising God and enjoying the favor of all the people. And the Lord added to their number daily those who were being saved (Acts 2:42-47).

Evident in this readily recognizable and often quoted passage of Scripture is a model for church program development and the skeleton of a practical application of the content and curricular issues that we have been discussing. As the early church apostles and fathers considered the course over which the disciples were to race, they drew their messages from the tradition of Moses, the prophets, and the rest of the Old Testament text. Additionally, the daily life and ministry experience of the apostles filled the church with awe as their stories were recounted. The needs of the congregation and how to address them were also vital components of the strategic plan devised for the growth and development of the church. Finally, in the intervention of the Lord, manifest in miracles and many salvations, we readily see his hand at work. Tradition, participation, observation, and inspiration were all utilized as integral sources in the establishment of the message and proclamation intended to produce disciples who worship Jesus.

Within this proclamation, there is also evidence of the use of all four forms by which a message may be communicated. The subject matter was primarily the apostles' doctrine but it also included "many other words" (See Verse 40). They created an environment that included fellowship in the temple courts and their individual homes, sharing life experiences in breaking bread, prayer, baptism, and praise. The apostles were the models to be imitated, and they provided the example that illuminated knowledge and inspired action in the disciples.

This intentional "curricular plan" included an emphasis upon Stage V learning experiences. The disciples were motivated to life change, and it was evident in activities and behaviors such as:

- Devoting themselves
- Sharing communion and community
- Meeting needs
- Meeting together
- Praising God and worshiping Jesus

Debates rage in some circles as to whether or not this first century model is appropriate and applicable for the twenty-first century church. As to the specifics of the structure and program elements employed, I will not enter that debate here. As to the principles and underlying universal concepts illustrated in the establishment of their curricular plan, however, I submit that they have left us a model worthy of emulation and imitation.

A Contemporary Application

With this biblical example setting the stage, let us observe a more contemporary application of curricular principles. We will look over the shoulder of a fictitious Sunday school teacher of middle-school students who observes and acknowledges a lack of genuine love among the young people of her class. Wanting to address the problem before it creates serious division and distraction, she formulates a plan to present a biblical perspective and prescription for living a life of love (Ephesians 5:1-7). As she makes notes that she will later expand into a complete strategy, she identifies the sources for the various messages and lessons she intends to incorporate in her curricular plan:

1) Texts from the Gospel of John, and the epistles of 1John and Ephesians;

2) Stories from her own life when love was absent and the consequences she endured, along with anecdotes that illustrate the positive impacts of loving behavior;

3) Testimonies from some of the students who had been hurt by unloving acts, as well as historical and contemporary illustrations; and

4) Group prayer, trusting that the Lord would speak to and inspire her students.

After determining the messages she believes the students need to hear, see, and experience, she spends time delineating and describing the forms in which these messages may be communicated. Her *subject matter* will include: a definition of love, biblical instructions and examples, contemporary illustrations and applications, and some independent student research. In creating an *environment* that facilitates and supports her messages of love, she intends to: greet each student with attention and affection at the door, place text posters in the classroom, create small groups with seating arrangements that place students in close proximity to each other, and go out of her way to make sure that her students know that she is available. In generating *life experiences* that help express and confirm the love message, she will: motivate her students to love one another by engaging in role plays, creating "agape boxes" to take to those in need, and generally utilizing dramatic and discovery methods of teaching. As the *teacher (model)* herself, her example will include behaviors such as telling her own story, calling each student during the week, and being on the lookout for opportunities to love and motivate her students to do the same. Finally, she addresses the sequence in which she can most effectively deliver the messages and creates lesson plans to facilitate her strategy.

While this example may not illustrate the extent or complexity of a formally developed curricular plan as I alluded to in this chapter, it does illustrate the kinds of thoughts, reactions, and intentions that the everyday Sunday school teacher, club leader, small group manager, coach, or caring parent have as they intentionally structure environments and activities of learning. In other words, whether formal or informal, large or small, organized or casual, or even natural or intentional, effective educators consider the sources and forms of their messages and lay out a course of exposures and experiences over which their students will race as they progress to the goal of the perfected and prepared life in Christ.

The Principal Principles

In conclusion and summary, discipleship ministries operate most effectively within the structure and guidelines provided by the principal principles I acknowledge in the Preamble to Part III. Numbers 4-6 provide a response to our second inquiry, "What Is the Content of (Christian) Education?"

Principal Principles:

In succinct review, Christian education:

4. contains messages that we choose to communicate in a curricular plan:
(Content controls curriculum).
Hebrews 12
5. determines its messages, primarily, through 4 sources:
(Tradition, Observation, Participation, Inspiration).
1Corinthians 2, 3; 2Peter 1:12-21
6. communicates its messages, primarily, in 4 forms:
[Subject Matter, Environment, Life (experiences),
Teacher (model)].
John 14:6

Prime Characteristic: Christian education is Bible-based.

(Based: "to establish the starting point or line for an action or undertaking")
Every element of Christian education must find support and justification in Scripture. This is especially true of an educator's choice of message(s) to present to the learner(s).

Essential Activity:

Construct a Curricular Plan

Reflection and Response

An Experience in Curriculum Design

Utilize this outline, adapted from Hilda Taba's sequence and incorporating all of the critical concerns addressed in this chapter, to facilitate the construction of a curricular plan or an educational program for institutional or individual use. Answer the "Discussion" questions in order to form the framework for your plan and then finalize and fix the details in a formal document for distribution.

Step 1: Diagnosis of need

Description: Analyze and assess the educational environment

Discussion: What essential issues do our mission and vision statements address?

- Discipleship
  - o Evangelism
  - o Education
- Worship

Step 2: Formulation of objectives

Description: Determine the competencies expected of disciple-followers

Discussion: What are the goals of this educational ministry?

- What do we want them to know? What attitudes do we want them to hold?
- What do we want them to be able to do? How will we address deficiencies?

Discussion: What are the intended outcomes in the lives of the learners?

- An Essential Knowledge Set consisting of...
- An Effective Skill Set consisting of...
- An Engaging Mindset preparing for...

Step 3: Selection of content

Description: Explore the possible origins of the content

Discussion: From what are the curricular messages extracted? Narrow the options by...

- TRADITION: the messages/lessons embedded in and extracted from the "heritage of the race" (J. M. Gregory, 1888) – corporate experience and tradition, transmitted in both oral and written expressions. The historical "stuff" that societies codify in their texts and contain in their treasures to describe and perpetuate their culture (the "content" of socialization)
- OBSERVATION: the messages/lessons embedded in and extracted from the learning activities of the student – the life experiences and needs of the followers as they are witnessed and interpreted by the teacher. The raw "stuff" that every individual brings to the educational experience to be refined and cultured. Banyan trees
- PARTICIPATION: the messages/lessons embedded in and extracted from the life experiences of the teacher – as they confirm and impact the lesson objectives. The refined "stuff" that each educator brings to the experience to share with others. Preach what you practice
- INSPIRATION: the messages/lessons embedded in and extracted from the instruction and direction of the Holy Spirit – the immediate inspiration the teacher receives from the divine source. The anointed "stuff" that the teacher receives from above to transmit here below; often perceived of as intuition or "insight" – an innate sense of what is necessary to communicate to the student

Step 4: Organization of content

Description: Select an ordered and organized framework
Discussion: How will these messages be arranged harmoniously?

- Once content has been determined, it must be organized into a functional framework. Content determines curriculum 'scope,' but the related issue of 'sequence' requires additional coordination.
    o Chronology (e.g., historical studies);
    o Complexity (e.g., simple concepts lead to more complicated ones, as in math);
    o Theory/thesis/theme (e.g., literature);
    o Pedagogy (e.g., from personal to remote events, or from concrete to abstract).

Step 5: Selection of learning experiences

Description: Determine the message(s) necessary to facilitate the competencies and fulfill the objectives

Discussion: To what will the students be exposed?

Discussion: In what will the students be experienced? Expand the opportunities through...

- SUBJECT MATTER: a reality replacement
  - o What will be "said" (or shown, to direct them to learn)?
- TEACHER (model): a representation of reality
  - o What will be done to demonstrate this truth?
- ENVIRONMENT: a framework for reality
  - o What will be "said" with facility, tone, and relationship?
- LIFE (experiences): a participation in reality
  - o What will the student(s) do to experience/practice this truth?

Discussion: Are these forms...

- "Balanced"? Are all four evident in the program?
- "Integrated or correlated"? Are they coordinated and aligned?
- "Congruent"? Do they "say" the same thing?

Step 6: Organization of learning experiences

Description: Formulate a strategy to communicate the curricular message(s)

Discussion: What courses and lessons will be offered?

Discussion: What will be the scope and sequence in which they will be offered?

- Identify what activities must be scheduled to facilitate these
- Create a plan (sequence, schedule, etc.) to accomplish this
- Administrative Concerns
  - o Mission & Vision, Communication, Coordination (Horizontal & Vertical Alignment)
- Educational Concerns
  - o Construct a Master Schedule/Calendar; Prepare a Faculty
- Management Concerns
  - o Resources, Budget, Facility

Discussion: **Review Steps 1-5, modifying the curricular plan as necessary and appropriate.**

Discussion: Decide whether or not a teacher should use published, written curricular materials.

Step 7: Determination of what to evaluate and the ways and means of doing it.

Description: Create a rubric for program evaluation

Discussion: How will the learning that has taken place be assessed?

- Determine what will be evaluated (when and how)
- Based upon what standard (e.g., Proverbs 2)

Ten
What Are the Processes of Education?

I love to swim, and I love the beach. I grew up in southern California, appreciating the mild weather and the benefits of having been born into a very loving, caring, and spiritual family. I enjoyed my church, and most of the time school was tolerable, if not agreeable. I played sports, developed friendships, started my career, and met my wife there. Overall, I have pleasant memories, but after three decades of being away from California, the one thing I truly miss is the beach. I miss Fourth of July beach parties, biking to Newport Beach on Saturdays, and walking along the shore at sunset. More than anything, though, I miss body surfing.

I am amazed, however, that I could be so enthralled with a sport at which I did not excel. Although I did take pleasure in it, I never took a lesson to learn how to properly swim or surf, and I never truly knew what I was doing. That is, until I took a college course in water safety instruction and senior life saving. That course formally introduced me to the proper techniques of the various strokes, and to pass the course I had to be proficient in each. It quickly became apparent that my self-taught strokes were not acceptable, and I had to learn how to swim all over again. I will never forget those first few days; everything right felt so wrong. I had bad habits to unlearn and new techniques to master.

I was unaware of it at the time, but as I reflect upon how I learned to swim correctly, I can now identify the five stages of the teaching-learning metamodel explored in Chapter 6 and how they played out in sequence:

I.   I willingly submitted to the instruction by taking the course,
II. Presented my senses to receive that instruction,
III. Engaged in critical thinking and reflective response as I considered the implications for my strokes,
IV. Improved my capacities with each lesson, and
V.   Ultimately became a more effective swimmer.

In this chapter, we will examine the conceptual context for the Proverbs 2 Teaching-Learning Metamodel and sharpen our perspective by focusing on the critical components of the educational process. If Chapter 6 was the microscope, allowing us to explore the details of the teaching-learning process, then this chapter is the telescope, allowing us to explore the universe in which it exists and operates. As previously, we will investigate concerns critical to the inquiry first, and then we will explore the activities essential to an application of the process question.

Concerns Critical to the Inquiry

Due to the nature and extent of the subject matter I will address in this chapter, a significant portion of the content is based upon or extracted from previously presented material. Repetition is therefore unavoidable. To minimize this, I have attempted to concisely summarize points wherever possible, to utilize notes, or to simply refer to the original discussion. With that proviso and the framework of the preceding nine chapters, we will commence our exploration of the critical processes of Christian education by addressing a number of concepts central to this conversation.

Identifying Some Central Concepts and Cautions

The first concern we must consider is actually a caution for teachers and leaders. They must be careful to avoid the deception of the seductive assumption that standing before a collection of disciple-followers and declaring a message insures that communication has occurred. Presenting information, even accompanied by illustrations and application suggestions, does not equal lessons learned. After all, simply seeing words does not constitute reading, hearing words does not constitute listening, and seeing movement or symbols does not constitute observing.

The corollary to this warning is the observation and resultant caution that neither the teacher nor the leader can be satisfied with going through the motions of fruitless activity. If learning has not occurred then there has been no teaching; if following has not occurred there has been no leading. It is true that there are educators who promote a less strident definition of teaching, in which the teaching process is separate from the learning process. The operational assumption taken in this book, however, is that to truly teach denotes that a student has truly learned. Scholars seriously debate this concept; however, as discussed at the end of Chapter 7, an investigation of the Hebrew language of the Old Testament reveals that significant terms for teaching and learning share the same root, *lamad*. While this may not close the case, it certainly provides evidence of a biblical base and support for the use of the hyphenated term *teaching-learning* process.

There are certainly other critical concepts and concerns that we need to address when considering the processes of an education that is Christian.

However, as previously stated, this book is intended to be more of a primer than a scholarly treatise, so we will move forward with an investigation of some of the impacting principles that underlie the processes of education.

Exploring Some Impacting Principles

This section will explore two categories of principles that have impact upon education. The first is a catalogue of the various approaches to the educational endeavor that identifies the strategies commonly implemented by teachers and educational administrators. This segment concludes with my recommendation as to which is the most effective approach. The second category of principles consists of observations from the biblical Scriptures. This segment concludes with a teacher's checklist of behaviors that are the logical applications of the principles identified in those observations.

Approaches to Education

Educators can approach their efforts from one of four primary perspectives. Perceived from a different paradigm, we can also view these approach options as teaching-learning strategies that provide assistance in the selection and organization of learning experiences, as found in a curricular plan. These four strategies include approaching education from the perspective of: 1) the *process*, or the methodology of teaching; 2) the *context*, or the environment of teaching; 3) the *people*, or the participants of teaching and learning; and 4) the *content*, or the messages presented in teaching and learning. We will briefly explore and assess each one.

The Process Approach: *A teacher commits to a specific methodology; every message is taught in the same manner.*

Educators who utilize the process approach have a firm conviction that every lesson is learned in basically the same way. We have all sat under a teacher who lectured at every opportunity or one who refused to lecture and preferred a Socratic, interactive dialogue with students. In part, this is the result of a teacher's understanding and definition of the educative process. As we discussed in Chapter 8, education can be perceived either as a pouring in process or a drawing out process. This underlying conceptual basis forms the argument for the transmissive versus constructivist teaching philosophies. It also forms the foundation for the practical ramifications and distinctions between primary and secondary learning's E. D. Hirsch suggested in his book, *The Schools We Need* (1999).

The process approach also generates a debate over the validity of a schooling model for Christian education versus that of a socialization model. The schooling model is familiar, and many of the educational programs of the contemporary local church are based upon it. Hence, we have rows of chairs and desks facing a focal point upfront, with students and teachers utilizing texts, including the Bible, as their primary source of information. Evident also is a memory and mastery understanding of learning. On the other hand, past religious educators like Horace Bushnell and contemporary scholars such as Larry Richards, John Westerhoff, and Thomas Groome (representing evangelical, mainline, and Catholic traditions, respectively), recommend and demonstrate a socialization model for religious education where communication of the Christian life is more relational than instructional.

I am a hearty proponent of outdoor education in all of its venues and forms, whether camps, recreation programs, sports programs, excursions, or outdoor adventure and wilderness activities. In fact, during my college years, I formulated a resident camping program that implemented a principle I refer to as "life laboratory." Since then, I have utilized this approach in four church education programs. I recognize, however, that natural education, and its reliance upon the forces of nature to instruct, limits the ability to accurately transmit detailed information and application. Most of these "natural" programs, therefore, rely heavily upon a trained and competent counseling, program, and instructional staff, and are thus mediated. In other words, even focused programs seldom utilize a single process, so many educators defer to one of the other strategic options.

The Context Approach: *A teacher commits to a specific environment; every message is taught in the same milieu or setting.*

Educators who utilize the context approach have a firm conviction that the environment and the instructional setting are the central components of the teaching-learning process. From the Christian perspective, one of the most prevalent educational ministries utilizing this approach is the Navigators' catalogue of resources for small group ministries. These materials assume their application will take place in a small group environment. Likewise, Serendipity House produces materials intended for small group use. On the other hand, there are those who prefer or insist upon large group approaches; this frequently occurs in mega-churches, where the programs tend to imitate and replicate the multi-thousands in the adult service even if the gatherings are smaller or with different age groups. I once served as the adult education pastor of a large church and spent a significant amount of my time recruiting and training a growing cadre of adult educators. One day, however, the senior pastor instructed me to reduce the number of classes and increase their size rather than continue to produce many small classes. He never informed me of the reason for this shift of emphasis, but the functional principle was a preference for large rather than small adult Sunday school classes; he expected every class to form and perform as a large group.

Granted, there are situations and circumstances in which the size of the group is predetermined by available facility or faculty. The educational approach is evident, however, when those are discretionary, and the organization has the opportunity to choose what size of buildings to build, classrooms to construct, and faculty to recruit.

Size, however, is only one of the factors. Whether education occurs in a formal context, such as a school, or an informal context, such as a camp, impacts the process as well. A *natural education* environment normally provides non-guided learning opportunities; a *discovery* environment employs guided learning with observation; *apprenticeships* utilize guided learning with observation and experience; and finally, *discipleship* offers guided learning with observation, experience, and the sharing of values. The underlying concept behind each of these approaches is that setting and environment matter. In fact, they are definitive in the construction and implementation of educational endeavors. Natural educators, continuing the example from the process approach, believe that life experiences are also the context and often the content of all learning. Progressive educators, in their purest iteration, also fit in this category.

The problem with the context approach is life, living, and learning seldom conform to preconceived or preferred notions. Therefore, even though I love camps and outdoor education ministries, along with small discipleship groups, I do not place myself in the position of expecting all educational activity to occur within those settings or environments. I employ the context, large or small, formal or informal, that I believe will facilitate the most effective learning.

The People Approach: *A teacher commits to a pupil-centered approach — where every message is determined by student's needs and experiences — or to a teacher-focused approached based upon the experiences, values, and goals of the instructor.*

Educators who utilize the people approach have a firm conviction that the needs of the pupil, or the knowledge of the instructor, drive the teaching-learning process. For example, one local school district expects their teachers to adjust the curriculum to the needs of the individual student rather than expecting the student to attain the proficiency level the standards of the district prescribe. The following quotation, taken from a "Talking Points on Board Policy – Kindergarten Entrance Age," issued by their Instructional Services Department in January 2003, exemplifies this stance:

> *All children who meet the age requirement may enter kindergarten. Neither principals nor teachers may discourage parents from enrolling their child in school regardless of the child's developmental readiness or abilities.*
>
> *With the wide developmental spans in children that exist at kindergarten and each of the other grade levels, the District recognizes the role of the school is to match instruction to the needs of each child rather than require the child to fit into a set of curriculum. The educational program will be adapted to meet each child's unique abilities, learning needs and interests.*

Many Christian educators believe that the Bible or the curriculum must be adapted to individual abilities, needs, and interests. This pupil-centered approach has many good motives and applications, but we have to be cautious when accommodating individual needs and preferences. We must be careful to mitigate the possibility of compromising the content to such an extent that we sacrifice the original intent of the message. This can create a situation where standards are not developed or lowered to a point where the quality and content of the curriculum is lost. This is one of the issues that the federal "No Child Left Behind" legislation attempted to rectify in addressing the declining standardized test scores of public school students.

The Content Approach. *A teacher commits to a specific message; every message is delivered utilizing the appropriate context and process for that lesson.*

Educators who utilize the content approach have a firm conviction that what matters is the message. How and where it is delivered or discovered are functional but secondary considerations. In other words, once a teacher has selected the message, he can then proceed to determine the most effective methods, materials, settings, and relationships to ensure the reception and mastery of the message by the student.

In this approach, messages are perceived as either *foundational*, with the student participating in activities that primarily promote "learning to live," or *experiential*, with the student participating in activities that primarily promote "living to learn." Utilizing the terms presented in Chapter 9, foundational content messages expose the learner to the forms of subject matter and teacher (model), while experiential content messages provide the learner with experiences in the forms of environment and life.

It is my considered conviction that the content approach to educational experiences is the most effective and efficient of the four. This is evident in both the suggested strategy for curricular plan development proffered in the previous chapter and in the recommended plan for teaching and learning presented here.

This discussion of the approaches to education constitutes only one of the "Impacting Principles" I will identify in this section on critical concerns. Since the greatest impact upon my understanding of educational process principles comes not from reasoning but from revelation, I will address in this section some selected observations from the Scriptures.

Observations on a Biblical Approach to the Teaching Ministry

The seminary where I teach recently initiated a Ph.D. program in apologetics and biblical studies. One of the first courses that the students are expected to take is a combined class on research techniques and college teaching methodology. The underlying assumption is that at some point in their careers doctoral students will be engaged in extensive research and expected to present the results of their study. I was selected to construct the segment on college teaching preparation and spent a significant amount of time over a summer break creating my course plan and agenda. During that time, I fine-tuned a number of previously produced materials, presentations, and student handouts, but the most exciting project was identifying the basic biblical underpinnings to the process of Christian education. I described them simply as "observations," but they were quickly converted into principles and practices that I labeled as a "teacher's checklist" of resultant and recommended behaviors.

Most of these foundations are not new to our investigation. Each of them received attention in previous chapters or sections of this book. Therefore, we will use the following set of notes to review eight biblical observations in order to lay the groundwork for a suggested sequence of steps essential to the processes of generating and producing life change.

Observation 1: The Teaching Ministry Demands Devotion

> *The gracious hand of his God was on him. For Ezra had devoted himself to the study and observance of the Law of the LORD, and to teaching its decrees and laws in Israel.*
> *Ezra 7:9, 10*

> *Cf. I Timothy 4:16: Watch your life and doctrine closely. Persevere in them, because if you do, you will save both yourself and your hearers.*

Description: Conceptually, as was noted in the study of the Ezra Experience, this observation is virtually axiomatic; it is so obvious that it requires no explanation. Practically, however, it is frequently ignored. Preachers and teachers do not spend enough time in the study and observance of the law, and consequently they experience ineffective teaching and unchanged lives.

A Teacher's Checkpoint: ☑ **Master Your Message**

Prescription: Before you stand before or sit among your disciple-followers, make sure you have something to say – something that you truly know they need because you have experienced in your own life.

Observation 2: The Teaching Ministry Demands Discipleship

> *The LORD disciplines those he loves, as a father the son he delights in.*
> *Proverbs 3:12*

> *For you know that we dealt with each of you as a father deals with his own children, encouraging, comforting and urging you to live lives worthy of God.*
> *1 Thessalonians 2:11, 12*

> *Cf. Mark 3:14, Acts 4:13, 1 Thessalonians 1:4-7; 2:6b-12:*
> *He appointed twelve – designating them apostles – that they might be <u>with</u> him and that he might send them out to preach.*
> *When they saw the courage of Peter and John and realized that they were unschooled, ordinary men, they were astonished and they took note that these men had been <u>with</u> Jesus*

> *You know how we lived among you... we were gentle among you, like a mother caring for her little children... You are witnesses, and so is God, of how holy, righteous and blameless we were among you who believed.*

Description: Although observed prominently in the ministries of Jesus and Paul, the necessity of being close to our disciples is evident throughout Scripture. From a father disciplining his son to an apostle planting a church, we see the disciple-making process contingent upon being "with" and "among" while engaging in the Communication > Choice > Consequence pattern of development and training. Ministry demands proximity and the immediacy of discipline to be truly effective in producing disciple-followers.

A Teacher's Checkpoint: ☑ **Discipline Your Disciple(s)**

Prescription: Before you can expect your messages to carry the transforming power of life change, you need to be close enough to your students to equip them with the potential of a "life worthy," and exercise the discipline necessary to develop and nurture it. Whether that discipline is educative or corrective, it trains and prepares the disciple for life change.

Observation 3: The Teaching Ministry Demands Design

> *Let us run with perseverance the race marked out for us. Let us fix our eyes on Jesus, the author and perfected of our faith.*
> Hebrews 12:1, 2

> *Cf. Acts 2:42: They devoted themselves to the apostles' teaching and to the fellowship, to the breaking of bread and to prayer.*

Description: Countless books and articles recommend the example of the early church in the book of Acts as a template for the program of the Church in any age. The reason for this is the conviction and belief that the biblical model is universal in application, and that there is a design available for all who would emulate it. This conviction applies to the teaching-learning process as well. In the creation of a course for our students to run over, we are duplicating and implementing the concept of design.

A Teacher's Checkpoint: ☑ **Create Your Curriculum**

Prescription: Before you stand or sit before your students, take the time to discern the design appropriate for the learner and the lesson to be presented. Although every situation is different, a curricular carrier implementing the principles and procedures discussed in Chapter 9 is possible for every educational opportunity.

Observation 4: The Teaching Ministry Demands a Proclamation

> *You must teach what is in accord with sound doctrine.*
> *Titus 2:1*

> *We loved you so much that we were delighted to share with you not only the gospel of God but our lives as well, because you had become so dear to us.*
> *1 Thessalonians 2:8*

> *Cf. Romans 15:18, 1 John 1:1: I will not venture to speak of anything except what Christ has accomplished through me ... by the power of signs and miracles, through the power of the Spirit. So... I have fully proclaimed the gospel of Christ.*
> *That which was from the beginning, which we have heard, which we have seen with our eyes, which we have looked at and our hands have touched—this we proclaim concerning the Word of life.*

Description: In his famous *The Seven Laws of Teaching,* John Milton Gregory (1973) describes a corollary to the Law of the Teacher: "What the teacher knows he must teach." Addressed as either a moral obligation or a natural consequence, this law is also virtually axiomatic from a biblical perspective.

A Teacher's Checkpoint: ☑ **Communicate your Content**

Prescription: Before you present yourself to your students, check your life message, be aware of the current condition of your students, and be sensitive to the Holy Spirit. Then select the messages that are appropriate, and share them with your students in such a way that they become common to the both of you.

Observation 5: The Teaching Ministry Demands a Plan

> *For this reason, since the day we heard about you, we have not stopped praying for you and asking God to fill you with*

> the <u>knowledge</u> of his will through all spiritual wisdom and
> <u>understanding</u>. And we pray this in order that you may <u>live a</u>
> <u>life</u> worthy of the Lord.
> Colossians 1:9-10

> Cf. Philippians 1:9-11: And this is my prayer: that your
> love may abound more and more in <u>knowledge</u> and depth of
> <u>insight</u>, so that you may be able to discern what is best and
> may be pure and <u>blameless</u> until the day of Christ, filled with
> the fruit of righteousness that comes through Jesus Christ -- to
> the glory and praise of God.

Description: The apostle's prayers for the disciples in Colosse and Philippi indicate a rather simple and straightforward approach to his ministry. Apparently in sequence, he prays for and anticipates: 1) an increase in knowledge, 2) a wise and discerning spirit, and 3) the practical application of these in life.

A Teacher's Checkpoint: ☑ **Prepare Your Plan**

Prescription: In preparing for the presentation of yourself and your message to your students, formulate a strategic plan that incorporates these three concerns in sequence. We will address how to do this in a section on creating a biblical template for a lesson plan later in this chapter.

Observation 6: The Teaching Ministry Demands a Procedure

> Whatever you have <u>learned</u> or received or heard from me,
> or <u>seen</u> in me—put it into <u>practice</u>. And the God of peace will
> be with you.
> Philippians 4:9

> Cf. 1 Thessalonians 1:4-7: For we know, brothers loved by
> God, that he has chosen you, because our gospel came to you not
> simply with <u>words</u>, but also with power, with the Holy Spirit
> and with deep conviction. You know how we lived among you
> for your sake. You became <u>imitators</u> of us and of the Lord; in
> spite of severe suffering, you welcomed the message with the joy
> given by the Holy Spirit. And so you <u>became a model</u> to all the
> believers in Macedonia and Achaia.

Description: These passages affirm the three critical processes of Christian education that we examined in Chapter 8. The proclamation of information, the provision of a model to imitate, and the promotion of practical experience and life change are the foundational building blocks upon which an effective procedure for every educational endeavor and teaching-learning experience can be constructed and implemented.

A Teacher's Checkpoint: ☑ **Implement Your Instruction**

Prescription: As you present yourself and your message to your students, do so with balance and congruence, integrating all three components. Information, identification, and experience provide all that is necessary for an effective methodology. We will address how to identify and select the appropriate instructional method for a teaching plan later in this chapter.

Observation 7: The Teaching Ministry Demands Assessment

> *Examine yourselves to see whether you are in the faith; test yourselves. Do you not realize that Christ Jesus is in you—unless, of course, you fail the test? And I trust that you will discover that we have not failed the test.*
> *2Corinthians 13:5, 6*

> *We do not dare to classify or compare ourselves with some who commend themselves. When they measure themselves by themselves and compare themselves with themselves, they are not wise.*
> *2Corinthians 10:12*

> *Cf. Acts 15:19, 36; James 1:3: It is my judgment, therefore, that we should not make it difficult for the Gentiles who are turning to God.*
> *Some time later Paul said to Barnabas, "Let us go back and visit the brothers in all the towns where we preached the word of the Lord and see how they are doing."*
> *...you know that the testing of your faith develops perseverance.*

Description: This biblical observation concerns the evaluation process that rouses fear in students and anxiety in teachers. Testing, trying, approving, and correcting are four of the biblical terms utilized to describe the process of assessing the learner prior to or as the result of a lesson, and the same ultimate reality that restricts our selection of curricular messages also forms the rubric by which all learning is assessed. It is not enough to be satisfied with our teaching and its results simply because it is better than another teacher's performance. It must be measured against the ultimate standard of the perfection of Jesus.

A Teacher's Checkpoint: ☑ **Evaluate Your Effectiveness**

Prescription: As you engage in the educational enterprise, you must remember that the standard of perfection presented by the Lord himself is the one against which both students and teachers will be judged. As the Apostle Paul recounts in Romans 14, it is to him alone that we stand or fall, and he will make us stand. At the same time, however, we are encouraged to test both ourselves and others to see how we are progressing in our faith development.

Observation 8: The Teaching Ministry Demands Anticipation

> *Paul and his companions [had] been kept by the Holy Spirit from preaching the word in the province of Asia. ... During the night Paul had a vision of a man of Macedonia standing and begging him, "Come over to Macedonia and help us." After Paul had seen the vision... we concluded that God had called us to preach the gospel to them.*
> *Acts 16:6-10*

> *Cf. Exodus 3:15-20: Go, assemble the elders of Israel ...*
> *The elders of Israel will listen to you. Then you and the elders are to go to the king of Egypt and say to him, "The LORD, the God of the Hebrews, has met with us. Let us take a three-day journey into the desert to offer sacrifices to the LORD our God." But I know that the king of Egypt will not let you go unless a mighty hand compels him. So I will stretch out my hand and strike the Egyptians with all the wonders that I will perform among them. After that, he will let you go.*

Description: The primary intention of evaluation, as explained in Observation 7, is to assess the students' learning, either as a preparation for the lesson to come or as an examination of the lesson to have been learned. In both instances, the practical effect is to give guidance to future educational endeavors. Thus, evaluating both the student's learning and the teacher's instruction is biblical and beneficial. This process is both the culmination of one educational event and the commencement of the next.

Therefore, this process generates an exceptionally high level of expectation and anticipation concerning the prospects before them.

As was discussed in the section on the sources of an educator's message, an assessment of the present conditions and experiences of our pupils is only one of the four primary ways in which messages are determined. In addition to tradition and the life experiences of the teacher, these selected scriptures also emphasize the guidance and direction of the Lord himself. They remind us of the importance placed upon the leader's responsibility to hear primarily from the Lord in determining a mission and vision.

Put simply, this observation identifies a primary principle for both teaching and leading: as you anticipate your next lesson, seek inspiration from the Lord as you establish direction, intention, and expectation for your endeavors.

A Teacher's Checkpoint: ☑ **Face Your Future**

Prescription: As you prepare to stand before your students with another lesson, take into consideration the learning that has occurred and where you need to go educationally from there. More than anything else, however, take the time to inquire of and receive direction from the Lord as you and your pupils face your future.

These eight biblical observations, and the checklist they generate, provide the basis for a suggested sequence of instructional steps that produce student learning. They are represented as a circular sequence in Display 12.

Display 12. Biblical Observations and the Checklist They Generate

A Suggested Sequence of Steps: Giving Guidance to Instruction

Based upon the biblical record and the principles we have been exploring in this book, we can identify seven steps that provide the Christian educator with an efficient and effective pattern for educational excellence:

Step 1: Dedicate Yourself

Step 2: Disciple your Students

Step 3: Discern your Strategy

Step 4: Assemble your Teaching Plan

Step 5: Assist your Students' Learning

Step 6: Assess your Teaching Effectiveness

Step 7: Select your Next Message

With the establishment of our critical concerns for this chapter, we now move to an examination of the activities essential to an application of the inquiry that we are addressing: "What Are the Processes of Christian Education?"

Activities Essential to an Application

When exploring the processes of education, the vast diversity of educational activity becomes evident. Learners utilize differing styles, preferences, and processing speeds, and teachers employ a catalogue of various approaches and preferred methods. Yet, somehow in the midst of this diversity and differentiation, people teach and people learn.

After examining, in Chapter 9, a prescription for a curricular strategy we can utilize to facilitate the proposed definition of education, we now turn our attention to the approaches and principles that facilitate the most effective means to disseminate those curricular messages. In doing so, we will address the essential activity of the process question and learn how to "Prepare a Plan for Teaching and Learning." We will examine this essential activity by investigating a series of five sequentially related and increasingly specific behaviors:

Behavior 1: Communicating – The Key to Teaching and Learning

Behavior 2: Implementing the Critical Components of Teaching and Learning

Behavior 3: Following a Suggested Sequence for Teaching and Learning

Behavior 4: Formulating a Preferred Plan for Teaching and Learning

Behavior 5: Evaluating Teaching and Learning

In this order, we will: 1) reaffirm that the key to every enterprise is communication and commence our study with a brief review of this essential activity, 2) take a more detailed look at another previously introduced concept, "The Biblical Model," which consists of three components, and 3) present a suggested sequence of activities that emanates from the biblical observations and teacher checklist generated in the previous section. After constructing this conceptual platform, we will: 4) explore in some depth the essential activity of actually preparing a lesson plan, and 5) examine some critical concepts for evaluating its effectiveness in facilitating student learning and the determination of future lessons.

Behavior 1: Communicating – The Key to Teaching and Learning

The essential activity of transmitting and receiving messages from one individual or group to another is the key to being a really good, really global, world-class educator. This anonymous, and apparently quite old, story illustrates not only the complexity but also the necessity of that process:

> About a century or two ago, the Pope decided that all the Jews had to leave the Vatican. Naturally there was a big uproar from the Jewish community. So the Pope made a deal. He would have a religious debate with a member of the Jewish community. If the Jew won, the Jews could stay. If the Pope won, the Jews would leave.
>
> The Jews realized that they had no choice. So they picked a middle-aged man named Moishe to represent them. Moishe asked for one addition to the debate. To make it more interesting, neither side would be allowed to talk. The Pope agreed.
>
> The day of the great debate came. Moishe and the Pope sat opposite each other for a full minute before the Pope raised his hand and showed three fingers. Moishe looked back at him and raised one finger. The Pope waved his fingers in a circle around his head. Moishe pointed to the ground where he sat. The Pope pulled out a wafer and a glass of wine. Moishe pulled out an apple. The Pope stood up and said, "I give up. This man is too good. The Jews can stay."
>
> An hour later, the cardinals were all around the Pope asking him what happened. The Pope said: "First I held up three fingers to represent the Trinity. He responded by holding up one finger to remind me that there was still one God

common to both our religions. Then I waved my finger around me to show him that God was all around us. He responded by pointing to the ground and showing that God was also right here with us. I pulled out the wine and the wafer to show that God absolves us from our sins. He pulled out an apple to remind me of original sin. He had an answer for everything. What could I do?"

Meanwhile, the Jewish community had crowded around Moishe. "What happened?" they asked. "Well," said Moishe, "First he said to me that the Jews had three days to get out of here. I told him that not one of us was leaving. Then he told me that this whole city would be cleared of Jews. I let him know that we were staying right here."

"And then?" asked a woman.

I don't know," said Moishe. "He took out his lunch and I took out mine."

We established earlier, and illustrated with Moishe, that communication must involve more than just the sending of a message (see and review the details of the process in Chapter 2). Since a message is first conceived in the soulish activities of thought, feeling, and decision-making, then transmitted via the senses to the soul of the receiver, effective communication involves the apprehension of meaning and understanding on the part of the disciple-follower. As Myron Rush suggests:

Communication can be defined as the process we go through to convey understanding from one person or group to another. Unless understanding occurs, we have not communicated. Therefore when people complain about poor communication, they are actually complaining about the lack of understanding and not about the lack of conversation, discussions, memos, or correspondence.

All too often we confuse the tools of communication with communication itself. Just because we have made the effort to communicate with someone, it doesn't guarantee that they'll automatically comprehend our message. Talking does not insure understanding, and written correspondence does not necessarily mean people understand the message (Rush 1983).

As the superintendent of a charter school, my board instructed me to improve communication between the administration and the school's families by instituting three forms of redundant communication. I did better and instituted five. These revisions, however, did not help the mother who came into our office one afternoon looking for the parent conferences scheduled for the next day. She had ignored the monthly newsletter and school newspaper sent to her home, an auto-dialer voice message left on her home phone, and the marquee announcement she passed when entering our offices. Her inattention to the message resulted in disrupted and broken communication.

The next spring, as we developed our strategic plan, the board once again asked me to improve communication with our families. I wholeheartedly agreed, but my suggestion to focus on the families' responsibilities in the receiving process rather than just adding more modes fell on deaf ears. They were convinced that a communication problem must be the result of ineffective one-way media. In truth, communication travels on a two-way street involving a variety of drivers and vehicles.

Elements of Communication

Traditional communication theorists suggest a linear model for the process that demands at least four elements: 1) a message; 2) a messenger or sender, the source; 3) a medium; and 4) a receiver. The Lord himself identified these very components in one of the most famous passages in the Bible, John 3:16: "For God (the Sender) so loved the world (the Message) that he gave his one and only Son (the Medium) that whoever (the Receiver) believes in him (Receiver's response/feedback) shall not perish but have eternal life (the Mission, the intent of the Message)." Some authorities include feedback in the model, and others expect an acknowledgment of the environment, including its conditions and obstacles or distortions.

The ability to communicate one's message effectively is the key to every relationship and activity of humankind. In fact, God observed that if people were of one mind, language, and plan, everything they attempt would succeed (Genesis 11:6). From an investigation of the activity of God in the Babel episode, we also discovered his perception of the situation and the only appropriate, proficient means to thwart Satan's plans – the disruption of communication networks through the confusion of language.

Christian leaders need not fear contemporary communication theories, models, and skills; many have a sound biblical foundation. Likewise, education-specific communication incorporates a variety of biblically based activities and processes. Therefore, the next essential behavior we will explore identifies three discrete components that constitute a biblical model for the education enterprise.

Behavior 2: Implementing the Critical Components of Teaching and Learning

If communication is the key to any enterprise, then the latch to the educational endeavor consists of the three crucial process components we may simply label the "Biblical Model." Although the term *model* may seem overused, it is the best term to employ because it describes how something works. These components, introduced in Chapter 8 and addressed as Biblical Observation 6, reveal how the education process unfolds, and expose another universal to add to a really good, really global Christian educator's tool belt.

The "Biblical Model"

Previously, we identified and labeled the three processes that constitute the biblical model as *information, identification,* and *experience.* We described them as:

1. the Transmission of raw data for constructing information and producing knowledge;
2. the Provision of an illustrative model to imitate; and
3. the Motivation to practical application and life change.

Among the many passages that illustrate their implementation, we can identify four as descriptive and prescriptive. They provide the Christian minister with a depiction of what the ancients practiced and a portrait of what contemporary educators can anticipate.

1 Thessalonians 1:4-7: the Model Described

> For we know, brothers loved by God, that he has chosen you, because our gospel came to you not simply with **words**, but also with power, with the Holy Spirit and with deep conviction. You know how we lived among you for your sake. You became **imitators** of us and of the Lord; in spite of severe suffering, you welcomed the message with the joy given by the

*Holy Spirit. And so you **became** a model to all the believers in Macedonia.*

Philippians 4:9: the Model Prescribed

*Whatever you have **learned** or received or heard from me, or **seen** in me—put it into **practice**. And the God of peace will be with you.*

Deuteronomy 6:1-7: the Model Illustrated - Shema

*Hear, O Israel: The LORD our God, the LORD is one. Love the LORD your God with all your heart and with all your soul and with all your strength. These **commandments** that I give you today are to be upon your **hearts**. **Impress** them on your children. Talk about them when you sit at home and when you walk along the road, when you lie down and when you get up. Tie them as symbols on your hands and bind them on your foreheads. Write them on the doorframes of your houses and on your gates.*

Acts 2:42: the Model Illustrated - Gospel

*With many other **words** he warned them; and he pleaded with them, "Save yourselves from this corrupt generation." Those who **accepted his message** were **baptized**...*

*They devoted themselves to the apostles' **teaching** and to the **fellowship**, to the breaking of **bread and to prayer**. Everyone was filled with awe, and many wonders and miraculous signs were done by the apostles. All the believers were together and had everything in common. Selling their possessions and goods, they gave to anyone as he had need. Every day they continued to meet together in the temple courts. They broke bread in their homes and ate together with glad and sincere hearts, praising God and enjoying the favor of all the people. And the Lord added to their number daily those who were being saved.*

In addition to these four texts, the term *manthano* affirms the concept of the model as well as its application.

Manthano

Our exploration of the Proverbs 2 Teaching-Learning Metamodel introduced us to the Greek term *manthano*. In defining and describing the term, *The Complete Biblical Library* (Gilbrant 1986) notes:

> *Manthano occurs in classical Greek with various meanings such as "to learn by instruction, practice, or experience." It can also mean "to acquire the habit" or "to understand." The Septuagint uses manthano to translate three different Hebrew words. In Exodus 2:4 Miriam watched in order to "learn by observation" (manthano) what would happen to Moses. The Israelites were to hear God's word so they might "learn by practice" or "acquire the habit" (manthano) of obeying god (Deuteronomy 4:10; 5:1; 14:23). In Deuteronomy 17:19 the people are to read God's Word and "learn."*

In the section examining New Testament usage, it is also reported that the term refers to at least two forms of learning:

> *In the New Testament manthano means "to learn by investigation" (Matthew 9:13) and "to learn from instruction" (Matthew 11:29; Colossians 1:7).*

Hence, we find that in the uses of *manthano* in both the New Testament and the Septuagint, a Greek translation of the Old Testament, there is a positive correlation to the three processes that constitute the biblical model we are examining. The authors and translators employed *manthano* to describe learning that is facilitated by:

- **Information:** which is provided as we learn by the Word and receive its instruction
- **Identification:** which is promoted as we learn by observation
- **Experience:** which is produced as we learn by practice and participate in investigation

Applying the Model

These three processes are not limited to Biblical support; they are amply attested to by contemporary educators, both Christian and secular. British educator Philip May provided the initial inspiration for identifying and labeling the processes in *Which Way to Educate?* (May 1975). In *Youth Ministry*, Larry Richards labels the same three activities as Bible, Body, and Life (Richards 1972).

In addition to these seminal works, supplementary illustrations of how these processes are applied in a variety of educational settings can be noted. For example, in *Testament of Vision*, Henry Zylstra observes that teaching composition requires illustration, example, and practice (1958), and the article on "Education" in the *Zondervan Pictorial Encyclopedia of the Bible* acknowledges three primary means of teaching: story-telling, modeling, and life situations (Tenney 1975). In my personal file, I have collected a number of illustrations taken from Sunday school teacher training manuals, juvenile residence programs, and children's ministry texts, among others. They ratify the conviction that these three processes are the essential foundation for every effective educational enterprise.

Effective education requires the communication of information and the provision of an example or model to follow, no matter how they are labeled or defined. William Frankena goes "out on a limb" to observe, "My guess is that most of the important things in education are passed on in this manner – by example and explanation" (Frankena 1968). The process, however, is not complete until the student has become a "doer" of the Word, and his mentor assesses his learning. Jesus, Paul, and James all refer to the necessity of a learner putting into practice what is being learned (cf. Matthew 7, James 1, 2, and Ephesians 4-6). This assertion has been attested to throughout our study; it has become essentially axiomatic.

Strategic Applications of the Model – Practice and Praxis

Affirming that education is a creative and flexible process, these activities may proceed from instruction to application or from practice to principle; in other words, either receiving information or having an experience may initiate the sequence. Students may accept instruction, view an illustration, and then attempt to practice it; this is a more traditional approach, and I give it the label of "practice." On the other hand, students may have an experience before it is explained to them. If they reflect upon that experience, learn from it, try again and repeat this process, they are participating in "praxis" (Groome 1980).

A friend and colleague, Jason, is a college instructor of communication studies. In one of his courses, the curricular plan calls for the students to first receive subject matter instruction concerning argumentation via class work and then to create a five-minute oral presentation addressing some sort of proposition. Later, each student presents an examination and evaluation of one of history's outstanding discourses. By identifying and assessing the utilization of the critical components of effective communication discussed in class, this assignment is designed to investigate and articulate what made the selected speech great. In his words, these two assignments require the students to "create" an argument and then to "evaluate" another one.

While scoring a recent collection of these student presentations, Jason observed the expected – the evaluation speeches were significantly superior to those of the initial creation assignment. He was, however, suspicious that this improvement was due to something more than just having experience and practice. He recognized that the speeches created for the first round were based solely upon class instruction and application, while those designed to evaluate were also influenced by the content and process modeled by outstanding speechmakers. His considered opinion was that the students' development was due in part to their exposure to and emulation of the world-class orations they were examining.

Providing instruction without a template to imitate yielded less than optimum outcomes, so he decided that in the future he would assign the evaluation speech first and expose the students to superior examples earlier in their study. In the language of our biblical model, he believed adding identification to information would contribute greatly to improved experience.

Jason's case illustrates a number of the principles we have encountered. First, he attempted to utilize a form of praxis by requiring the creation experience before the evaluation exercise (which would have provided the model with which to identify and imitate). When that apparently failed to produce satisfactory results, he shifted to a practice mode and facilitated instruction, illustration, and implementation in that sequence. Whether by way of practice or praxis, regardless of the sequence in which they are experienced, the proclamation of information, the provision of an example to imitate, and the promotion of practical experience and life change, are the foundational building blocks of every educational endeavor and teaching-learning experience.

We can also observe in his experience the dynamic, creative, and flexible nature of the educative process. Students can learn in a variety of ways, but some approaches and methods appear to work better than others in a given venue.

Finally, Jason adhered to the content approach to education. He allowed the subject matter to drive the setting and the environment, the sequence of activity, and the selection of instructional methods.

Behavior 3: Following a Suggested Sequence for Teaching and Learning

The Christian educator must implement the essential activity of communication, facilitated by the processes of the biblical model, with specific and practical procedures laid out as a course over which the student(s) will race.

The biblical observations noted earlier in this chapter generated a checklist that in turn produced a suggested sequence of instructional steps. The following exposition will show how the answer to the process question can be facilitated in real time educational venues and situations by implementing these steps.

Giving Direction to Instruction

I call this seven-step sequence, "Giving Direction to Instruction." Its intention is just that – to provide an instructor with the guidance necessary to structure a successful teaching-learning experience. A succinct description of each step follows.

Step 1: Dedicate Yourself

Corresponding with Biblical Observation 1, this step addresses the prerequisites necessary for an effective and successful educational experience. Adhering to the directive of the Apostle Paul to his apprentice Timothy, the Christian teacher is to "Watch your life and doctrine closely. Persevere in them, because if you do, you will save both yourself and your hearers" (1Timothy 4:16). In other words, leaders should master their doctrines and model their lives, as discussed in Chapter 7 and the lessons we learned from the example of Ezra.

Step 2: Disciple your Students

In implementing the principles addressed in Chapter 5, and noted in Observation 2, a teacher fulfills this step. In brief summary, it is at this stage that it is important to know the students and to develop their capacities well enough to apprehend the current lesson message. Asking questions such as these can facilitate this: Who are they? Are they trained? Are they ready to learn? Which style do they prefer?

This step is complete when the pupils are trained and have developed their capacities in preparation for the learning experience to come.

Step 3: Discern your Strategy

After assuring that both teacher and pupils are prepared and ready for the lesson, the teacher embarks upon the adventure of establishing the curricular plan that satisfies this strategic step.

A condensed and simplified review of the process may be helpful. Begin by identifying intentions and expectations. Follow that with an exploration of the sources of tradition, participation, observation, and inspiration. Then, select from the options by identifying them, weighing the alternatives, and choosing those most appropriate for the lesson. Next, envision the forms the message will take and utilize subject matter, environment, life experiences, and the model of the teacher, to communicate it. Finally, create the curricular plan itself and facilitate the laying out of a unique learning experience by formulating specific lesson plans.

Step 4: Assemble your Teaching Plan

The teacher's creation of a plan for a specific lesson or unit can be based upon and extracted from what Larry Richards (1970) calls the "Colossians Cycle" and the pattern as it is reproduced in the letter to the Philippians. As identified in Observation 5, this cyclical pattern consists of three primary stages: increased knowledge, followed by perceptive insight and wisdom, and culminating in practical application and life change. The instructor implements this biblical template through the use of a formalized and structured lesson plan, such as the preferred one introduced following the presentation of this suggested sequence. Having a plan, however, simply sets the stage. The teacher must also be concerned about actual learning and progress to Step 5 in the sequence.

Step 5: Assist your Students' Learning

In implementing the teaching-learning metamodel of Proverbs 2, and utilizing instructional methods to do so, teachers engage in five primary activities that promote and produce student learning. These activities are summarized in the following outline:

1. MOTIVATE YOUR STUDENTS
   Extract their interest, to hold their attention
2. COMMUNICATE WITH YOUR STUDENTS
   Excite their senses, to penetrate their soul
3. INSPIRE YOUR STUDENTS
   Expand their knowledge, to promote wisdom

Engage the student's learning, by promoting and directing the development of…

The Cognitive Dimension
Stimulate higher-level thinking and comprehension
The Affective Dimension
Encourage growth and responses from and within the "inner states"
The Psycho-Motor Dimension
Expect increase and maturation in choice and application of appropriate skills

4. ELEVATE YOUR STUDENTS
Extend their limits, to reach their potential
Evaluate your student's learning
Establish a Valid Rubric, Examine the Student's Work, Evaluate According to the Rubric

5. ACTIVATE YOUR STUDENTS
Explore applications, to enrich their lives

After assisting the student's learning, the teacher assesses both the teaching and the learning in order to establish the lesson in the learner and to provide information and direction for the instructor concerning the next message to be addressed.

Step 6: Assess your Teaching Effectiveness

In this, the philosopher and the theologian both agree: the examination of one's life is a necessary component in the perpetual quest for personal fulfillment and achievement. Therefore, the next responsibility of the teacher is to answer two critical questions: "Did my instruction increase and elevate student achievement?" and "Did it facilitate the curricular plan and the mission and vision statements?"

Evaluating the teaching-learning process, as suggested in Observation 7, provides vital directive and corrective action for the future, as well as confirming the validity and effectiveness of the present lesson.

Step 7: Select your Next Message

Lastly, the teacher looks ahead in anticipation and expectation to the next lesson message the students will encounter as they race over the course of prescribed exposures and experiences of the curricular plan.

Behavior 4: Formulating a Preferred Plan for Teaching and Learning

In order to facilitate the implementation of Steps 4 and 5, numerous authors and authorities, including curriculum publishing companies, have constructed and suggested a variety of preferred strategies and approaches to lesson planning. After investigating dozens of these, I have come to two simple conclusions: 1) virtually all of them utilize a four-stage lesson plan structure, following Findley Edge's decades-old template (Edge 1956) and 2) the Hook, Book, Look, Took, lesson planning guide offered by Larry Richards in *Creative Bible Teaching* has provided an efficient and effective structure for formulating a plan for teaching (Richards 1970).

A Recommended Template

Richards' plan consists of: an attention-getting introduction (the Hook), the presentation of information (the Book), interaction with the text and fellow students to discern implications (the Look), and the practical implementation of the lesson (the Took).

A simple two column, four row format, providing one column for teaching methods and a second for learning activities, with four rows for the Hook, Book, Look, and Took stages, is not novel, as authors before and since have utilized similar formats, but it fulfills the necessary requirements. Its ease-of-use can be illustrated by simply folding a regular piece of paper once along the length axis and twice along the width, unfolding into a neat pattern of eight boxes; two columns and four rows produces an easy to construct and useful worksheet.

While I recognize the value of alternative structures and formats, my file cabinet is filled with HBLT formatted lesson plans for Sunday school, home Bible studies, devotionals, camping Bible programs, and even sermons. I have found it to be both efficient and effective in assembling a teaching plan that leads the learner through the five stages of the Proverbs 2 Teaching-Learning Metamodel. In fact, my current lesson plan template utilizes that language. The correlation of the stages of learning – and the three crucial processes – with the phases of the plan can be summarized simply:

- The **Hook** facilitates STAGE I
  - o "Accept my words"
- The **Book** facilitates STAGES II and III while proclaiming information
  - o "Turn your ear and apply your heart"

- The **Look** facilitates STAGES III and IV while providing an example to imitate and exploring implications
  - "Then you will understand"
- The **Took** facilitates STAGE V while promoting practical experience and life change
  - "Thus you will walk"

It should be readily apparent why this template and others that emulate it can be eminently useful to the rookie teacher and the veteran as well. In fact, even a casual perusal will note the structural similarity to the formatting I utilized in this written work. I labored diligently on the introduction to each chapter in my desire to provoke interest in the matter we were to address (the Hook: "Accept my words"). I then produced and presented each chapter (the Book: "Turn your *eyes* and apply your heart"), and illustrated it in such a way that the possible implications and applications would be evident (the Look: "Then you will understand"). Finally, I concluded each chapter with an opportunity to reflect and respond to a component of the written "lesson" (the Took: "Thus you will walk"). I intentionally implemented each of the four steps in an effort to make this work truly educative.

Methods of Instruction

Instructional methods are the techniques utilized by a teacher to implement the transmission of a curricular message and facilitate the processing of that message by the learner. Methods, therefore, are the containers that hold both teaching materials and learning activities, as discussed in Chapter 9. Materials are the physical resources utilized to facilitate the methods; they include visual aids, auditory assists, technology, arts and crafts, costumes, equipment, and printed resources, among others. Learning activities are the behaviors and activities of the student; they include listening, thinking, analyzing, assessing, responding, and making decisions.

In implementing a lesson plan, a teacher utilizes instructional methods to encourage and facilitate the learning activities of the pupils. These techniques can be sorted by categories, and despite being artificial and unofficial, they provide a convenient and condensed catalogue of the available options. The following notes provide a taxonomy of methods and offer assistance in the selection of the most effective means of implementing the biblical model through the application of a planned lesson.

Demonstration Methods

These techniques involve learners in the observation of examples, models, displays, and illustrations of the lesson; they constitute a relational observation of an exhibition. This is the original method of teaching. "To show how to do" has a long and glorious tradition; it should be prominent in the educator's tool kit.

Demonstration methods should not be confused with dramatic methods. While dramatic methods are symbolic and representational, demonstration methods are actual. A role-play, however, is a hybrid, demonstrating the actual while dramatizing the potential, while a "lab" is a combination of demonstration and discovery.

Some biblical examples include: Matthew 6:9-13 (Lord's Prayer); John 14:1-15 (Jesus showed his love, washed feet, and provided example); and 1Corinthians 11:1 (imitate me).

Lecture Methods

These techniques involve learners in the reception of subject matter conveyed by inscribed composition or an oral presentation of the lesson; they constitute an impersonal transmission of information. They facilitate what Slavin (2006) refers to as "direct instruction."

Sermons, speeches, addresses, historical accounts, and the traditional lecture represent this category. They are not to be confused with the manner of delivery, resources utilized, or the content presented; a lecture may be facilitated, for example, by a guest speaker, a personality on film or video, and it may be presented as a story or a testimony.

Media may enhance a lecture. Providing a book, magazine, or pamphlet, however, is not a method, the method consists of the student actually reading and responding to them.

Some biblical examples include: Matthew 5:1, 2 (direct, verbal speech); Luke 18:1, 2 (information through stories); Acts 17:22 (guest speaker); Nehemiah 8 (reading the Law); Hebrews (sermon manuscript?); and all of Jesus' anecdotes and stories.

Socratic Methods

These techniques involve learners in interaction with facts, concepts, and perceptions that produce new insight, clarification, or understanding of the lesson; they constitute an interpersonal exchange of ideas. Socratic methods include discussion, question and answer, and dialogue as well as conversation. They do not primarily transmit information; they facilitate understanding. Information may be disseminated in a group, but that only provides the data necessary for discussion and the essential interaction that constitutes the Socratic method.

Groups formed for brainstorming should not be confused with these methods as they do not facilitate understanding but do engage participants in activity.

Some biblical examples include: Matthew 21:24-27 (use of questions); John 4:7-10 (answers>questions); John 8:12-13 (expression of doubts); John 14 (dialogue with the disciples); and John 3, 4 (dialogue with individuals).

Discovery Methods

These techniques involve learners in an encounter with data facilitated by activities that explore the lesson; they constitute an intrapersonal investigation of information. Discovery in its purest form is natural education; however, enhanced by guided exploration (utilizing worksheets and reflection exercises) or experimentation (as in project-oriented instruction, laboratory work, or research), it has a place in the classroom as well. Interviews, and other forms of observation, would be included in this category.

Discovery methods should not be confused with individualized learning activities, which by definition are personal or possibly inter-personal if the experience is explored or shared later in an interactive group setting.

Some biblical examples include: Acts 16:6 (guided journeys); Luke 18:31-34 (they had to do it); Mark 14:72 (discovery); Luke 9:1-6, 10 (the Twelve sent out); and Luke 9:20 (you are the Christ).

Dramatic Methods

These techniques involve learners in the participation in or observation of simulated or imitated life experiences or lessons applied; they constitute a communal interactive expression of issues. Plays, sketches, vignettes, role-plays, and skits are common dramatic methods. Simply observing a presentation, even exciting drama, comes perilously close to lecture, but if it is done right, it allows a student to vicariously participate in a representation of the experience; e.g., plays can evoke emotion and while field trips are observational, they can easily become participatory.

Dramatic methods should not be confused with entertainment or amusement (*a* = not + *muse* = think); a true dramatic method involves students actively, whether physically or mentally.

Some biblical examples include: Acts 21:11 (visual prophecy); Luke 22:17ff (Lord's Supper); and Prophetic enactments (Jeremiah, Hosea).

Practice Methods

These techniques involve learners in the acquisition or affirmation of an ability or proficiency addressed in the lesson; they constitute personal application of knowledge or acquisition of a skill. Practice methods are attempts to implement, confirm, and validate the learning; they may be utilized to enhance skill, facilitate behavior modification, or apply a lesson to life. These methods are commonly employed in sports, drama, music, and virtually the rest of the arts to train and discipline as well as perfect performance. They also represent and facilitate Stage V learning by being "doers" of the word and putting it into "practice."

Practice should not be confused with methods that facilitate the discovery or revelation of truth; they are a response to that discovery.

Some biblical examples include: Luke 10:28 (do this and live); Luke 22:19 (do this in remembrance); Philippians 4:9 (put it into practice) Deuteronomy 6:7 (talk, walk, come and go); 2Peter 1:5 (add to your faith): 1Timothy 5:4 (put religion into practice) cf. also Ezekiel 33:31, 31; Matthew 5:19, 23:3; and Luke 8:21.

While virtually any method could be employed in any of the phases of the plan, there does seem to be an apparent correlation between the six categories of methods and the three critical processes of education introduced in Chapter 8 and reproduced in this chapter as "The Biblical Model." For example, to proclaim *information*, an instructor may want to consider utilizing, primarily, Lecture and Discovery. To provide *identification*, priority could be given to Demonstration and Socratic methodologies. Finally, to promote *experience*, the teacher may want to have students participate in Dramatic and Practice activities. The correlation of the suggested lesson plan structure with the three processes, implemented by the six categories of methods, provides a seamless integration of the teaching-learning experience.

Methods and Variety

I was sitting at my desk preparing for an evening meeting and training session with a group of departmental leaders. While assembling the plan, I included an activity I had used countless times. A sudden inspiration, however, interrupted me, and I was struck with the thought, "That won't work with these people." Motivated by this realization, I quickly changed plans and also reflected on why I should use a variety of methods in my teaching ministry.

I concluded that there are at least four reasons for not using the same method all the time. First, an understanding of diversity and learning styles demands it. The research is patent; we all learn differently and are in need of differentiated instruction. Second, as we noticed in the section on Stage II of the learning model, brain research affirms that variety stimulates the brain and facilitates learning. Third, our understanding of how people learn and grow – and the differences between learners, whether children or adult – informs us that as people change so do their responses to methods. Finally, just as light encountering a prism reveals a multitude of facets, so also a variety of methods reveal a multitude of features and enrich the lesson before the disciple-follower.

Differentiated Instruction

Working with individuals who are at the extreme ends of the auditory-visual continuum of preferred learning styles is a constant challenge. I encountered such a situation during one of my administrative assignments – one of the staff members was an auditory learner, and another was a visual learner. When I wanted to conduct a meeting that involved both of them, I would first meet with each separately, asking one to read any appropriate information relating to the agenda and the other to listen as I literally read it aloud. If I had to go to that much trouble to assure understanding and a sense of agreement with only two individuals, think about how difficult it must be for the classroom instructor who addresses thirty students, the pastor of a mega-church who preaches to thousands, or the businessperson who works with a vast array of customers and clients.

The concept and practice of differentiated instruction offers a solution to this dilemma. Guided by general principles such as respective tasks, flexible grouping, and ongoing assessment and adjustment, teachers can differentiate at least three critical components of the process: they can alter the content, method, or expected outcome of a given lesson. According to a student's readiness, interests, and learning styles and preferences, the creative and differentiated instructor varies the methods utilized to address the learning profile of the disciple-follower (Tomlinson 1999).

Foundations for Learning Styles: Sensory Input

In planning for differentiated instruction, it is helpful to realize that the most common and frequently utilized catalogues of learning styles are based upon two primary foundations. The first foundation supporting learning styles is that of sensory input preference – acknowledging that one of the five senses is dominant in the life of the learner. The Institute for Learning Styles Research provides one of the better summaries of this approach (http://learningstyles.org 2003):

> *The term "Learning Style" is used in a variety of ways in the teaching and learning process. Generally, it refers to the uniqueness of each learner. Individual difference might include personality, mental processing, confidence, attitude, sensory intake processes or some complex combination of these and other differences.*
>
> *The threshold of learning is receiving new information; therefore, sensory intake deserves special attention. Measuring the seven elements of the perceptual modality of learning styles can give the learner valuable information about their sensory processes...*
>
> *Perceptual learning styles are the means by which learners extract information from their surroundings through the use of their five senses. Individuals have different "pathways" that are specific to them. When information enters that "pathway" the information is retained in short term memory. Repeated exposure and use promote retention in long term memory. The seven perceptual modes (pathways) included in this theory are:*
>
> > **Print** - *refers to seeing printed or written words.*
> > **Aural** - *refers to listening.*
> > **Interactive** - *refers to verbalization.*
> > **Visual** - *refers to seeing visual depictions such as pictures and graphs.*
> > **Haptic** - *refers to the sense of touch or grasp.*
> > **Kinesthetic** - *refers to whole body movement.*
> > **Olfactory** - *refers to sense of smell and taste.*

Hence, styles are initially categorized according to how data or information is acquired by the learner (i.e., by seeing, hearing, touching and manipulating, etc.). The two staff members I noted identified their preferred auditory and visual learning styles by this sensory-based approach.

Foundations for Learning Styles: Soul Work

The teaching-learning model presented in Chapter 6, however, recognizes that the stimulation of the senses is simply a precursor to the work of the soul – where the learning actually occurs – so a complementary foundation consists of how the learner processes the data acquired. The second approach to learning styles is therefore based on psychological profiles, personality types, and character traits and is readily applicable to a variety of cognitive, affective, and volitional interactions and transactions. It is from this perspective that McCarthy and Lefever identify the categories of learners as: *imaginative, analytic, common sense,* and *dynamic* (Lefever 2001). Bill Huitt (2000) provides one of the better summaries of this approach:

> According to Bernice McCarthy, developer of the 4MAT system, there are four major learning styles, each of which asks different questions and displays different strengths during the learning process.
>
> These styles are based on the work of Gregorc & Butler (1984) and Kolb (1984). The Index of Learning Styles Questionnaire developed by Solomon and Felder (Felder, 1993) provides data relevant to this theory. The Myers-Briggs Type Indicator (MBTI) and the Kiersey Temperament Sorter II define an associated theory for personality style and temperaments.
>
> The Concrete-Random or "Imaginative Learner" demands to know "Why" he or she should be involved in this activity. This temperament is similar to the SP (Sensing/Perceiving) temperament in the MBTI. The Abstract-Sequential learner wants to know "What" to learn and is similar to the NT (Intuitive/Thinking) temperament. The Concrete-Sequential learner wants to know "How" to apply the learning and is similar to the SJ (Sensing/Judging) temperament. The Abstract-Random learner asks "If" this is correct how can I modify it to make it work for me. This is similar to the NF (Intuitive/Feeling) temperament. In the language of the ancient Greeks, these are the Sanguine, Choleric, Melancholy, and Phlegmatic temperaments, respectively. The DISC personality system has a similar categorization.
>
> Each learning style is associated with both left- and right-brain learners. Left-brain learners are logical, rational, sequential, serial, verbal learners. Right-brain learners are intuitive, emotional, holistic, parallel, and tactile learners.

Again, the two staff members differed; one was *common sense*, one was *analytic* – longing for action and craving information, respectively.

Framework for Learning Styles: Curricular Preference Options

Regardless of the sensory or psychological style that accommodates receiving and processing instructional information, every student also has a preferred curricular strategy and methodological approach. In other words, learners have distinct preferences for the manner by which curricular exposures and experiences are encountered in the course of study. Based upon personal penchants and perceived successes, students make educational decisions as to whether they learn best in a group or alone, and whether they prefer that information is mediated and conveyed or extracted by discovery and reason. Some students, for example, learn more effectively in independent study and investigation while others excel in group settings and interaction. Likewise, some learners prefer direct instruction such as in-class lectures or personal mentoring, while others would prefer to mine the lesson and reflect on it, regardless of whether they are alone or in cooperation with fellow learners.

Thus, in addition to the two common taxonomies of learning styles, this third approach provides a framework for identifying the preferred curricular context for the work of the senses and the soul in the learning process. The discovery of this framework was an unexpected consequence of my exploration of the possibility of a correlation between the commonly accepted foundational learning styles, regardless of the descriptive titles they are given, and the four quadrants of the dimensions of education first presented in Chapter 8 and illustrated in Display 8. As a result of this preliminary research, a hypothesis emerged: students prefer to facilitate the processing of a lesson in one of the four combinations of the transmission-reflection and individual-corporate dimensions.

There have been a number of creative attempts to identify and label learning styles – from colors, to animals, to descriptive phrases. I have settled, however, upon four simple descriptors: *Broadcast, Narrowcast, Contemplate,* and *Collaborate*. Coupled with explanatory phrases, these descriptors concisely reflect the educational activities by which students prefer to receive and respond to instruction. These combinations are identified in Display 8b.

Display 8b. The Dimensions of Education and Curricular Preference Options

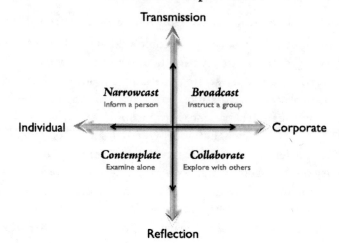

My thesis postulates that this framework supports the foundations inherent in the traditional learning styles. In fact, the application of this approach identifies and encourages the commonalities within learner diversity; for example, although their sensory input and processing preferences were diametrically opposed, my two staff members were both collaborative learners. While this thesis is still in its early stages of research, the concept of acknowledging and addressing variety in our learners' styles and preferences is a valid and necessary component of our endeavor.

Applications of Learning Styles

When Displays 8 and 9 were first presented in Chapter 8, I provided a number of examples to illustrate the dynamics of each quadrant. We will now explore some possibilities of how these dynamics function as curricular and learning style preferences in a specific venue – an adult Sunday school class. The common perception of one adult lecturing a group caters to those who prefer a corporate-transmissive approach to education, and breaking into small groups to discuss the lesson facilitates those who prefer a corporate-reflective learning style. For those with more individual learning leanings, the teacher could allow and encourage personal meditation or provide a small library for individual independent research and set aside class time to accomplish both activities. Additionally, teachers can utilize differentiated instruction, and facilitate multiple learning styles, by engaging students in activities such as: outside biblical research (Individual-

Transmission), writing a position paper or opinion piece on a topic of theological interest (Individual-Reflection), then making a presentation (Corporate-Transmission) or leading a workshop (Corporate-Reflection) exploring possible applications of the doctrine or text being studied.

Learning Style Profile

In summary, learning styles and preferences are cataloged according to three different taxonomies:

1) Those that are **sensory-based** and focus upon how a student receives instructional input are *Perceptual Learning Styles*. They are utilized to enable the learner, by way of physical perceptions, to accept the information contained in the curricular message. "Turning your ear" (Prov. 2:2a).

2) Those that are **psychology-based** and focus upon how a student processes the input received are *Procedural Learning Styles*. They are utilized to enable the learner, by way of psychological processes, to reflect upon the implications of the curricular message. "Applying your heart" (Prov. 2:2b).

3) Those that are **curricular-based** and focus upon how a student prefers to facilitate the processes of learning are *Preferential Learning Styles*. They are utilized to enable the learner, by way of favored exposures to and experiences with the instructional environment and delivery systems, to respond to the curricular messages.

When combined, these three components provide a profile of learning preferences and styles that enable the learner to most efficiently and effectively process instruction and for the teacher to choose the appropriate methods and differentiate the instructional environment for the most effective and life-changing teaching-learning experience.

Teaching Applications

Teachers adapt their methods to the kind of educational experience intended as well as the personality and preference of their learners; therefore, it may be helpful to consider the roles a teacher may adopt in facilitating student preferences. For example, the TC (Broadcast) quadrant learner benefits most when the instructor performs as a tour guide; the TI (Narrowcast) learner profits from a reference librarian; the IR (Contemplative) learner appreciates the contribution of a life coach; and the CR (Collaborative) learner is inspired by a corporate motivational speaker. Sports teams also provide an illustration: they incorporate a head coach, position coaches, trainers, and a chaplain to facilitate the varieties of instruction and support. A little creativity and ingenuity can produce a vast array of ways in which educators can utilize this curricular taxonomy of styles as a framework or context for the sensory and personality approaches.

To assist the differentiated instructor in comprehending and utilizing learning styles and preferences, a host of material is available from a variety of sources. Literally thousands of texts, journal articles, websites, and videos available on the Internet are readily accessible. Additionally, numerous sources offer free self-assessments and inventories to help students determine their preferred learning style. One of the most common resources available and utilized by Christian educators is Marlene Lefever's popular work *Learning Styles* based upon Bernice McCarthy's 4-MAT system (Lefever 2001).

Concerns

Before we leave this topic, I feel compelled to address a couple of concerns or cautions. First, I am concerned that acknowledging preferential learning styles can label students and put them in boxes that restrict or even hinder their efforts. In this regard, I would recommend an expenditure of some time investigating those scholars and researchers who have come to the conclusion that while differentiated instruction is essential, learning styles are a myth (Willingham 2008).

The second, and closely related, concern is whether it was the Creator's original intention for a learner to be so preferential in the activity of learning. Our students may be better served by learning in a variety of ways rather than being restricted to a preferred style or approach. Perhaps the diversity that the Lord employed in declaring his messages was not a response to learning style preferences, but an intention to utilize the prism effect and shed light on the multiplicity of facets of his revelation to us. It was not an intentional concession to preference or weakness; rather it was a conscious and strategic choice to convey the message most effectively. Differentiated instruction, learning styles, and preferences should also be critical components in the human teacher's toolkit as the most effective and efficient means of education are pursued.

Learning Activities

As we conclude our discussion of lesson planning, a reminder is in order: a teacher must not be confused or deceived by the assumption that a student is learning just because an instructional method has been implemented or provided. A well-respected colleague recently stated that it took him three years to realize that his "teaching" did not ensure student learning. He now realizes teacher activity can never replace the learner's soul work of cognition, affection, and volition.

In this same vein, a teacher cannot be satisfied with preparing, and implementing, a well-designed plan that focuses upon lower levels of learning. Likewise, a teacher cannot be content without knowing the outcome in the learners' lives.

Behavior 5: Evaluating Teaching and Learning

In a declaration directed to the Jewish nation, the Apostle Paul provides a simple and concise statement of the biblical model and intention for evaluation. Utilizing this model in an educational environment affects the assessment of past performance and anticipation of future lessons.

> ...*if you know his will and approve of what is superior because you are instructed by the law; if you are convinced that you are a guide for the blind, a light for those who are in the dark, an instructor of the foolish, a teacher of infants, because you have in the law the embodiment of knowledge and truth – you, then, who teach others, do you not teach yourself? You who preach against stealing, do you steal? (Romans 2:18-21).*

Paul presents a relatively simple process and three keys words – *will, approve,* and *instructed* – provide a succinct summary. The teacher determines and declares a standard, a rubric ("his will") by which the educational endeavor is to be judged, and then imparts instruction. Subsequently, "because you are instructed by the law," an evaluation ensues, and approval or disapproval of "what is superior" is attained. It is informative to note that the Greek term here translated *superior* is the same term that is often translated *value*, the root of evaluation. In this brief but instructive passage, we find a framework for a biblical approach to the evaluation process. A positive correlation with the four stages of the administrative function *control* is not accidental – administrators and educators both attempt to ensure progress toward the goal by evaluating the advancement of the disciple-follower as well as their contribution to it.

A number of different terms are utilized in the Scriptures to describe this process; it may be helpful for us to examine them for direction and suggestion. The extracted Greek definitions referred to in this section are from *Strong's Exhaustive Concordance*.

The term *evaluation* denotes the process of ascertaining the value of something, appraising it carefully. Although the word is not specifically used in English translations of the Bible, the Greek word for "value" is found there, and is commonly translated "what is superior" or "that are excellent" (Romans 2:18, Philippians 1:10). In other words, its purpose is to assess worth or value.

Examination is necessary, therefore, as a tool to determine the worth of an attitude, idea, experience, or process. The *Merriam-Webster Dictionary* defines it as "a careful search, inquiry or inspection; to inquire into the qualification, capabilities, knowledge." One of the Greek New Testament terms for examine, *dokimazo*, signifies to test, prove, or even scrutinize, with the purpose of making a decision. This implies, of course, that a standard has been set as a basis for the examination itself and for the rubric applied in the assessment.

Testing (or trying) is a common New Testament concept utilized in a variety of settings with an almost equal number of purposes and procedures. The dictionary definition of a test as a means to discriminate seems to justify one's testing of an individual's behavior. The usage of the term in testing faith in James 1 refers to the process of piercing a container to probe its contents and determine its substance and viability. To employ a common analogy, the implication is that circumstances and temptations test our faith by probing it with a measuring stick to check its level and determine if additional content is necessary and appropriate.

Correction is a word found often in situations commonly referred to as "discipline." Yet, since "discipling" is the root from which discipline comes, the idea of correction must be prominent in education and evaluation. Because a teacher corrects work as a regular duty, whether in a classroom, coaching a skill, or even sharing a hobby, it behooves us to take a biblical look at this responsibility.

It would be beneficial to examine the challenge presented by Paul:

> ...*if you know his will and approve of what is superior because you are instructed by the law; if you are convinced that you are a guide for the blind, a light for those who are in the dark, an instructor of the foolish, a teacher of infants, because you have in the law the embodiment of knowledge and truth—you, then, who teach others, do you not teach yourself?* (Romans 2:18-21).

In summary, Paul acknowledges this four-step procedure:
a. A standard is set - his will
b. Instruction/communication is given - the law

c. Results are evaluated - what is superior, i.e., of value

d. Approval is determined or Correction is pursued

Paul's reference to the corrective activity of the Scriptures in 2Timothy 3:16 utilizes a term that has a root meaning of being upright or erect and implies its purpose is to "straighten up" or better to "straighten up again" (i.e., a rectification). The restoration of an erring brother's lifestyle has parallels to the classroom teacher's responsibility to correct a student's academic error.

Correcting and restoring to perpendicular is an educational concern; simply stating that an error has been made or discovering a fault, without rectifying it, is not biblical evaluation. The four-step procedure acknowledged previously in Romans 2 and Observation 7 provides a fine template for any teacher to utilize in this process.

Evaluation as Education

During my studies for a Master of Arts in Christian Education, I wrote a research paper on the biblical principles of evaluation from which the preceding discussion emanates. One principle stood out most dramatically, and that was the implication that the evaluation process should be educative; in other words, we should perceive evaluation as education.

The evaluation process is intended to be directive as much as it is corrective; therefore, it is also intended to be educative. In my dissertation on the socialization of home-schooled students, I included the following paragraph as a conclusion to the description of the research design implemented in the study. It is interesting to note the connections the evaluation process makes with other components of the processes we studied in this chapter:

> *Finally, the researcher anticipated that the research methodology itself would provide an educational opportunity for home schoolers. The processes of identifying and assessing the movement's attitudes toward socialization, and its perceptions of its own effectiveness, provide an environment in which critically reflective thinking may result in the transformation of the movement's—or an individual's—theory and practice. Evaluation as education provided the respondents with internal motivation for their participation.*

Putting It All Together

I love my son. I love to swim. I love to teach. What could be better than teaching my son to swim? Well, I tried. Nevertheless, Michael was just not motivated; he was not interested, and four of the other six principles that motivate did not apply to him as well. Although he loved the sand, he did not enjoy the water at the beach, and when we moved to Michigan from southern California, the lack of an ocean for swimming did not trouble him. The only thing I had going for me was the fact that the house we purchased had a swimming pool. So, as it happened, one afternoon when my wife, Sharyn, was entertaining friends and sitting by the pool, Michael decided he wanted to get in the water. My son was in his swimming suit, and my wife was not. There was, however, no time for her to change clothes, as he might change his mind and the opportunity would be lost. So street clothes and all, Sharyn jumped in and took advantage of the teachable moment. Ministry demanded proximity and she responded; for the next hour, she engaged our son in a teaching-learning experience that exemplifies most of the principles that we have addressed in this chapter or have been referred to and suggested in the rest of this book.

In choosing her messages, Sharyn took into consideration not only the content of swimming instruction, but also the life needs and present condition of her pupil as well. She incorporated, with balance, all four potential forms of her message: subject matter (learning to swim), environment (friends and family who were swimming), life experience (he was actually in the pool), and a teacher-model (mom) were all present.

As to the utilization of teaching methodology, my wife clearly incorporated lecture in the transmission of her lesson's message, and she Socratically allowed for interaction. She demonstrated the techniques of the strokes constantly, and in Michael's attempts to swim, he participated in the discovery of something new each time. If we take into account the "role-plays" of imitating the stroke on the side of the pool before he entered the water, one could say he even experienced dramatic methods. Finally, he practiced all that he was learning, and put it into immediate application in his life.

The impromptu lesson, of course, was spontaneous, but it nonetheless incorporated the essential four steps of a lesson plan:

1. The Hook: he was motivated and initiated the lesson himself
2. The Book: he received vital instruction with a variety of methods
3. The Look: he saw its implications and applications,
4. The Took: he jumped in and tried it himself

Additionally, it implemented the three critical processes of every successful educational endeavor: Sharyn provided information, identification, and experience, by telling him how to swim, showing him how to swim, and allowing him the opportunity to actually swim.

Finally, we can also see how the five stages of the teaching-learning process, provided by Solomon in Proverbs 2, were implemented in this learning experience: Michael...

- Chose to enter the lesson and accept the words of his instructor (Stage I);
- Turned his ear – indeed, his entire body (Stage II);
- Applied his heart in thinking, feeling, and choosing to practice (Stage III);
- Increased the level of his learning as he went (Stage IV); and
- Took a giant leap in his ability to swim (Stage V).

He successfully navigated the five stages and learned a lesson, acquired a skill, and experienced a change in his life. It may not have been a perfect lesson, and to this day he does not enjoy swimming nearly as much as I do, but he can save himself if necessary and has a recreational skill for life – the capacity to swim for enjoyment when he so chooses. Being teachers as well as parents, Sharyn and I were both satisfied that this was a successful lesson.

Because life and learning are dynamic and every opportunity is unique, this illustration may not have covered all of the lessons of this chapter. The fact, however, that such a simple experience readily illustrates so many principles leads to the conclusion that these principles work. I wholeheartedly encourage a review of the whole of Part II and the process section of Chapter 8. The truths presented there are invaluable and should become embedded in an educator's mind and skill sets; they can assist a teacher in being prepared for the spontaneous teachable moments as well as the more predictable opportunities within an organization or classroom.

The Principal Principles

In conclusion and summary, discipleship ministries operate most effectively within the structure and guidelines provided by the principal principles I acknowledge in the Preamble to Part III. Numbers 7-9 provide a response to our third inquiry, "What Are the Processes of (Christian) Education?"

Principal Principles:

In succinct review, Christian education:

7. *involves the communication of 3 elements:*
(Information, Identification, Experience).
Genesis 11; Philippians 4:9
8. *entails a learning process of 5 stages:*
(Choice, Content, Curriculum, Consequence, Change).
Proverbs 2
9. *incorporates a teaching process of 4 phases:*
(Introduction, Information, Implication, Implementation).
Colossians 1:9-12

Prime Characteristic: Christian education is Application-designed.
(Designed: "formed or conceived in the mind; to have intention or purpose")
Education is not complete until a person has applied and experienced the teaching received (in the classroom setting). Education ministry will be focused on life and the Christian's experience—becoming, in essence, a "life laboratory."

Essential Activity:
Prepare a Plan for Teaching and Learning

Reflection and Response

Contemplations on Educational Process

Reflect upon and record your responses to the following,
considering the impact upon your present educational ministry:

1.   Which of the **approaches** to education do you utilize most frequently? Why? What is attractive about that approach? Are you satisfied with the results?

2.   Think about the most recent educational settings in which you have been involved (as teacher or student). What was done to see that all three of these **processes** were implemented?
   a.   Information
   b.   Identification
   c.   Experience

3.   Most teachers communicate *information* as a primary activity in teaching. What can you do, in your next opportunity to teach, to include *identification* and *experience*? Which methods may help?

4.   How many of the eight **biblical observations** have had an impact upon your teaching ministry? Which ones? In what ways?

5.   Make a list of the various **methods** and materials you have used (or seen used) in the last month. Have you identified what **style**(s) most effectively facilitate your students' learning?
   Which (categories) were most effective? Why?
   What new method (or style) would you be willing to implement?

6.   With which **learning activities** are your students most often involved? Is this what you desire for them? If not, what can you do to change it? Be specific.

7.   As a result of this chapter, what changes in **lesson planning** or presentation will you make in the upcoming months?

Dr. Michael R. Mitchell

Contemplations on Learning Styles Theory

*Bill Huitt, as noted in the text, has provided one of the most concise
summaries of the foundations for psychology-based learning theories, illustrated
by McCarthy's 4MAT system.
I reproduce it here for your consideration and reflection upon the questions
that follow.*

According to Bernice McCarthy, developer of the 4MAT system, there are four major learning styles, each of which asks different questions and displays different strengths during the learning process.

These styles are based on the work of Gregorc & Butler (1984) and Kolb (1984). The Index of Learning Styles Questionnaire developed by Solomon and Felder (Felder, 1993) provides data relevant to this theory. The Myers-Briggs Type Indicator (MBTI) and the Kiersey Temperament Sorter II define an associated theory for personality style and temperaments.

The Concrete-Random or "Imaginative Learner" demands to know "Why" he or she should be involved in this activity. This temperament is similar to the SP (Sensing/Perceiving) temperament in the MBTI. The Abstract-Sequential learner wants to know "What" to learn and is similar to the NT (Intuitive/Thinking) temperament. The Concrete-Sequential learner wants to know "How" to apply the learning and is similar to the SJ (Sensing/Judging) temperament. The Abstract-Random learner asks "If" this is correct how can I modify it to make it work for me. This is similar to the NF (Intuitive/Feeling) temperament. In the language of the ancient Greeks, these are the Sanguine, Choleric, Melancholy, and Phlegmatic temperaments, respectively. The DISC personality system has a similar categorization.

Each learning style is associated with both left- and right-brain learners. Left-brain learners are logical, rational, sequential, serial, verbal learners. Right-brain learners are intuitive, emotional, holistic, parallel, and tactile learners.

Huitt, William. 2000 A. *Individual differences: The 4MAT system. Educational Psychology Interactive.* Valdosta, GA: Valdosta State University. *Retrieved from* http://chiron.valdosta.edu/whuitt/col/instruct/4mat.html

1. How valid for church ministry is a system based upon business and formal education models?
2. How valid for Christian education is a system based upon ancient, secular Greek philosophy?
3. Are personality types and character traits valid foundations for a learning system?
4. How would you integrate preferences based on sensory input into a psychology-based system?
5. How can you integrate learning style and preference theory into your present educational ministry?

For Further Research on Curricular Preference Options

Investigate, consider, and record your responses to the following, reflecting upon the impact upon your present educational ministry:

1. Explore the correlation between the popular temperament/personality trait assessments with the proposed curricular preference options (review Display 8b and the Huitt quote above).

2. Explore the correlation between the popular learning style inventories with the proposed curricular preference options.

3. Investigate the Scriptures and identify instances of learning occurring in each of the four quadrants.

4. Identify current examples of the instances of learning that occur in each quadrant, building upon but expanding the examples given in the text.

5. Propose descriptive identifiers and behaviors that illustrate each quadrant, converting them into a questionnaire to function as an inventory of preferred curricular preferences.

Eleven
What Is the Context of Education?

In the telling of a story, the setting frequently provides an additional and distinct voice. When it does, the backdrop moves to the foreground, and the encompassing environment becomes an essential character in the script. For example, in the New Testament of the Bible, the Roman Empire is omnipresent and affects virtually every aspect of the content and presentation of the Gospel narrative. Likewise, in *Gone with the Wind*, the dramatic ambience provided by the plantation Tara and the Civil War are palpable influences upon the plot and the characters. The impact of the setting upon the views of life, emotional reactions, and decisions made is readily evident in each of these masterpieces. Whether they tell their tales orally, literarily, or with rhythmic movement, storytellers share the conviction that setting is one of the critical elements in the construction of a good story.

Similarly, in the articulation and implementation of a curricular plan for teaching and learning, context carries a significant voice and establishes the educational environment. In fact, the contribution is so dramatic that the environment is frequently referred to as the hidden curriculum.

The intention of this chapter is to expose and explore the underlying principles and practices that shape a biblical construct for a successful setting for teaching and learning. By investigating this essential component of education, we will address the fourth inquiry that gives structure to the discipline: "What Is the Context of Christian Education?" To facilitate this examination, we will acknowledge both critical concerns and essential activities.

Concerns Critical to the Inquiry

In Chapter 8, we explored the idea of creating an environment in which a student just might learn as a critical concern in the attempt to define education. In that discussion, we acknowledged the existence and essence of two dimensions of education – individual and corporate. We observed that disciple making involves both, and that teachers must take each of them into consideration as they create an environment in which learning might occur. We expended, however, little to no effort in identifying the components of a context that promotes individual discipleship and encourages group development. Therefore, the first critical concern that we must address involves identifying the foundations for, and possible implications of, such an endeavor. Following this segment, we will explore some impacting principles and then conclude our exploration of the critical concerns by considering some of the components of context.

Establishing the Foundations: Individual and Corporate Contexts

Fostering growth and development in individuals and in the groups of which they are a part produces complete and mature persons who contribute to the creation and establishment of a Christian community. Stated simply and illustrated easily, incorporating both the individual and corporate dimensions of education satisfies a critical concern and provides the central components for an answer to the context question.

The story of a young man I will call Larry offers an illustration of individual discipleship. He was a volunteer servant in a number of different positions for our comparatively young and growing church, and when he came to me asking for additional responsibilities, my initial reaction was to assign him to our struggling nursery program. When I offered him the opportunity to become the coordinator, Larry eagerly accepted it, and our adventure began.

As we worked together over the next quarter, two dramatic changes began to unfold. One change was visible to everyone – the nursery program flourished and prospered beyond our wildest expectations. The second, however, was equally impacting within a narrower sphere – the mentor-mentee relationship flourished as well. The young man's maturation and growth in both leadership and ministry skills occurred in front of my very eyes, so I was able to witness the results of my discipleship efforts. Sadly, but equally informative, when I left that church the relationship was altered because of the separation. Indeed, as we have noted before, ministry demands proximity.

The home Bible study for young married couples introduced in Chapter 3 provides an illustration of corporate educational context. My wife and I had no idea what we were getting into when we began this study. The original intention for the establishment of the group was to conduct a training program for a new ministry at the church. Within a few months, however, a number of the couples had dropped out of the ministry but remained a part of the small group. The reason was simple: the relational impacts were profound and no one wanted to leave, even if they were no longer part of the training program.

During the year we were together, both the individuals involved and the group as a whole experienced the highs and lows of life. Three of the couples struggled at times with marital difficulties. In fact, there were evenings when the entire session was devoted to serious counsel involving the issues that were causing the problems. In other words, what began as a training program and preparation for a certain ministry evolved into ministry itself.

For months the group flourished, but there came a time when, in exercising control as discussed in Chapter 3, my wife and I realized that the group had lost its focus, and we were diverting from the original and stated mission. Regretfully, we were forced to choose between altering the mission and discontinuing the group. Given the factors, we chose to leave in order to focus on the ministry we believed to be the higher priority at that time.

The group attempted to stay together, but they were not successful and soon disbanded. Within months, the three couples that had struggled did indeed separate, and one of them even divorced. As my wife and I discussed these events, she asked me, "Why do you still believe in small groups? They obviously don't work – just look at those three couples." Without much hesitation I replied, "Quite the contrary; the group did work for over a year. While we were together, the couples had the support necessary for a fighting chance. As soon as the group disbanded, these people lost a critical resource for their lives and marriages." Corporate context is crucial to individual discipleship; consequently, I believe that groups do "work."

Anecdotal evidence, however, is not sufficient to state the case; as Christian educators, we must look to the biblical record to provide a surer footing and foundation. Hence, it is to that record we turn our attention.

The Scriptures provide us with some hints and, consistent with our preliminary observation, it appears that God has utilized both individual and corporate models for organizing, ordering, and arranging people to fulfill his mission. Selected scriptures listed below identify the variety of relationships that facilitate individual discipleship and suggest analogies that describe the kind of educational metaphors and models available to our corporate ministries today.

Biblical Foundations for the "Individual Context"

The context for individual Christian education is a proximity-oriented relationship based upon the metaphors and models biblical leaders employed in establishing a venue for personal discipleship resulting in the complete man. The following list provides some of the impacting biblical references and consequent concepts that inform our inquiry. They selectively demonstrate the variety of environments and relationships utilized in the disciple-making process.

Personal ministry is facilitated when people are in contexts such as the following:

- ✓ Proximity: someone they can be with
  Allelon: "One anothering"
- ✓ With, among
  Mark 3:14 and Acts 4:13; 1Thessalonians 1-3
- ✓ Parent/child; Paul,
  1Thessalonians 2
- ✓ Teacher/student; Ezra,
  Nehemiah 8
- ✓ Leader/follower: Moses,
  Exodus 1-5
- ✓ Master/disciple: Jesus,
  John 13-17
- ✓ Elder/younger: Peter,
  1Peter 5:1-7
- ✓ Shepherd/sheep: Jesus,
  Jeremiah 37, 38
- ✓ Model/example: Jesus, Peter, and Paul
  1Corinthians 11:1; Mimeomai: Imitate; follow

Biblical Foundations for the "Corporate Context"

The context for corporate Christian education is a community, born of communion and based upon the organizational model God utilized in establishing what is known in professional literature as "job design." In Numbers 2-5, for example, we find the Lord identifying the work, the workers, and the workplace. He also provided direction and instruction in caring for the tabernacle and preparing for the march as they traversed the wilderness for forty years. In the language of Part I, he even distinguished managers from leaders.

Focusing our investigation, we find in the Scriptures a catalogue of references to the context and environment in which God operates. Passages such as these inform our inquiry:

- Ephesians 3:9 (Created all things)
- Colossians 1:15-17 (Creator, sustainer)
- Genesis 1 (the Natural family)
- Genesis 12, 15; Exodus 1 (the National family)
- Ephesians 2:19ff (the Spiritual family)
- Jeremiah 31:8; Malachi 2:10 (Jehovah as father)
- Isaiah 54:5, 62:5; Jeremiah 2:2 (Jehovah espoused to Israel)
- Psalm 68:6 (Jehovah places the lonely in families)
- John 14:18 (No longer orphans)
- 1 Timothy 1:2, 1Peter 5:13 (Son in the faith)
- Mark 3:14; cf. w/ Acts 4:13 (With)
- 1 Thessalonians 1:5; 2:7-11 (Among)

Having established a biblical foundation for the structure, organization, and context for our ministries, let us build upon it.

Exploring Some Impacting Principles

Through a profound and personal event, I came to realize that the first impacting principle I must acknowledge is that order, a harmonious arrangement of parts, is primarily a result of interactive relationships rather than a static organizational structure. A serendipitous encounter with the Lord, and the educational process that ensued, aligned my perceptions with his and transformed my understanding of the context question.

Establishing Order: Competing Concepts

I was on a horseback ride with a group of junior campers in the high country of the Colorado Rocky Mountains. We were on a ridge with a view of the Continental Divide to the left and an active beaver pond on the right. As I started to take a closer look at my surroundings, I noticed a mix-and-match of colored wildflowers growing everywhere among tall and short grasses, a sprinkling of Aspen and Pine trees randomly scattered in every direction, and an intermingling of a variety of high country wildlife surrounding the beaver pond. While observing this incredibly gorgeous setting, I reflected upon a mental picture of my own backyard; it was a rectangular, perfectly symmetrical, mowed, and clipped landscape with evenly spaced trees, shrubs, and flowers lining the fence in a planned and orderly fashion. That image of my yard was in sharp contrast to what I perceived as the natural disarray that, despite its beauty, was attracting my attention.

This was the perfect context for critical thinking and personal reflection. I had frequently taught about the Lord's order, yet as I pondered this contrast, I realized I did not fully comprehend the concept behind how he accomplishes it. His idea of order was certainly different from mine. In the midst of my contemplation, I was struck by an inspired realization: God establishes order in relationship, whereas I attempt to create order in organization. In his backyard, each of the elements exists and thrives in a mutual interdependence; in mine, they are assigned an independent and specific location and function.

This realization was timely, as I was in a state of personal turmoil regarding my job description and placement on the organizational chart at church. As a result of this mountaintop experience, the Lord impressed on my heart his perception for my ministry. I was inspired to be like a backpacker wandering through the woods and serving the Lord by ministering to his creation. Utilizing the gifts in my bag, I was to serve whomever and wherever I was needed. I was not to accept the limitations imposed by carving out a niche for my ministry and restricting myself to a corner of the forest. Confirming this final impression, I visualized the beautiful campground where we were staying as no more than a niche that humans cut out for themselves in the midst of God's creation. This reminded me of the Babelites in Genesis 11 who refused to disperse and chose to settle for a city with a tower, so they could make a name for themselves.

Later, after we returned home from the camp, I looked up the word *order* in the *Merriam-Webster Dictionary* to discover the implications of what God had ministered to my heart. To my surprise, I encountered a great definition: order is "a harmonious arrangement of parts." While it is possible to facilitate this harmonious arrangement by organization, it had become clear to me that the Lord primarily utilizes relationships to arrange the parts. This is one of the cardinal concepts that undergird my suggestion in Chapter 3 to postpone job descriptions and orgchart positions until the personnel are in place and relationships are established. To put it another way, form follows function.

Establishing Order: Complementary Components

The second impacting principle informing our inquiry is actually a set of four dyads, the components of which are often perceived of as conflicting with one another, much as organization and relationship compete to define order. While in practice they may appear to be in opposition, it would be more helpful to see them as complementary components facilitating the establishment of order.

Grace and Government

Balancing the grace of God (allowing humankind to exercise choice and will) with his governmental structures (restricting the options to maintain order) provides a solution to the perceived conflict between freedom and control. Grace provides freedom of choice and movement, which is facilitated by the functionality of the structure that supports it. I employ the phrase "organize for freedom" to identify and describe my desire for, and conviction that, organizational structure or context can actually facilitate freedom of movement in ministry. Through careful planning, organizing, and staffing, we prepare ourselves for the flexibility and maneuverability needed when we encounter surprising or unusual ministry circumstances. To revisit an analogy, the more clubs leaders have in their bags, and the more capable they are of using them, the more effective the shot, no matter where the ball lies.

Organization and Administration

I have a number of friends and family members who are incredibly good at organizing items, whether shopping lists, storage boxes, bookshelves, closets, or an occasional garage. They vary, however, in their ability to maintain and manage their organization. In a manner similar to how leaders depend upon managers to manipulate the necessary resources, organization depends upon administration to facilitate order. For example, when someone removes something from a shelf, it must be replaced so it can be found easily the next time. If someone removes a document from a file folder, it should be returned to the same file folder and put in the same place so that it can be retrieved again. This functional distinction between organization and administration, whether implemented by leadership or management, supports the development of the educational context.

In a church, school, or any institution, organization is the process that puts people and things into order, while administration is the process that implements the intention of the institution through effectively utilizing the instruments that facilitate that order. This idea may seem in conflict with God's intention that order comes out of relationship, but order does come from organization when it is the result of identifying relationships and then formulating a structure that facilitates them.

Whether the relationship is between individuals, items to be stored or cataloged, or tasks to be accomplished, the process is the same: administration facilitates organization, and organization supports administration. They may constitute a comparative continuum, but they need not be in conflict.

Organization and Organism

Much has been written and discussed concerning the perception that organization is distinct from, if not adversarial to, organism. In most dictionary definitions, however, the two terms define each other, as noted in our earlier discussion concerning the leader's administrative function of organization. The denotations do not conflict; they work in harmony with each other.

As if to imprint his own perception and intention, the Creator provides most life forms with an organizational house, such as a human's skeleton or a turtle's shell. These "houses," however, are of little value without a living entity. For example, seashells become merely decorations washed up on the shore of the beach. Whether we are talking about human beings, systematic theology, or organizational structure, energy without a constraining and directive framework is usually wasted, and a framework without energy is simply a waste.

Open and Closed Systems

We explored the concepts of systems thinking and analysis previously. In this segment, we will address two distinct types of systems, open and closed, and consider how they affect ministry. Using a simple analogy, closed systems operate like the cooling system of an automobile; the same coolant circulates through the engine continuously. It may lose a little to leaks and evaporation over time, but basically the same coolant is in the car today that was there yesterday. An open system operates more like the engine and the fuel supplied from the gas tank; once the engine uses the fuel, it is gone and must be replaced. To illustrate, consider the Sunday school teacher who came by my office requesting some additional roster forms for her class. For five weeks she had taken attendance regularly and noticed two critical bits of data: 1) she never had more than 30 students in the class at a time, and 2) in those five weeks she had 135 different names of students who attended. The math told her all she needed to know: of 150 possible different students (five weeks times 30 different students each week), only 15 students had attended more than one time. That is an open system. On the other hand, consider the small Baptist church in which I was raised. The same people attended Sunday worship, Sunday school, Wednesday prayer meeting, and we seldom saw a visitor. That was a closed system.

Implications should be obvious. The nature of the system affects everything from ministry methods to communication networks. Open systems invite diversity, while closed systems protect continuity. Identifying the kind of system that appears to drive the organization would be a profitable investigation and consideration.

These four dyads, grace and government, organization and administration, organization and organism, and open and closed systems, provide helpful language and structure to assist leaders and teachers as they anticipate and arrange for the order they desire for their ministries.

The Organizational Chart

The third influential principle we will address in this section is the role of a management tool known as the organizational chart (or orgchart). Its impact upon our discussion of context, order, and organization cannot be overstated. An organizational chart is a graphic display designed and intended to reflect the structure, form, and administrative flow of the institution, division, department, group, or collection it represents. It can be employed either to represent the current actual condition or to provide a vision for the entity's potential or preferred future composition and configuration. The description and purpose statement found at orgchart. net states it simply and clearly:

> An organizational chart is a diagram that shows the structure of an organization as well as the relationships and relative ranks of its positions. The term "chart" refers to a map that helps managers navigate through patterns in their employees. Charts help organize the workplace while outlining the direction of management control of subordinates. Increasingly a necessary management tool, organizational charts are particularly useful when companies reorganize, embark on a merger or acquisition, or need an easy way to visualize a large number of employees.
>
> Organizational charts provide the greatest value when used as a framework for managing change and communicating current organizational structure. When fully utilized, org charts allow managers to make decisions about resources, provide a framework for managing change and communicate operational information across the organization.

In this brief section, we will explore the impact of these charts by considering the two most common forms, the business orgchart and the family tree. Both neatly represent the connections between the various levels of responsibility and relationship, but there are a number of differences between them that can be identified by exploring inquiries such as: How does a person get on an orgchart or family tree? How do the horizontal relationships work? Does it represent an open or a closed system?

There are two notable distinctions I wish to address here. The first is that while the organizational chart may represent a business's potential configuration, the family tree represents the generational relationships that actually exist. As noted above, an administrator utilizes the orgchart to facilitate decision-making, problem solving, and resource allocation, among other activities, in order to facilitate change and promote the fulfillment of a vision. A family member, on the other hand utilizes a family tree to identify relationships, both past and present, to facilitate the harmony that is the mark of order. The strength of such a tool is that the arrangement of the members can be represented visually:

> *Genealogical data can be represented in several formats, for example as a pedigree or ancestor chart. Family trees are often presented with the oldest generations at the top and the newer generations at the bottom. An ancestry chart, which is a tree showing the ancestors of an individual, will more closely resemble a tree in shape, being wider at the top than the bottom. In some ancestry charts, an individual appears on the left and his or her ancestors appear to the right. A descendancy chart, which depicts all the descendants of an individual will be narrowest at the top (http://www.ask.com).*

The second distinction is in the flow of administrative service. Who serves whom is the critical question. The business orgchart usually anticipates that the personnel on each level of the chart serve those in the positions above. The family tree, however, anticipates that each generation on the tree serves those below, and to the side, as well as those above. As I stated in Chapter 3:

> *In the business world, the typical organizational chart implies those on the lower levels serve those who are above them, but Myron Rush reminds us, "The Christian leader is to serve those under him by helping them to reach maximum effectiveness. And the higher up in an organization a person*

goes, the more he or she is to serve. In fact, the head of the organization is to be totally at the service of those under him (like a slave is to a master)" (Rush 1983).

While writing this section, and reflecting upon how to best express and illustrate this concept, I took a short break to collect my thoughts. I decided to leave my office and take a walk, and as I entered a common area, I was surprised to see a young man bending over a table, changing the diapers of his recently born son. I cannot think of a better illustration of the service expected of an administrator or someone residing on a higher branch of the tree; after all, even the heavenly father cares for, nurses, child trains, and disciplines his children (cf. Hebrews 12).

Another possibly helpful perspective on the issue of service entails the recognition that the first ones to be placed on either an orgchart or a family tree are challenged to serve and minister to those who come after, rather than to expect to be served by them. A final observation, however, may actually state the biblical case most effectively. Many experienced business leaders have suggested that the fewer levels on the organizational chart, the better. One of my students, in fact, recommends the provocative, and no doubt arguable, proposition that everyone below Jesus should be perceived on one flat line – we are all equal in his sight, all brothers and sisters within the same heavenly family. Irrespective of the number of levels, in this perception, everyone serves everyone else, just as we are instructed in Ephesians 5:21 and strongly encouraged by Jesus in Luke 22, when he directed his disciple-followers, even as rulers, to be servants. Without sacrificing structure and support (rulership), they were to facilitate relationship and order (service).

Not surprisingly, by its very nature, the family tree has the better potential for creating order out of relationship, providing structure for life, integrating both open and closed systems, and allowing grace within its government. It is no wonder, as we will see in more detail, that God chose to employ the family metaphor when creating organizations, and their necessary structures, to accomplish his purposes.

Considering the Components of Context

We were getting ready to enroll our son in first grade, when we noticed that a private Christian school in our neighborhood expanded and built new buildings. Believing this might be a great opportunity for him, we scheduled an appointment to meet with the principal and tour the new facilities. When we visited the classroom to which he would be assigned, we were impressed with the freshly painted walls, the new carpet on the floor, and the glistening new desks. There was only one problem: this new facility virtually screamed, "Look all you want, but don't touch." It projected a cold and uninviting environment. Dismissing that first impression, we enrolled him.

When he came home after his first day of school, we were disappointed that he was not more excited and seemed to be even a little discouraged or depressed. By the third day, we knew the reason. The staff told him more than once that he could not talk even at their meal times, and his teacher was regularly screaming at the class. We met with the principal to discuss the issues and her responses only confirmed that this was not the place for our son. The next day, we were looking for another option for his education.

After a bit of investigation, we discovered that the public school kindergarten teacher he had so appreciated the previous year had been reassigned to first grade. Following a brief conversation with her principal, and with the assurance that Michael could indeed be in her class again, we took another tour. This time we were looking at a decades old, well worn, and badly in need of repair first grade classroom. We noticed the patched walls, the frayed carpet, and student work and school supplies piled everywhere. This old facility screamed, "Don't just look, please touch and use me." When his teacher greeted Michael with a hug and a welcome back pat, we knew he was home. The environment of education speaks volumes. In this case, a functional and practical facility affirmed the relational order established by a knowing and caring teacher.

Which message does the disciple-follower hear, "Use me" or "Do not touch me"? In order to craft a satisfactory response to that question, educators create environments conducive to ministry by addressing and establishing four contextual components: educational, physical, relational, and familial. I will very briefly acknowledge each and then explore possible implementations.

An Educational Environment

An educational environment promotes and provides the opportunity for learning to take place. It is stimulating and collegial, challenging but not overbearing, supporting the biblical learning model, and implementing the variety of principles we discovered in the previous chapter on the processes of education.

It would be a profitable experience to review the various observations, guidelines, and checklists we have explored and turn them into an environmental rubric. This rubric can be a useful tool to assess the kind of messages that we send.

A Physical Environment

Whether it is formal or informal, natural or structured, indoors or outdoors, for a large group or a small one, every educational ministry opportunity takes place in some kind of a physical environment. To ignore that reality, and allow the physical environment to go unnoticed or unchecked, eliminates from consideration one-quarter of the potential forms in which our message can be communicated.

To put it simply, regardless of the age and wear of the facility, environments and educational contexts need to be inviting and attractive to pupils. They need to enhance and support the relational order being established. A review of the sources and forms of messages that we discussed in creating a curricular plan would enhance a reflection upon the significance and value of an environment conducive for learning.

A Relational Environment

Ministry demands proximity, and discipleship is enhanced when the mentor is with and among the disciples. Whether in individual or corporate settings and groupings, our contexts need to be facilitating growth in personal relationships. Teachers need to be providing students with opportunities to observe exemplary lives that are consistent with the words spoken in the lessons presented. The teacher-model ministering in close proximity to students, and treating them as if they were natural offspring, is an intended outcome of an intentional, educational, and relational environment.

A Familial Environment

The Scriptures declare that every time God intervened in the affairs of men to accomplish some task, such as filling and subduing the earth, blessing all the nations of the earth, or fulfilling the Great commission, he organized them by placing them in families: natural, national, and ultimately, spiritual. From the prophetic analogy of Jehovah as both the Father and espoused husband to Israel, to the simile of Paul as both a mother and a father to the Thessalonian church, we find the family metaphor utilized throughout Scripture.

The noted anthropologist Edmund Leach once stated in an interview with *Psychology Today* (July 1974), "It is not the presence of people which is needed, but the obligations of kinship that are wanted." In other words, as much as presence and proximity are necessary, it is the kind and quality of the relationships that matter. In describing wanted relationships, he utilized the phrase "obligations of kinship" to describe their nature.

Metaphors and Context

"If churches were parks" is the subject of a brief essay written by Linda Cannell in the recent text *Children Matter*. In it, she indicates how a church and its children's ministry would be impacted if ministry was conducted outdoors, in open, welcoming, flexible, and friendly conditions. The picture she paints is not idyllic but it is idealistic. Her imaginative alternative to present conditions is one woman's vision of what could be if the environment was different.

In order to paint this powerful and poignant picture, Cannell utilized a metaphor, a "literary device using analogy or comparison that affects our perception of reality" (May 2005). The volume in which she writes suggests that it is beneficial to identify the dominant metaphor utilized in local educational ministry contexts because it often evolves into a functional model, even if unconsciously:

> *No metaphor, micro or macro, perfectly represents a ministry setting or its people. Yet helpful insights result when the metaphors of a context are identified, because metaphors matter. They matter a lot.*
>
> *Although often more subtle or implicit, these metaphors tend to shape everything that is done, even without the awareness of the leadership staff. The dominant metaphor tends to become the ministry model (May 2005).*

To illustrate this assertion, we need only to consider two of the more frequently utilized metaphors for ministry context. Many churches conceive of themselves as either an army or a hospital. In the former, the focus is on preparation for or participation in battle; the culture wars and political activism are dominant themes, with training and teaching as expected practices. In churches with a hospital motif, pastoral care and counseling concerns dominate the church program.

Occasionally, a church will attempt to blend or merge the two, and the concept of a "wounded warrior" dominates their vocabulary and influences a service mentality. These two well-worn metaphors are illustrative of the various symbols used to describe the environment in which ministry is expected to occur. Utilizing them to articulate the underlying assumptions about ministry regularly exposes the members of a staff and congregation to the ministry's priorities and practices. This idea lends credence to the often-quoted, and previously noted, dictum that the setting is the "hidden curriculum" embedded within the educational environment.

Examining the Family Metaphor for Ministry

Personal study, practical experience, and professional observation of effective ministry contexts lead me to the conclusion that the family metaphor provides the most effective, efficient, and biblical approach to bringing order to educational environments and contexts. Before examining this proposition in some depth, an introduction to the foundations upon which the assertion rests and the concepts upon which it is built are in order. We will then turn our attention to potential and actual applications.

Foundation: God-Ordained Institutions

As acknowledged earlier in this section, God chose at various times throughout the history of humankind to intervene and direct the implementation and fulfillment of his purposes. Three of those times bear directly upon the discussion before us. At those moments of divine intervention, we find not only the activity of God in fulfilling his intentions, but we also see the establishment of the institutions through which God chose to fulfill those purposes.

The first mention of these interventions occurs in the story of the Garden of Eden when God gave the command to fill and subdue the earth. In order to facilitate this commission, God provided man with a partner. This union of husband and wife established the first of what I refer to as the "God-ordained institutions."

The Lord founded the institution of marriage upon the threefold union of the bodies, souls, and spirits of a man and a woman. Established in Genesis 1:26-29 and 2:18-24, he formed this trinitarian union for a threefold purpose. The first, reflecting the physical union and its consequences, was to fill and subdue the earth. The second, reflecting the soulish union of the couple, was to complete and complement each other. The third, reflecting the spiritual union, was to illustrate and represent the oneness of Jesus Christ, the head of the church, with his bride, the body (see Ephesians

5:31-33). Thus, we see that the first intervention of God in the affairs of men produced a marriage and the resultant *natural family*.

Perusing the sacred text further, we observe a second institution inaugurated by the Lord in his dealings with humankind. He established a *national family* in the lineage of Jacob, also known as Israel. The Lord's desire was to bless all of the nations of the earth through the offspring of Abraham, and in the process, he revealed some of his perception of the nature and purpose of government and authority (see Genesis 12:1-3 and Exodus 1:1-9; review Romans 13 and 1Peter 2, 3 concerning governments).

Finally, in the New Testament (specifically in Ephesians 2:19-24 and 3:14), we discover the third direct intervention by God in establishing an institution designed to fulfill his purpose. In this case, he delegated the ministries of reconciliation and the uniting of all humankind under one head to a *spiritual family*, the church of Jesus Christ.

The natural, national, and spiritual families are the God-ordained institutions established to implement the divine mission and vision. While each of these deserve a full volume of their own, let it suffice for this discussion to observe that they provide a fair representation of the kind and nature of context the Lord himself chose to utilize.

Application: Man-Inspired Organizations

A preferable environment for both leadership and education appears to be a tight-knit group of people who are in proximity to each other and functioning like a family. Since the family is the cornerstone upon which society is constructed, organizations are wise to build upon this same foundation when creating a contextual framework in which to implement their intentions.

A good place to begin our discussion of the implications of this assertion is to acknowledge a simple but profound observation: virtually every organization that is successful prides itself on functioning like a family. In other words, the most commonly imitated structure is the one God himself instituted. Biblical models, observations of scholars, and a plethora of historical and contemporary illustrations support this perception and proposition.

Biblical Models

As pointed out earlier in this chapter, the scriptures utilize a variety of metaphors to describe the types of service that occur within education and ministry environments. Additionally, we referenced the two paradigms of schooling and socialization at various points in this work. These paradigms and biblical metaphors provide the Christian educator with a multitude of possible environments that may be constructed to support educational ministry:

> *The wide range of models for children's ministry could be represented by many metaphors. Some currently prominent metaphors or models will be discussed in the section: School, Gold Star/Win a Prize, Carnival, Pilgrims Journey, and Dance with God. The last two metaphors may be unfamiliar in many churches, but they have qualities that make them worthy of careful consideration (May 2005).*

A simple concordant search, though, helped me identify the metaphors and paradigms with the most support. Thinking through the possibilities, I assumed the beloved and commonly utilized figures of speech such as shepherd, bread of life, body, and warfare would find the most usage and application in the New Testament's description of the church and its ministry. I was surprised to realize that many of these terms actually had limited use. The Apostle Paul, for example, employs the analogy of body in only four of his epistles, and I found just two references to struggles and wars outside of the combat in the book of Revelation. I did encounter nearly twenty references to shepherds, sheep, and flock, as analogies and metaphors, but I expected more. When I searched the "Household of God" motif, however, and considered terms in the faith analogies such as father, son, brother, marriage, bride, groom, orphans, and children, I encountered dozens of entries. The search affirmed family as the dominant metaphor of the New Testament. When I considered the Old Testament as well, the numbers multiplied.

This brief survey of representative scriptural texts affirms, even when based exclusively on numbers, the preferred biblical approach is the utilization of the family metaphor in establishing both organizational and ministry contexts. Classic organizational advice given by Jethro to Moses in Exodus 18 may well be the dominant illustration of family-based counsel and implementation. It is, however, not alone. In the early chapters of the book of Numbers, we find the nation of Israel organized around families and tribes, with tribal responsibilities and marching sequence a natural consequence. We find an additional parallel in the familial responsibilities allotted in the rebuilding of the city walls in the books of Ezra and Nehemiah, and perhaps even in the assignment of the Levite family to priestly duties and responsibilities.

In terms of ministry models, we find a multiplicity of examples. The Lord himself compared his relationship to the nation Israel as one of betrothment (Cf. Isaiah 54:5; 62:4; and Psalm 68:6), and this analogy is reiterated in the New Testament where the church is perceived as the bride of Jesus Christ. Jesus further affirmed the family analogy when he told his disciples that he would not leave them as orphans when he left (see John 14). Finally, the apostles Peter and Paul acknowledged the familial relationship they had with their disciples by referring to them as "sons in the faith" who were to be nursed, encouraged, and child trained (see, for example, 1Peter and 1Thessalonians).

Theoretical Suggestions

In addition to these biblical foundations, I would like to note three quotations, which reflect a more theoretical and scholarly orientation, from sources that influenced me early in my ministry. The first comes from Larry Richards's *Theology of Christian Education*. He states,

> While all Christian education is not to take place in the home, a family relationship or family feeling is to be of concern in every teaching/learning setting (Richards 1975).

In Gene Getz's contribution to the text *Childhood Education in the Church*, he asks a series of questions designed to get the church educator to think about the connection between the Sunday school and the home. One of those questions was,

> Does learning take place in closely knit groups that simulate family units? (Clark 1975).

Finally, in Dennis Guernsey's *A New Design for Family Ministry*, he makes a case for the compensatory work the church must do when natural family life breaks down. In it, he declares,

> But what we must understand is that to minister effectively to those without viable Christian families we must build new family structures for them. Socialization takes place best in the compelling structure of a family, whether that family be natural or surrogate (Guernsey 1982).

Historical Illustrations

Two ancient cultures exemplify the incorporation of the concept of family into the educational nomenclature. They represent and illustrate a tradition found in the biblical milieu. In the school for scribes located in the nation of Sumer, teachers were known as "fathers" while the students were referred to as "sons." The Hebrew schools, meanwhile, were called "Houses of Life," with the ones attached to synagogues called "Houses of the Book." Additionally, the advanced school was labeled the "House of Study." Even the ancients regarded "family" as a worthy metaphor to model in their educative efforts.

Contemporary Illustrations

We can also catalogue contemporary anecdotes and illustrations of the implementation of the family metaphor in real time and real life environments.

When NASA lost the Columbia space shuttle in February of 2003, the administrative team addressed the deaths of the crew by lamenting, "We just lost members of our family." Schools also illustrate the family metaphor. Some students of the charter school approached me one day voicing concern for harsher discipline for their classmates who were abusing drugs and alcohol, characterizing them as "stepping out of the lifestyle of the family." Consider also country singer Miranda Lambert, who said her band was a family and that music was the only place she could find that relationship (2006).

Two other personal experiences caught my attention as I considered the family metaphor and some of its implications. During my college years, I worked for a city Parks and Recreation Department. For every park and playground in the city, the department assigned a team composed of one male and one female recreation leader. Later, a group therapist participating in a training program for small group leaders in our church informed me that at one time the cutting edge of group therapy included one male and one female therapist in each group. Although these illustrations do not directly implement a family model or suggest specific structures such as team teaching, they do provide evidence that the relational balance that Edmund Leach recommended was an intentional context and program element.

These anecdotes and illustrations highlight the suggestion that staffing with teams, building relationships, and treating one another as if they were members of a family create a positive and effective environment for learning.

Activities Essential to an Application

I was on the staff of a growing church that was moving into a new facility the same weekend that I was meeting with a group of two dozen prospective children's ministers, and communication with maintenance obviously broke down. Despite the fact that I was given assurances that the room would be ready for the children's ministry Sunday school orientation that was about to begin, nothing was cleaned or prepared for our arrival. I was devastated. The meeting room was in total disarray, with construction equipment and debris scattered everywhere. Facility construction and program renovation characterized everything we were doing, and the reconstruction of a neglected children's ministry was high priority in our strategic plan. Thankfully, the introduction and orientation meeting was scheduled to last an entire morning, because it took me nearly an hour to get the room ready and then another hour to win back the attention of my audience that had been lost due to the delay.

I had done everything that I could think of to fulfill the "Getting a Great Start" checklist that I recommended in Chapter 4 (Display 5). More than anything, the final recommendation to make good first impressions was on my mind. The initial sessions of a group, class, or even a committee, impact the members' receptivity and responsiveness, and I knew that getting off to a good start with this meeting was critical to the first few months of the project to strengthen our children's ministry program.

Laying the Foundation: First Impressions

The impressions and relationships established at the beginning may not be permanent, but they certainly can be persistent. I have vivid memories of the fear that engulfed my seventh grade English class as we entered the room of a teacher who had a reputation for being harsh and cruel. A theology professor established a similar atmosphere in my first year of my Masters studies. On the other hand, taking courses taught by close associates dissipated the worry and enhanced my level of comfort and confidence.

As a leader-teacher, I always give special attention to that first class session, group meeting, program orientation, or even personal introduction. It provides the foundation upon which the rest of my ministry is constructed. Therefore, the essential activity of the context question, "Establish an

Environment for Education," is initiated by getting a great start and leaving positive first impressions – do it right and do it well. Upon this foundation, an educator constructs an effective context for teaching and learning.

Constructing the Context: Critical Components

First impressions matter because they affect how we get started. Lasting impressions, however, affect how we continue and ultimately finish. When erecting our ministry contexts, we need to give careful attention to a number of factors, because each one of them contributes to whether or not the environment will be educative and inviting to our students. These factors include the physical, emotional, and relational components that contribute to the context under construction and influence how easily and effectively it can be utilized.

The construction procedures for two facilities that I was involved with personally are in essence similes for the process of creating educational settings for our families. The first was a project near to my heart – building the future home for my family. I drove by the house nearly every day while it was under construction. I knew the contractor very well, and he involved me in virtually every critical decision as it was being built. Working with him and the subcontractors, I was able to customize and individualize the house where my family would live for the next thirteen years. The result was a home that met our personal needs and was a comfortable place to live and grow together.

The second facility was a building our church constructed for the children's ministry I was serving as an associate pastor very early in my career. In contrast to our home, I did not feel very welcome around the construction site. Therefore, like Nehemiah, I participated in clandestine surveying trips. On one of these visits, I noticed a door and window set installed backwards. Although this was not a big deal to the workers, this led the electrician to install the light switch to correspond with the misplaced door. I faced a dilemma because exposing the problem would reveal that I had been checking out the work. Even though my input would not have been welcome, I am, nonetheless, embarrassed to admit that I chose not to point out the problem. The result was a defect in that room that caused inconvenience for years to come, including to myself when I taught a class there. To this day, teachers have to cross the room to turn on the lights. There were also other issues in that building that arose from the lack of involvement of those that would be working and ministering there, effecting both the teachers and students.

Although Gregory's assertion is debatable, there is still validity in his declaration that, "the true function of a teacher is to create the most favorable conditions for self-learning" (Gregory 2003). In creating these favorable conditions, we must address and provide for the four dimensions introduced earlier in this chapter: educational, physical, relational, and familial.

Encouraging an Educational Environment

The notion of creating an environment to facilitate learning was introduced in the exploration of our first question: "What Is Christian Education?" Here, we recognize it as a plea to establish and provide an educative environment for our scholars and disciple-followers. I do not believe it is an overstatement or exaggeration to state that this process is exactly what our study is intended to accomplish. If we take the principles and practices we have discovered seriously, an educational environment should be the minimal result.

Providing a Physical Environment

Creating an inviting atmosphere that begs the student to "use me" rather than "don't touch me" obviously implies an engagement with the physical environment. In addition to the evident concerns of cleanliness, functionality, appropriate equipment in size and in function, suitable flooring and lighting, wall coloring, and age-appropriate décor, the educator concerned with facility also addresses a number of other issues.

Numbers, for example, are a critical concern. How large is the organization? How many people are expected to utilize the building and individual classrooms? A church administrator who was responsible to oversee the construction of a children's ministry wing for his church contacted me for help. He asked me to review the floor plans and provide any feedback or recommendations that might be appropriate. The very first thing I noticed was that the hallway was less than six feet wide. I asked him how many people would be utilizing the building at any given time and suggested that a six-foot wide corridor would not be enough. When he replied that the footprint had already been established and that to gain space in the hall would mean a smaller classroom, I checked the size of the classrooms next to see if they had room to spare. To my disappointment, I noticed that there was not only no room to spare, there was no room for cabinets and storage space. Additionally, there was no room or provision made for water to any of the classrooms. Apparently, the architect felt that all that was necessary for children's ministry was space in which they could sit at desks and do coursework.

Another critical concern is how many and when different groups will use the facility. Who "owns" the white board, the cabinet space, the supplies found within the cabinet, and the vacuum cleaner? Ownership, as discussed in the transformative phase of leadership in Chapter 2, generates responsibility and commitment that translates into concern and care for the setting in which ministry occurs. I actually have fond memories of getting down on my hands and knees and picking up glitter off the floor because I had ownership of my ministry, but I did not own a vacuum cleaner.

Realizing a Relational Environment

The relational environment of our educational settings consists of two distinct dynamics, individual and institutional. The primary principle that addresses the individual dynamic is a proximity orientation that focuses on the need to be with and among those to whom one is ministering, so that personal attention may be provided. Individual relationships in the Christian education context, however, also require an additional principle to guide them.

The Scriptures are used to nurture and train children in a simple dictum, and it is appropriate for adults as well: do unto others, as you would have them do unto you. A corollary, from the familial perspective, is to treat them as if they were your own. One of my personal applications of this principle in the institutional dimension is in the recruitment and selection of faculty. A critical question I frequently ponder is, "Would I want my child(ren) in this person's class or group?" If not, I will not appoint them. I always wanted my children's teachers and coaches to regard them that way, and I felt it was appropriate to view and treat others in a like manner.

From the corporate perspective, many other issues converge as we acknowledge the need to create a relational environment for our educational settings. We have discovered certain key words and concepts such as *koinonia, community,* and *context* that imply and affirm that the Christian life cannot be lived alone; indeed, God did not design it to be. We also examined an organization as a group and suggested the value of the study of group dynamics. Additionally, in the team development section of our discussion of a leader's role in staffing, I presented a seven-step approach to building team unity. Each of these concepts and concerns deserve attention and time devoted to them.

Facilitating a Familial Environment

The idea and vision for a ministry based on the metaphor of family came at a point in my life when I was at a crossroads and about to make some important decisions. It was one of those classic crisis moments of adult education, when a learner becomes almost painfully aware that change is necessary and an educational event is about to unfold. In my case, I was about to leave the church of my childhood and embark upon a spiritual adventure as a young adult. At the same time, I was finishing the first phase of my educational training and setting out upon a professional adventure. In addition to the encouragement from my family, I also received valuable assistance from one of my seminary professors, Norman Wakefield. While taking a walk one afternoon with Norm, he shared two bits of advice that changed my life.

The first was concerning the process of decision-making and has little bearing upon the topic before us, but had a profound influence on my growing understanding of both leadership and education. In brief, Norm suggested that I discern whether my decisions concerned unchanging, life altering, foundational principles, or simply personal preference. In other words, I had to ascertain what was negotiable in my life and what was not. Once I made that determination, the rest was easy.

The next topic in our conversation, however, had a tremendous impact upon my ministry. It was in that conversation that Norm originally suggested that the biblical, historical, and contemporary illustrations presented in this chapter could have a church-based, educational environment application. He suggested that I should view educational groupings such as Sunday school classes and small group ministries as mini-families where the participants treat each other as brothers and sisters and "fulfill the obligations of kinship." We dreamed of teachers who could build long-term personal relationships with their students and create environments in their classrooms that, as recommended by Gene Getz, simulated the relationships found in family units. Due to the fact that it was one walk with many topics, we did not get much further in our discussion that day, but the seed was planted. Two years later, I became the children's pastor of a local church, and the opportunity to implement the principles inherent in that dream became possible.

In the next two sections, I would like to further explore the family metaphor and consider some of the practical implications that it generates. I will begin with a formal description of the concept. However, to prevent the possibility of confining, restricting, and possibly distorting the perception and application of this idea, I will not refer to it with any more specificity than the family metaphor. I will leave it to individual churches or educational organizations to provide a specific title according to the uniqueness and intentions of their program. For example, a camping or outdoor education ministry may include the concept in its vision statement, influencing how cabin groupings are arranged, yet not give it a formal programmatic title (e.g., referring to a collection of cabins as a "unit" rather than the more familial "tribe").

The Family Metaphor Described

The family metaphor facilitates a functioning model for the immediate, educational environment of a local church or related Christian ministry. It normally consists of individuals or a team of teacher-leaders, who unite with disciple-followers in mutual ministry within a family-like environment, which finds its order in relationships, rather than in organizational structure. An extended spiritual family is formed when the natural family members, along with the gifted leaders of the ministry such as administrators, programmers, and resource specialists, contribute to the nurture and the development of the group and its members.

The Implications Discussed

Considering how the family metaphor can be implemented practically within a local church or organization reveals a vast array of possible implications. As a result of actually implementing the family metaphor in church and Sunday school programs, camping ministries, and compulsory education day schools, I have identified a number of organizational and general implications that appear to be prominent. In this section, I will address five general categories that give direction and guidance in considering the impact of the family metaphor. These categories include: the validity of the concept, structural concerns, relationships, curriculum, and facilities. In the Reflection and Response section at the end of this chapter, there will be an opportunity to personalize responses to some of these issues.

Validity of the Concept

One of the first items on my job description as the pastor of a children's ministry for a church in southern California was to create an audiovisual room for my teaching faculty. In my investigation of what it should look like and what it should contain, I was invited to examine the resource room of a local public school. Taking advantage of the offer, my Resource Room Coordinator and I visited this model supply room. The trip exceeded our expectations, and we gathered much needed information and direction for creating our resource room.

As we were leaving, our host, who happened to be a math teacher, called me aside to read a recent correspondence from the Education Department of The State of California. The memorandum instructed math teachers in the state to "deemphasize the new math." Given that the department had spent millions of dollars on curriculum planning and faculty development, this was a significant pronouncement. They were giving up on the approach because it had proven to be ineffective in the math education of most California students. This announcement had little direct impact upon my ministry or me personally. Thirty minutes later, however, I had an experience that shocked me, and I have never been the same because of it.

As we were driving away, I rolled down the window and enjoyed the sunny southern California afternoon, and basked in the knowledge of some newfound wisdom and direction for ministry. All of a sudden, I panicked. I remembered the memorandum, and I was petrified at the thought of one day, ten or fifteen years in the future, receiving a memo from the Lord himself instructing me to deemphasize the family metaphor and the applications that I had spent years developing in my church. Thankfully, the Lord assured my heart that I had built my ministry upon his word, and it endures forever. I had no reason to panic, and I had every reason to suspect that he would bless my efforts and the ministry they produced. That day, the Lord addressed and ratified the validity question in my heart.

For over three decades now, I have been practicing and teaching the biblical principles required to emulate and simulate the ministry found and exemplified in the God-ordained institution of family. Educators can anchor their convictions and labors upon this timeless wisdom. Since today's students, especially children, are subjected to a vast array of societal issues that affect their growth and development, the need for godly and biblical contexts for their nurture is vital and patent.

Structure

Curricular plans constructed upon the family metaphor are highly dependent on classroom teacher-leaders, just as natural families rely upon parents. Consequently, over the years I have reached the conclusion that I must attempt to enlist teachers whose lives are worthy of imitation and whose hearts are committed to the concept that ministry demands proximity, because order emanates from relationship, not organizational structure.

Recruiting teachers, group leaders, camp counselors, or any form of ministry leadership as a team rather than as individuals provides a supportive structure when ministry philosophy or circumstances, such as size, location, or program, dictate the need for more than one teacher. Therefore, I also recruit people who are able to work well with others.

Relationships

Although Edmund Leach asserted that having relationships is more critical than simply being present, it is equally important to note that in conclusion he stated, "Kin groups can function effectively only if most members are clustered in one place. Apparently we must choose between curtailed social mobility and an isolated, stress-ridden family life" (Leach 1974). Therefore, in our leadership practices and educational endeavors, the relationships we nurture are to manifest certain characteristics. One is the need for proximity; we need to be close to our students and disciple-followers. This implies spending time with and among them, getting to know them, and allowing ourselves to be known by them, as we have seen exemplified in the life and ministry of our Master and model. We cannot allow ourselves, due to benign neglect or intentional decision, to become distant or withdrawn from our charges.

I once served with a pastor who chose not to participate or share in the Lord's Supper, water baptisms, or virtually any other form of fellowship. After some nudging by congregants and staff alike, he decided to lead the Communion service during one of the midweek services. After the service, a member approached him and asked what the pastor perceived to be a challenging question, and he stormed off stating, "This is exactly why I never participate." The member, who simply wanted a conversation with his pastor, was left stunned and disillusioned. This pastor had a stage presence that attracted hundreds and thousands of visitors every year, but the church never grew beyond a plateaued state; I do not believe he ever made the connection.

The "individual dynamic metaphors" with which we opened this chapter provide hints as to other characteristics found in the kind of relationships expected within the church family. Others are available, for example, in Paul's exposition of a "life worthy" located in the Ephesians 4-6 passage we briefly explored in Chapter 8. Disciple-followers, who are in a mutual submission relationship with their leaders (Ephesians 5:21), often operate in heterogeneous, intergenerational groupings where distinctive and disparate ministry styles and giftings are present.

Each of these characteristics represents an attitude and a resultant behavior found in exemplary family life. They mark the kind of relationships produced within effective discipleship ministries as well.

Curriculum

Curriculum selection within the family metaphor is no different from the procedures discussed previously for a more traditional or formal classroom environment. The sources and forms of the teacher's message are as valid a consideration in a family as they are in the schoolroom. The advantage of a family metaphor model is that the life experiences of both teacher and pupil are valued highly and not relegated to extra-curricular status at the end of the lesson. The idea of life as a laboratory for learning allows the environment as the hidden curriculum to promote growth and development equally as well as the formal activities of teaching.

Facilities

The final implication of the family paradigm is its impact upon facilities. As natural families create living arrangements and environments that are as unique as the nature of the inhabitants, so also are the room arrangements for organized classes built upon the family metaphor unique to the needs of the students and the nature of the curricular plan.

The purpose of the family environment is to sustain, encourage, and support the relationships being built and developed there. In creating a family-like environment to accomplish this goal, teachers usually consider more open, flexible, spacious, and even modular classrooms. To accommodate a team teaching situation that also provided a teacher of a different gender for students in the two classes at one Christian school, we cut doors through the walls between classrooms in order to allow the class of a male teacher on one side to interact with the class of a female teacher on the other.

Teachers can also provide spaces that simulate "living rooms" or areas for small groups of students to gather and read, converse, or even study together. Of course, home Bible studies or other assemblies in private homes, such as house churches, have a natural advantage in creating familial environments, but with creativity and ingenuity formal classroom educators can likewise establish relational environments for their students.

How to Implement the Family Metaphor

In reviewing and utilizing segments of Scripture taken from the Epistle to the Ephesians, we discover a pattern of church development that proposes a strategy and sequence of behavioral steps to support the nurture and development of an educational environment, whether naturally or formally organized (Table 16). Teachers and leaders can employ this suggested sequence in conjunction with the seven-step process for team building, and can utilize it with any number of communication and group resources.

The following table is one of two resources provided to encourage and facilitate the implementation of an educational model using the family metaphor, especially in formal environments. They consist of a chart and a checklist, providing a strategy and a set of behaviors to use as guides for creative thinking and master planning.

Table 16. A Suggested Strategy for Facilitating the Family Metaphor

Scripture	Definition	Function	Practices
Ephesians 2:19-20	Physical components assembled	Acquire the information necessary to build relationships	Get names, addresses phone #'s, interests and hobbies. Reproduce in a database
Ephesians 2:1-22	Initial interaction of the members	Interact with members on two levels: cognitive and affective	Use group building techniques to grow the group and become aware of the other members
Ephesians 4:1-14	Relationships result in growth	Participate in activities to develop mature Christians (the whole man)	Experience the curriculum, together, to learn, meet needs, and grow in Christ and His way of life.
Ephesians 4:15	Having grown up into Him in all things		

The far right columns recommend specific functions and practices in which a teacher or leader may engage to facilitate the process. This table, however, is intended to be suggestive and a tool to generate ideas, not a rigid set of steps or prescribed behaviors.

Practices for Facilitating a Family Metaphor

The second resource is a simple list of behaviors recommended for a classroom teacher, small group leader, sports team coach, camp counselor, or anyone interested in facilitating a familial and relational environment for education.

Every time a teacher or leader gathers with disciple-followers, whether in a formal meeting or in those spontaneous moments of ministry, there is an opportunity to:

1. Acknowledge each member by name
2. Come to know something new about each member
3. Let that person get to know something about you
4. Show care and concern
5. Pray for each person
6. Communicate God's message for each person
7. Plan for the future together
8. Grow your group

In Conclusion

"To be a Christian school, not just a school with Christians in it!" In Chapter 8, I identified this statement as a vision for a private, Christian, K-8 school. Formal structures may vary, but this statement reflects a universal commitment to create an environment in which discipleship produces worship. Regardless of the content or the processes utilized, the context fashioned for an educational ministry, in large measure, contributes to its success. To create an effective educational environment, the context must be:

1. Marked by elevated expectations and is high achieving,
2. Known by its order and organization and is disciplined,
3. Recognized for its care and concern for each student and is relational,
4. Dependent upon mutual interaction and involvement and is familial, and
5. Committed to providing the appropriate resources and is stimulating.

"Creating an environment in which a student just might learn" is one of the objectives of every capable educator. In the creation of an effective environment, the scriptures have provided a framework for us to consider. When God chose to intervene in the affairs of humans, he always utilized the organizational construct of family (Genesis 2; Genesis 15 & 17; Ephesians 2:19). The contemporary Christian educator can do no better than to implement this metaphor by designing an environment that treats the students as if they were members of the family.

The Principal Principles

In conclusion and summary, discipleship ministries operate most effectively within the structure and guidelines provided by the principal principles I acknowledge in the Preamble to Part III. Numbers 10-12 provide a response to our fourth inquiry, "What Is the Context of (Christian) Education?"

Principal Principles:

> In succinct review, Christian education:
>> 10. *is founded upon an organizational metaphor of "family."*
>> *Genesis 12, 15; Ephesians 2:19*
>> 11. *builds a "corporate dynamic" context in the group.*
>> *Ephesians 2*
>> 12. *provides a "personal dynamic" context for modeling relationships.*
>> *1Thessalonians 1, 2; Mark 3:14 and Acts 4:13*

Prime Characteristic: Christian education is Family-oriented.
> *(Oriented: "to direct towards the interest of a particular group")*
> *The Divinely ordained method of organization and structure is firmly established upon a metaphor of "family." Each system formed for the purpose of ministry, including class groupings, ought also to be based on that same family model.*

Essential Activity:
> *Establish an Environment for Education*

Reflection and Response

An Exercise in Family Thinking

Take a moment and reflect upon ministry metaphors:

* Which ministry metaphors resonate with you personally? Professionally?

* Which metaphor is dominant in your organization?
> Is it biblically based? Upon which passages?
> How does it impact the educational, relational, and physical dimensions of the environment?
> What is unique to your program(s) because of it?

* Describe the attitudes, actions, and vocabulary that are characteristic of this metaphor.
> Have they become the model for your ministry?

Now, take some time to reflect upon the family metaphor.
Brainstorm some responses to questions 1 and 2. Write down the ones that appear to influence you.

1. If you or your ministry took the family metaphor seriously, what (actions, attitudes, values, etc.) would you expect to see in people who are "in family"?

2. In what activities must people be involved in order to experience the obligations of kinship (i.e., how do we get the above behaviors, feelings, etc.)?

Finally, utilizing ideas generated by these responses, personalize your efforts to create a "family environment" in your teaching ministry.

3. Which of these activities are you doing (or can you do) in your present educational situation?

4. Which would you like to be doing? Make plans to start this week. How will you do them? Write out your strategy.

An Exercise in Facility Thinking

Access the booklet *Spaces: Room Layout for Early Childhood Education* available from Community Playthings at www. CommunityPlaythings.com. Even if you are not an early childhood educator, you will still find most of the concepts and suggestions appropriate for any age group.

After reviewing and reflecting upon this resource, consider...

1. What messages are your facilities sending?
2. What changes would facilitate the messages you desire to send?
3. What can readily be done (given space, finances, etc.) to accomplish these?

Twelve
Who Are the People Involved in Education?

"It all comes down to people." Tom Peters, the coauthor of the best-selling *In Search of Excellence*, contends in the introduction to the book's video companion that this simple assertion affects every aspect of leadership (1985). Although he articulated his proposition nearly three decades ago, the sentiment is timeless. In the end, it all comes down to people.

Peters affirms this conviction when he observes in his syndicated column, "On Excellence," that the way you deal with people even affects the retention of customers.

> Consider some meticulous research done by the Forum Corp. It analyzed business customers lost by 14 big manufacturing and service companies (e.g., banks). Fifteen percent of those who switched to a competitor did so because they "found a better product" – by a technical measure of quality. Another 15% changed suppliers because they found a "cheaper product" elsewhere. Twenty percent hightailed it because of the "lack of contact and individual attention" from the prior supplier; and 49% left because "contact from old supplier's personnel was poor in quality."
>
> It seems fair to combine the last two categories, after which we could say 70% defected because they didn't like the human side of doing business with the previous product or service provider (Peters 1994).

People are the focus of leadership, and working with and for them is so critical that John Maxwell wrote *Be a People Person* specifically to foster "effective leadership through interpersonal relationships" (Maxwell 1989). It is appropriate, therefore, that we conclude our investigation of the five questions that inform and shape the structure of the discipline that is education with this concern: "Who Are the People Involved in Christian Education?"

Two affirming observations provide a reflective introduction to this investigation. The first is that regardless of the concept under consideration, it is patent that the common denominator present in every anecdote, illustration, or example provided in this book is people. Relational concepts such as proximity, with and among, and the family metaphor framed the pictures painted in the portraits of the processes, contexts, and content of the discipline. The teaching-learning strategies we implement, the environmental organizations we order, and the courses over which our students run are all instigated for, and influenced by human beings. People are indeed the integral and essential component.

As easy as it is to anthropomorphize our institutions, it is important to recognize that they are constructed entities that exist only because of, and are the products of, creative humans. This second observation highlights the fact it is people who make up these organizations and formulate policies and procedures; they are not manufactured by inanimate objects or mechanisms. "We, the people" even founded and formed our nation's governmental structure and all of its bureaucracy. Therefore, as people change, so does the makeup and personality of the institution. People are the creative and critical component.

Concerns Critical to the Inquiry

Observations such as these frame the investigation of the people question conducted in this chapter. We will commence our examination with the concerns critical to the inquiry – the perceptions, principles, and practices that have had the most profound impact upon countless leaders and are now embedded in effective ministry with and for people. Specifically, we will address and assess the involvement of three persons: the Master, the mentor, and the mentee. Contributions of the members of the Godhead will be acknowledged first, then the attributes of the teacher-leader, and finally the definitive characteristics of the disciple-follower, who is the focus of our educative efforts. We will then conclude our study by identifying the essential activities necessary to "Have a Heart for and Serve People."

Some Contributions a Minister Must Acknowledge

> *Now may our God and Father himself and our Lord Jesus clear the way for us to come to you. May the Lord make your love increase and overflow for each other and for everyone else, just as ours does for you. May he strengthen your hearts so that you will be blameless and holy in the presence of our God and Father when our Lord Jesus comes with all his holy ones (1 Thessalonians 3:11-13).*

With this benediction, the Apostle Paul addresses each of the categories of people involved in Christian education: God, you, others, and us. I acknowledge the role of other individuals and influences, both physical and spiritual, but for this concluding chapter I will focus on the Trinity, the teacher, and the taught.

Roles of the Godhead

The Old Testament contains numerous references to Jehovah as a teacher, and the New Testament Gospels regularly refer to Jesus as a rabbi. The Apostle John, in the fourteenth and sixteenth chapters of his gospel, calls our attention to the teaching ministry of the Holy Spirit. Hence, the Scriptures portray all three members of the Trinity as being active in educational endeavors. Many commentaries and analytical works on the members of the Godhead and their functions are available for anyone who desires to pursue further study. I will address, however, two particularly influential texts – one from the Apostle Paul and another from H. H. Horne.

All three members of the Godhead are personally and sovereignly engaged in, and give direction to, the ministries that occur within the Body of Christ. Their functions are described in the three verses in 1Corinthians 12 that I quoted in Chapter 8 concerning the people who make education Christian:

> *There are different kinds of gifts, but the same Spirit. There are different kinds of service, but the same Lord. There are different kinds of working, but the same God works all of them in all men (1Corinthians 12:4-6).*

The Holy Spirit distributes and empowers the gifts; the Lord Jesus determines and directs where and how they are exercised; and the Father takes responsibility for the outcomes and consequences. This last observation is based upon the wordplay and interaction between the terms *working* and *works*, with the latter signifying the results. What an encouragement for the Christian educator. Both the novice volunteer and the seasoned professional depend upon the same source: the present and active involvement of God.

It is also interesting to note the involvement of the Godhead in leadership behaviors. The Holy Spirit is clearly involved in the leader's responsibility to determine and declare the mission. He guides and leads to truth and reveals what has hitherto been unknown (cf. 1Corinthians 2:9, 10). Jesus, as the head of the church, selects and directs his administrators and authorizes them to lead and manage the church as they direct the mission. The final task of an administrator, control, is evident in the work of the Father as he works "all of them in all men." Once again, the parallel and complementary natures of teaching and leading find a common source and inspiration, in this case the activity and involvement of the entire Godhead. The need for a truly Christian educator to seek direction and guidance in discerning the revelation of the will of God is obvious.

The second text I will mention is *Teaching Techniques of Jesus* by Herman Harrell Horne (1971). In his book, Horne describes the qualifications of a "world-teacher" modeled after Jesus. Considering the emphasis I place upon being really good, really global, i.e., "world-class," educators and administrators, his condensed descriptions of the critical components of Jesus' ministry are worthy of our consideration and emulation. Horne suggests that the Master's ministry incorporated:

- A vision that encompasses the world
- Knowledge of the heart of man
- Mastery of the subject taught
- Aptness in teaching
- A life that embodies the teaching

This brief depiction of the distinctive nature of Jesus' ministry provides a concise summary of the characteristics necessary for success in any teaching ministry. It also serves as a segue to a more detailed discussion of the fifth characteristic, "A life that embodies the teaching."

Some Qualities a Minister Must Acquire

Inducing others to come and influencing them to follow is, by definition, the primary function of a leader. Inspiring people to participate in a mission is an essential component of administrative activity. In the processes of successful transformative leadership and effective recruiting efforts, three critical and core components of the leader's lifestyle are evident: a *manner*, a *method*, and a *message*. As a result of these, three corresponding responses are typically generated: disciple-followers *watch*, *follow*, and *imitate* their leader. I call these elements the Pillars of Personal Ministry.

The Pillars of Personal Ministry

In the New Testament, especially in the life and leadership of Jesus and his apostles, we find these three components and their responses illustrated. In examining them, we can discover hints and suggestions as to how to be effective in leading and ministering to people. To explore these essential columns and the consequences they generate, we will revisit some familiar texts of Scripture and reflect on several anecdotes to illustrate them. We will begin by discovering the foundation upon which these pillars stand.

"I have hidden your word in my heart that I might not sin against you" (Psalm 119:11) is the personal confession of the psalmist, and the cornerstone upon which the three pillars are constructed. In this prayer, he also exposes two critical ingredients necessary to buckle the tool belt of the contemporary Christian teacher or leader: an attitude and an aptitude. When Paul exhorts the Philippians that "Your attitude should be the same as that of Christ Jesus" (Philippians 2:5), he encourages the establishment of a godly mindset. Increasing our knowledge and hiding God's Word in our hearts equips us with a unique and godly perspective on life, leading, and learning that is necessary for a minister in Christ's service.

The psalmist, however, does not stop there. He asserts that this wisdom is designed to produce an aptitude in response to the attitude. The intention of hiding God's word in our hearts is that we "...might not sin against you [him]." Paul captures this expectation in his encouragement to the Ephesian church to "live a life worthy of the calling you have received" (Ephesians 4:3). In order to do so, a Christian educator must:

> *Watch your life and doctrine closely. Persevere in them,*
> *because if you do, you will save both yourself and your hearers*
> *(1 Timothy 4:16; cf. 1 Thessalonians 2:8).*

The mindset and accompanying skill set that form the foundation for this life worthy will be identified further as we address the three characteristics that constitute the pillars of personal ministry. In doing so, we will explicate the biblical perception and description of godly ministry, summarize its consequences, and outline our study with the following observations: you are being watched, followed, and imitated.

You Are Being Watched

One day while in college, I was walking down the campus's main boulevard when a young woman I recognized as a classmate came up beside me. As we made our way to our next class, we engaged in the usual small talk until she stunned me with the statement, "I want to tell you how much you encouraged and inspired me last night." It took me a moment to remember that I had served as a volunteer counselor at a Billy Graham Crusade. It actually had been a rather uneventful evening for me. I had the opportunity to share with only one young couple that had come forward to rededicate their lives to Christ, and by the time we were finished talking, there really was nothing left to do, so I made my way home. I quickly replayed the entire evening trying to discern any reason why my behavior could have been an encouragement or inspiration, but I came up empty. I no doubt gave her a blank look and simply responded, "How so?"

She answered that she had been watching my behavior, body language, and facial expressions, and her observations had spurred in her some form of spiritual response. I thanked her and expressed my appreciation for her encouragement. Then I asked, "Where were you sitting?" "In the third deck," she replied. Her answer and its implications were life altering for me. From the third deck of the 50,000 seat outdoor stadium, she was able to identify me and observe my behavior. That got my attention. It was a true awakening to realize that people could actually be watching my life that closely.

Fast-forward a half dozen years. I was walking down a dirt path on the last day of a family camp. As I was strolling from the cabins, a mother of one the children who had participated in the program during the week stopped me to chat. We engaged in the usual pleasantries, and she thanked my staff and me for the job that we had done in the children's program that week. She continued, "But do you know what I appreciated most? It was watching you work with the campers; you taught me how to be a better mother by the way you ministered to my children this week." She was not in the third deck, but she was watching just the same.

Those two incidents had a profound influence upon my perception of both ministry and ministers. It became evident that how we conduct ministry is just as impacting as the content of ministry. To use language with which we are now familiar, the bridge from information to experience is the identification with a model or an example to imitate. This mother had read the books and attended the workshops, and she had plenty of opportunity to minister to her children. What we provided that week was the example that she needed to see how it was actually done. Others are watching what we do, and observing how we do it. Our lifestyle is therefore the first pillar, or component, of personal ministry.

People Are Attentive to a Manner

> *He appointed twelve – that they might be with him and*
> *that he might send them out to preach… When they saw the*

*courage of Peter and John... they were astonished and **they
took note** that these men had been with Jesus.*

*You know how we lived among you for your sake... we were
gentle among you, like a mother caring for her little children...
You are witnesses, and so is God, of how holy, righteous and
blameless we were among you who believed (Mk. 3:14; Acts
4:13; 1 Thess. 1, 2).*

We have explored these passages before, focusing our attention upon
the ministry of proximity practiced by a leader or teacher who is with and
among the students. Here, we will highlight the words that are in bold,
"they took note" and "you are witnesses." While we have emphasized the
necessity of the leader-teacher being close, we must now acknowledge that
the disciple-follower is witnessing our manner, and even our enemies are
taking notes. This should not surprise us; the Master was closely scrutinized
throughout his entire ministry, and he appeared to welcome it.

The Master's Model

One selected incident from the Gospel of Luke illustrates the fact that
Jesus was being watched. People were observing him closely and expecting
him to do something. He did not disappoint them.

*One Sabbath, when Jesus went to eat in the house of a
prominent Pharisee, he was being carefully **watched**. There in
front of him was a man suffering from dropsy... So taking hold
of the man, he **healed** him and sent him away (Luke 14:1-4).*

So, this question must be asked: what do people see when they watch
you? What do they observe in your manner? The follow-up is just as
penetrating: what do you see when you turn around and look behind you?

You Are Being Followed

Two single moms, whom I will refer to as Rachel and Sheila, attended
home Bible studies and church services in a smaller church that I pastored
years ago. Sheila even brought her young daughter with her to sleep on the
couch as we studied. Although both of these women and their families were
obviously ministered to by the studies and counsel they received, we had no
idea of the impact of our ministry in their lives. When my season of ministry
in that church was over, I packed up my family and moved halfway across
the country. Not until a few days before we left were we aware that both

of these young women had intentions of literally following us in this move. Within a year, both of them made the move and joined the church where I had taken a staff position. Their lives continued to flourish in the new environment, and the personal ministry between our families continued for years. Not only are leaders and teachers in Christ's kingdom being watched, they are being followed as well. The second pillar, therefore, consists of the behaviors that influence others to follow. To put it in Maxwell's language, "becoming a person people want to follow" (Maxwell 1989).

People Are Attracted to a Method

> *The apostles **performed** many miraculous signs and wonders among the people… As a result, people **brought** the sick into the streets and laid them on beds and mats so that at least Peter's shadow might fall on some of them as he passed by (Acts 5:12-16).*

People are not only attracted to a manner of living; they are also attracted to a method of ministry. During the time of the ministry noted, Sheila brought a young woman I will call Cathy to our home for counsel, and a thirty-year relationship ensued. This association, however, had a very rocky beginning that almost ended it. Late one Saturday evening, just as I was putting the finishing touches to my sermon preparation, and Sharyn was putting Michael to bed, we heard a knock at the door. Cathy, who had been at our home once before for counseling, was standing there, car keys in hand, asking us to keep her for the night; she was on drugs, fearful for her life, and apparently willing to do anything to escape her present condition. She spent that night with us and stayed for the week that followed. She came off the drugs, started the difficult process of recovery, and received the necessary ministry to grow in a relationship with Jesus Christ. To this day, Cathy continues on that path and although she did not follow us physically when we moved, she followed us in spirit and by phone. She became like a sister to my wife and to this day, she still calls me her pastor.

I certainly make no claim to a ministry that equals that of the apostles noted in Acts 5, but in a small way we did indeed see the miraculous and experienced people bringing their friends to receive the small loaves and fishes of ministry that we did have to share. Not only do people watch a manner, they also follow a method; it inspires and motivates them to bring their friends to be healed.

The Master's Model

The Gospel stories contain many exciting accounts of miracles large and small, of lives changed young and old, and decisions made both good and bad. The Acts of the Apostles continue the story and thrill us with the potential and possibilities of lives empowered by the Holy Spirit. One may wonder what motivated those early disciples not only to watch Jesus, but also to follow him. Luke records the response and reaction of one man, Simon Peter, and his companions who were "astonished at the catch of fish they had taken" when Jesus directed them to cast their nets on the other side of the boat because their attempts had yielded no results. Jesus' miraculous method caught more than fish, he also netted disciple-followers.

> ...*When they had done so, they caught such a large number of fish that their nets began to break... When Simon Peter saw this, he fell at Jesus' knees and said, "Go away from me, Lord; I am a sinful man." For he and all his companions were* **astonished at the catch of fish** *they had taken... Then Jesus said to Simon, "Don't be afraid; from now on you will catch men." So they pulled their boats up on shore, left everything and* **followed** *him (Luke 5:4-11).*

Disciple makers are watched and followed; if their manners and methods imitate those of the Master, their disciple-followers will, as Paul noted to the Corinthian church, "Be imitators of me as I imitate Christ" (1 Corinthians 11:1).

You Are Being Imitated

Seeing one's self reflected in the attitudes, behaviors, and even language of other people can be an enlightening experience. The awesome reality of Jesus' observation that when a disciple is fully taught he becomes just like his teacher hits home with force (Luke 6:40). The words and actions one is really saying and doing become manifest. A leader cannot hide behind wishful thinking or doing.

Disciples who worship Jesus are the goal of our ministry; if I am that kind of disciple, there is a very good chance that I will see that model reproduced in others. As I think of the people I have influenced in the increase and development of their ministry skills, I am thankful for the little bits of myself showing up here and there. As I think about certain people, such as the two women who were observing me as I ministered to others, I trust that my influence was positive, and today they are living fruitful lives in part because of the tiny role that I was able to play.

On the other hand, I can also think of situations in which my less than exemplary attitudes and behaviors were reflected in the actions of others. I have struggled at various times over the years, for example, with proper submission to authority, and when I see that manifested in my disciple-followers' lives I have to wonder how much I contributed to it. The good news is that in the Lord's curricular plan for my life he has addressed and corrected that issue. Now I can stand before my followers and not only talk about, but also illustrate, proper submissive attitudes and actions. In receiving and responding to corrective action, and being honest about it before my disciple-followers, I am providing an illustration of proper behaviors and the correction of improper ones. This is obviously important because the simple reality is that they do not only imitate what we do right.

People Are Accepting of a Message

If people watch a manner and follow a method, what prompts them to imitate another? As strange as it may seem, the Scriptures indicate that a message, an articulated mission or vision, has the power to generate imitative behavior. We have seen in Part II, and Chapter 9, that in accepting a message, the disciple-follower precipitates a process that eventuates into not only imitating another but also providing a pattern for others:

> You became **imitators** of us and of the Lord; in spite of severe suffering, you **welcomed the message** with the joy given by the Holy Spirit. And so you **became a model** to all the believers (1 Thessalonians 1:6, 7).

The power of a persuasive message should never be underestimated in terms of its impact upon followers and learners. History is replete with examples of both positive and negative leaders who inspired, motivated, and even manipulated followers into patterns of behavior that enabled them to imitate their leaders. Proximity in many of these cases is artificial, but followers perceive it as real, and receive the leader's words are as if spoken personally to the disciple. The psychological proximity of a persuasive content message, delivered by an inspirational messenger, can overcome a lack of physical proximity due to geographical or chronological separation. The study of "cognitive proxemics" includes this phenomenon, and it would be a worthwhile expenditure of time to investigate the implications and applications of the concept in ministry environments.

The Master's Model

> *I have revealed you to those whom you gave me out of the world. They were yours; you gave them to me and they have obeyed your **word**. Now they know that everything you have given me comes from you. For **I gave them the words you gave me and they accepted them**. They knew with certainty that I came from you, and they believed that you sent me. I pray for them. I am not praying for the world, but for those you have given me, for they are yours (John 17:6-9).*

When we discussed the John 17 People in the staffing section of our discussion of leadership, we noted that what attracted the disciples to Jesus was his message and their perception that it was of God. Likewise, our followers accept and imitate our life message because they believe it is of God, and then their lives become models imitated by others. This was exactly what Jesus had in mind when he spoke with his father concerning his disciples: "My prayer is not for them alone. I pray also for those who will believe in me through their message" (John 17:20).

The Master's model, therefore, consists of three steps: hear from the Father, communicate with the follower, and motivate the faithful. They, in turn, follow his example and become the template for others to imitate. To be a model that is worthy of emulating, one should:

- **Be someone worth watching!**
  Live among (1 Thessalonians 1:5) your disciple-followers with courage and care, heeding Paul's concern that we imitate Christ (1 Corinthians 11:1).
- **Do something worth following!**
  Perform among (Acts 5:12) your disciple-followers with activity and achievement, following the example of Jesus (Matthew 20:34; Mark 10:52; Acts 8:11, 13; et al).
- **Say something worth imitating!**
  Share among (1 Thessalonians 2:8) your disciple-followers with a message and a model, acknowledging Jesus' observation that they will become like you (Luke 6:40).

We have now addressed two of the three prominent categories of people who are involved in Christian education, the members of the Godhead and godly leaders. We now turn our attention to the learner, or disciple-follower, and explore the nature and nurture of human beings.

Some Questions a Minister must Answer

Teachers and leaders carry certain perceptions regarding their disciple-followers and how they are to be treated. Seven of these perceptions are critical and worthy of identification and assessment. In this section, we will address them by posing questions educators must answer regarding the students they serve. To guide our discussion, I will ask the question, restate it in a more descriptive manner, and provide a biblical perspective.

I am also going to exemplify an application of each of the concepts by reference to a story, anecdote, principle, or personal example previously encountered in this book. My intention, therefore, is not only to summarize and illustrate, but also to integrate educational concepts with these theological presuppositions.

Reflections on the Learner

Teachers should consider how they view their students. Are they perceived to be:

Created or Evolved?

Are we advanced animals or something different (or more)?

> *And God said, "Let the land produce living creatures according to their kinds: livestock, creatures that move along the ground, and wild animals, each according to its kind." And it was so. God made the wild animals according to their kinds, the livestock according to their kinds, and all the creatures that move along the ground according to their kinds. And God saw that it was good.*
>
> *Then God said, "Let us make man in our image, in our likeness, and let them rule over the fish of the sea and the birds of the air, over the livestock, over all the earth, and over all the creatures that move along the ground."*
>
> *So God created man in his own image, in the image of God he created him; male and female he created them (Genesis 1:24-27).*

I affirm the biblical contention that God created the human race separate and distinct from the animal kingdom.

In the Tower of Babel episode, we observed people collaborating, communicating, and planning a major undertaking. The chapter we spent exploring the idea of a curricular plan depended upon the assumption that a teacher has the capacity to engage in complex critical thinking and planning. So far, science has yet to observe animals communicating and planning anything resembling a tower, a curricular plan, or something requiring ability beyond the rudimentary and instinctive level. The implications and applications of this distinction are vast, but our next question illuminates one of them.

Image-bearers or Blank Slates?

Are we imprinted or awaiting impressions to determine who we are and the value we hold?

> *Then God said, "Let us make man in our image, in our likeness, and let them rule over the fish of the sea and the birds of the air, over the livestock, over all the earth, and over all the creatures that move along the ground."*
>
> *So God created man in his own image, in the image of God he created him; male and female he created them* (Genesis 1:26, 27).

I affirm the biblical contention that God created the human race, and he created it in his own image. That image enables and enhances the human ability to interact with the creator.

The Apostle Paul declared that human beings have the requirements of the law "written on their hearts" (Romans 2:15). These words lay the foundation for experiences such as the one shared about junior-age campers who were able to meditate and reflect upon God's creation. Even in their youth, they were able to see, hear, and sense not only the presence, but also the pronouncements of God embedded in a starlit sky, an overhanging forest, and animal noises in the night. That ability, painfully and discouragingly, is often distorted and interrupted by another characteristic of humanity.

Innocent or Evil?

Are we predisposed to making appropriate or inappropriate decisions and choices?

> *For I know my transgressions, and my sin is always before me.*

> *Against you, you only, have I sinned and done what is evil in your sight, so that you are proved right when you speak and justified when you judge.*
>
> *Surely I was sinful at birth, sinful from the time my mother conceived me (Psalm 51:3-5).*

I affirm the biblical contention that despite being created in God's image, men and women choose to rebel and resist his work and intervention in their lives.

The sinful nature resident in humans is not hard to identify or exemplify. Probably the most obvious case we have encountered here is the story of the rebellious high school girl who would not do her homework or participate in any way in her educational experience.

Single or Multi-part Individuals?

Are we a collection of (coordinated) components or a unitary structure?

> *May God himself, the God of peace, sanctify you through and through. May your whole spirit, soul and body be kept blameless at the coming of our Lord Jesus Christ (1 Thessalonians 5:23).*
>
> *For the word of God is living and active. Sharper than any double-edged sword, it penetrates even to dividing soul and spirit, joints and marrow; it judges the thoughts and attitudes of the heart (Hebrews 4:12).*

I affirm the biblical contention that "God is spirit, and his worshipers must worship in spirit and in truth" (John 4:24), and, because of discipleship, that worship engages body, soul, and spirit.

The overarching goal of Christian education is making a disciple who worships. In the process of becoming a disciple, there is a constant conflict between the senses and the spirit for control of the soul (with, for example, its effect upon the mind in Romans 8:5). In the process of becoming a worshiper, the educational goals of knowing, loving, and obeying God are fulfilled by the soulish activities of acknowledgment, adoration, and acts of service to the Lord. It is a presupposition of this work that the image of God includes a constitutional representation of him as a trinitarian being. This perception has impact upon marriage and communication as well as education and worship.

Individual or Corporate in Life and Learning?

Are we designed to live and learn in isolation or social settings?

> And let us consider how we may spur one another on toward love and good deeds. Let us not give up meeting together, as some are in the habit of doing, but let us encourage one another—and all the more as you see the Day approaching (Hebrews 10:24, 25).

I affirm the biblical contention that "one anothering," as illustrated in the frequent and contextual use of the Greek term *allelon*, is a critical component of effective Christian ministry.

It was in a corporate environment that the young business administrator and I worked together to learn the distinction and complementary nature of the roles of leadership and management. It was also in a highly social and corporate context that the basketball team learned the interpersonal skills they were lacking and then modeled these behaviors for others. The many references we have made in this study to the concept of "with and among" imply involvement in a corporate learning environment.

Passive or Active in the Learning Process?

Are we the recipients of messages or the constructors of knowledge and/or meaning?

> My son, if you accept my words and store up my commands within you... (Proverbs 2:1).

I affirm the biblical contentions that a disciple receives and accepts the message of the master but is nonetheless accountable to think clearly and choose wisely, engaging not only the senses to receive, but also the soul to reflect. We discussed the distinction between active and passive learning in Chapter 8, and returning to that section for a brief review would no doubt be beneficial.

One of the recommendations I made when we were studying the Proverbs 2 metamodel was to do a word study on the use of the term *receive* in the Bible. I also suggested that one of the characteristics of the John 17 Person was that the disciple-follower chose to accept the message transmitted by the teacher.

On the other hand, I applauded the active reflection and construction of meaning by Jack Sherwood, the science teacher, as he created his own interpretation and application of the material he chose to receive.

Event or Process Oriented?

Is there anything about the process unique to the developmental stages or the manner in which they learn?

> *These commandments that I give you today are to be upon your hearts. Impress them on your children. Talk about them when you sit at home and when you walk along the road, when you lie down and when you get up. Tie them as symbols on your hands and bind them on your foreheads. Write them on the doorframes of your houses and on your gates.*
>
> *Teach them to your children, talking about them when you sit at home and when you walk along the road, when you lie down and when you get up. Write them on the doorframes of your houses and on your gates (Deuteronomy 6:7-9; 11:19, 20).*

I affirm the biblical contention that there is a distinction between children and adults and the way they learn.

We encountered the concept of education as a cycle of events and processes in Chapter 8. As a brief review, consider how life begins with an event, conception, followed by a nine-month process. The event of birth then precipitates another series of processes, growth and development. This sequence – event then process – continues in early childhood until approximately the age of five, at about the time compulsory education or schooling begins. At that point, we find the sequence reversing itself, with educational processes preparing students for the events of life. This continues until adolescence, the onset of young adulthood, at which time the sequence again reverses itself and events precipitate the process of education. In other words, each learner continually finds himself at a point along a developmental continuum. Infants learn through events that precipitate a process. Grade school children learn through the process of preparing for events. Finally, adults learn through a process precipitated by events.

In conclusion, the answers an educator provides to these seven inquiries frame and inform an understanding of the pupils to whom the teacher will be ministering. In summary, among other characteristics, this educator affirms a biblically based perception of a learner as a created human being, in God's trinitarian image, fallen in sin, yet choosing correction and submission to discipline, in order to worship Jesus.

Activities Essential to an Application

We referred to them as "Daddy-Daughter Dates" (or "3-D Dates"), and they began quite by accident. I came home for lunch one day to find that my homeschooled daughter had done exceptionally well that morning in her school activities, so I decided to take her out for lunch as a commendation. A few days later, when Carrie once again performed exceedingly well, I took her out to lunch and inadvertently established a tradition. Whether it was these lunches, birthday putt-putt adventures, attending a Colorado Rockies baseball game, or even years later during her teen years receiving pop culture music lessons while driving together to volleyball or basketball games, Carrie and I shared countless "3-D Dates."

Seldom was there an ulterior motive beyond that of blessing and receiving a blessing from my daughter. The reality underlying it all, however, is that proximity, being with and among, and exercising mutual ministry are elements of a familial relationship that is a biblical response to and application of the process and context questions, while equally reflecting components of the people question. When I share my "3-D Dad" experiences with other families, I consistently receive knowing nods and smiles in return. Whether or not it is one's own natural daughter or a student in the church, school, or group that one leads, it all comes down to caring for and caring about people. Thus, the essential activity produced by the answer to the people question is simply "Have a Heart for and Serve People."

Two resources came to my attention early in my career and provoked me deeply in my investigation of this final question of the five. John Claypool's short but provocative work *Stages* provided illustration of the necessity to "keep my eyes and ears open" to students in need (Claypool 1977). His work also suggested the need for the church to participate in compensatory work when the natural processes of family life have broken down; in other words, the church was to be a substitute spiritual family. Further, the film *Cipher in the Snow* confirmed the need to have a heart for my students. Based upon a true story by Jean Mizer, the tale of Cliff Evans and the effects of neglect and abuse in his life have inspired me to never leave a person feeling like they are a zero. Many texts pick up the theme, but these two works touched my heart and still profoundly influence my attitude and approach to people.

Bruce Wilkinson, in his "Teach with Style" video series, reminds educators that they must be to their students whatever is necessary for the successful communication of their message. To be willing to be "all things to all men" is a vital mentality for a Christian educator (1 Corinthians 9:22) and illuminates a heart and mind motivated by service to people. Having a heart for and serving people are the essential activities that inform and shape the answer to the people question. Leaders and teachers implement them by working for and with people.

Working for People

Working for people is simply another way to express the idea of service. When Jesus told his disciples that being great in the kingdom involved service not lordship, he set a new standard and established the rubric by which his administrators would be determined and evaluated. In Chapter 2, I introduced an acrostic to highlight seven critical characteristics of a servant. I expand them here with descriptions and additional scriptural resources. I also suggest some connections and correlations between Paul's behaviors, as he recounts them in 1Thessalonians, and the SERVANT descriptions. I would encourage leaders and teachers to examine their ministries – are examples such as these readily evidenced in their attitudes and behaviors toward disciple-followers?

A SERVANT is one who:

S: Shares his life message (2 Cor. 2:3-8; 1Tim. 4:16)

1Thess. 2:8 contains the definitive statement: Paul shared the Gospel and his life as well.

This characteristic received ample attention in our study, but I wish to enrich the discussion by observing that this trait is a manifestation of nothing more or less than love. Scriptures such as John 3:16 and other passages define love as the giving of oneself by laying down a life for another. In sharing our lives with our disciple-followers and by showing Christ's love to them, we are indeed laying down our lives and modeling its messages.

E: Exemplifies that message (Phil. 3:17; 1Cor. 11:1)

1Thess. 1:6 suggests that Paul was a model worthy of imitation.

The idea of "example" in Scripture is evident in two concepts and contexts, roughly corresponding to usage as a verb or a noun. Its function as a noun occurs when the Greek word that is literally translated "exhibition" or "sample" is used. For example, Jesus employed it when he was illustrating the life expected of one of his followers. A second more commonly used Greek term is translated "example" but literally refers to a "type" or "pattern" (Strong 2004). Derived from the practice of striking a blow to force an object on some material to make an impression, becoming a mold for others, our English "type" comes from this action word. In other words, our lives are to be samples, making an impression upon others and establishing a standard.

Some other scriptures that may be instructive in this regard include: John 13:15; 1Peter 2:21; 2Thessalonians 3:7; and Luke 6:40.

R: Represents his master correctly (1John 4:20; 1Peter 2:12)

1Thess. 2:4 indicates that the Lord approved of Paul's behavior.

To "represent" also involves two concepts or behaviors. The first is the natural extension of being an example – you live your life as a representation or image of the master for which you are a messenger. In the case of Christian ministry, our lives are an imitation of Christ.

The second concept embodies representation as an ambassador, presenting the master's message to an assigned audience. In a very practical sense, this requires that we pay attention to the language that we use and the methods that we utilize. They must be appropriate to the individual or group we are addressing while not distorting the heart and intention of the message.

Reflect upon and consider the following scriptures: Matthew 5:14-16; John 8:12, 9:5; and Colossians 2:8.

V: Verbalizes his master's thoughts (1Cor. 5:20; 1Peter 4:10, 11)

1Thess. 1:5 indicates that Paul presented the gospel first in words.

As ambassadors representing Jesus Christ or the human leaders he has ordained, it is our assignment to make sure that we are clearly and accurately representing the Master's words. In the apostle's first letter, Peter instructs everyone that when they speak they should do so as one speaking the very words of God (4:11). He, in essence, cautions us to watch our words and to do our homework before we speak. While this is primarily a verbal characteristic, ministers affirm and confirm it by their behavior as well.

A: Acquiesces to authority and shares leadership (2Cor. 1:24; 1Peter 2:13 – 3:7)

1Thess. 1:7, 8 illustrate the emerging role of the Thessalonians.

In the Great Commission, Jesus reminds us that all authority is his. Therefore, in Peter's challenge to the elders, he reminds them that a shepherd will not lord his position and authority over those entrusted to him. While it is true that a leader may indeed rule (Luke 22:25), he does so as a servant under another's authority and not as a lord attempting to dictate his will into another's life or ministry. Paul illustrates the same attitude in 2Corinthians 1:24, as he reminded the church that he worked with them rather than lorded it over them. Jesus himself made the definitive declaration in Mark 10:42, when he called his disciples together and informed them that whoever wanted to become great must first become a servant.

N: Needs are met (Acts 4:32-35; 2Cor. 8)

1Thess. 2:6 suggests the care and concern that meets needs.

It should virtually go without saying that one of the components of servant leadership is to address and meet needs. The classic biblical example is the activity of the deacons in Acts 6. Jesus' instruction to give a cup of cold water to anyone in need is the rubric and benchmark by which he assesses our service. His implied insistence is that to be a neighbor like the Samaritan is standard operating behavior in his kingdom.

Passages that develop this theme include Acts 2:44-45; Acts 4:34; and 2Corinthians 8.

T: Teaches and trains (Acts 20:20, 27; Titus 2; 1Tim. 3:2; 2Tim. 2:2, 14)

1Thess. 2:12, 4:1 reveal the intentions of the teaching ministry.

These two terms, and the concepts they represent, have received significant attention so they need very little further clarification. Suffice it to say, teaching and training are vital components and elements of a leader-educator's toolkit.

Additional scripture references addressing the teaching/training ministry include Proverbs 22:6; John 14:26; and 1Timothy 4:13.

The nature and function of servant leadership virtually defines working for people. Considering and giving attention to these seven characteristics and their implications or applications in an administrator's life and ministry will go a long way toward establishing credibility and identity as a servant leader.

Leadership, however, is not always about doing things for people. It is also accomplishing tasks with them.

Working with People

An ability to work with people is a critical component in four of the five habits of highly effective leaders, as Becky Brodin articulates in an article published by *Discipleship Journal* (1993):

Five Habits of Highly Effective Leaders:
- *Effective Leaders Tolerate Diversity*
- *Effective Leaders Develop People*
- *Effective Leaders Make Decisions*
- *Effective Leaders Welcome Feedback*
- *Effective Leaders Care About People*

Working for people establishes and affirms the mindset of a leader, but working with people challenges the skill set. I hope that our study together has enabled some increase and maturation in both. To summarize, let me provide a synopsis of the disciple maker's charge and challenge that it all comes down to people.

From the leader's perspective, working with people includes:

- **Working** with People: Tasks to Accomplish and Lives to Change
  The leader-educator focuses upon the mission
- Working **with** People: Relationships to Develop and Activities to Share
  The leader-educator facilitates the vision
- Working with **People**: Needs to Meet and Potentials to Actuate
  The leader-educator fulfills the commission

From the teacher's perspective, in the interaction between teacher and learner, there must be...

Something to **Say:**
The leader-educator determines the mission's message and has a word for listeners

Something to **Show:**
The leader-educator declares the mission's message and has a heart for learners

Something to **Share:**
The leader-educator directs the implementation of the mission's message and has an eye for leaders

It all comes down to people.

> *Thus, we have come full circle. Christian leaders have long known of their biblical responsibility to be committed to the people they lead. What we need to continually remind ourselves is that failure to adhere to these biblical priorities also deprives the organization of its opportunity to achieve its potential (Habecker 1989).*

With that affirmation, we conclude our exploration of the final question to give shape and structure to the discipline. With that concluding observation, we terminate our investigation of ancient wisdom for contemporary Christian education and leadership.

The Principal Principles

In conclusion and summary, discipleship ministries operate most effectively within the structure and guidelines provided by the principal principles I acknowledge in the Preamble to Part III. The last three provide a response to our final inquiry, "Who Are the People Involved in (Christian) Education?"

Principal Principles:

> In succinct review, Christian education:
>> 13. *requires all three members of the Godhead:*
>> (*the Spirit anoints, the Lord Jesus directs, and the Father determines the results*).
>>> *1Corinthians 12:4-6*
>> 14. *includes leaders ("masters") who serve the community through instruction and influence:*
>> (*with something to say, show, and share*).
>>> *Luke 22:25ff*
>> 15. *focuses upon students ("disciples") who are created in the image of God, yet immature and choosing to learn.*
>>> *Genesis 1:27; Proverbs 17:16*

Prime Characteristic: Christian education is Others-focused.
> (*Focused: "to concentrate attention or effort"*)
> *Christian education is not an isolated or individual education. It is an education that is dependent upon relationships. The teacher must give adequate attention to the development and growth of the group as well as the individual.*

Essential Activity:
> *Have a Heart for and Serve People*

Reflection and Response

Reflections on the Learner

This chapter provided a number of bulleted lists and sequences of questions to be considered and addressed by the Christian educator.

For this activity, focus upon the seven questions that educators must ask concerning their pupils. Reflect upon each question, identify pertinent scripture references, and write out a two-paragraph response. In the first, summarize your position; in the second, identify implications for ministry.

Are human beings:

Created or Evolved?
Are we advanced animals or something different (or more)?
 Informing Scripture:
 Ministry Implications:

Image-bearers or Blank Slates?
Are we imprinted or awaiting impressions to determine who we are and the value we hold?
 Informing Scripture:
 Ministry Implications:

Innocent or Evil?
Are we predisposed to making appropriate or inappropriate decisions and choices?
 Informing Scripture:
 Ministry Implications:

Single or Multi-part Individuals?
Are we a collection of (coordinated) components or a unitary structure?
 Informing Scripture:
 Ministry Implications:

Individual or Corporate in Life and Learning?
Are we designed to live and learn in isolation or social settings?
 Informing Scripture:
 Ministry Implications:

Passive or Active in the Learning Process?
Are we the recipients of messages or the constructors of knowledge and/or meaning?
Informing Scripture:
Ministry Implications:

Event or Process Oriented?
Is there anything about the process unique to the developmental stages?
Informing Scripture:
Ministry Implications:

Reflections on the Learner, Continued

Marcia Bunge has provided an instructive illustration of this process in her article "A More Vibrant Theology of Children" found in the 2003 edition of Christian Reflections published by The Center for Christian Ethics at Baylor University. In this provocative essay, she identifies three dyads of almost paradoxical ways in which children are perceived in the Bible. She asserts that, "These six central ways, taken together, present a complex picture of children that can provide a solid foundation for more creative religious education programs, more serious theological and ethical reflection on children, and renewed commitment to serving and protecting all children."

As you read and reflect upon her observations, take note that most of these are also applicable to young people and adults, thus rendering them useful for a full-orbed Christian education ministry. Note also how many of the seven questions are either directly addressed or have implications implied.

It all comes down to people, and Bunge's theology of children provides a framework for the reflection and response critical to the construction of "a solid foundation for more creative religious education programs":

> **"The Christian tradition represents children in complex, almost paradoxical ways, as**
> **gifts of God and signs of God's blessing,**
> **though they are sinful and selfish;**

as developing creatures in need of instruction and guidance,
yet as fully human and made in the image of God;

and as models of faith, sources of revelation, and representatives
of Jesus,
though they be orphans, neighbors, and strangers who need to
be treated with justice and integrity."

If you accept her articulation of these "six central ways," how will your
ministry be affected and the manner in which you treat children (or adults)
altered?

Epilogue

LOOKING BACK: *What Was this Book About?*

I was enjoying a pleasant walk one sunny afternoon when my mind began to wander, and I found myself reflecting upon my legacy. Specifically, I was wondering what of significant value I would leave behind. As I contemplated the possibilities, I felt the strong impression in my heart that if I left nothing behind but my children that would be enough; they are world changers. For a moment, I was satisfied, encouraged, and affirmed; my children are indeed a blessing to me and to others. Then, I started comparing myself to them and realized that I was almost jealous because they are so talented in so many ways. For example, they both inherited artistic and musical leanings from their mother, who plays piano by ear. They both are intelligent and creative (my son has two Masters degrees, writes music and produces one-man puppet shows, and my daughter has a J.D. and was a published journalist as an undergrad), while it seems like all I do is produce outlines for study and presentation.

At that moment in my reflections, a second impression came to me vividly. An image of one of my outlines formed in my mind. I could see the major headings identified with a Roman numeral, followed by an indented line started with a capital letter immediately below it, and then a series of indented sub points. It was dry, methodical, and mechanical; I guess one could say it was just short of boring. Suddenly, however, the outline rotated horizontally, and I began to picture the image differently – now it resembled a sheet of music. The words that initially flowed from top to bottom now read from side to side. The outline indentions now appeared as the ebb and flow of musical measures, creating a melodic tune. With the textual notes transforming into musical notes, it reminded me of a musical score.

The impact was life affirming; I realized I am also an artist. My teaching outlines and study guides are how I express my educational creativity. I no longer perceive of them as mundane, routine, or lifeless. On the contrary, they overflow with life. My legacy, therefore, is my life message. The life I have lived and am reproducing in my children, along with what I know and am reproducing in part here, constitute the life and doctrine in which I persevere. My ministry is to share them with any who will take the time to listen. I want to thank you for being one of them; I trust there has been something profitable in this expanded outline of thoughts expressed as a symphony of words.

A Life Message

My life verse of Psalm 119:80 offers this prayer: "Let my heart be sound in thy statutes, that I be not ashamed" (KJV). Consisting of what I have learned and what I have experienced, the response to this petition is my life message, and remaining sound in it brings salvation to my disciple-followers as well as myself (1Timothy 4:16). From commencement to conclusion, one underlying and constantly recurring theme has driven me. This commitment, the driving thesis of my lifetime of ministry, can be summarized by the simple assertion that I have something to say, show, and share with my children and my students. To paraphrase yet another Pauline pronouncement, I love them so much that I am delighted to share with them not only the Gospel of God but my life as well, because they have become so dear to me (1Thessalonians 2:8).

The Pauline Memoirs: 1Thessalonians 1:1 - 4:12

Paul's ministry memoirs have inspired me from the beginnings of my ministry. I find them to be a source of both personal and professional inspiration. Personally, they provide a template for my behavior and a rubric for its assessment. Professionally, and I am not surprised to observe this, the apostle's recollection of his ministry with the believers in Thessalonica addresses many of the principles and practices we have discovered and discussed. His ministry attended to, and provided suggestive answers to, the five inquiries that have provided our structure for Part III. He utilized and modeled for us the use of all four forms in the delivery of his message. His teaching promoted and led his disciple-followers through the five stages of the Proverbs 2 metamodel for learning that we explored in Part II. Finally, his ministry exhibited the five characteristics and requisites of effective leadership that we discussed in Part I. Paul illustrated all this in three and one-half chapters of his first letter to the Thessalonians, the original design for discipleship.

Paul was therefore both a fountain of pertinent information and a formidable model to imitate. In essence, by penning his educational memoirs, he prompted both the style and substance of this book. I can think of no better way to conclude our study than to briefly review one man's effective ministry and another's attempt to emulate it.

We will frame our exploration by observing how Paul addressed and practically answered the five questions that provide a structure for the discipline of ministry. Although throughout Part III we have referred to educational ministry questions, for this examination of Paul's ministry model we will utilize more generic Christian ministry inquiries.

What Is Christian Ministry?

Early in the epistle, Paul addresses the goals and components of Christian ministry: discipleship and worship.

> to **live lives worthy of God,** *who calls you into his* *kingdom and glory.*
> (Discipleship, 2:12)
> *you* **turned to God from idols** *to* **serve the living and** **true God.**
> (Worship, 1:9)

Both of these issues have been addressed in some depth previously, but here I would like to make the observation that Paul's ministry generated discipleship at all four levels commonly identified in discipleship taxonomies.

He Generated all Four Levels of Discipleship

1. **Apprentice** (competency training)

A participant in the process of skill development (live a life worthy)

2. **Student** (information acquisition)

A participant in the process of knowledge development (receive the Gospel)

3. **Scholar** (philosophical inquiry)

A participant in the process of professional development (become a model)

4. **Follower** (discipleship)

A participant in the process of life development (at work in you)

Paul placed an emphasis upon the development of Christian life skills, a mastery of biblical knowledge, a formation of a comprehensive worldview, and the establishment of a bond between the discipler and the disciple that neither time nor distance can diminish. Making disciple-followers who worship Jesus was clearly Paul's intention and modus operandi, and it influenced his message and method selection.

What Is the Content of Christian Ministry?

1:5, because our gospel came to you

4:1, Finally, brothers, we instructed you how to live

4:3, It is God's will that you should be sanctified: that you should avoid...

4:9, Now about brotherly love we do not need to write to you, for you yourselves have been taught by God to love each other.

Having identified Paul's intention and goal, we logically ask the question, "What messages did he need to communicate in order to fulfill his goal?" In Paul's case, the Gospel of salvation, the instructions for sanctification, and the encouragement to love one another provided the content and the framework for the curricular plan he constructed and implemented. In doing so, Paul utilized, in balance and in congruence, all four forms that a message may take, and he identifies each of them in three verses of Chapter 1. To make them clear, I have highlighted them in bold and abbreviated them in brackets: SM: Subject Matter; E: Environment; L: Life Experience; TM: Teacher Model.

He Utilized all Four Forms of a Message: SMELT

...because our gospel came to you not simply with words[SM], but also with power, with the Holy Spirit and with deep conviction. You know how we lived among you [E] for your sake. You became imitators of us and of the Lord [TM]; in spite of severe suffering [L], you welcomed the message with the joy given by the Holy Spirit. And so you became a model to all the believers in Macedonia and Achaia (1:5-7).

After establishing his intentions and selecting his messages, Paul implemented the three primary processes that we labeled the "Biblical Model" while following the five stages of the Proverbs 2 Teaching-Learning Metamodel.

What Are the Processes of Christian Ministry?

It has been clearly articulated, and I trust abundantly affirmed, that the three processes consisting of the proclamation of information, the provision of a model to imitate, and the promotion of practical experience and life change, are the foundational building blocks upon which an effective procedure for every educational endeavor and teaching-learning experience can be built. The apostle agrees, reminding the Thessalonians of the message that rang out through the declaration of the Gospel, the example of his life, and the experience of theirs. It is also worth noting the correlation of the three processes with the four forms of the message.

> For we know, brothers loved by God, that he has chosen you, because **our gospel came to you** ... [and] You know how we **lived among you** for your sake. You **became imitators** of us and of the Lord; in spite of severe **suffering... you became a model** to all the believers in Macedonia and Achaia. The Lord's message rang out from you not only in Macedonia and Achaia—your faith in God has become known everywhere (1:4-8).

Not only were the three processes evident, but so also were the five stages of the learning metamodel. In fact, he acknowledges them in sequence and provides another biblical illustration of the validity and practicality of the model.

He Facilitated all Five Stages of the Proverbs 2 Metamodel

> And we also thank God continually because, when you **received** the word of God [I], which you **heard** from us [II], you **accepted** it not as the word of men, but as it actually is, the word of God, which is **at work in you** who believe [III]. For you, brothers, **became imitators** of God's churches in Judea [IV], which are in Christ Jesus: You **suffered** from your own countrymen the same things those churches suffered from the Jews [V] (2:13, 14).

It appears that Paul spent a significant amount of time creating and establishing an educational, physical, relational, and familial environment. To create an environment in which a student just might learn by experiencing the five stages was more than just a theoretical construct.

What Is the Context of Christian Ministry?

> As apostles of Christ we could have been a burden to you, but we were gentle among you, like a mother caring for her little children. We loved you so much that we were delighted to <u>share with you not only the gospel of God but our lives as well</u>, because you had become so dear to us.
> You are witnesses, and so is God, of how <u>holy, righteous and blameless we were among you</u> who believed. For you know

that we dealt with each of you as a father deals with his own children, <u>encouraging, comforting and urging</u> you to live lives worthy of God (2:6-12).

How many ministers, or their ministries, actually serve rather than burden? How many create relational environments that are gentle? Caring? Loving? Sharing? How many create educational ones that actually encourage and motivate or familial ones that foster obligations of kinship while treating their followers as their own children? Paul did, and he has left a template for others.

He Established a Familial Environment

Contemporary twenty-first century Christian ministers cannot complain about a lack of appropriate ministry models; we have one in this first century apostle's life message. Among other valuable revelations, Paul discloses the metaphor he used to create a context in which his students just might learn. It is that of a family, with its nurturing and supportive relationships and serving structure.

Who Are the People Involved in Christian Ministry?

Now may our God and Father himself and our Lord Jesus clear the way for us to come to you. May the Lord make your love increase and overflow for each other and for everyone else, just as ours does for you. May he strengthen your hearts so that you will be blameless and holy in the presence of our God and Father when our Lord Jesus comes with all his holy ones (3:11-13).

We opened the critical concerns section of Chapter 12 by quoting this paragraph. It seems appropriate to conclude by reviewing its implications. Seen here are five categories of people involved in Christian ministry: God, us, you, everyone else, and all his holy ones. For our discussion, we combined *you* with *everyone else* and chose not to address the holy ones. This left the Godhead, the teacher-leader, and the disciple-follower. That all of them would be included within three sentences indicates the kind of respect Paul holds for them and the responsibility that each shares in the discipleship process. It is as if he already knew 2000 years ago that it all comes down to people and working for and with them. In doing so, Paul's ministry to the Thessalonians reveals and exemplifies the five requisites of effective leadership. We also observed these requisites in the case study of

Joshua defending the Gibeonites and as a directive in Paul's instruction to Timothy (see Chapter 4).

He Met the Five Requisites of Effective Leadership

Hard work, commitment, preparation, power, and time comprise the requisites of leadership. Reflecting upon how they are implemented and illustrated in Paul's ministry and taking the time to consider their impact upon present ministry would be a worthwhile endeavor.

*1:4 For we know, brothers loved by God, that he has chosen you, 5 because our gospel came to you… with **power**, with the Holy Spirit and with deep **conviction**. You know how we lived among you for your sake.*

*2:4 we speak as men **approved** by God to be entrusted with the gospel.*

*9 Surely you remember, brothers, our toil and **hardship**; we **worked night and day** in order not to be a burden to anyone while we preached the gospel of God to you… 13 And we also thank God continually.*

The Educational Memoirs: in Conclusion

A legacy, in short, is something of real value passed from one person to the next. In this work, I have attempted to emulate the model of Paul and pass along, through my "educational memoirs," a design for discipleship ministry – a valuable understanding of ancient wisdom that is applicable in contemporary education and leadership. The extent to which this transfer has been successful will be evident in the lives and ministries of those who have traveled with me in this continuation of my pilgrimage and the commencement of theirs. The disciple-followers who travel with them, however, are the ultimate beneficiaries.

Thank you for joining me in this adventure of learning to lead, teach, and make disciples.

Appendix A
FACTORS THAT FRAME: *A Graphic Model*

The following graphic depiction (Display 13) represents the five lines of inquiry that define, describe, and direct the philosophy of Christian education, or discipleship ministries, presented in Part III.

Consisting of the "Factors that Frame the Investigation" and concisely identifying the necessary Biblical Foundations, Theological Pre-Suppositions, Philosophical Concerns, Scientific Considerations, and Educational Assumptions and Praxis for each of the five questions, each component of the graphic contains a representative sample of the issues and concerns that inform the investigation. Although no attempt has been made to be exhaustive in scope or depth, I have tried to acknowledge the critical components I addressed in my personal research. Most of these issues can be explored in a comprehensive manner by exposure to the sources catalogued in the Works Cited Reference List in Appendix B. I recommend, especially, Knight's *Philosophy and Education* (1998), Pazmiño's *Foundational Issues in Christian Education* (1997), and Estep, Anthony, and Allison's A *Theology for Christian Education* (2008).

Imagine, viewing from above, a five-leaf clover laying flat on the ground. Now, imagine, similar to the rings in the Olympic logo, each of the leaves as overlapping circles. Within each of these individual circles, envision five statements inscribed to represent the foundational factors that frame and inform the inquiry. Every circle contains the Scripture reference, theological concept, philosophical issue, scientific insight, and educational assumption that pertains to and explicates that question.

Display 13. A Graphic Model: the Structure of the Discipline

Toward a Philosophy of Christian Education:

THE STRUCTURE OF THE DISCIPLINE

a MODEL combining the essential elements of
Biblical Foundations, Theological Pre-Suppositions, Philosophical Concerns, Scientific Considerations, and Educational Praxis

christ-centered

Genesis 1, 2: the "Mission"
Matthew 28:19, 20; Hebrews 13:15, 16

Making Disciples who Worship Jesus
WHAT IS CHRISTIAN EDUCATION?

Christo-Centric
Philosophy

Christology
Completed Work of Christ
Object of Man's Response

Ecclesiology
Continuing Work of the Church
Brotherhood of Believers

family-oriented
Genesis 1, 12, 15: the "Model"
Ephesians 2:19ff; 1 Thessalonians 1, 2:7-11
Establishing an Environment for Education
WHAT IS THE CONTEXT OF CE?

Creation-Oriented
Metaphysics

others-focused
Genesis 1, 2: the "Ministers"
Genesis 1:27; 1 Corinthians 12:4-6
Having a Heart for and Serving People
WHO ARE THE PEOPLE OF CE?

Worship Focused
Axiology

Ed. Psych

Development

Environment

Pneumatology

Anthropology
Man's Response to the Message
Recipients of the Message

Assessment

Cognition

Theology (proper)
Fatherhood of God
Source of the Message

Revelation
Methods of the Message

Revelation
Content of the Message

WHAT ARE THE PROCESSES OF CE?
(REVEALED truth)
Revelation-Based
Epistemology
Preparing a Plan for Teaching & Learning
Philippians 4:9; Colossians 1:9-12
Genesis 3, 11: the "Method"
application-designed

WHAT IS THE CONTENT OF CE?
(revealed TRUTH)
Revelation-Based
Epistemology
Constructing a Curricular Plan
Hebrews 12:1, 2; John 14:6
Genesis 1-3: the "Message"
bible-based

© 2000 Michael R. Mitchell

422

Appendix B

REFERENCE LIST: *Works Cited*

Adams, Carmine, and Gerstein. 1982. Instructional strategies for studying content area texts in the intermediate grades. *Reading Research Quarterly* 18, 27-53.

Alderman, L. H. and A. Kaplan. 2008. The role of interpersonal relationships in student motivation: Introduction to the special issue. *The Journal of Experimental Education* 76 (2): 115-119.

Anderson, Margaret. 1999. What is educational psychology? Retrieved from http://snycorva.cortland.edu/~andersmd/whatis.html.

Anthony, Michael J. and James Estep, Jr. 2005. *Management essentials for Christian ministries.* Nashville, TN: Broadman and Holman Publishers.

Augustine. 1997. *On Christian teaching.* Translated by R.P.H. Green. World's Classics Series Oxford: Oxford University Press.

Barlow, Daniel Lenox. 1985. *Educational psychology: The teaching-learning process.* Chicago: Moody Press.

Barna, George. 1997. *Leaders on leadership.* Ventura, CA: Gospel Light, Regal Books.

Beechick, Ruth. 1982. *A biblical psychology of learning.* Denver: Accent Books.

Bennis, Warren and Burt Nanus. 1985. *Leaders: the strategies for taking charge.* New York: Harper and Row Publishers.

Biehler, Robert F. 1978. *Psychology applied to teaching,* 3rd ed. Boston: Houston Mifflin Company.

Bigge, Morris L. and S. Samuel Shermis. 1999. *Learning theories for teachers,* 6th ed. New York: Addison Wesley Longman, Inc.

Blackaby, Henry and Richard. 2001. *Spiritual leadership – Moving people on to God's agenda.* Nashville: Broadman and Holman Publishers.

Bloom, Benjamin S., ed. 1956. *Taxonomy of educational objectives.* New York: David McKay Company.

Butterweed, G. Johannes, and Helmer Rigger, eds. John T. Willis, translator. 1974. *Theological dictionary of the Old Testament.* Grand Rapids: Eerdmans.

Bower, Robert K. 1964. *Administering Christian education.* Grand Rapids: Eerdmans Publishing Company.

Bredfeldt, Gary J. 2006. *Great leader great teacher: Recovering the biblical vision for leadership*. Chicago: Moody Publishers.

Brother Lawrence. 1985. *The practice of the presence of God: Revised edition*. Translation by Robert J. Edmondson. Orleans, MA. Paraclete Press.

Burns, James MacGregor. 1978. *Leadership*. New York: Harper & Row Publishers, Inc.

Chadwick, Ronald P. 1982. *Teaching and learning*. Old Tappan, NJ: Fleming H. Revell Company.

Childs, John L. 1950. *Education and morals*. New York: Arno Press.

Clark, Robert E., Lin Johnson, and Allyn K. Sloat, eds. 1991. *Christian education: Foundations for the future*. Chicago: Moody Press.

Clark, Robert E. and Roy B. Zuck, eds. 1975. *Childhood education in the church*. Chicago: Moody Press.

Collins, Jim. 2001. *Good to great: Why some companies make the leap... and others don't*. New York, NY: HarperCollins.

_____. 2001. *Good to great and the social sector*. Boulder, CO: Jim Collins.

Colburn, A. 2007. Constructivism and conceptual change, Part 1. *Science Teacher* 74 (7): 10.

Colson, Howard P. 1969. *Understanding your church's curriculum*. Nashville: Broadman Press.

Davis, Barbara Gross. 1993. *Tools for teaching*. San Francisco: Jossey-Bass.

De Pree, Max. 1989. *Leadership is an art*. New York: Bantam Double Day Dell Publishing Group, Inc.

DeSilets, L. D. 2007. Using objectives as a road map. *Journal of Continuing Education in Nursing* 38 (5): 196-197.

Drakeford, John W. 1964. *Psychology: In search of a soul*. Nashville: Broadman Press.

Eavey, C. B. 1940. *Principles of teaching for Christian teachers*. Grand Rapids: Zondervan Publishing House.

Edge, Findley B. 1956. *Teaching for results*. Nashville: Broadman Press.

Eims, LeRoy. 1981. *Be a motivational leader*. Wheaton, IL: SP Publications, Victor Books.

Eldridge, Daryl. 1995. *The teaching ministry of the church*. Nashville: Broadman and Holman Publishers.

Estep, James R. Jr., Michael J. Anthony, and Gregg R. Allison. 2008. *A Theology for Christian Education*. Nashville: B&H Academic.

Estes, Daniel. 1997. *Hear, my son: teaching and learning in Proverbs 1-9*. Downers Grove, IL: InterVarsity Press.

Falwell, Jerry. 2005. *Building dynamic faith*. Nashville: World Publishing, Inc.

Farmer, K.A. 1991. Who knows what is good? In *International theological commentary*. Grand Rapids: Eerdmans.

Ford, Leighton. 1991. *Transforming leadership: Jesus' way of creating vision, shaping values and empowering change*. Downers Grove, IL: Intervarsity Press.

Forrest, Benjamin K. 2008. Proverbs 2 as a metamodel for an integration of biblical and psychological learning theories. Liberty University.

French, John P. R. Jr., and Raven, Bertram. 1960. The bases of social power. In D. Cartwright and A. Zander (eds.), *Group dynamics*. New York: Harper and Row.

Gagne, Robert M. and Leslie J. Briggs, 1974. *Principles of instructional design*. New York: Holt, Rinehart and Winston, Inc.

Gangel, Kenneth O. 1970. *Leadership for church education*. Chicago: Moody Press.

_____. 1974. *Competent to lead*. Chicago: Moody Press.

_____. 1997. *Team leadership in Christian ministry*. Chicago: Moody Press.

Gannett, Lynn. 1991. Teaching for Learning. In *Christian education: Foundations for the future*, eds. Clark, Robert E., Lin Johnson, and Allyn K. Sloat, 105-119. Chicago: Moody Press.

Gilbrant, Thoralf, ed. 1986. *The complete biblical library*. Springfield, MO: World Library Press, Inc.

Gonzalez, Justo L. and Zaida Maldonado Perez. 2002. *Introduction to Christian theology*. Nashville: Abingdon Press.

Graendorf, Werner C. 1981. *Introduction to biblical Christian education*. Chicago: Moody Bible Institute.

Greenblat, C. S. and Richard D. Duke. 1975. *Gaming simulation*. Hoboken, NJ: John Wiley & Sons Inc.

Greenleaf, Robert K. 1977. *Servant leadership*. Ramsey, NJ: Paulist Press

Gregory, John Milton. 2003. *The seven laws of teaching unabridged edition*. Moscow, ID: Charles Nolan Publishers.

_____. 1972. *The seven laws of teaching*. Grand Rapids: Baker Book House.

Groome, Thomas H. 1980. *Christian religious education: Sharing our story and vision*. San Francisco: Harper & Row, Publishers.

Guernsey, Dennis B. 1982. *New design for family ministry*. Colorado Springs, CO: Cook Communications Ministries Intl.

Guiness, Oz. 1993. *Dining with the devil: the megachurch movement flirts with modernity*. Grand Rapids: Baker Books.

Habecker, Eugene B. 1987. *The other side of leadership*. Wheaton: SP Publications, Victor Books.

Habermas, Ronald, and Klaus Issler. 1992. *Teaching for reconciliation*. Grand Rapids: Baker Book House.

Hanson, Victor Davis and John Heath. 2001. *Who killed Homer?: the demise of classical education and the recovery of Greek wisdom*. San Francisco: Encounter Books.

Hardy, Lee. 1990. *The fabric of this world: Inquiries into calling, career choice, and the design of human work*. Grand Rapids, MI: William B. Eerdmans Publishing Company.

Havighurst, Robert J. 1972. *Developmental tasks and education*. United Kingdom: Longman Group.

Harris, Laird, ed. 1980. *Theological wordbook of the Old Testament*. Chicago: Moody Press.

Hergenhahn B.R. 1988. *An introduction to theories of learning*, 3rd ed. Englewood Cliffs, NJ: Prentice Hall.

Hersey, Paul, Kenneth H. Blanchard, and Dewey E. Johnson. 2001. *Management of organizational behavior: Utilizing human resources*, 8th ed. New Jersey: Prentice Hall.

Hesselbein, Frances, Marshall Goldsmith, and Richard Beckhard, eds. 1996. *The leader of the future*. Drucker Foundation Future Series. San Francisco, CA: Jossey-Bass Publishers.

Highet, Gilbert. 1973. *The art of teaching*. New York: Alfred A. Knopf.

Hirsch, E.D. 1999. *The schools we need: And why we don't have them*. New York: Anchor Books.

Horne, Herman Harrell. 1971. *The teaching techniques of Jesus*. Grand Rapids, MI: Kregel.

Hull, William. Church Educator, April 1995.

Imhof, M. 2001. How to listen more efficiently: Self-monitoring strategies in listening. *International Journal of Listening* 15: 2-19.

Jackson, Phil. 2004. *The last season: a team in search of its soul*. New York: The Penguin Press.

Klausmeier, Herbert J., and William Goodwin. 1966. *Learning and human abilities*. New York: Harper & Row, Publishers.

Knight, George R. 1998. *Philosophy and education*, 3rd ed. Berrien Springs, MI: Andrews University Press.

Kolb, David A. 1984. *Experiential learning*. New York: Prentice-Hall.

Kotter, John P. 1996. *Leading change*. Boston; Harvard Business School Press.

Kouzes, James M. and Barry Z. Posner, eds. 2004. *Christian reflections on the leadership challenge*. San Francisco: Jossey-Bass Publishing.

Krathwohl, David, ed. 1964. *Taxonomy of educational objectives: Handbook II – Affective domain*. New York: David McKay Company.

Kuhn, D. and D. Dean, 2004. Metacognition: A bridge between cognitive psychology and educational practice. *Theory into Practice* 43 (4): 268-273.

Kurtz, Paul. 1980. *A secular humanist declaration*. Amherst, NY: Prometheus Books.

LeBar, Lois. 1995. *Education that is Christian*. Colorado Springs, CO: Chariot Victor Publishing. Cook Communications.

Lefever, Marlene. 2002. *Learning styles*. Colorado Springs, CO: David C. Cook.

Maguire, Jack. 1990. *The care and feeding of the brain*. New York: Doubleday.

Malphurs, Aubrey. 1995. *Maximizing your effectiveness*. Grand Rapids: Baker.

Maxwell, John C. 1998. *The 21 irrefutable laws of leadership*. Nashville: Thomas Nelson Publishers.

_____. 1989. *Be a people person: Effective leadership through interpersonal relationships*. Wheaton, IL: Victor Books.

May, Scottie, Catherine Stonehouse, Beth Posterski, and Linda Cannell. 2005. *Children matter: Celebrating their place in the church, family, and community*. Grand Rapids, MI: William B. Eerdmans Publishing Co.

Means, James E. 1989. *Leadership in Christian ministry*. Grand Rapids: Baker Book House Company, Baker Books.

Melchert, Charles F. 1998. *Wise teaching: Biblical wisdom and educational ministry*. Harrisburg, PA: Trinity Press.

Moran, Gabriel. 1997. *Showing how: The act of teaching*. Valley Forge, PA: Trinity Press International.

Murphy, Elizabeth 1997. Personal website. Retrieved from http://www.stemnet.nf.ca/~elmurphy/emurphy/cle.html.

Murphy, Roland Edmund and Elizabeth Huwiler. 1999. *Proverbs, Ecclesiastes, Song of Songs*. New International Biblical Commentary, 12. Peabody, MA: Hendrickson Publishers.

Nanus, Burt. 1992. *Visionary leadership*. San Francisco: Jossey-Bass Inc, Publishers.

Niremberg, Jesse. 1963. *Getting through to people.* Englewood Cliffs, NJ: Prentice-Hall, Inc.

Noe, John R. 1986. *Peak performance principles for high achievers.* New York: The Berkley Publishing Company.

Pazmiño, Robert W. 1997. *Foundational issues in Christian education: An introduction in evangelical perspective.* Grand Rapids, MI: Baker Books.

Peters, Thomas J. and Robert H. Waterman, Jr. 1982. *In search of excellence: lessons from America's best-run companies.* New York: Harper and Row, Warner Books, Inc.

Pollock, David R. 1996. *Business management in the local church: Revised and expanded.* Chicago: Moody Press.

Potter, Charles Francis. 1930. *Humanism: A new religion.* New York: Simon and Schuster.

Rainer, Thom; and Eric Geiger. 2006. *Simple church: Returning to God's process for making disciples.* Nashville, TN: Broadman & Holman.

Richards, Lawrence O. 1983. *A theology of children's ministry.* Grand Rapids: Zondervan Publishing House.

_____. 1976. *Expository dictionary of bible words.* Grand Rapids: Zondervan Publishing House.

_____. 1975. *A theology of Christian education.* Grand Rapids: Zondervan Publishing House.

_____. 1972. *Youth ministry.* Grand Rapids: Zondervan Publishing House.

_____. 1970. *Creative Bible teaching.* Chicago: Moody Press.

Richards, Lawrence O. and Clyde Hoeldtke. 1980. *A theology of church leadership.* Grand Rapids, MI: Zondervan.

Robertson, William H. 2007. *Christian perspectives in education* Volume 1, Issue 2, Article 5. "The Greatest Constructivist Educator Ever: The Pedagogy of Jesus Christ in the Gospel of Matthew in the Context of the 5Es." The Berkeley Electronic Press. http://digitalcommons.liberty.edu/cpe.

Rush, Myron. 1983. *Management: a biblical approach.* Wheaton: SP Publications, Victor Books.

Ryan, Kevin and Cooper, James M. 2001. *Those who can, teach.* 9th ed. Boston: Houghton-Mifflin Co.

Santrock, John W. 2001. *Educational psychology.* New York: McGraw-Hill Companies, Inc.

Schwartz, Christian. 2006. *Natural church development: A guide to eight essential qualities of healthy churches*. Saint Charles, IL: Churchsmart Resources.

Seymour, Jack L. and Donald E. Miller. 1982. *Contemporary approaches to Christian education*. Nashville: Abingdon.

Sire, James W. 2004. *Naming the elephant: Worldview as a concept*. Downers Grove, IL: InterVarsity Press.

Slavin, Robert. 2006. *Educational psychology: theory and practice*. 8th ed. Needham Heights, MA: Allyn and Bacon, Inc.

Smith, M. K. 2000. "Curriculum theory and practice" in *The encyclopedia of informal education*. www.infed.org/biblio/b-curric.htm.

Spears, Paul D. and Steven R. Loomis. 2009. *Education for human flourishing: A Christian perspective*. Christian Worldview Integration Series. Downers Grove, IL: InterVarsity Press.

Stanley, Andy and Lane Jones. 2006. *Communicating for change*. Portland: Multnomah Publishers, Inc.

Stover, Allen. 2004. *Learning architecture online: New directions for distance education and the design studio?* Unpublished master's capstone project, University of Maryland University College. Available: http://home.comcast.net/~abstover/learning_arch.

Strauch, Alexander. 2006. *Leading with love*. Littleton, CO: Lewis and Roth Publishers.

Swanson, Richard A. (1994). *Analysis for improving performance*. San Francisco, CA: Berrett-Koehler Publishers.

Taylor, Allan. 2003. *The six core values of Sunday school: A philosophical, practical, & passionate approach to Sunday school*. Canton, GA: Riverstone Group Publishing.

Tenney, Merrill, ed. 1975. *Zondervan pictorial encyclopedia of the Bible*. Grand Rapids: Zondervan.

Tomlinson, Carol Ann. 1999. *The differentiated classroom*. Englewood Cliffs, NJ: Prentice Hall.

Towns, Elmer. 1992. *The eight laws of leadership*. Church Growth Institute: Lynchburg, VA.

Tozer, A. W. 2008. *Man: the dwelling place of God*. Goodyear, AZ: Diggory Press, Incorporated.

Tubbs, S. L. 2004. *Systems approach to small group interaction*. 8th ed. New York: McGraw Hill.

Vine, W. E., M. F. Unger and W. White. 1996. *Vine's complete expository dictionary of Old and New Testament words*. Nashville, TN: Thomas Nelson.

Westerhoff, John. 1994. *Spiritual life: The foundation for preaching and teaching*. Louisville, KY: Westminster/John Knox Press.

Wilhoit, James C., and John M. Dettoni, eds. 1995. *Nurture that is Christian: Developmental perspectives on Christian education*. Wheaton, IL: A Bridgepoint Book.

Wilkinson, Bruce. 1992: *The seven laws of the learner: Textbook edition*. Sisters, OR: Multnomah Press, Questar Publishers, Inc.

Willard, Dallas. 1988. *The spirit of the disciplines: Understanding how God changes lives*. San Francisco: HarperSanFrancisco.

Willard, Dallas and Richard Foster. 2005. "The making of the Christian." Interview by Agnieszka Tennant. ChristianityToday.com. September 16, 2005.

Willingham, Daniel. 2008. Learning styles don't exist. University of Virginia; retrieved from http://www.youtube.com/watch?v=sIv9rz2NTUk.

Witkin, B.R. and J.W. Altschud. 1995. *Planning and conducting needs assessments: A practical guide*. Thousand Oaks, CA: Sage Publications.

Woolfolk, Anita E. 2006. *Educational psychology*. 10th ed. Needham Heights, MA: Allyn and Bacon, Inc.

Yount, William R. 1996. *Created to learn*. Nashville: Broadman and Holman Publishers.

Yount, William R., ed. 2008. *The teaching ministry of the Church*, 2nd Ed. Nashville: Broadman and Holman Publishing Group.

Zodhiates, Spiros. 1984. *The Hebrew-Greek key study Bible*. Chattanooga, TN: AMG Publishers.

Zylstra, Henry. 1958. *Testament of vision*. Grand Rapids, MI: Wm. B. Eerdmans Publishing Company.

Appendix C
ACKNOWLEDGEMENTS: *Decisions and Influences*

Before we conclude our adventure together, I want to acknowledge a number of decisions and influences that informed and shaped the content and style of this work. First, no doubt you noticed immediately that I utilize a first person writing style. This is due to two primary factors: 1) It is a highly personal work, rooted in my own study and experience; virtually all of the outlines, procedures, and conclusions are mine. I am not simply rearranging other's thoughts, and 2) I did not attempt a primarily scholarly or theoretical work but a practical one. Although I do believe it is based on sound research, I desired to speak personally to the emerging leader and teacher as much as professionally to the seasoned. Much of the teaching section of this work, for example, was originally prepared for home educators, and most of the leadership section was designed to train volunteer department coordinators in a local church setting. I would appreciate the acceptance of my labors by scholarly peers and colleagues; but, it is not only to them I write.

Second, concerning the anecdotes and stories, I affirm that, except where noted otherwise, the people, places, and particulars are all true as I recollect them. Nonetheless, I have utilized aliases in the situations where I referred to people by name. I am willing to be held accountable for what I have produced here, but I am not so comfortable doing so with others who may recall the incidents differently or draw alternate conclusions.

Next, I would like to make the usual acknowledgements of those human resources that influenced, inspired, and assisted me in this undertaking. Without doubt, my entire family is my most important and honored influence. My father was the greatest Christian man I have ever known, and my mother was a most gracious and supportive partner. My wife, Sharyn, a gifted woman in her own right, has provided me with all a man could need or want in a "soul mate." She is my primary inspiration, critic, and editor; she has influenced the content, format, and the entire concept of this work. Her example as an educator inspires me. Without her, this book probably never would have been written. My children, Michael and Charis, daily bless and inspire me; if I could not write a book, they would be the entire legacy I would need to leave behind. Both were English majors and each played a role in the editing process. Their contributions were always a welcome addition. Michael made significant suggestions regarding the structure and flow of

Parts I and II. Carrie's support and encouragement affected this work and me in countless ways as she proofread the entire manuscript. Together, they provided the model of the emerging minister I desired to inform. The Mitchell family has been my heart and soul for half a century; I would not want to lead or teach without them.

Bill Bynum and Norm Wakefield were my early educational guides and mentors, with Warren Benson and Dennis Williams serving as later influences. The voluminous contributions of Larry Richards also inspired me in my formative years, along with a host of authors of commentaries and works on teaching and leading, too numerous to mention.

For over ten years, Stuart and Betsy Marlatt were close friends and companions in my work. They have been a constant source of inspiration for my family and me. Without them this would have been a different work altogether. We live in different states now, but their influence remains nearby. A mutual friend and fellow elder, Axel Johnson was a constant source of support and inspiration as well; our discussions of leadership were always thought provoking. He and Stuart illustrated and confirmed that elder is a verb, and their example of servant leadership is seldom matched. They authenticate and affirm the principles and practices I have presented here.

The core membership of Emmanuel Community Church in Arvada, Colorado, along with Pastor Gary Witkop of Community in Christ Lutheran Brethren Church, was a constant source of encouragement and blessing in the early phases of writing. Thank you, Randy and Barb, Tom and Pam, Axel and Pam, Don and Jenn, Mark and Barbara, David and Jackie, Alea, Sarah, Jeremy, and Ryan.

Finally, at various stages of writing and finalizing the text, four colleagues and five students made helpful observations and suggestions; their contributions were invaluable. Thank you, Dave Hirschman, Ben Forrest, Jason Leverett, Derrick Turrentine, Adam Moore, Danielle Kearney, Tiffany Fitzgerald, Stephen Cribb, and Kristi Finch. You each blessed me in countless ways.

At twenty-four years of age, I was asked to direct the children's ministry of a megachurch in the center of the Jesus Movement. When I responded, "Why me?" Pastor Chuck Smith of Calvary Chapel of Costa Mesa answered, "We just want the man God wants!" I have never forgotten and that is all I have ever wanted to be.

Thank you all for helping me.

CPSIA information can be obtained at www.ICGtesting.com
Printed in the USA
LVOW041953200911

247100LV00002B/3/P